Christianity and Monasticism in Northern Egypt

Christianity and Monasticism in Northern Egypt

Beni Suef, Giza, Cairo, and the Nile Delta

Edited by
Gawdat Gabra
Hany N. Takla

A Saint Mark Foundation Book
The American University in Cairo Press
Cairo New York

The American University in Cairo Press
113 Sharia Kasr el Aini, Cairo, Egypt
420 Fifth Avenue, New York, NY 10018
www.aucpress.com

Exclusive distribution outside Egypt and North America by I.B.Tauris & Co Ltd.,
6 Salem Road, London, W2 4BU

Dar el Kutub No. 25739/15
ISBN 978 977 416 777 5

Dar el Kutub Cataloging-in-Publication Data

Gabra, Gawdat

Christianity and Monasticism in Northern Egypt: Beni Suef, Giza, Cairo, and the Nile Delta / Gawdat Gabra, Hany Takla.—Cairo: The American University in Cairo Press, 2017.

p. cm.
ISBN: 978 977 416 777 5
1. Egypt—Church history
2. Monasticism and religious orders—Egypt
I. Takla, Hany (jt. auth.)
270.25739

1 2 3 4 5 21 20 19 18 17

Designed by Jon W. Stoy
Printed in the United States of America

This volume is dedicated to the memory of
Yassa 'Abd al-Masih (1898–1959),
who gave serious attention and care
to the manuscripts of the Coptic Patriarchate,
the Coptic Museum, and the monasteries of Egypt

Contents

Illustrations

Figure

Contributors

Krzysztof Babraj holds a PhD from the University of Warsaw. He has participated in a number of archaeological missions in Egypt (Naqlun, Kom al-Dikka, Tell Atrib). He is head of the Department of Mediterranean Archaeology at the Archaeological Museum in Krakow. Since 2010, he has been head of the mission at Marea/Philoxenite, near Alexandria. He is the author of seventy articles in the fields of Coptic, Byzantine, and early Christian art.

David Brakke is Joe R. Engle Chair in the History of Christianity and professor of history at the Ohio State University. He is the author of several books and articles on early Egyptian monasticism, including *Athanasius and the Politics of Asceticism* (1995), and president of the International Association for Coptic Studies (2016–2020).

Sherin Sadek El Gendi is professor of Coptic art and archaeology and head of the Tourism Guidance Department in the Faculty of Arts of Ain Shams University. She is a member of the International Association for Coptic Studies, and a member and researcher in the Ain Shams Center of Papyrological Studies and Inscriptions.

Frank Feder is senior academic researcher at the Göttingen Academy of Sciences and Humanities and directs the project for the complete digital edition and translation of the Coptic Sahidic Old Testament. He studied Egyptology and classical philology in Berlin and Lyon, and obtained his PhD from the Martin-Luther-University Halle-Wittenberg for the critical edition of the Jeremianic Corpus in Sahidic. He has worked for the Dictionary of Ancient Egyptian project at the Berlin-Brandenburg Academy of Sciences and Humanities in Berlin, and taught Coptology at the University of Münster.

Mary Ghattas is a PhD candidate at Claremont Graduate University. Her dissertation is entitled "Towards a Modern History of Eastern Christianity: The Coptic, Syriac, and Armenian Communities in Egypt, 1805–Present." After completing her BA in history at UCLA, she completed her MA at Claremont Graduate University in 2012. She is the assistant managing editor of the *Claremont Coptic Encyclopedia*.

James E. Goehring is professor of religion at the University of Mary Washington in Fredericksburg, Virginia. He has authored numerous works in the field of early Egyptian asceticism, including *Ascetics, Society and the Desert: Studies in Early Egyptian Monasticism* (1999) and *Politics, Monasticism, and Miracles in Sixth Century Upper Egypt* (2012).

Tomasz Górecki is an archaeologist, and a graduate of the Academy of Catholic Theology in Warsaw. He has been on the staff of the National Museum in Warsaw since 1976, where he is responsible for Eastern Christian art in the Collection of Ancient and Eastern Christian Art. He has taken part in many archaeological missions in Egypt, including Alexandria, Tell Atrib, Naqlun, Abu Fano, and Shenhur. Since 2003 he has directed the excavations at Sheikh Abd al-Gurna (Luxor), a joint project with the Centre of Mediterranean Archaeology of the University of Warsaw.

Gisèle Hadji-Minaglou is an architect and archaeologist, and a researcher at the Institut français d'archéologie orientale (IFAO) in Cairo. She is in charge of the IFAO and Louvre Museum excavations at Bawit; chief excavator of the IFAO and Milan University mission in Tebtynis, Fayyum; and a member of the IFAO mission at Balat in Dakhla Oasis.

Karel C. Innemée is an affiliated fellow at the Faculty of Archaeology, Leiden University (Netherlands). He is the project director of the Leiden Wadi al-Natrun project, which includes excavation at Dayr al-Baramus, survey at the site of Dayr Abu Maqar, and conservation work at Dayr al-Surian.

Michael Jones is associate director for conservation projects at the American Research Center in Egypt (ARCE), Cairo. He directs the Red Monastery Conservation and Site Management Project at Sohag and was responsible for ARCE's conservation work at the Red Sea monasteries of St. Anthony and St. Paul. He has published articles and books on conservation of cultural heritage in Egypt and Cyprus.

Mary Missak Kupelian is an associate professor in the Faculty of Tourism and Hotel Management, Helwan University, Egypt. In June 2010, she was awarded a PhD in Tourism Guidance under the joint supervision of Helwan and Leiden universities. Her research interests include Coptic art and archaeology, Armenian heritage and history in Egypt, and pedagogy in museums.

Bishop Kyrillos hold a BS in communication studies from UCLA, a Juris Doctor degree from the Georgetown University Law Center, an MTS and ThM from Holy Cross Orthodox School of Theology, and a PhD in the history of Christianity from the University of Notre Dame School of Theology. In 2016 he was consecrated as an auxiliary bishop in the Diocese of Los Angeles. He currently oversees Christian education in the diocese and serves as dean of the St. Athanasius and St. Cyril Theological School at Claremont University.

Bishop Martyros is General Bishop in the Coptic Orthodox Church in Cairo. He was formerly the hegumen of the Syrian Monastery in Wadi al-Natrun. He is a frequent contributor to international conferences of Coptology. He has authored multiple books on Coptic monasticism in Wadi al-Natrun.

Adel F. Sadek is a lecturer at the Institute of Coptic Studies, Anba Ruways, Cairo. For many years he participated in the restoration of mansucripts of the Coptic Patriarchate and many monasteries. He has authored a number of books in Arabic about the history and heritage of several Coptic dioceses. He is currently a member of the editorial board of *Bulletin of Rakoti: Spotlight on Coptic Studies*, published in Arabic in Alexandria.

Ashraf Alexandre Sadek, professor of Egyptology, Coptology, and biblical archaeology at the University of Limoges (France), is the author of many books and articles of research in these fields and editor of the cultural collection *Le Monde Copte*. He also teaches in several faculties of theology in Europe and Egypt and gives lectures in many countries.

Ibrahim Saweros is a lecturer in Coptology at Sohag University (Egypt). He recently obtained his PhD from Leiden University (Netherlands). His PhD research dealt with the Sahidic corpus attributed to Athanasius of Alexandria. His research interests include Coptic literature and Middle Egyptian.

Caroline T. Schroeder is professor of religious and classical studies at the University of the Pacific. She received her PhD from Duke University and AB from Brown University. Her research primarily concerns asceticism and monasticism in early Christianity, with a particular focus on Egypt. She is the author of numerous books and articles, and co-founder of the online platform Coptic Scriptorium, dedicated to open-source and open-access texts and technology for the study of Coptic language and literature.

Mark Sheridan, originally from Washington, D.C., is a Benedictine monk of Dormition Abbey in Jerusalem and professor emeritus in the Faculty of Theology of the Pontificio Ateneo S. Anselmo, Rome, where he served as dean of the Faculty of Theology (1998–2005) and Rector Magnificus (2005–2009) of the Athenaeum. He continues his research in the areas of Coptology and ancient Christian literature.

Adel Sidarus studied philosophy and Christian studies in various Arab and European countries, and received his PhD in Oriental studies in 1973 from the University of Munich. Retired from the University of Evora (Portugal) as professor of Arabic and Islamic studies, he is currently a member of the Institute of Eastern Studies, Faculty of Arts, Portuguese Catholic University at Lisbon. Since 2014, he has been a member of the Accademia Ambrosiana in Milan.

Hany N. Takla is founding president of the St. Shenouda the Archimandrite Coptic Society, director of the St. Shenouda Center of Coptic

Studies, Coptic language instructor at the Pope Shenouda III Theological College in Los Angeles, and a member of the board of trustees for the St. Mark Coptic Cultural Center in Cairo. He is currently a Coptic language lecturer at the University of California, Los Angeles (UCLA).

Daria Tarara is a professional architect with the Polish Archaeological Mission in Egypt. She has worked on key sites in Marea, Alexandria, Palmyra, and Erbil, undertaking the survey, site drawings, record-keeping, and documentation of excavation activities and interpreting the excavation material to enable CGI reconstruction and visualization of the structures. Ms. Tarara has also worked on 3D animations of ancient architecture for documentaries and exhibitions.

Fr. Teddawos Ava Mina holds a BSc in agricultural science, and has pursued master's-level studies in archaeology at Kafr El-Sheikh University. He has served as representative of St. Menas Coptic Orthodox Monastery to several Egyptian organizations, such as the Ministry of Culture and the Supreme Council of Antiquities, as well as to UNESCO and other international organizations.

Asuka Tsuji is a postdoctoral research fellow of the Japan Society for the Promotion of Science at the Institute of Advanced Studies on Asia, University of Tokyo. She received her PhD from the University of Tokyo in 2014. Her current research interest is the history of the Coptic Church in the medieval period.

Jacques van der Vliet is professor of Egyptian religion at Radboud University, Nijmegen, and lecturer of Coptic at Leiden University, the Netherlands. His research covers most aspects of the literary culture of Egyptian and Nubian Christianity in late-antique and medieval times, with a particular focus on Gnostic and apocryphal scripture, magic, epigraphy, and papyrology.

Fr. Awad Wadi is a Franciscan friar and, since 1986, researcher in the Franciscan Oriental Christian Studies in Cairo. He teaches patrology in the Coptic Catholic Seminary and in the Theological Institute in Cairo. He is the author of many articles and books in the field of Christian Arabic heritage.

Youhanna Nessim Youssef is associate professor in the University of Divinity of St. Athanasius College, and research fellow at the Centre for Early Christian Studies at Australian Catholic University. He is the author of many books and book chapters on the subjects of hagiography, liturgy, Arabic Christian studies, art history, and patristics.

Ewa D. Zakrzewska holds an MA in Egyptology and a PhD in linguistics. She is an affiliated member of the Amsterdam Center for Language and Communication (ACLC) of the University of Amsterdam and a subject specialist in the university library. She seeks to apply insights from functional-typological linguistics, text linguistics, and contact linguistics to the study of Coptic, especially Bohairic.

Foreword

THIS IS THE SEVENTH VOLUME of the series *Christianity and Monasticism in Egypt*. It contains the essays presented at the seventh international symposium of the St. Mark Foundation for Coptic History Studies and the St. Shenouda the Archimandrite Coptic Society. The symposium was held on February 8–12, 2015 in the Monastery of Saint Menas (Dayr Mari Mina) near Alexandria. It was His Holiness St. Cyril VI who revived monasticism in the famous Late Antique pilgrimage site of the shrine of St. Menas. In February 1962 some of the relics of St. Menas were translated from his church in Fumm al-Khalig to the new monastery. The monastery continues to flourish and hundreds of monks enjoy their monastic life there. In addition to a number of Egyptians, the invited scholars, who represent a variety of academic disciplines, come from Australia, England, France, Germany, Japan, the Netherlands, Poland, and the United States.

I am greatly blessed and grateful to His Holiness Pope Tawadros II for his continued support to the St. Mark Foundation. It was an unforgettable experience when His Holiness performed the Mass in the ancient site of the great martyr St. Menas. He personally inaugurated the symposium, welcomed its participants and attendees, and encouraged them to promote knowledge about Egypt's Christian legacy. The symposium was hosted by Bishop Kyrillos Ava Mena, Abbot of the Monastery of St Menas.

I would like to express my heartfelt thanks to His Grace for his unparalleled generosity.

The most recent International Congress of Coptic Studies (Claremont Graduate University, July 25–30, 2016) has shown how useful are the proceedings of the symposia of our foundation, which were used by many of the participants in that congress. I am indebted to all the contributors of this volume for their invaluable chapters that greatly enrich our knowledge about Christianity and monasticism in Beni Suef, Giza, Cairo, and the Nile Delta. I am looking forward to the next symposium, "Christianity and Monasticism in Alexandria and Its Surroundings, and in the Eastern and Western Deserts," which will be hosted by His Holiness Pope Tawadros II at the Monastery of St. Pshoi in Wadi al-Natrun in February 2017.

I would like to give my special thanks to Sherif Doss and Shahira Loza for their unfailing support. As always, I thank the symposium's organizing committee: Faheem Wassef, Akhnoukh Fanous, and Ashraf Nageh, as well as Hoda Garas, who finalized the contacts with the contributors.

Finally, I extend my thanks to the American University in Cairo Press, and especially to Nigel Fletcher-Jones, director, Neil Hewison, associate director for editorial programs, Nadia Naqib, managing editor, and Johanna Baboukis, who has done a magnificent job of copyediting.

Fawzy Estafanous, President
The St Mark Foundation for Coptic History Studies

Introduction

THIS VOLUME, *Christianity and Monasticism in Northern Egypt: Beni Suef, Giza, Cairo, and the Nile Delta*, contains the papers that were presented at the seventh international symposium of the St. Mark Foundation for Coptic History Studies and the St. Shenouda the Archimandrite Coptic Society. The symposium was held at the Monastery of Saint Menas (Dayr Mari Mina) near Alexandria, February 8–12, 2015. Because of the security situation in Egypt, a number of prospective participants could not attend and deliver their papers. Fortunately, they were kind enough to submit their work for publication to ensure that this volume would provide a more complete picture of the history and institutions of the region being studied. This area runs from the northern governorates of Upper Egypt—Beni Suef and Giza—to the entire Delta region of Lower Egypt. Alexandria, having its own unique and rich history, was excluded and will be covered in the upcoming volume in this series.

The collection of twenty-six chapters included in this volume represents a broad picture of Christianity and monasticism in terms of the history, literature, language, art and architecture, and people of these regions from the first century to the late twentieth century. They cover the more significant events, people, and regions rather than forming a complete survey of the entire area.

The book is arranged in the same way as each of the previous volumes in the series: language and literature; art, archaeology, and material culture; and preservation. The chapters within each category are arranged alphabetically by the author's last name. As usual, the majority of the chapters (twenty-one) were in the first category. They cover not only topics of language and literature in the areas being studied, but also the history that we can draw from such literature in the classical languages of Christian Egypt: Coptic, Arabic, and Greek. A shorter section (four chapters) deals with art and architecture, and the volume concludes with a single chapter in the category of preservation.

In the first section, Ashraf Alexandre Sadek's chapter reviews the Holy Family's flight to Egypt and the tradition preserved in Coptic sources about the places they visited in the Delta. Two other chapters in this section deal with the two most important monastic settlements in northern Egypt, Kellia and Nitria. Fr. Mark Sheridan surveys the history of monasticism in the region of Nitria based on the literary sources available. Jacques van der Vliet's chapter on Kellia investigates the monasticism in this region based on the wall inscriptions left by the monks. James Goehring's chapter deals with the monasteries in Lower Egypt that were part of the Pachomian Federation of Upper Egypt. Mary Ghattas describes the most prominent of these Pachomian monasteries, the Hennaton monastery or Dayr al-Zujaj, and the debates about its exact location. Sherin Sadek El Gendi's chapter covers another of the important monastic sites in the region, St. Mina Monastery—Abu Mena's world-renowned fourth-century pilgrimage center—as recorded in the Arabic sources.

Three important components dominated the life of the Church of Egypt in its golden age: the Alexandria hierarchy, monks, and the famous Theological School of Alexandria. David Brakke's chapter describes the close relationship between the patriarchs and the monks, in particular those of northern Egypt. The most famous of the patriarchs of Alexandria is the twentieth, St. Athanasius the Great. Ibrahim Saweros's chapter examines four Sahidic manuscripts of Athanasius's works preserved in the famous Hamuli Collection from Archangel Michael Monastery in Fayoum and discusses how they preserved his memory, even though their attribution is doubtful. Continuing this theme of the three components, Caroline Schroeder's chapter examines the significant papyri find in the ancient St. Arsenius monastery in Tura, which yielded a wealth of writings in Greek from one of the most prominent heads of the Theological School of

Alexandria, Didymus the Blind.

This area also produced several literary figures in addition to those of the Theological School of Alexandria. The careers and writings of three of these authors are discussed. The first of these chapters, by Bishop Kyrillos, examines the history of John of Barullos (sixth–seventh century) and the writings attributed to him. Another literary figure who was also a bishop lived in the early thirteenth century, Yuhanna al-Samannudi. Adel Sidarus's chapter examines this bishop's pioneering contribution to Coptic philology, which documented the fundamentals of the Coptic language in order to preserve it for generations to come. Frank Feder introduces the so-called Bashmuric dialect of Coptic as part of his examination of the history of the famous Bashmuric revolts. The third literary figure examined in this section is Butrus al-Sadamanti al-Armani. Fr. Awad Wadi examines the career of this author, who enriched the Christian Arabic literature of Egypt later in the thirteenth century with many important works. Butrus's Armenian heritage serves as a link to Mary Kupelian's chapter, which examines the relationship between the Coptic and Armenian churches in Egypt in the nineteenth and twentieth centuries.

No discussion of the literary heritage of this region can be complete without the important genre of hagiography, the lives of the saints of the Church. This type of literature is not limited to the works dedicated specifically to the lives of these saints, but extends to the later social history of the Copts, their liturgical hymns, and even their modern institutions. Ewa Zakrzewska's chapter examines the function of the *Acts of the Martyrs* preserved in Bohairic, which played a very influential role in the life of the Church at times, despite their historical inaccuracies. Youhanna Youssef examines a case history of one of these late hagiographic compositions attributed to Julius of Aqfahs, the *Martyrdom of John and Simon*, documenting the historical shortcomings of this text. Hany Takla discusses in his chapter two different manuscript traditions of the *Miracles of St. Menas* in Arabic, one based on the shorter Sahidic version and the other reflecting a later, longer Arabic recension. Three other chapters deal with the Arabic hagiographic tradition concerning thirteenth-century Coptic saints. The first is by Asuka Tsuji on a little-known saint from the Delta, St. Hadid, which sheds light on aspects of his life according to the preserved vita. The second is about the more famous St. Barsoum the Naked (Anba Barsouma al-Arian); Bishop Martyros examines the veneration of this saint near Cairo, in a monastery originally known as Dayr Shahran. The third chapter is by Adel Sadek, on another famous saint from that period, Anba Ruways, and the history related to the foundation of the St. Mark Cathedral in Cairo over the site of his monastery. The last chapter in this genre is by Fr. Teddawos Ava Mina and Youhanna Youssef, about the life of Pope Cyril VI (Anba Kyrillos VI), the 116th patriarch of Alexandria, from his youth to his great contributions that included the foundation of the modern monastery of St. Menas and the building of the new St. Mark Cathedral in Cairo.

The second and third categories in this volume include five chapters on some of the art and architecture of places in northern Egypt, as well as efforts to conserve their remains. The first one is by Tomasz Górecki, describing an excavation of a Byzantine church in the old town of Athribis in modern-day Benha, which has yielded artifacts but whose architecture has not yet been revealed. The next two chapters deal with the famous monastic region of Kellia, which was addressed from a literary perspective earlier. Gisèle Hadji-Minaglou describes the architecture of this famous monastic settlement north of Wadi al-Natrun; Karel Innemée discusses the artistic elements excavated at the site. The third site is Marea/Philoxenite, the subject of the excavation campaigns by the Polish Mission in Egypt during the period of 2000–14. Krzysztof Babraj and Daria Tarara document the history and the architecture of the site settlement, including its large ancient cathedral, situated forty-five miles southwest of Alexandria. The last chapter, by Michael Jones, describes in detail the preservation efforts undertaken by the American Research Center in Egypt on the famous murals, preserved in the Cairo Coptic Museum, which were originally excavated in Apa Jeremiah's Saqqara monastery and Apa Apollo's Bawit monastery. These wall paintings have traditionally been considered the principal symbols of Coptic art.

Our heartfelt thanks are due to all the authors for their valuable contributions to this volume. Our special thanks go to Dr. Fawzy Estafanous, president of the St. Mark Foundation, for supporting the symposium and its proceedings. We would also like to express our thanks to the staff of the American University in Cairo Press for their interest and professionalism in publishing the proceedings of the symposia on Christianity and Monasticism in Egypt, and especially to Nigel Fletcher-Jones, Neil Hewison, Nadia Naqib, and Johanna Baboukis.

Finally, it is our pleasure and honor to dedicate this volume to Yassa 'Abd al-Masih in acknowledgment of his lifelong devotion to the Coptic heritage.

1 John of Barullos (540–615)

Bishop Kyrillos

Introduction

There are many notable leaders in the annals of Coptic history whose names are well known. John of Barullos is not one of them. The Synaxarium entry for 19 Kiyahk mentions only that John was the bishop of Barullos, and author of some articles. This chapter is only a preliminary survey of John of Barullos, intended to open up doors for future research into his life and writings.[1]

Barullos

The name of the region John was from is as obscure as his life. Al-Barullos is equated with many Greek variants (Parallos, Parallou, and Parhalos), as well as Coptic ones (Nikedjoou [O'Leary 1937b: 168]; Naqizah (Coquin and Martin 1991d: 1174b–1175a, citing Maspero and Wiet 1919; and Nafwah[2]). The north-central Delta contained two cities with similar names: al-Burlus and al-Burlus al-Ramla (Kosack 1971: 49, cited in Vivian 2008: 342n138). According to ancient hieroglyphic records, at least one of these cities is situated on a peninsula that connected Lake Barullos with the sea (Budge 1920: 2:1030: "Sai Ta her sept Uatch ur"). But it seems that the Barullos associated with John was situated somewhere between present-day Baltim and al-Burj, on the eastern shore of Lake Barullos, in the northern Delta (Stewart 1991c: 2:427).

The city seems to have had an important religious role in the life of the Copts. According to a homily delivered by Bishop Zakariya of Sakha (seventh–eighth century), Barullos was the location of the fig tree where the Holy Family rested during their flight to Egypt.[3] Moreover, St. Thecla, the disciple of St. Paul, was associated with the city when the story of this most popular female virgin martyr in late antique Egypt was assimilated into the native Egyptian veneration of the martyrs (Armanios 2003: 109–10, citing Davis 2001: 172).

A diocese was located in al-Barullos as early as the beginning of the fourth century, until at least the eleventh century (Stewart 1991c, citing Munier 1943a: 28). One of its earliest bishops was Athanasius, who attended the Council of Ephesus in 431 (Stewart 1991c, citing Munier 1943a: 15). Al-Barullos was the hometown of Patriarch Isaac (686–89), the dwelling place of the hermit George during the papacy of John IV (775–79), and the hometown of the recluse Christodoulus, who became the sixty-sixth pope of Alexandria, from 1047 to 1077. Among the most notable of its bishops was John, who lived from around 540 to 615.

Early Life

John of Barullos was probably born around 540, of a respected clerical family of Lower Egypt.[4] Like his parents, he was recognized for his charity (O'Leary 1937b: 427; *al-Siniksar* 1978: 211–12 [19 Kiyahk]). As a young man, John used his inheritance to build a shelter for pilgrims and the sick (Stewart 1991c; Budge *Synaxarium*: 223). He learned Greek, Coptic, and probably Syriac. Encouraged by one of the monk-pilgrims who probably visited his home (*al-Siniksar*, 19 Kiyahk), John entered the Monastery of St. Macarius in Shiheet, under the leadership of St. Daniel the Hegumen (Müller 1991b: 5:1367, citing *al-Siniksar*, 19 Kiyahk).

The Coptic and Ethiopian Synaxaria recall that while John lived in a secluded building, Satan painfully attacked him so that he was sick for several days. After his miraculous healing, he was called to be a bishop, probably by Pope Peter IV in 576 (Müller 1991b: 5:1368), at one of the most challenging periods in the history of the Coptic Church.[5]

Writings

John was one of the most significant Coptic theologians of his time. He used all available means to root out various heresies—delivering homilies, writing articles, or visiting monasteries to burn the heretical books he found there (Müller 1991b: 5:1368). He even journeyed abroad to Syria for about four months to resolve the dogmatic controversy between Pope

Damian of Alexandria (570–607) and Peter of Callinicum (also known as Peter III of Raqqa [Taylor 2006: 15n1], or Petrus of Antioch).[6] Unfortunately, only a few of his writings survive in Coptic, Arabic, and Ethiopic (Armanios 2003, citing Müller 1991b: 1367–68).

Homilies

Perhaps John is most famous for his homilies concerning the Resurrection and the Last Judgment, the *Book of Adam*,[7] and "On the Archangel Michael and on Heretical Books,"[8] most of which are responses to heresies that emerged from the Sa'id with Gnostic claims of secret revelations. One such Gnostic writer claimed to have been visited by the prophet Habakkuk.[9] When a monk from Upper Egypt claimed that Archangel Michael revealed to him certain mysteries in *The Book of the Investiture of the Archangel Michael*, John refuted the heresy in his homily noted above (Budge *Synaxarium*: 223).

These homilies seem to be directed toward priests (Müller 1954b: 242). In his homily on Archangel Michael, John often expresses his desire to equip the "servants of God" to prevent the heretics who are confusing the "simple people" or the "uneducated" in the villages, and the zealots (Σπουδαῖοι) in the cities (Stewart 1991c, citing *al-Siniksar*; Kelly 2004: 237).

While much of the heresy at this time involves Gnosticism, several issues involve Trinitarian theology. At one point in his Archangel Michael homily, John refers to the uncreated, eternal divine nature (Lantschoot 1946: 321n16). He also speaks of the orders of angels, which he lists as the "innumerable orders of angels and archangels, cherubim and seraphim, the four creatures with multiple eyes, the dominions and virtues" (Lantschoot 1946: 321).

Primarily, John is reliant on scriptures and emphasizes precisely what is *not* revealed therein to mark the limitations outside of which the Gnostic, apocryphal, or heretical works venture to describe. Mainly from the work of Lantschoot, we have come to realize that John also seems to rely heavily on the writings of Origen, St. Basil, St. Gregory Nazianzen, St. John Chrysostom, and John the Grammarian.[10] Perhaps the greatest influence of the arguments contained in this homily (as well as his homily on the Resurrection and the Last Judgment) is seen most directly in the *Homily on Riches* attributed to Peter of Alexandria, which contains an encomium on the Archangel Michael (82–117), sandwiched between two sections on the Judgment and Resurrection (75–81, 118–19) (Pearson and Vivian 1993: 15–25).

Synaxaria

The second main work attributed to John of Barullus are the Coptic and Ethiopian Synaxaria.[11] While the prologue of the Coptic Synaxarium lists among its authors "John, bishop of Barullos," this is probably *not* the same figure as the sixth-century bishop who lived from 540 to 610 or 620. The bishop of Barullos, in this prologue, explains that after observing the ruins of his church in Za'farana, he spent much time thinking about investigating the lives of the martyrs of the Church, until a saintly monk visited him with old and damaged books, seeking repair. The text reads as follows:

> I was bishop of Barullos and I had always attended the church in Za'farana.[12] I saw that it was in ruin because of the passing of time and the destruction of people. Thus it came to my mind that I should investigate the lives of the martyrs of this church. After some time passed, as I thought more about this matter and was unable either to eat or sleep because of my preoccupation, a saintly monk from Dayr al-Mayma[13] came to me. He carried old and damaged books from that church. . . . He said "Father, take these books in order to prepare the orders of the church since you are our father and have authority over this church." . . . I was overjoyed and I searched in the books and found the orders of the church, in both Coptic and Arabic. While I searched, I [also] found the story in question, the hagiography of the saint martyr Dimyana. . . . I began to transcribe it, as it had been written in the handwriting of a boy from the slave of Julius al-Aqfahsi, whose name was Ikhristodolo.[14]

The mention that these books were in the Coptic *and* Arabic languages suggests that this is not the sixth-century Bishop John of Barullos, but a much later figure. We are aware that John knew Coptic and Greek, and perhaps Syriac. But 541 is far too early to see the Synaxarium in both Coptic and Arabic. According to Cardinal Angelo Mai's work on the Arabic Synaxarium, its reputed compiler was Michael, bishop of Atrib and Malig in 1425 (Burmester 1938: 249); Michael's work was then adopted by most scholars working on the Arabic and Ethiopian Synaxaria (Burmester 1938: 249, citing Zotenberg 1877: 152; Wüstenfeld 1879: 152; Hyvernat 1909: 362; O'Leary 1937b: 32).

While it is nearly impossible that the entire Synaxarium can have been composed by John, at least two manuscripts do attribute the life of St.

Dimiana to John of Barullos.[15] If this is the case, then some revision must be made to the introductory preface of the current Coptic Synaxarium.

Other writings

Two other works deserving of scholarly attention are attributed to John. Ibn Kabar's (d. 1324) catalog attributes thirteen anathemas to John, without express citation or elaboration.[16] The only other mention of this seems to be the *Antiphonarion*, which praises John for delivering the apostolic canons to the faithful. I have not yet been able to locate these anathemas in any collection. A lesser-known work is the Coptic life of Pope Damian attributed to the bishop of Barullos, found in the White Monastery.[17]

The Divine Fire Motif in the Life of John of Barullos

One of the unique features of John's Synaxarium entries is their strange infatuation with fire. We are told that every time John would celebrate the Divine Liturgy, his face and his body would flush red, as if in a furnace. He wept at beholding the heavenly Host on the altar.[18] When he placed his finger on the chalice to make the sign of the cross, he found the cup hot with fire.[19] In the Ethiopian version, John would also find the *korban*[20] burning like fire (Budge *Synaxarium*: 224).

In the Coptic Synaxarium, John excommunicated those who would partake of the mysteries without fasting. According to the Ethiopian version, these "evil men and heretics . . . [would] offer up the Offering twice a day, after they had eaten."[21] After John excommunicated them, "God sent fire from heaven and consumed their leader; when those who remained saw this, they feared exceedingly and entered the True Faith."

What is the reason for this strange emphasis on fire in the Coptic and Ethiopian accounts? One possibility could be that in the Ethiopian Synaxarium, the entry for John of Barullos on 19 Tahisas (28 December) is followed by that for the Three Holy Youths, Ananias, Azarias, and Misael. Yet this does not seem to provide an adequate connection to John, since the Ethiopian account is a translation from the Coptic, which commemorates the Three Holy Youths five months later, on 10 Bashans (18 May). Perhaps the inclusion of the Three Holy Youths on a different date in the Ethiopian version could be the *effect* of the emphasis on fire, rather than its *cause* or explanation.

Another possibility comes from the fourteenth-century manuscript concerning the life of St. Pisentius (Psenthaisus or Psenda), a contemporary of John of Barullos, who is also described in a very similar manner.[22] Pisentius also had a strong connection to Pope Damian (who ordained him) and was known for his generosity to travelers. We are told that when he ascended the altar, his face glowed like fire while he watched the Holy Spirit descending on the oblations. Yet the Coptic Synaxarium entry on 13 Abib only mentions that he used to see the angels flying—without any mention of fire or the Holy Spirit. Fortunately, this manuscript does give some explanation for this fiery theme—the personal connection between Bishop Pisentius and Elijah the Prophet.[23] The bishop was drawn to the monastic life by Abbot Elijah the Great, the head of Abu Fam Monastery on the mount of Shama (Malaty 1993: 114). The passage also relates an apparition of Elijah to the monk Pisentius in his cell (Malaty 1993: 115), in which the latter was "enflamed" with the monastic life. While none of these stories or descriptions is found in the Coptic entry, we do find a similar entry at the same period in the Russian tradition. The fourteenth-century hermit and mystic, Abbot Sergius, has a vision of a twisted flame that enters the chalice before he communes, and his face glows after he is visited by the Virgin Mary and Sts. Peter and John (Bulgakov 1997: 66; Fedotov 1969: 82; Fanning 2001: 46–47). Thus this second possibility is that this motif is a characteristic of many accounts of fourteenth-century mystics, at least in Ethiopia and Russia.

Yet another possibility for this fiery motif comes from the Byzantine Eucharistic tradition. In the Byzantine rite, the famous Communion prayer attributed to Symeon Metaphrastes speaks of the fire of the Eucharist that either consumes or cleanses. This notion of the fire of the divinity active in the Eucharist is a native feature of the Byzantine liturgical tradition that may be due, at least in part, to the pouring of hot water into the chalice, usually interpreted as a type of the Divine Essence as a consuming fire (see Taft 2000: 488; Hawkes-Teeples 2011: 151). But again, how can Symeon's comments be related to John of Barullos? Symeon was secretary and chancellor of the imperial court at Constantinople, about 900, and wrote the biographies of 122 saints and martyrs. For our purposes, one of the most important of these biographies is that of Peter I of Alexandria.[24] In the Coptic homily on the Epiphany attributed to Peter of Alexandria, the author relates that he sees a flame of fire above the throne in the altar—a hidden flame which is explained by Hebrews 12:29, "Our God is a consuming fire."[25] Even though several ancient authors may have made the same correlation, it seems more than possible that Symeon was inspired by this theme when composing the Prayer for Communion, which itself had a deep and long-standing tradition in Byzantine Eucharistic theology. While the theory is admittedly speculative, it is possible that the fiery motif in the story of John of Barullos could be the result of the influence of Symeon Metaphrastes, who did edit many other Coptic lives. This fascination with the divine fire remained not only in these Coptic lives, but also in the Byzantine rite as well.

The narratives of John also contain the motif of divine fire related to the judgment of those who partook of the Eucharist several times in one day without fasting. Surely, this notion of divine punishment originates with the strange fire of Nadab and Abihu (Exodus 24) and the fire that consumes the 250 men of Korah (Numbers 26:10). A similar story is mentioned in the life of Pope Benjamin I (623–62), who called down fire from heaven upon some notorious offender.[26]

Conclusion

What, then, can be said regarding John of Barullos with any certainty at this stage?

We know he was bishop of al-Barullos, a city which remained quite an active diocese for several centuries.

We also know that his main work was to respond to heresies (primarily Gnostic) that seem to target the uneducated within the Sa'id. It was his response to these heresies, at least in part, which prompted Pope Damian to entrust him with some advisorial capacity, possibly in regard to Syria.

Related to these heresies is his concern for the saints. Although he is believed to have been one of the compilers of the Synaxarium, at this point we can only verify his composition of the life of St. Dimiana, and his concern for Archangel Michael, especially relating to his day of commemoration. It is not unreasonable to assume that John of Barullos saw the necessity of reviewing and/or composing the lives of the saints, since they often result in conveying false doctrines or inexact spiritual truths, which often creep into these hagiographical traditions.

The motif of divine fire in the Coptic and Ethiopian entries for John of Barullos seems most likely to be the result of some type of the appropriation of the life of his contemporary St. Pisentius, who seems to be compared with Elijah the Prophet sometime before the fourteenth century. This may be the result of a long-standing tradition of Eucharistic visions that date at least to Peter I, which seem to have influenced Byzantine Eucharistic theology through Symeon Metaphrastes in the tenth century.

As is clear from the above, much work still remains to be done on the life and teachings of John of Barullos.

Notes

1 I must express my gratitude to Fr. Wadi Awad and Hany Takla for their assistance in finding some of the Coptic texts and references related to him.
2 Coquin and Martin 1991d: 1174b–1175a, as found in the *History of the Patriarchs*.
3 Davis 2008: 146–47, citing *Kitab mayamir wa 'aja'ib al-'adhra'*, 71; see also Stewart 1991c: 427.
4 Müller 1991b: 5:1367. Many of his relatives were believed to be priests: O'Leary 1937b: 168.
5 This is emphasized in the Ethiopian Synaxarium (Budge *Synaxarium*: 223).
6 *History of the Patriarchs* mentions that John of Barullos was held in high admiration by Pope Damian. According to some accounts, Petrus Callinicus was consecrated by Pope Damian. John of Ephesus heard that Peter was consecrated by Damian in Alexandria, while Michael the Syrian (copying Denys of Tell-Mahre) reports that the Eastern bishops, in agreement with the Alexandrians, ordained Peter in the Monastery of Mar Hanina (Ebied 1981: 4–5). In this controversy, Damian accused Peter of Tritheism while Peter accused Damian of Sabellianism.
7 Müller 1991b: 1368; Mai 1831: 198. MS 90 is dated to AM 934 or AD 1218. See also *Book of Adam* and *Apocalypse of Moses* in Helmbold 1967: 86.
8 This was originally published by Evetts 1907a: 213 (= PO 1.4: 477). It was followed by a French translation by Arnold van Lantschoot (Lantschoot 1946), and a German translation by C.D.G. Müller (Müller 1954a: 102–103, 150–56).
9 *The Investiture of (Archangel) Michael, the Apocryphon of John, Jubilation of the Apostles, Apocalypse of Adam, and the Dialog of the Savior* (Lantschoot 1946: 298).
10 Lantschoot 1946: 322n18. He compares the orders of the angels in John of Barullos and John the Grammarian in *De opifio mundi*, 1.10.
11 The Ethiopian manuscripts include the name of "the honorable father John, bishop of the city of Burlus, and the other holy and honorable fathers." Burmester 1938: 250.
12 According to Crum, this is located south of the Monastery of al-Mayma. Crum 1899–1900: 51.
13 According to her hagiography, St. Dimiana was baptized at the age of one at Dayr al-Mayma. Armanios 2003: 80.
14 Awad 1948: 56. Ikhristodolo may have been one of the three hundred young men believed to have assisted Julius with the tasks of preserving the stories and bodies of the saints. See *al-Siniksar* 1978: 47–48.
15 Strassburg MS 4.180, and St. Shenouda the Archimandrite Coptic Society ML.MS.146. See also Forget 1963: 165–66. I am grateful to Hany Takla for these references.
16 Riedel 1902. Burmester 1938 lists extant manuscripts from Zotenberg 1877: 124 MS 111.
17 Lucchesi 2003: 232. See also Müller 1986: 139n75.
18 The Ethiopian Synaxarium explains that this would take place when reciting the "Holy, Holy, Holy" (Budge *Synaxarium*: 224).
19 According to the Coptic Synaxarium, this happened three times; in the Difnar (Mattaos 1985) and the Ethiopian Synaxarium, it happened *each* time.
20 *Korban* is the Arabic word for the sacramental bread offering.

21 Budge *Synaxarium*: 224. Archdale King claims that these heretics were accustomed to commune twenty times a day. King gives no citation, and may have just misread the account (King 2007: 416).

22 Malaty 1993: 115, citing Manuscript 97-470 History 18, Library of the Coptic Museum (=Coptic Museum Hist. 470), from the fourteenth century, published by Nabil Selim (in Arabic).

23 Malaty 1993: 115, citing Manuscript 97-470 History 18, Library of the Coptic Museum (=Coptic Museum Hist. 470), from the fourteenth century, published by Nabil Selim (in Arabic).

24 Schaff 1859: 472. Symeon is also believed to have edited the *Philokalia* and paraphrased the homilies of St. Macarius the Great. Agapios 1957: 848n76, concerning the Holy and Ecumenical Fifth–Sixth or Sixth Synod.

25 St. Peter of Alexandria, *On the Epiphany*, 28–29 (Pearson and Vivian 1993: 167).

26 Unfortunately only a small fragment of the life of Benjamin survives. See Butler 1978: 173n2, citing Bodleian Library MS. Copt. Clar. Press b. 5; Amélineau 1889. We are never told exactly what crime prompted Benjamin to call down fire upon him.

2 The Relationship between the Monks of Northern Egypt and the Patriarchs of the Egyptian Church

David Brakke

On the evening of 8 February 356, imperial soldiers surrounded the Church of Theonas in Alexandria. They sought to apprehend Athanasius, the bishop of Alexandria, whom three church councils had recently condemned and deposed. According to Athanasius himself, he was able to escape thanks to "the monks who were with us and some of the clergy."[1] For six years Athanasius eluded capture. While one source reports that he hid within the city, others tell us that he took refuge with desert monks (Brakke 1995: 130). Athanasius describes himself as "living in the desert" during this period.[2] Most likely, because imperial officials continued to search for him, Athanasius moved among a variety of hiding places, both in the city and among the monasteries. Monks certainly played an important role in preventing the agents of the emperor Constantius II from arresting the bishop and sending him into exile in some far location. This incident provides a dramatic example of solidarity between the patriarch of Alexandria and the monks of northern Egypt.

We should not, however, take this close relationship for granted. Certainly Athanasius did not. Instead, Athanasius and his successors had to work to create and maintain a productive connection between the monks and the patriarchate. This chapter surveys how bishops Athanasius, Theophilus, and Cyril interacted with the monks of northern Egypt. Although at times Kellia, Nitria, or Scetis will be discussed in particular, for the most part the chapter will speak generally of monks resident in the semi-eremitical communities of the north. It is often difficult to determine from our sources precisely where the monks that they name were located, and the settlements at Kellia often served as a subset or more withdrawn version of other communities in Nitria. Kellia in particular was most populous in the sixth and seventh centuries, but I will discuss primarily the fourth and fifth centuries, when the relationship between the monks and the patriarch was first established.

The most significant areas or themes of the interactions between these monks and the patriarchs were proper ascetic practice, appointment to the episcopate, and the promotion of orthodoxy and the suppression of heresy and paganism. For the most part the patriarchs and the monks created a respectful and mutually supportive relationship. But tensions could develop between the patriarch's interest in building up the Church and the monks' goals of seclusion and prayer. At times the association could have real problems, and it seems that Theophilus had the most contentious and ambiguous interactions with the desert fathers.

Athanasius (r. 328–73) was the first patriarch for whom the growth of monasticism became an important area of concern.[3] Although he was not a desert monk, Athanasius does appear to have led an ascetic lifestyle before his consecration, and thus he was sympathetic to the new monastic movement. In his earliest *Festal Letters* the new patriarch praised virginity and the ascetic life: the saints, he wrote in his second letter, "remained alone, living virtuously," for they understood the power of "quietness and withdrawal from human beings in the troubles of life."[4] Still, he was concerned to make sure that monks remained firmly connected to the wider Church and that their teachings and practices supported orthodoxy as he understood it. His *Life of Antony* depicted the ideal monk as orthodox in faith, subordinate to the episcopate, and hostile to heretics and pagans (Brakke 1995: 135–37, 245–48). It was Athanasius who established the precedents for patriarchal involvement in the monasteries and who created the close relationship between the Alexandrian church and the desert monasteries south of the great city.

First, Athanasius wrote letters to monks that gave them directions on proper ascetic practice. In a letter to Ammoun of Nitria, Athanasius condemned monks who absented themselves from the Eucharist after a nocturnal emission, and in another letter to an unknown monk, now called *On Sickness and Health*, he criticized the practice of extreme sleep deprivation (Brakke

1995: 86–99). In both cases Athanasius was concerned that monks had gone too far in their ascetic disciplines, and he urged moderation. Moreover, the patriarch feared that monks who practiced severe asceticism might overestimate their superiority to ordinary married Christians. Although Athanasius agreed that the monastic life was holier than marriage, this difference was only a matter of degree. As he did in other works, Athanasius drew upon the different yields in the Parable of the Sower (Matthew 13:1–8) to make this point: the married person yields fruit "thirtyfold," but the celibate does so "a hundredfold."[5] All Christians, both monks in the desert and lay people in the world, are sacred members of the Church.

Likewise, Athanasius encouraged monks to support orthodox doctrine and to oppose heresy. Because monks emphasized the life of solitude, obedience, and prayer, they could lose interest in matters of church doctrine, and the monastic virtues of humility and hospitality sometimes made monks reluctant to judge other ascetics in matters of belief. Even a pagan priest could receive monastic hospitality and offer spiritual wisdom.[6] Athanasius, however, urged monks not to pray with or offer hospitality to monks who adhered to Arian teachings or who associated with Arians (Brakke 1995: 129–38). Monks should participate in the struggle to defend the orthodox faith against dissenters, as indeed those monks did who helped to rescue Athanasius in February 356 and granted him shelter in the following years.

We have little or no evidence as to how the monks responded to Athanasius's interventions regarding ascetic practice and monastic hospitality, but we do know that the patriarch faced monastic resistance to his third important initiative—appointing monks as bishops. Monastic literature, including the *Apophthegmata Patrum* or *Sayings of the Desert Fathers*, expresses great ambivalence about ordination. Monks resisted being drawn back into the world that they had renounced, and they feared that ordination to church offices would lead them into sinful pride (Brakke 1995: 103–104). As Evagrius of Pontus taught, the priesthood could very well be a temptation from the demon of vainglory.[7] In 354, when Athanasius tried to make the monk Dracontius bishop of Hermopolis Parva, just north of Nitria, Dracontius refused. In his letter to the monk, Athanasius stressed the unity of the Church. "Teaching and preaching" are not "an occasion for sin," he wrote,[8] nor does monastic withdrawal exempt someone from responsibility to the wider family of Christians. Athanasius cited Moses, Jeremiah, and Paul as men who were reluctant to preach and serve their communities, but who nonetheless obeyed God's call to do so (Brakke 1995: 99–110).

Dracontius did accept appointment as the bishop of Hermopolis Parva, and he suffered exile to the desert because of his support for Athanasius. Both of his successors in that see were Nitrian monks. We know that Athanasius successfully appointed monks as bishops in numerous cities and towns throughout Egypt. Nonetheless, monastic resistance to the episcopal office endured. According to a famous story that Palladius tells, when Timothy I (r. 380–85) and the people of a certain city tried to make the monk Ammonius a bishop, the monk cut off his left ear so as to make himself ineligible. When the patriarch and the people persisted, Ammonius threatened to cut off his tongue as well, and so Timothy and the people relented.[9]

The close bond between the Alexandrian patriarch and the desert monks that Athanasius forged continued during the reign of his successor Peter II (r. 373–80). Peter spent most of his seven-year reign in exile for his pro-Nicene beliefs, and numerous monks who supported him went into exile as well (Davis 2004: 62).

Leaving aside Theophilus for a moment, I turn now to the career of Cyril, who reigned from 412 to 444. Here we no longer find the patriarch struggling to persuade monks to accept ordination as bishops, nor did Cyril instruct the monks on specifically ascetic matters, as Athanasius did. By this time the varieties of monasticism had become much more stable, and the place of monks within the Church was less uncertain. Rather, Cyril's letters to monks show a strong concern for orthodoxy in doctrine, and the patriarch was eager to involve monks in his own efforts to oppose views that he considered heretical. The patriarch's *Letter to the Monks of Egypt* is traditionally placed first in the collection of his ordinary rather than festal letters. Written in the spring of 429, it marks the opening of the conflict between Cyril and Nestorius, the patriarch of Constantinople, which culminated in the Council of Ephesus of 431 (McGuckin 2004: 32–34; Wessel 2004: 76–82). In the letter Cyril warned monks against those who might question whether Mary should be called the Mother of God, and he encouraged them to remain in solidarity with him and the Alexandrian church (Davis 2004: 77–78). Cyril identified himself as the monks' "spiritual father," and he argued that orthodox belief must be the foundation for proper asceticism: "Those who have chosen to live the glorious and beloved way of life devised by Christ must first be adorned with simple and unblemished faith, and so then add virtue to their faith."[10] In defense of applying the title "Mother of God" to Mary the Virgin, Cyril cited the writings of Athanasius, who remained a revered figure among Egyptian

Christians in general and among the monks in particular: "Athanasius is a man worthy of trust and deserving of confidence, since he did not say anything that is not in agreement with Holy Scripture."[11]

The *Letter to the Monks of Egypt* was just the first of several letters that Cyril wrote to groups of monks, monastic leaders, and individual monks, all of which addressed matters of orthodoxy and heresy. While that famous letter did not mention Nestorius by name, in *Letters* 26 and 55 Cyril specifically referred to him as a danger to orthodox faith; in the latter he expounded the Creed of Nicaea as the touchstone of correct doctrine. In *Letter 81* the patriarch echoed his uncle Theophilus's condemnations of Origen, which I will discuss below; Cyril criticized Origen's teachings on the resurrection of the flesh and the preexistence of souls. Four letters (106–109) address a monk named Victor, sometimes along with bishops: according to the Coptic work that preserves these letters, the addressee was the Victor who served as archimandrite of the Pachomian *koinonia* based at Pbow in Middle Egypt and who sources report accompanied Cyril to the Council of Ephesus in 431 (Bouriant 1892; Coquin 1991h). The Victor who received these letters was an important ally of Cyril in his anti-Nestorian efforts leading up to and including the council. But Cyril's *Apologeticus* to Emperor Theodosius II mentions another "beloved monastic Victor" whose role in these events was more ambiguous. According to Cyril, this Victor was said to have made accusations against Cyril, but the monk dramatically swore that he did no such thing as "most of the holy bishops stood around him."[12] This might be another monk Victor, one from northern Egypt, for in a letter whose addressee is uncertain, Cyril names a "Victor" (not called a monk) among the "offal" of Alexandria that "speak ill of me" in Constantinople (not Ephesus);[13] perhaps this Victor, who came from Alexandria, not Middle Egypt, is the monk of the *Apologeticus*. Historians debate whether we are dealing with a single monk named Victor or two or more Victors (Kraatz 1904; Schwartz 1928). Whichever is the case, in addition to Victor of Pbow, other monks, including Shenoute of the White Monastery near Panopolis in Middle Egypt, accompanied Cyril to Ephesus.

Monks traveled to Alexandria to support the patriarch in his conflict with the Roman governor Orestes as well (Davis 2004: 71–73). This incident took place early in Cyril's episcopate; in 415 monks of Nitria came to the city and protested against Orestes, who believed that Cyril was illegitimately extending his power beyond that of the Church into the city's secular affairs. According to Socrates Scholasticus, a monk named Ammonius injured Orestes with a stone, and when Ammonius was arrested, he died under torture. Cyril proclaimed Ammonius a martyr. Not all Christians agreed that Ammonius deserved such recognition, and tensions escalated in Alexandria. Soon thereafter a mob of Christians murdered the philosopher Hypatia.[14] Monastic support of the Church and its patriarch had extended beyond opposing Christian heresy to confronting secular rulers and pagans.

The popularity of both Athanasius and Cyril among the monks of Nitria, Scetis, and Kellia is apparent in their few appearances in the *Sayings of the Desert Fathers*. The *Sayings* depict both men as paragons of orthodoxy who enjoyed congenial relationships with monks and with such ecclesiastical leaders as Epiphanius of Salamis.[15] The *Sayings* do not portray Theophilus (r. 385–412), Cyril's predecessor and uncle, so positively. On the one hand, unlike Athanasius and Cyril, Theophilus actually has a set of sayings attached to his name in the alphabetical collection. And in several of these, wise and thoughtful teachings about the monastic life are attributed to the patriarch.[16] On the other hand, Theophilus's interactions with monks are just as often awkward, and a few monks seem to show little respect for him. When Theophilus asks Arsenius for a saying, the monk tells him, "Wherever you hear Arsenius is, do not come near."[17] Pambo refuses to speak to the patriarch, suggesting that the bishop would learn neither from the monk's speech nor from his silence.[18] In yet another anecdote, Theophilus invites monks to Alexandria to tear down pagan temples. When he serves the visiting monks veal, the monks politely eat it—until the patriarch points out that it is veal, at which point the fathers refuse to eat any more of it.[19] In this story the monks accede to the bishop's request for help in his anti-pagan activities, but Theophilus shows little sensitivity to the monks' ascetic discipline.

This ambivalent portrayal of Theophilus in the *Apophthegmata Patrum* reflects the tumultuous nature of the patriarch's relationship with the monks of northern Egypt (Watts 2010: 198–200). Theophilus intervened more directly in the monasteries than any of his predecessors, and more than his successor Cyril. It was Theophilus who urged the monks to expand their support for the Church from opposing internal heresy, as we see in the career of Athanasius, to fighting paganism, which we see in the career of Theophilus's successor and nephew Cyril. With the Nicene–Arian conflict well behind him, Theophilus could turn his attention to the worship of pagan gods that still remained in Alexandria. He aggressively stirred up conflict with pagans, and he famously led an attack on the Serapeum, which pagan militants had made their fortress. Theophilus recruited monks to help him in vandalizing the temple and converting it to a church dedicated to John the Baptist and Elijah. He encouraged monks to make it a monastic residence. He did the same at the pagan pilgrimage site at Canopus, east of Alexandria. Here too Theophilus built a church and settled monks (Davis 2004: 64–65). Clearly some monks supported and participated in these anti-pagan activities, but others did not approve of them or felt ambivalent about monastic involvement in such events. These mixed feelings appear in multiple monastic sayings and stories, including the anecdote about the veal mentioned earlier (Brakke 2008). Monks should not "in the cities act shamefully," as one monastic father puts it.[20]

Even more controversial are Theophilus's actions during the so-called Origenist controversy (Clark 1992: 43–84; Davis 2004: 66–70; Russell 2007: 18–34, 89–174). As we have seen, both Athanasius before Theophilus and Cyril after him worried about heretical people and doctrines circulating among monastic communities. While Athanasius was concerned about Arians and Manichaeans, in Cyril's day the dangers were Nestorianism and Origen's teachings about the resurrection and the origin of the soul. Theophilus was the first patriarch to identify Origenism as a danger among the monks of Nitria, Scetis, and Kellia.

In 399 Theophilus used his annual *Festal Letter* to criticize an anthropomorphic conception of the divine: God, he said, has no body and so fundamentally differs from created beings, which are corporeal by nature.[21] Denial of divine anthropomorphism, however, could be understood to call into question prayer focused on an image of God, the goodness of the physical body, and the resurrection of the flesh. A group of monks traveled to Alexandria to protest. Theophilus then reversed himself: allegedly declaring to see "the face of God" in those of his monastic critics, Theophilus anathematized books of Origen, whose allegorical interpretation of the Bible allegedly undermined a more literal understanding of humanity's creation "in the image of God."[22] The patriarch violently expelled leading "Origenist" intellectuals from the monastic communities; when these refugee monks sought shelter with John Chrysostom in Constantinople, they initiated events that enabled Theophilus to get his ecclesiastical rival condemned and exiled.

John Cassian was in Egypt when Theophilus issued his anti-anthropomorphite *Festal Letter*. Cassian later presented as the paradigmatic "anthropomorphite" an elderly monk named Serapion whose "ignorance and rustic naiveté" led to the error of imagining that God has a human body.[23] Socrates Scholasticus likewise characterized the monks opposed to Origen's ideas as "simpler."[24] Following their lead, modern scholars have tended to attribute anthropomorphite ideas and practices to the origin of Egyptian monasticism among illiterate Egyptian monks (Serapion is an Egyptian name); their conception of an embodied God would have reflected their background in Egyptian paganism. "Origenism," then, entered the Egyptian desert with the arrival of learned Greek speakers like Evagrius of Pontus, who died shortly before the dramatic events of 399. Theophilus's expulsion of the Origenist intellectuals represented the removal of a later and foreign element from the simple faith of Egyptian monks. Cassian, a disciple of Evagrius, looked back on this episode with regret.

Recent scholarship has challenged this traditional interpretation. On the one hand, the earliest Egyptian monks were more literate and philosophically inclined than previously thought: the letters of Antony the Great indicate that, although his *Life* presented the legendary hermit as illiterate and uneducated, he in fact wrote sophisticated monastic epistles and pursued ascetic self-transformation within a cosmological theology indebted to Origen (Rubenson 1990). Monks in Nitria and Kellia read the Bible spiritually, to aid their contemplation of God, in the Alexandrian tradition of exegesis that included Philo, Clement, and Origen (Sheridan 2002). Evagrius's spirituality, which sought a knowledge *(gnosis)* of God beyond all images, may have been distinctive, but it was by no means foreign to previous Egyptian monastic tradition (Brakke 2006: 112–14). On the other hand, visionary experiences of God in human form appear not to have been remnants of paganism, but were rooted in a long tradition of learned Jewish and Christian prayer and speculation based on biblical passages that suggested divine anthropomorphism. Evidence for such exegetically based mysticism and for Christologies that emphasized the glory of God in human form appears in a range of monastic and other contemporary literary sources, and thus the attribution of anthropomorphism primarily to uneducated monks is no longer persuasive (Golitzin 2003; Patterson 2012).

The anthropomorphite episode of the first Origenist controversy, then, arose from the diversity of the monastic movement in Egypt. These different traditions of prayer and exegesis had existed among the monks of Nitria, Scetis, and Kellia for decades. Theophilus's intervention brought these traditions into conflict, with tragic results. Later monks may have agreed with Theophilus that Origen's teachings were unacceptable, but his violent approach to the problem damaged the monastic communities.

As unfortunate as this event was, it is nonetheless anomalous within the history of the relationship between the patriarch of Alexandria and the monks of northern Egypt during the fourth and fifth centuries (Bartelink 1987). Even Theophilus retained a measure of respect in some monastic traditions. If one monastic anecdote shows Arsenius of Scetis refusing to see Theophilus and telling him to go away, another depicts the dying patriarch as having learned from the old man and praising him as "blessed of God" for always keeping the moment of death before his eyes.[25] The close connection that Athanasius created faced testing during the long reign of Theophilus, but Cyril turned away from his uncle's tendency to intervene aggressively in monastic life, and he was able to build a strong relationship with the monks and rely on them at critical moments.

Some 275 years after Athanasius took refuge with monks in northern Egypt to escape imperial arrest, another patriarch of the Egyptian church did the same. When the emperor Heraclius reclaimed Egypt from the Persians in 629, he pursued a renewed policy aimed at bringing anti-Chalcedonian Christians into the larger Byzantine church: the opponents of Chalcedon should be able to live with the language of "two natures" if they were granted the doctrines of "one activity" and "one will." Pope Benjamin (r. 626–65) and his anti-Chalcedonian flock would have none of this, and so when the emperor appointed Cyrus as Chalcedonian patriarch of Alexandria in 631 and charged him to implement this policy, Benjamin fled into exile in the monasteries of Kellia and Scetis, where he remained for ten years (Davis 2004: 115–21). The fall of Egypt to the Muslims in 641–42 allowed him to return to Alexandria. Benjamin set about reconstructing damaged monastic settlements, and he consecrated a new church at the Monastery of St. Macarius (Swanson 2010: 11–12). This moment renewed the close relationship between the patriarchate and the monks of northern Egypt.

The important role that monks play in the life of the Egyptian church today has developed over centuries, but such patriarchs as Athanasius, Cyril, and Benjamin laid the foundation for it during Late Antiquity.

Notes

1 Athanasius, *Defense of His Flight* 24 (Szymusiak 1987: 234–36).

2 Athanasius, *Letter to Serapion on the Holy Spirit* 1.33.1 (DelCogliano, Radde-Gallwitz, and Ayres 2011: 103).

3 The following discussion recapitulates chapter 2 of Brakke 1995. See also Davis 2004: 55–63.
4 Athanasius, *Festal Letter* 24 (=2) (Brakke 1995: 320–21).
5 Athanasius, *Letter to Ammoun* (Joannou 1963: 69).
6 *Sayings of the Desert Fathers* 11.109 (Wortley 2012: 210).
7 Evagrius, *Talking Back* 7.3, 8, 26, 36, 40 (Brakke 2009: 148–56).
8 Athanasius, *Letter to Dracontius* 10 (*Patrologia Graeca* 25: 533).
9 Palladius, *Lausiac History* 11.1–3 (Meyer 1964: 46–47).
10 Cyril, *Letter* 1.2–3 (McEnerney 2010a: 3–4).
11 Cyril, *Letter* 1.9 (McEnerney 2010a: 16).
12 Cyril, *Apologeticus* (*Patrologia Graeca* 76: 485).
13 Cyril, *Letter* 10.7 (McEnerney 2010a: 57).
14 Socrates Scholasticus, *Ecclesiastical History* 7.13–15 (Hansen 1995: 357–60); Davis 2004: 71–73.
15 Athanasius: *Sayings of the Desert Fathers* 3.32; 10.17; Epiphanius 1; Sisoes 25. Cyril: *Sayings of the Desert Fathers* 10.178; 18.5; Motius 2.
16 See especially *Sayings of the Desert Fathers* Theophilus 1, 4–5.
17 *Sayings of the Desert Fathers* 2.6 (Wortley 2012: 16).
18 *Sayings of the Desert Fathers* 15.59 (Wortley 2012: 262).
19 *Sayings of the Desert Fathers* 4.76 (Wortley 2012: 52–53).
20 *Sayings of the Desert Fathers* Bessarion 4 (Wortley 2014: 78–79).
21 This letter does not survive. Rather, scholars follow a summary of what seems to have been this letter given by Gennadius of Marseilles, *Illustrious Men* 33 (*Patrologia Latina* 58: 1077–78).
22 Socrates Scholasticus, *Ecclesiastical History* 6.7 (Hansen 1995: 322).
23 Cassian, *Conferences* 10.1–4 (Ramsey 1997: 371–73).
24 Socrates Scholasticus, *Ecclesiastical History* 6.7 (Hansen 1995: 324).
25 *Sayings of the Desert Fathers* 3.15 (Wortley 2012: 28).

3 Saint Mina Monastery in Arabic Sources

Sherin Sadek El Gendi

St. Mina the Egyptian, or the Miracle Worker, is one of the most important Coptic saints in Egypt from the Roman period (Krause 1991a: 1589b–1590). His monuments are visited by a large number of believers, and a large artistic collection, discovered in his monastery in Mareotis[1] (Miedema 1913; De Cosson 1935; Bagnall and Rathbone 2008: 109, 116–19, figs. 4.2.1, 4.3.1), is displayed in Coptic monasteries (Kaufmann 1920; Leroy 1982; Lyster 1999: 19; Gabra 2002: 59, 77, 91; Bolman 2002; Van Moorsel 1995: 1–2; Van Moorsel 2002), in Coptic churches, and in the Coptic Museum in Cairo and other international archaeological museums. This chapter begins with a short historical introduction to St. Mina, the meaning of his name, his feasts, and his monasteries and churches in Mareotis[2] west of Alexandria, in Fumm al-Khalig, in the Delta, and in Upper Egypt according to the Arabic sources.

St. Mina and His Namesakes

St. Mina is well known in Egypt and abroad because of a biography written for the first time most probably in the eighth century AD, and later in several historical sources (Atiya 1959: 2:313; Abu al-Makarim 1895: 103; 'Abd al-Malek 2009: 28–57), in addition to some Greek and Coptic manuscripts.[3]

According to his biography, his mother, Euphemia, was barren. One day, she went to pray in the church in front of the icon of the Holy Virgin

Mary, who appeared to her and told her "Amen," which means "answered." The Greek name of St. Mina was taken from the word "amen" (Hooff 1884: 258–70; Basset 1909: 3:293–98; Kaufmann 1910b: 34; Meinardus 2002b: 168–70; 'Abd al-Malek 2009: 28–57). He is also known by titles such as: ⲁⲡⲁ or ⲁⲃⲃⲁ ⲙⲏⲛⲁ, meaning 'Father Mina' in Coptic; αγιος Μήνας, meaning 'St. Mina' in Greek; μεγαλο μαρτήρος Μήνας, 'the great martyr Mina'; Μήνας του Θαυματουργου, 'Mina the wonder-worker,' in the Greek church; Abu Mina (Abu al-Makarim 1895), Bu Mina (Cairo Coptic Museum Ms. Hist 469), Bumnah, Mar Mina, or Mari Mina. In the ecclesiastic references, he is known as St. Mina al-Bayadi (Mar Mina Monastery 2003: 15, 18–21).

At different times, Mina's name was given to various monks, bishops, and several patriarchs. In Upper Egypt, specifically in Akhmim, there was a Coptic monk named Mina who passed away on 17 Amshir as mentioned in the Coptic Synaxarium (Coquin 1991f: 1589) after the Arab conquest of Egypt by 'Amr ibn al-'As in AH 21 (AD 641–42). We must mention also St. Mina of al-Ashmunayn or St. Mina the Ascetic,[4] the martyr who was killed after the Arab conquest, and St. Mina the bishop of Tmuis, who was a native of Samannud in the Delta. There are also Sts. Mina of Qus, of the Metanoia Monastery, and of the St. Apollo Monastery, and St. Mina of Benevento in Italy (Mar Mina Monastery 2003: 497–511). Nor can we forget Pope Mina I, the forty-seventh Coptic Orthodox patriarch (767–74),[5] Pope Mina II, the sixty-first patriarch (956–74),[6] and Pope Cyril VI, the 116th patriarch (1959–71), who undertook the construction of the new Monastery of St. Mina in King Maryut and in Fumm al-Khalig.

Sometimes St. Mina the Miracle Worker is confused with St. Mina who was the abbot of the Monastery of St. Apollo (Coquin 1991e: 1588b–1589a) at Bawit. He is also sometimes confused with another saint bearing the same name who was born in Athens (Coquin 1991f: 1589).

Biography of St. Mina

According to several Ethiopian, Greek, Coptic, and Arabic sources, St. Mina was born in the village of Qetwa in Greek (Cotyée in French) (Kaufmann 1910a: 33). This village is located in Phrygia in Asia Minor. Others believe that he was born in Nikyius (Νικευς in Greek, or Νιχιω in the *Itinerary of Antonius* [Abu al-Makarim 1895: 103]); in the village of Ibshadi (in Coptic ⲡϣⲁϯ) in the district of Manf (Abu al-Makarim 1895: 103); or in Tala, near Zawyat Razain village in Munufiya governorate[7] to the east of the Rosetta branch of the Nile (Amélineau 1893: 277–83), not far from Kafr al-Zayyat in Gharbiya where his monastery was built later in Ibiyar (Abu al-Makarim 1895: 103; Viaud 1979: 5, 29–30, no. 11). Others think that he was born in the third century AD of rich Christian parents in Alexandria (Shafiq 2003: 14–15).

Being a native of Nikyius, Mina's father Eudoxios[8] was appointed governor of the province of Africa. In fact, during the lifetime of the Roman emperor Carus (282–83), St. Mina's father left Egypt and went to Phrygia, which is why many think that St. Mina was born and martyred there (Drescher 1942: 58). After the premature death of his father Eudoxios, he joined the Roman army and became the prefect of Pentapolis[9] as his father's successor. He was very close to the Roman emperor, but when he became a Christian, Mina left the Roman army to escape from the cruel persecution of the Roman emperor Diocletian (r. 284–305) against the Copts. A few years later, when Galerius (r. 305–10) had become emperor, Mina returned to his garrison, where he was persecuted, tortured, and beheaded on 15 December 307, at the age of twenty (Shafiq 2003: 16, no. 6), because of his attachment to the Christian religion (Budge 1909: 1–2, 22–23; Delehaye 1922; Cabrol and Leclerq 1925–53: 1:2, 15:2; Drescher 1946; Maraval 1985: 82; Coquin 1991f: 1589; Jaritz 1993: 22, no. 10; D'Orléans 2002: 2:403; Iskandar 2005: 10–68, 188–91; 'Abd al-Malek 2009: 28–57). He was buried near Lake Mareotis (Abu al-Makarim 1895: 102, fol. 29b). Others believe that St. Mina was killed in Asia Minor (Bagnall and Rathbone 2008: 109–16).

Later, orders were given to his colleagues to suppress the rebellions of the Bedouins in the Desert of Maryut. They took St. Mina's body with them, carrying it on the backs of camels. In King Maryut, the camels suddenly stopped and refused to continue walking. The soldiers understood this to mean that it was the desire of the saint to be buried there near the village of Asset (Hyvernat 1886a: 1:171; Drescher 1942: 59; Forster 1990: 284–91; Mar Mina Monastery 2003: 29–83; 'Abd al-Malek 2009: 28–57). The story of the camels is also mentioned in the biography of Piroou and Atom, who died in Psarion on 8 Abib. Others think that St. Mina suffered martyrdom in Qetwa. The church bearing his name there is their evidence.

Four years after his death, St. Mina's miracles (Devos 1960a: 275–305) appeared to the natives of the area, particularly curing different diseases and solving several problems (Zotenberg 1877: 203; Crum 1905: 156–57, no. 340; Delehaye 1925: 46–49; Devos 1960a: 275–308; Devos 1960b: 156–59), especially after the appearance of a spring of healing water at the site. A small chapel covered by a cupola was built over his tomb. Many pilgrims flocked to this site from all over the world to be baptized, to be cured of diseases, and to obtain the blessing of St. Mina, especially during feasts. Because of his miracles, his monastery in King Maryut became one of the ancient pilgrimage centers from the end of the Roman period.

Although the Coptic patriarch Athanasius (r. 326–78) ordered the construction of a church to St. Mina on this site, it was built later by the Roman emperors Valentinian and Valens (r. 364–78). In the time of the archbishop Theophilos (r. 385–412), the Roman emperor Arcadius (r. 395–408) built a church which is wrongly identified with the Great Basilica, which was one of the biggest churches in Egypt (Kaufmann 1910b; Grossmann 1982: 131–54). Later, the Roman emperor Zeno (r. 474–91) sent a garrison of soldiers to protect the pilgrims (Amélineau 1888; Grossmann 1986: 9). The monastery flourished and took its final shape in the late fifth and the first half of the sixth century AD (fig. 3.1).

Grossmann states that the body of St. Mina was brought to Egypt to a place named "Nepaeiat al-Bayadi," meaning "Libya" and used usually to describe the region west of Alexandria (Grossmann 1986: 8–9). At the end of the fourteenth century AD, the relics of St. Mina (Mar Mina Monastery 2003: 131–60) were transferred to his church in Fumm al-Khalig or Zahraa Misr al-Qadima (Mar Mina Monastery 2002: 132), also called the church of Bu Mina, in al-Hamra near the Roman fortress of Babylon. It was rebuilt during the rule of al-Walid ibn Rifa'a in AH 117/AD 735, and again in the time of the Mamluk sultan al-Nasir Muhammad ibn Qalawun (r.

Fig. 3.1. Remains of ancient Monastery of St. Mina in King Maryut (Sherin Sadek El Gendi).

AD 1310–41) (Abu al-Makarim 1895: 102; al-Maqrizi 1835: 1:303, 2:512; Wüstenfeld 1847: 3:50–120; Butler 1884: 1:47–74; Delehaye 1910: 117; Drescher 1941: 19–32).

St. Mina's Monasteries and Churches in Arabic Sources

Fifteen kilometers southeast of Burg al-'Arab, Dayr Abu Mina is in the area known to the Arab Bedouins as Karm Abu Mina (Dutilh 1904: 38–52, 56–68, 69–73; Krause 1990: 3:cols. 1116–58; Shoucri 1991b: 706b–707a) or Abuh Minnah (Grossmann 1986: fig. 1). According to Coquin, the word *dair* or *dayr* describes any dwelling place of Christians or cenobites (Coquin 1991a: 695a). St. Mina's Monastery in King Maryut is about forty-three kilometers southwest of Alexandria (Stephen 1998: 303–39; Chaillot 2005: 12) and parallel to the area of Bahig (Grossmann 1986: 7; Shafiq 2003: 33).

According to Abu al-Makarim, there was another monastery dedicated to St. Mina located in Ibiyar about one kilometer away from Kafr al-Zayyat. This monastery is also called Dayr al-Habis, as a hermit was living within it. The Ayyubid sultan al-Kamil Muhammad Nasir al-Din (r. AH 615–36/AD 1218–38), son of al-'Adil Abu Bakr Sayf al-Din (r. AD 1200–18), visited this monastery (Abu al-Makarim 1895: 108; Viaud 1979: 5, 29–30, no. 11).

Describing the Monastery and the Church of St. Mina in al-Hamra, Abu al-Makarim confirmed that the monastery named after the martyr Mina, the owner of the three crowns which came down to him from heaven, who was a native of Nikyius, and whose pure body is buried in the church at Maryut, was restored during the caliphate of Hisham ibn 'Abd al-Malik ibn Marwan, when al-Walid ibn Rifa'a was *wali*, at the expense of all the Christians who lived in that quarter (AH 106/AD 725). This took place after the conflict with the Arabs, when the Christians complained to the *wali* that their women and children were not secure from molestation while going to and returning from the churches in Misr, especially on the nights of the Forty Days' fast (Abu al-Makarim 1895: 102, fol. 29b). In consequence of these outrages, a great number of the Arabs were killed. In this quarter, there were many prominent men among the Christians, so they were allowed to restore their churches; they began to rebuild al-Hamra, and to repair what had been destroyed there (Abu al-Makarim 1895: 103). They renovated the Church of St. Mina, and they made precious vessels of silver and other things for it. They also bought much property, including a garden in which there were two wells with waterwheels; all of this property was occupied by houses.

In the church, there was a large baptismal font dedicated to St. Mina. Several chapels in the upper story were rebuilt, including the chapel of St. George, which is said to have been originally dedicated to St. Theodore.[10] In the big Church of St. Mina, there was the body of the martyr St. John, on a stand of solid wood. The river was near this church, but it later receded from that place and changed its course until it reached the Church of St. Theodore at Damanhur Shubra close to Cairo on the river, and damaged it. Later the body was moved to the church of Our Lady at Shubra. The chapel of St. John was restored after the fire of al-Fustat, by order of Shawar, by Shaykh Ibn Abu al-Fada'il ibn Abu Sa'id (Abu al-Makarim 1895: 104, fol. 30a), during the caliphate of al-'Adid. The Church of the Holy Nativity looks out on the courtyard of the big church, as does a very small chapel renovated by Abu Ghalib ibn Abi al-Makarim al-Bilbaisi, and named after St. Mercurius (Abu al-Makarim 1895: 105, fol. 30b; Vansleb 1677b: 178).

In the big Church of St. Mina is a colored marble ambo, the greater part of which is red and transparent. It is supported by marble pillars of skillful workmanship. There is also a wooden episcopal chair. Near the ambon, on the north side, an altar is dedicated to the martyr Mercurius, donated by Shaykh Abu al-Fadl, son of the bishop, which has a wooden tablet upon it. Above the altar there is a wooden cupola supported by marble pillars, and upon this altar too there is a wooden tablet.

Near the church is the monastery, entered by a separate door; it houses a number of nuns in separate dwellings. In the monastery, there is a well of running water, which was dug and furnished at the expense of Shaykh Abu Zakari al-Sayrafi, during the caliphate of al-Hafiz. Within the chapel was the entrance to the bake house (Bayt al-'Ajin, or House of Dough), where the Eucharistic breads are prepared, and in which there is an ancient tomb. Shaykh al-As'ad Salib ibn Mikha'il, the son of the hegumen,[11] separated the bake house from the chapel and made it a church dedicated to St. George, with a separate door near the large church as well as a door from the chapel. The finished church was consecrated by Mark, bishop of Cairo, in the presence of St. John the seventy-second patriarch (r. 1147–67) (Abu al-Makarim 1895: 106, fol. 31a) and the liturgy was celebrated in it. This church stands among gardens and is much frequented by the monks and others (Abu al-Makarim 1895: 106, fol. 31a).

The chapel of St. John, which has already been mentioned, built above the big Church of St. Mina, was restored later by Abu al-Fada'il, known by the name of Ibn Dukhan, and was consecrated and the liturgy was celebrated in it. In front of the church, Ibn Dukhan also began to rebuild a three-story tower which was old and had fallen into ruins. This and the furnishings of the church were (partly) paid for by Shaykh Salib, mentioned above. The tower was not completed, because of interference from Abu al-Barakat, son of Shaykh Abu al-Fakhr ibn Sibuwaih. While the Church of St. Paul was being restored, the greater part of the monastery was destroyed. Shaykh Salib dug a well for a waterwheel and built the first story of the tower and half of the second story. He was making efforts to finish it when he was stopped by Abu al-Barakat, who said: "None shall finish this work but me, with my own money."

The rest of the monastery and the pavilion remain unfinished. There are burial grounds in the courtyards outside the church. Five wells have been dug in this monastery and in the surrounding courtyards, which belong to it. The greater part of the houses and the shops, bought for this monastery when it was restored, were ruined; those that remained were left deserted (Abu al-Makarim 1895: 107, fol. 31b). Abba Mark, bishop of Misr, sold them to a man who demolished them and carried away the bricks and the timber. Thus the monastery was left in the midst of ruins.

There is also, in the Hamra al-Wusta, a church named after St. Colluthos (25 Bashans/20 May) (Abu al-Makarim 1895: 108, fol. 32a),[12] built during the caliphate of al-Amir, and under the government of Suwarr in Rifa'a, on ground bought by the Christians from the tribe of Banu Fahm. It stood near the baths of Ibn Najah and the alley named Zuqaq ibn 'Aqil (Abu al-Makarim 1895: 108, fol. 32a; Ibn Duqmaq 1893: 4:33) between al-Fustat and Cairo, in the Hamra, later known as Qanatir al-Saba'. A church and monastery of Abu Mina still exist, but are better known today as Mari Mina. Under the rule of the sultan al-Nasir Muhammad ibn Qalawun during the eighth/fourteenth century, the monastery and church of Abu Mina were wrecked; but they have since been restored (Abu al-Makarim 1895: 102, fol. 29b; al-Maqrizi 1835: 2:513). It is said that the grave of St. Mina at Lake Mareotis remained unknown for some time, until a princess was cured of leprosy by mold from it. The king then erected a church over it, which was replaced by a larger church built by Arcadius and Honorius (Abu al-Makarim 1895: 103; Amélineau 1890: 90).

On the shores of Lake Mareotis, a church dedicated to Abu Mina was flourishing after the Arab conquest, but seems to have fallen into decay before AD 1376. Some remains on the borders of the lake, however, still bear the name (Abu al-Makarim 1895: 102, fol. 33b; Amélineau 1893: 241–43). In addition, Abu al-Makarim reports the existence of the church of Abu Mina built by Shaykh Sa'id al-Dawla Abu Minga ibn Bu Zikri ibn al-Sarid (Abu al-Makarim 1895: 102, fol. 33b).

Following Abu al-Makarim, al-Maqrizi (d. AH 845/AD 1441) mentions again that the chief act of al-Walid ibn Rifa'a was to allow the Copts to rebuild the Church of St. Mina in the Hamra in Old Cairo (al-Maqrizi 1835: 1:303; 1998b: 196), in which a feast was celebrated every year. This church was divided into three chapels for the Jacobites, the Syrians, and the Armenians (al-Maqrizi 1998b: 194). It existed until the rule of al-Nasir Muhammad ibn Qalawun (AD 1285–1341).

Providing additional details, al-Maqrizi also wrote about the churches of Bu Mina, the Apostles, and the Archangel Michael in the village of Shaqalqil in the district of Abanub in Asyut (al-Maqrizi 1998b: 221). He also mentions another church dedicated to Bu Mina in Huwwa in Nag' Hammadi near the western mountain in Upper Egypt (al-Maqrizi 1998b: 224). Meinardus mentions Bu Mina in Abanub as follows: "Among the once abandoned monasteries east of Asyut, the Monastery of St. Mina (Dair Abu Mina) near Abnub has been reactivated" (Meinardus 2006: 47).

'Ali Mubarak writes about the Monastery of St. Mina built south of Cairo near the dam. He confirms that it included a church containing a chapel for the Syrian Orthodox, and that some of them were buried within it. The monastery was surrounded by an enclosure wall and a big garden. Its church was restored by Ibrahim al-Guhari and then by Tadros Guirguis Halabi (Mubarak 1887: 6:81). There are other monasteries of St. Mina in Sanabu and Hiw, in addition to churches in Basyun, Tahna Mount, Taha, Nazlit Hirz, Nazlit sons of Morgan, al-Makhila, and Bayt al-Kallaph (Mar Mina Monastery 2003: 395–405).

Monasteries and Churches of St. Mina in Recent Studies

In modern times, several travelers, scholars, and art historians have visited, excavated, and recovered the site of Abu Mina west of Alexandria, which had been abandoned from the late ninth century AD. Pacho was the first one to visit it, in 1820. In 1904, the Italian Annibale Evaristo Breccia excavated the site in addition to the site of Dikhaylah (Breccia 1907: 93, fig. 2/5; 'Abd al-Malek 2009: 23). In 1905, Kaufmann[13] and his assistant Ewald Falls arrived at the pilgrimage center of Abu Mina (Gabra 2008: 16; 'Abd al-Malek 2009: 23). Kaufmann called the site "the ancient Christian acropolis."

In 1926–27, Breccia visited the site again to restore the monastery. Antony de Cosson arrived at the monastery in 1935 and published its first map in 1936. The archaeological excavations had been continued in the meantime by the members of the Greco-Roman Museum in Alexandria (1925–29) and then by the German scholars Deichmann and Von Gerkan (Mohamed 2005: 2–3; 'Abd al-Malek 2009: 23). In 1942, the British archaeologist Perkins undertook some excavations in the Monastery of St. Mina in Maryut. In the same year Abuna Mina al-Baramusi al-Mutawahhid came to live at the monastery (Meinardus 1970: 231–32; Atiya 1991e: 1913–20; Van Doorn-Harder 1997: 231–44; Meinardus 2002a: 70; Meinardus 2002b: 168–79; Chaillot 2005: 25, 152–53). In 1945, Hegumen Yuhanna al-Subki the Antonian visited the monastery and described it. In 1951–52 Pahor Labib, the former director of the Coptic Museum, completed the excavations in the pilgrimage site of Abu Mina ('Abd al-Malek 2009: 24). It was visited in 1957 by Abba Theophilos and a group of monks from the Monastery of the Syrians in Wadi al-Natrun (Mohamed 2005: 3–4).

Pope Cyril VI, elected as the 116th Coptic patriarch in 1959, ordered the construction of the new monumental cathedral and monastery (Meinardus 1970: 44; Meinardus 2002a: 70; Meinardus 2002b: 168–79; Chaillot 2005: 25, 152–53; Gabra 2008: 88–89) in Maryut, where he transferred the relics of St. Mina in March 1962 (Khater 1961–62: 161–81; Jaritz 1993: 452). In 1964, the Deutsches Institut excavated the site in collaboration with the Coptic Museum in Cairo and later with the Franz Joseph Dölger-Institut in Bonn. After the death of Pope Cyril in 1971, his remains, along with those of his close disciple Bishop Samuel, were transported from St. Mina's Monastery in Old Cairo to this one in King Maryut and placed under the main altar (Meinardus 2006: 46).[14] Since 1974, the excavations have been carried out by the Deutsches Institut alone.[15] During the UNESCO meeting that took place in Luxor on October 22–27, 1979, the site was listed on the international patrimony list (fig. 3.2).

During all the excavations that have taken place in the archaeological site of Abu Mina, scholars have discovered arches, baths, streets, workshops, presses for oil and wine (Meinardus 2006: 46), a factory, and an oven (*Les fouilles* 1906: 59, fig. 38; Kaufmann 1908: 58–59; Falls 1913; Miedema 1913; *Tatwir* 1987: 14). The oven was most probably used to produce St. Mina flasks (fig. 3.3) (Metzger 1981; Kiss 1989; Krause 1991a: 1589–90; Gabra 1999: 47–48, 108; El Gendi 2007: 499–546; 'Abd al-Malek 2009: 95–98), children's toys, amphorae, storage jars, bowls, dishes, ewers, and terra cotta.

Fig. 3.2. New Monastery of St. Mina in King Maryut (Sherin Sadek El Gendi).

Nowadays, the Copts celebrate annually several feasts of St. Mina the Miracle Worker: 15 Ba'una/22 June, the date when his monastery was consecrated in King Maryut (Basset 1922b: 566–67; Viaud 1979: 19); 15 Hatur (Basset 1906: 2:293–98; Drescher 1942: 57), which corresponds to November 11 in the Greek and Roman Catholic Churches (Delehaye 1922: 85; Drescher 1942: 57; Meinardus 2002b: 168), the day of his martyrdom; 15 Hatur/24 November (Delehaye 1910: 117; Drescher 1941: 19–32; Khater 1961–62: 161–81; Viaud 1979: 19; Chaillot 2005: 120–52). These feasts are celebrated in Cairo, Qetwa, and Constantinople, where his church was built by the Roman emperor Constantine (r. 306–37) over the remains of an ancient temple dedicated to the Greek god Poseidon (Delehaye 1922: 120; Schmidt 1986: 258–59). Some scholars believe that the church in Constantinople is dedicated to St. Minas the Greek, who was born in Athens, and not to the Egyptian St. Minas (Dutilh 1904: 40). Starting from the beginning of the eighteenth century AD, various Coptic, Greek, and Armenian artists produced many icons decorated with the iconography of St. Mina to immortalize his memory (Van Moorsel, Immerzeel, and Langen 1991).

In conclusion, the life of St. Mina the Egyptian appears in several Greek and Coptic manuscripts. It is evident that his monasteries and churches are mentioned in several ancient historical Arabic sources, especially from the Fatimid and the Mamluk periods. Because of the religious, historical, and archaeological importance of these monuments, they have been renovated

Fig. 3.3. St. Mina pottery flask. The Coptic Museum, Cairo (Gabra 2014: 234).

at different periods starting from the eighth century AD, and excavated by archaeologists beginning in the nineteenth century. In the course of these excavations, many precious artifacts were discovered and were transferred to the Coptic Museum in Cairo and to other museums abroad. At present, the site of Abu Mina west of Alexandria, his monastery at Fumm al-Khalig, and his other churches in the Delta and Upper Egypt are visited by pilgrims seeking his intercession, especially at his feast days.

Notes

1 ⲘⲀⲢⲒⲰⲦϨⲤ in Coptic.
2 This is the Greek name of an ancient city, a district, and a lake in Egypt (Mubarak 1887: 6:61; Stewart 1991f: 1526b–1527b).
3 The Coptic manuscripts of al-Hamuli, preserved in the Pierpont Morgan Library and the New York Library (Cod. M575, M585 and M590).
4 His feast is celebrated on 17 Amshir (Coquin 1991f: 1589b).
5 Originally from Alexandria, he was a monk in St. Macarius the Great Monastery at Wadi al-Natrun (al-Maqrizi 1998b: 68; Labib 1991h; Isidorus 2002a: 268, 428).
6 Born in the village of Sandala, he was a monk in the Monastery of St. Macarius the Great (Labib 1991h; Isidorus 2002a: 429).
7 There is another village with the same name, to the east of the first one (Ramzi 1960: 1:463; 2.2:171, 217; Shafiq 2003: 13).
8 Eudoxios was the brother of Anatolius. Their father was *wali* (governor) during the time of the Roman emperor Probus (r. 276–82).

9 Located in Libya, Pentapolis consists of five cities: Apollonia, Berenike, Cyrene, Tocra, and Barcaia or Berca. This was the homeland of St. Mark the Evangelist, who preached Christianity in Egypt in the middle of the first century AD, according to the Coptic Orthodox tradition. The patriarch Athanasius (r. 326–73) visited this place. Pope Shenouda III also visited twice, in 1972 and in 2003.

10 It is not certain whether this is St. Theodore the Greek or Western (28 Amshir = 22 February), St. Theodore the Eastern (12 Tuba = 4 January), or St. Theodore of Shutb (20 Abib = 14 July). There is also a church named after the martyr St. John. (There are four martyrs by the name of John in the Coptic calendar, commemorated respectively on 11 Abib = 5 July, 19 Abib = 13 July, 14 Ba'una = 8 June, and 7 Tut = 4 September.)

11 ἡγούμενος in Greek is a more common form of the Arabic word *qummus*. The hegumen is, properly speaking, the abbot of a monastery, and the office of the ordination of the hegumen refers entirely to the duties of an abbot. However, the title of hegumen is also often given to priests of a superior rank, for instance, to the priest in charge of the patriarchal church of Cairo.

12 Colluthos was a priest; his sister was married to Arianus, governor of the Thebaid under Diocletian. Colluthos suffered martyrdom by decapitation, after terrible tortures (Georgii 1794; Zoega 1810: 237, cod. 41; Amélineau 1890: 21; Abu al-Makarim 1895: 108, fol. 32a).

13 A famous archaeologist, born in 1872 in Frankfurt and died in Ramstadt in 1951. He wrote about twenty-eight scholarly works in German (Falls 1913; Merkle 1932; 'Abd al-Malek 2005: 2.26–28; Mohamed 2005: 2; 'Abd al-Malek 2009: 23).

14 Bishop Samuel was assassinated on October 6, 1981, with President Muhammad Anwar al-Sadat (Shoucri 1991b: 707a).

15 For more information about the German excavations, see Kaufmann 1908; Grossmann and Jaritz 1982: 203–27; Grossmann 1986: 131–54; Grossmann 2004b: 33–43, pls. VII–X.

4 The Bashmurite Revolts in the Delta and the 'Bashmuric Dialect'

Frank Feder

The Bashmurite Revolts in the Delta

It is not completely clear which regions in the Delta belonged to the land of the Bashmurites, or al-Bashmur, because their territory might have changed over time. The Arab historian Ibn Hawqal (tenth century) mentioned that the lake of Nastarawa was also called 'lake of Bashmur.' This would place the region of the Bashmurites not far from the lake of Burullus northward of Kafr al-Shaykh. Abu al-Fida (fourteenth century), however, locates al-Bashmur in the northeastern Delta between the Damietta Nile branch and Ashmum Tanah (today called Ashmum al-Rumman). During the uprisings in the eighth and ninth centuries, it seems that the Bashmurites controlled the marshy region of the northern Delta extending from Fuwwa in the northwest to Ashmum al-Rumman in the northeast. In 749, they attacked Rosetta in the west Delta and went as far as al-Farama (Pelusium) in the east. In the time of Abu al-Fida, al-Bashmur was apparently confined to the eastern Delta (cf. Gabra 2003: 114–15; Stewart 1991a: 349; Megally 1991: 349–50).

The Bashmuric revolts were recorded by Coptic and Arabic medieval historians and became known to European scholars as early as the beginning of the nineteenth century (Quatremère 1808: 147–214). In the eighth and ninth centuries, the population of the Delta revolted very successfully for a longer period against the Arab rule and administration. The marshy land of al-Bashmur with its low-lying sand banks had two unbeatable advantages: inaccessibility, especially to larger hostile forces, and economic self-sufficiency (Gabra 2003: 114; Megally 1991: 350). Historians and the *History of the Patriarchs* saw the reason for the revolts in the insupportable fiscal demands and the unjust treatment of the Christian population by the Muslim governors (*walis*). Between 693/94 and 832, nine revolts of the Copts against Arab authority are recorded (Gabra 2003: 115–16; Megally 1991: 350). But only the Bashmuric revolts attracted so much attention and involved even the caliph himself.

In the last years of the Umayyad rule over Egypt, the revolts in Egypt flared up intensely. In 720, a Byzantine army landed briefly in the northern Delta, which was then obviously not under full Umayyad control. According to the *History of the Patriarchs*, the last Umayyad caliph, Marwan II (r. 744–50), appearing in Egypt himself with an army and a fleet, was unable to quell the revolt in 749 after his governor had failed to suppress the uprising. His campaign was a disaster. Although the Coptic patriarch, Michael I (r. 744–67), was taken hostage in Rosetta, the insurgents took the stronghold and destroyed it. In response, Marwan ordered the pillage and destruction of Coptic villages and monasteries in the Delta.

When the Abbasids took over power in Egypt in 750, an amnesty was declared and the Bashmurites were exempted from taxes for this and another year. But in 767 they revolted again (cf. Mikhail 2014a: 121), this time together with simultaneously revolting Arab settlers. They defeated a new expedition, which the *wali* Yazid ibn Hatem had sent against them. The rebellion reached its peak in 832 (cf. Mikhail 2014a: 125). The caliph al-Ma'mun (r. 813–33) sent a strong army commanded by the Turkish general Afshin to suppress the revolt once and for all. After successfully regaining the eastern Delta and Alexandria, this campaign was also stopped by the Bashmurites. Afshin asked the Coptic patriarch to intervene, and the latter sent bishops with letters to the rebels; however, these envoys achieved no success. The caliph himself appeared on the scene accompanied by Dionysius, Patriarch of Antioch, who, together with the Coptic patriarch, was supposed to persuade the Bashmurites to surrender. When all these efforts failed, al-Ma'mun mustered a strong army guided by locals and launched a systematic attack on the rebels. As a result, the losses on both sides were extremely high and the caliph offered an armistice that was finally accepted by the Bashmurites. But the rebels were no longer able to resist the pressure of a much bigger and better organized force. Armed men were slaughtered, land and villages burned, children and women deported to Baghdad or sold as slaves in Damascus. The Bashmurite uprising was deeply inscribed in the memory of the Copts and is regarded as the last great attempt to oppose Muslim rule over Egypt. The suppression of the revolts was followed by harsh repressions on the Copts and forced a considerable part of the Christian population to convert.[1]

Whatever the judgment of the historians over the results of this insurrection may be (cf. Mikhail 2014a: 189–91), the Bashmuric revolts are an important witness to the resistance of native Christian Egyptians against oppression of freedom and exploitation by foreign rulers.

The Bashmuric 'Dialect'

The appearance of the Bashmuric dialect is first noted in the description of Athanasius of Qus (fourteenth century) in his Coptic grammar written in Arabic:

> and you know that the Coptic language is distributed over three regions, among them the Coptic of *Misr* which is the **Sahidic**, the **Bohairic** Coptic known by the *Bohaira*, and the **Bashmuric** Coptic used in the country of *Bashmur*, as you know; now the Bohairic Coptic and the Sahidic Coptic are (alone still) used, and they are in origin a single language. (Kasser 1991: 47)

Following this description, early scholars (beginning in the seventeenth century) studying Coptic manuscripts tried to apply Athanasius's division of the Coptic language to the Coptic texts. Thus, first Fayoumic and then also Akhmimic texts were referred to as "Bashmuric" simply as the third distinguishable dialect besides Sahidic and Bohairic, which had already been clearly identified. It was Ludwig Stern, following a much earlier judgment by Quatremère (1808), who stated in his *Koptische Grammatik* of 1880 that there was not a single textual witness of a Bashmuric dialect. Consequently, the idea of a Bashmuric dialect fell into oblivion (Kasser 1991: 47–48).

As it was more or less clear that the land of al-Bashmur was situated in the northern and northeastern Delta, interest in the Bashmuric dialect revived when W.E. Crum, in 1939, published (or republished) four documentary texts dated approximately to the eighth century. These texts were believed to come from the eastern Delta, because in the first document (a letter: Vienna, Nationalbibliothek, Papyrussammlung, K 1785), a place called Thennesou, most probably identical with Tinnis in the eastern Delta, was mentioned (Crum 1939b: 249–54; Kasser 1975: 406).

Besides the particularity that these texts were written in Greek letters only, that is, without any of the graphemes borrowed from Demotic, which mark the difference between the Greek and the Coptic alphabet, the idiom of these texts shares most features with the Bohairic dialect. Might we have here the vestiges of the lost Bashmuric dialect? Crum also cited the opinion of Eutychius that "those speaking Bushmuric were by race not Egyptians but Greeks" (Crum 1939b: 253).

With his unique ability to identify in each Coptic document, whose writing differed somehow orthographically from a major dialect, a new subdialect or, as in this case, a new dialect of its own, Rodolphe Kasser decided,

> Nous même, après avoir examiné ces textes, nous avons eu l'impression très nette, puis la conviction, qu'ils attestaient l'existence d'un dialecte copte particulier, que nous avons appelé "dialecte G" (sigle *G*), et que nous avons identifié, d'une manière hypothétique, au "bachmourique." (Kasser 1975: 407)

Having given a detailed dialectal description of *G*, together with a profound analysis and translation of the texts published by Crum (Kasser 1975), Kasser nevertheless had to conclude in his *Coptic Encyclopedia* article that "the history of the Bashmuric dialect is in large measure that of a 'phantom dialect'" (Kasser 1991: 47). Since we are left with those few documentary texts whose exact provenance, dating, and historical context we do not know, their identification with 'Bashmuric' is a mere guess. Although we should not deny the possibility of a once spoken Bashmuric dialect (of the Delta?), because Athanasius of Qus told us so, there is not much hope that we will find any written documentation thereof revealing itself as Bashmuric, let alone any kind of literature.

Notes

1 Gabra 2003: 115–18; Megally 1991: 350–51; but see Mikhail 2014a: 75–76, who points out that the significance of the revolts in regard to religious conversion has been greatly exaggerated.

5 Toward the Localization of the Hennaton Monastic Complex

Mary Ghattas

As localization tends to be a general problem for monasteries in Egypt, there is no single claim to the locale of the Hennaton—it remains shrouded in mystery. In an ideal situation, literary documentation, monumental ruins, and archaeological evidence would converge to point to a locale. Sometimes, only literary attestations of a monastic settlement survive without satisfactory archaeological evidence; sometimes the evidence remains while the documentation is silent; and sometimes artistic depictions leave traces behind, vouching for what once was a grand monastic center, one that attracted pilgrims and believers from Egypt and the whole world. The Hennaton or Dayr al-Zujaj (as it is designated today) was one such monastic center of Byzantine and medieval Egypt (Gascou 1991a: 954). Its prestigious reputation inspired kings to leave behind their earthly kingdoms, attracted pilgrims from all over the world, drew native Egyptians into the ascetic life, and finally, produced both patriarchs and saints whose memory is immortalized in the history of the Coptic Orthodox Church.

The sources indicate that the Hennaton monasteries lay along the ninth milestone mark on the road from Alexandria leading to the Western Desert, its location lending its name.[1] Although all primary sources point to this same locale, it has not been an easy task to identify its present-day location with precision. Nevertheless, the primary sources situate the Hennaton in its historical context and provide insight into its importance in the history of the Church of Alexandria. The various archaeological expeditions carried out over the course of the twentieth and twenty-first centuries, as well as the epigraphic data discovered in the early twentieth century, have shaped the current state of research in offering compelling suggestions for localizing the Hennaton.

From the primary sources, it appears that the Hennaton monasteries were unlike the communities of Pachomius and Shenoute in Upper Egypt, but rather appear to be a complex of loosely related settlements—each called by different names—along the ninth milestone mark. This model of ascetic settlement appears to have functioned either like the *laura* systems in Eastern Orthodox monastic organization or the *koinobia* of early Egyptian monasticism. It also appears that the Hennaton monasteries had their heyday in the sixth century and survived the Arab conquest of Egypt in 641 CE. Reviewing the different names used for Hennaton will point to the current issues regarding its localization, as will become evident.

It would be helpful to elucidate here the different names the primary sources use to refer to the Hennaton, as they provide insight as to how the center functioned. Although little is known regarding its origin, the earliest references to the Hennaton come from the legendary Coptic *Martyrdom* of Apa Kradjon, which records that Patriarch Theonas, during the Great Persecution of Diocletian's reign, ordained a monk by the name of Theopemptos as bishop for a monastery outside Alexandria called the Monastery of the Fathers *(Ton Pateron)*, home to about six hundred monks. Another contemporaneous reference is the commemoration in the Arabic Synaxarium of Bishop Sarapamon of Nikou on 28 Hatur (Basset 1971a: 349), which names the same locale Dayr al-Zujaj. Both early sources mention Patriarch Theonas (18, r. 282–300) as a central character in order to provide historical context, a technique employed by writers of Coptic history. The commemoration of Bishop Sarapamon recounts how the subject traveled from his native Palestine to Alexandria in order to be baptized by Patriarch Theonas. He then embraced the monastic life at Dayr al-Zujaj (Timm 1984b: 836; Basset 1971a: 350). Whether these sources prove credible or not, it can be argued that they hold the first references to the Hennaton and that monastic life outside the city of Alexandria was on the rise at the end of the third century.[2]

At the time of the death of Emperor Marcian (457), the Hennaton was under the leadership of Abba Longinus. This hegumen was the subject of a hagiographical life recorded by Bishop Basilius of Oxyrhynchos, in which the author recounts that the Monastery of the Holy Abba Gaius was not initially included in the Hennaton but was added later on.[3] The *Vita* also states that this Abba Gaius was originally from Corinth and eventually became the head of the monastery by the ninth milestone mark from Alexandria. According to the *Life* of Severus of Antioch penned by Zacharias the Rhetor, the characters Stephanus and Athanasius were students and writers of the celebrated Salama, who inhabited a monastery within the enclosure of Hennaton which was later named after him—the Monastery of Salama. The same Stephanus was attributed his own monastery in Hennaton. John of Ephesus clarifies the appellation "Monastery of the Fathers" in the sixth-century lives of the monks Peter and Photius. John describes the two as being "of Hennaton by Alexandria, which is also called the Monastery of the Fathers."[4] John of Ephesus also attributes the Monastery of Abba Andreas to the Hennaton in the Western Desert (Timm 1985: 1286). John Moschus also confirmed the existence of the Monastery of Salama during his visit to Egypt and lodged in the Monastery of Abba John the Eunuch in Hennaton. Other names of sixth-century *koinobia* include the Three Cells, home to the great ascetic Abba Zenon; the Monastery of the Epiphany; the Monastery of the Antonians; and the Monastery of Dalamatia (Gascou 1991a: 955). Sophronius, bishop of Jerusalem in the seventh century, dedicated his twenty-first *Anacreonticon* to the abbot and *oikonom* Theonas of the Monastery of Tugara in Hennaton (Timm 1984b: 842). In the eighth century a church in one of the monasteries of Hennaton was dedicated to Patriarch Simon I and was also the site of his burial. This same church housed the body of Severus of Antioch. The *Life* of Abba Christodoulus (66, r. 1047–77) in *The History of the Patriarchs* mentions a Monastery of the Holy Severus in Hennaton. From the name it appears that the site of Severus's burial and subsequent veneration grew into its own *laura* or *koinobion* over time (Timm 1984b: 846). By the fifteenth century, al-Maqrizi acknowledged that Dayr al-Zujaj was also called al-Hanatun and dedicated by the name of (A)Bu Gurg the Elder (Timm 1984b: 846). This is the only reference to a monastery by the name of George the Elder in Hennaton and the first equation of Dayr al-Zujaj with Hennaton. Fewer names for the monasteries at Hennaton were used as the center steadily declined, attesting to both its prime and its gradual end.

In addition to the names of different *laura*s or *koinobia*, there exist renderings of 'Hennaton' in different languages. For example, John of Nikiou in his *Chronicle* reports the name 'Bantun' when describing Justinian's election of Apollinarius, a reader of the Monastery of Salama, to the

Chalcedonian patriarchate (Timm 1984b: 837). The name 'Bantun' appears to be an Ethiopian rendering of the Arabic al-Hanatun, which in turn is an arabicization of the Greek 'Hennaton.' In the *Life* of Abba Peter IV (34, r. 567–69), the *History of the Patriarchs* describes the arrival of Peter's successor, Damian, at Bihanatun, which is also called Tunbatarun. Both names are arabicized renderings of the hybrid Greek/Coptic 'Pi-Hennaton' and of the Greek 'Ton Pateron' respectively. Though it is unclear when the Coptic expression 'Monastery of the Glassmakers' (Pimonastrion nte ni(c)a-n-abajoni) was first used, it is the Arabic rendering, Dayr al-Zujaj, which is used to the present day. Finally, eighteenth-century manuscripts of the work entitled "The Miracles of Abba Mina" are generally attributed to a certain Archimandrite Mardarius of Gabal al-Niaton. The editor of the manuscript in 1993 saw a similarity between al-Niaton and Natrun, but the name also bears a significant resemblance to the Arabic rendering of the Greek Hennaton (Jaritz 1993: 160 and n715). In addition, Hennaton proves to be closer to Dayr Abu Mina than the monasteries of Wadi al-Natrun; in terms of proximity, this would allow a monastic leader at Hennaton to be well acquainted with the miraculous happening in Mareotis. The earliest date of this work attributed to Mardarius is 1363 (Coptic Museum Hist. 469), by which time Arabic had become the language of the Egyptians, at least in the Delta. On the character Mardarius and the interesting title he bears of archimandrite (few figures in Coptic history bear such a title), additional research will surely elaborate. For now, the survival of these names allows us a more complete illustration of the site's history and also allows us to link together the different appellations used over the course of that history.

In addition to the structure of the Hennaton and the different names used to refer to the monastic center, the primary sources also elucidate the general atmosphere following the famed Council of Chalcedon of 451. The Synaxarium for 21 Tuba commemorates Hilaria, the daughter of Emperor Zeno (r. 425–91) (Basset 1971b: 621; Drescher 1947: 74).[5] Abba Pambo's response to the young princess's desire to embrace the monastic life at Scetis is recorded. He advised her: "But if you want to embrace the monastic life, go to *El-Ainatoun*; because it is moderate; there is at this time a group of wealthy people who have made themselves monks; they live without fatigue; they find consolation."[6] From Abba Pambo's recommendation, one can infer that proximity to the metropolis of Alexandria might have been a factor that afforded the monastics of the Hennaton an easier life compared with the harsh inner desert of Scetis.

Hilaria's father, Emperor Zeno, was best known for his *Henoticon*, or Edict of Union, published in 482 with the approval of Acacius, Patriarch of Constantinople, in order to quell the heated doctrinal war that pitted Diophysites and Monophysites against each other in the aftermath of the Council of Chalcedon (Ostrogorsky 1969). The Hennaton is remembered as a stronghold of what is now called Miaphysite Christology. A closer reading of the primary sources will illustrate that although the Hennaton was indeed a refuge for important Miaphysite figures of the early sixth century, pro-Chalcedonians lived alongside opponents of the council in a system that may have functioned similarly to the contemporaneous *laura* of Sabas in Palestine (Griffith 1997).

The Coptic and Greek traditions in the years immediately following the Council of Chalcedon evidence considerable influence despite doctrinal differences, though the Coptic tradition is understandably silent regarding the Greek influence at Hennaton. Hilaria, the abovementioned daughter of Emperor Zeno and a princess of the Byzantine court, came to Egypt to embrace the monastic life. The fact that a Byzantine royal would come to a land depicted as the stronghold of Monophysitism to become a monastic illustrates that the situation following the council was not strictly dichotomous.[7] In addition to Hilaria, a fifth-century Eastern Orthodox saint known as Theodora of Alexandria lived at the Hennaton (Gascou 1991a: 957). By the sixth century the anti-Chalcedonian John of Nikiou reported in his *Chronicle* that the emperor Justinian (r. 527–65) sent a letter to Agathon, the prefect of Alexandria, to ordain Apollinarius from the Hennaton as patriarch of the Chalcedonians of Alexandria and the other cities of Egypt (Timm 1984b: 837). The Greek tradition knows nothing of Justinian's order but reports that Justinian sent a treatise to the monks in Hennaton by Alexandria in 542/543 (Timm 1984b: 837), congratulating them on having returned to the Chalcedonian communion of the archbishop Zoilus. It appears that Justinian chose Apollinarius to succeed Zoilus because of his moderate views and docile manner (Gascou 1991a: 957). Justinian's own marriage to Theodora, remembered for her Monophysite leanings, might be used to prove the fluidity of the Chalcedonian/non-Chalcedonian divide. While traveling in early seventh-century Egypt, John Moschus visited many Chalcedonian ascetics, more precisely of the Monastery of Tugara. The monks of this particular *laura* told John Moschus about Abbot Mina, the abbot of Hennaton at the time, and about the Chalcedonian patriarch Eulogius (r. 581–608) (Timm 1984b: 840). The

Monastery of Salama must have been a Chalcedonian settlement at that time as well (Timm 1984b: 840). It has already been mentioned that the Chalcedonian bishop of Jerusalem in the seventh century, Sophronius, dedicated his twenty-first *Anacreonticon* to the abbot and *oikonom* Theonas of the Monastery of Tugara in Hennaton (Timm 1984b: 840). This Theonas seems to be Abbot Mina's successor (Timm 1984b: 840). Sophronius is said to have traveled with John Moschus to Egypt. After the Persian invasion of 619, the Greek *Vita* of John V the Merciful or the Almsgiver states that this Chalcedonian patriarch sent the Chalcedonian hegumen Ktesipp of Hennaton to Jerusalem in order to ransom captive Christians. The Coptic sources are silent regarding this incident (Timm 1984b: 841). The Hennaton must have been a theologically fluid monastic center for some years after Chalcedon.

But there are of course instances of strong disagreement with Chalcedon and its followers. Following the Council of Chalcedon, soldiers of Emperor Marcian tried to force the Tome of Leo on the monks of Hennaton and failed because the leader of the monasteries, Abba Longinus, strongly resisted.[8] The Coptic life of this same hegumen states that he gathered the monks of the Hennaton, the Oktokaidekaton, and the clergy of Alexandria to inaugurate Timothy II Aelurus as the new patriarch (26, r. 458–80) following the death of Emperor Marcian in 457 (Timm 1984b: 834). The most illustrious guest of the Hennaton was undoubtedly Severus of Antioch, who visited the monastic settlement following his deposition from the See of Antioch in 518, accompanied by Julian of Halicarnassus (Gascou 1991a: 956). John of Ephesus in either 534 or 541 stayed at Hennaton and testified to the force of attraction the monastic center exerted (Timm 1984b: 837). In the sixth century, the monastic colony served as the seat and refuge of the Coptic Patriarchate (Timm 1984b: 838). Abba Peter IV (34, r. 567–69) was secretly ordained there because pro-Chalcedonians dominated the capital city, forbidding Abba Peter access to Alexandria (Timm 1984b: 838). Peter and his successor, Damian (35, r. 569–605), carried out their patriarchal duties from the Hennaton, particularly in the Church of Joseph (Timm 1984b: 708; Gascou 1991a: 957).

Damian's new Syrian counterpart did not recognize Damian's ordination (Timm 1984b: 839). It was not until after the stay of the bishops Thomas of Harquel and Paul of Tellia that the intense relations between the Syrian sister church and the Hennaton were overcome (Timm 1984b: 839). In 616, it was perhaps the site where the reconciliation between the Jacobite churches of Alexandria and of Antioch was cemented (Timm 1984b: 839; Gascou 1991a: 957). During their stay at the Monastery of the Antonians in the beginning of the seventh century, Thomas of Harquel collated a Syriac translation of the New Testament with Greek manuscripts and Paul of Tellia translated the Septuagint into Syriac after Origen's *Hexapla* (Gascou 1991a: 957).

Back to a small note on Damian: A recent discovery of a wall painting on layer two of the northern wall of the *khurus* in the Monastery of the Syrians is thought to be of Damian (Innemée and Van Rompay 2002). He wears elaborate liturgical vestments and has a youthful appearance, attesting to his consecration at a young age. Behind him are depictions of what may be churches of a monastery. It is possible that this representation illustrates the Hennaton, where Damian spent his patriarchate.

The History of the Patriarchs does not confirm that Damian's successor lived at the Hennaton, but does confirm that Andronicus (37, r. 612–22) resided in Alexandria thanks to his good relations with the civil authorities (Timm 1984b: 841). *The History of the Patriarchs* reports that there were six hundred monasteries by Hennaton. This seems to be an exaggeration, in view of the attestation that the Persian invasion of 619 razed the complex to the ground, killed all the monks, and plundered all its riches, leaving nothing but ruins (Timm 1984b: 841). The number could instead refer to all monasteries outside of Alexandria at the time. From Patriarch Benjamin's (38, r. 622–61) *Homily on the Wedding of Cana*, one can glean that the monastic colony was renovated, again inhabited by monks, and still standing at the time of the Arab Conquest of Egypt in 641 (Timm 1984b: 841).

Following the Arab conquest, the Hennaton still survived as a monastic settlement, but one receives the impression that the once grand colony began a steady decline (Gascou 1991a: 957). Two more patriarchs emerged from the Hennaton: Simon I (42, r. 689–701) and his successor, Alexander II (43, r. 705–30). Simon was of Syrian origin; his parents gave him to a monastery west of Alexandria where the body of Severus lay. He took the name John during the course of his monastic life and served as the hegumen of Hennaton before his election to the patriarchate (Timm 1984b: 842). Simon's Syrian origins attest to Hennaton's international character following the Arab conquest, although one cannot help but think it became a predominately Miaphysite center (Gascou 1991a: 958). The Synaxarium commemorates, on 14 Tuba, a certain Theophilius, a Greek prince who became a monk during Marwan ibn 'Abd al-'Aziz's tenure, and who in turn inspired his father and mother to abdicate the throne in favor of the monastic life at Hennaton (Timm 1984b: 843–44). Although there are many legendary elements in this account, it attests to the survival of a women's monastery at Hennaton. Patriarch Alexander II appears to be the last patriarch who received a monastic education at Hennaton, but on two occasions hegumens of the settlement were selected for the patriarchate: Hegumen John in 689 and Hegumen John ibn Tirus in 1066 (Gascou 1991a: 958; Timm 1984b: 845). At the death of Patriarch Shenoute II (65, r. 1032–46), only forty monks were living in Hennaton (Timm 1984b: 845), giving the impression that the Hennaton was reduced to a single monastery at this time. Al-Maqrizi reports that in the fifteenth century the custom that required a newly elected patriarch to make a visit or stay at Hennaton, if he was not previously a monk there, was extinct (Timm 1984b: 846). This custom is first attested to under Mark II (49, r. 799–819) (Gascou 1991a: 958). Al-Maqrizi is the last author to write of Dayr al-Zujaj (Gascou 1991a: 958).

While the many attempts to localize the Hennaton in the twentieth century have offered compelling data, they all seem to build on one another without ever arriving at a final answer. Part of the reason may be that modern Alexandria is built on top of the ancient metropolis: all attempts to localize the Hennaton cite this issue as problematic, as no proper starting point from the city traveling west can be pinpointed. Building on Gustave Lefebvre's work (Lefebvre 1907), Walter Ewing Crum, in the same year, identified twelve gravestones housed at the Museum of the Archaeological Society of Alexandria as belonging to a cemetery of Hennaton. The location where these gravestones were acquired was the village of Dikhaylah, which he argued corresponded sufficiently to the ninth milestone mark west of the ancient city (Breccia 1907). In addition, the names of the monasteries on the gravestones correspond to John Moschus's description of them in his work, *Spiritual Meadow*. Moreover, the gravestones date to the period in which these monasteries flourished (524–90). Evaristo Breccia, again in 1907 and guided by previous discoveries, began his own work in the area and believed that his discoveries of fourteen inscriptions and other objects confirmed the locale. While his discoveries of pillars and column capitals remain impressive, he gleaned important information from local Bedouins: a few kilometers west of Dikhaylah exists a hill named Kom al-Zujaj. Local Bedouins were able to confirm the existence of a Kom al-Hanadun, not far from Kom al-Zujaj. (The name bears a striking similarity to what was referred to as Dayr al-Zujaj after the Arab conquest or Hennaton in the Byzantine era). Breccia would later, in 1914 and again in 1919, publish more gravestones of monks believed to have lived at the Hennaton (Breccia 1914; Breccia 1919). In addition, he discovered several ruins in a small village called al-Dayr, four or five kilometers west of Kom al-Zujaj.

In Leclerq's 1920 "Dekhela" entry in the *Dictionnaire d'archéologie chrétienne et de liturgie*, the author completely equates Hennaton with Dikhaylah, stating that Breccia's findings of a Christian edifice sufficiently correspond to the fragments dated by Crum (Leclerq 1920: col. 514).

E. Schwartz's work on epigraphs in the 1920s suggests that Dikhaylah was most likely the site of the ancient Pempton Monastery (on the fifth milestone mark). The Hennaton, he argued, would probably be the site of Kom al-Zujaj, a few miles west of Dikhaylah on the *taenia*, the coastal strip that separates the Mediterranean from the western tip of Lake Mareotis. This discovery is important because, historically, the Hennaton had at its disposal a sea anchorage and access to Lake Mareotis (Gascou 1991a: 954).

Hishmat Messiha's work in the 1970s clarified the connection between the different appellations of the Hennaton. He argues that from the sixth century onward a monastery was called Dayr al-Zujaj, or the Monastery of the Glassmakers (Messiha 1975: 65). He reports that in 1948 the Coptic Museum undertook excavations at the desert west of Nagada and found an important collection of fragments of glass vases and chalices, proving that the glass industry prospered in Lower Egypt (Messiha 1975: 65). He quotes the *Life* of Abba Alexander II (43, r. 705–30) in the *History of the Patriarchs*, which records the patriarch's request that priests use glass vases and chalices in liturgical services (Messiha 1975: 66). From Messiha's work, it can be gleaned that Dayr al-Zujaj could possibly have been a plant at the Hennaton. At the end of his very short article, Messiha calls for more excavations at two different sites that he believed could be the locale of Dayr al-Zujaj: Kom al-Zujaj and a site (yet unnamed) between the twentieth and thirtieth kilometer marks.

In 1988, Stefan Timm equated the Pempton monasteries with the modern-day Alexandrian train station called al-Maks and suggested that it be used as a reference point from which to conduct studies regarding the localization of the Hennaton complex (Timm 1988: 1889).

In 2002, Peter Grossmann discovered what is believed to be the cathedral of the Hennaton monastic settlement, building on G. Haeny's work and providing a floor plan of the church. He specifies the location of this finding by the modern-day town of Dikhaylah (Grossmann 2002: 488).

Messiha's 1975 article may have inspired the work of the Hungarian Expedition led by the archaeologist and Egyptologist Gyozo Vörös in the early twenty-first century. While his work treats the site of Taposiris Magna as well as a temple of Osiris and a Roman fortress, the treatment of the site as Dayr al-Zujaj proves unfounded. One glass furnace was found by the expedition, leading to the conclusion that Taposiris Magna must have been the site of the Hennaton. This conclusion does not agree with previous work on localizing the prestigious monastic center, completely ignoring earlier work on the site, at Dikhaylah, and the historical attestations to the Hennaton at large (Bianchi 2003). While Gyozo Vörös's work indeed confirms the site of a church, and while it would be a plausible site for the ancient monastic complex, given its vastness and distance from any modern dwellings, a larger historical context is needed to arrive at a better understanding of the site.

Grossmann and Timm tackle the claims of the Hungarian Expedition regarding the site by historically contextualizing Taposiris Magna. Grossmann addresses the claim that in the late fourth century, a military camp was converted into a temple of Osiris at Taposiris Magna (Grossmann 2002: 488). The discovery of this church temporarily earned the site an erroneous identification with a monastery, which he considers unfounded because of the prohibition of the exercise of pagan cults by Theodosius I (r. 379–95) (Grossmann 2002: 488). Timm also explores all ancient attestations of Taposiris Magna—sources that treat the site as an entirely different locale from that of Hennaton. The seventh-century *Chronicle* of John of Nikiou mentions a place that is called in the Ethiopian version Dafsir, west of Alexandria (Timm 1992: 2516). In the eighth-century Syriac *History* of Peter the Iberian, it is stated that the pro-Chalcedonian faction imprisoned the non-Chalcedonian patriarch Timothy II Aelurus (26, r. 458–80) in Tafosiris,[9] some thirty Roman miles west of Alexandria, which corresponds to forty-five kilometers today (Timm 1992: 2515–16). *The History of the Patriarchs* reports, in the *Life* of Abba Christodoulus of the eleventh century, a Monastery of Tafsir, west of Alexandria (Timm 1992: 2517), which could possibly correspond to the previously mentioned Syriac Tafosiris and Ethiopian Dafsir. Both Timm's and Grossman's work provide a wider historical context to situate Taposiris Magna as a site separate from the Hennaton.

The different names associated with this monastic complex have proved invaluable in attempts to localize the Hennaton, even though it is not precisely known when the appellation 'Dayr al-Zujaj' began to circulate apart from the Arabization of Egypt, a process that spanned two centuries. It is telling as to its meaning and why this particular locale came to be known as such, especially because the names 'Kom al-Zujaj' and 'Kom al-Hanadun' survive to the present day outside the borders of the ancient city of Alexandria, a few miles west of the modern-day village of Dikhaylah.

There have been many attempts to localize the Hennaton, and for good reason. This once prestigious center has seemingly vanished into thin air. Comparing the known history of the monastic complex against the history of Egypt at large could offer many plausible theories as to its decline. For now, it remains an intriguing mystery.

Notes

1 Commonly spelled 'Enaton' to resemble the Greek word for nine, εννέα. Throughout the course of this paper the spelling 'Hennaton' will be used to account for the Greek rough breathing and because this sound is eventually arabicized as the letter ح.

2 Timm discusses the reasons why the Coptic *Martyrdom* of Apa Kradjon is not a credible source: his second reason can be explained by the traditional relationship of the Alexandrian patriarchate with Egyptian monks, which scholars agree began with Athanasius I (20, r. 326–73).

3 Timm 1984b: 835. It is unclear if this event took place while Abba Longinus served as hegumen.

4 Timm 1984b: 838. John of Ephesus's *Life* of John of Hephaistos recounts how all monks were expelled from the monasteries of Peter the Iberian in Gaza and found refuge in Hennaton. He does not include a new name for Hennaton, but rather affirms its locale at the ninth milestone west of Alexandria.

5 Drescher adds in a footnote: "The author evidently has no love for the Enaton communities." In Drescher's version, Hennaton is spelled Enaton, not al-Ainatoun, as in Basset's Synaxarium version.

6 Basset 1971b: 629. Translation from the French: "mais si tu veux embrasser la vie monastique, va à El-Ainatoun; car il est modéré; il y a en cet endroit une troupe de riches qui se sont faits moines; ils y vivent sans fatigue; ils y trouvent des consolations."

7 Other sources that illustrate these blurred lines include Menze 2008, Steppa 2002, and Mikhail 2014b.

8 Timm 1984b: 835. See also Basset 1971b: 764. In the same vein, a letter entitled "One is the Redeemer," penned by Patriarch Dioscorus while in exile in Gangra, addresses the monks of the Hennaton, encouraging them to remain strong in the faith of the One Lord Jesus Christ—fully human and fully divine—to hold onto the confession of the fathers, and not to heed the heretics who teach otherwise.

9 In Syriac, p = f.

6 The Pachomian Federation and Lower Egypt: The Ties that Bind

James E. Goehring

THE ESTABLISHMENT of the Pachomian movement as the preeminent expression of cenobitic monasticism in the broader history of Egyptian and thence Christian monasticism arose from three fundamental and interrelated facts: first, the movement's early origins in the fourth century, which generated a sense of its originality; second, the successful publication and distribution of its narrative story, which engendered and spread knowledge of the enterprise; and third, the early and abiding connections that formed between the Pachomians in Upper Egypt and the ecclesiastical institutions in Alexandria, which guaranteed its integration into the story of the Church.[1] While each element played an essential role in the fashioning and success of the final product, namely, the history of the Pachomian movement as we know it today, its connections to the Alexandrian church proved particularly important. Although the connections would eventually lead to the loss of the historical federation's[2] place in the emerging post-Chalcedonian discourse of the Coptic Orthodox Church, they had by that time cemented its place in the history of monasticism. In the discourse of Coptic Christian history, replete with its sharp anti-Chalcedonian polemics, the Pachomians retain their place as part of the golden age of monastic origins from which their movement transitions seamlessly into a more general post-Chalcedonian, post-Pachomian cenobitism.[3]

The history of this development began in the formative years of the movement. The seeds of the later Pachomian presence in Lower Egypt and their growing influence in the ecclesiastical politics of Alexandria were sown early in the movement's history in Upper Egypt. The flow of Alexandrian ascetics and ascetic wannabes up the Nile River into the Thebaid to the new Pachomian cenobia prepared the way for the later Pachomian expansion downriver to Alexandria. While the impetus for the initial connections to Alexandria remains uncertain, it is hard to imagine the subsequent presence and impact of the Pachomians in Lower Egypt without them.[4] Within the vita tradition, apart from the account of Athanasius's visit to the Thebaid circa 329–30, the first direct reference to a connection to Alexandria involves the arrival of the Alexandrian Theodore at the central Pachomian monastery of Pbow, which occurs after the foundation of the second group of monasteries circa 340, some seventeen years into the federation's existence and six to seven years before Pachomius's death. According to the account, a delegation of Pachomian monks had come by ship to Alexandria to visit the archbishop. During their stay, they came into contact with a young lector named Theodore, who sought permission from the archbishop to return south with the Pachomians to their monastic federation. Having gained Athanasius's approval, Theodore embarked with the Pachomians on their ship back up the Nile. When they arrived at Pbow, since Theodore spoke only Greek,[5] Pachomius placed him in a house with an old monk who knew Greek and could thus communicate with him. As he progressed in the monastic life and his abilities became clear, he rose to become housemaster of the house of foreigners[6] who, according to the Bohairic *Life*, "were coming to be monks" (SBo 89; Veilleux, 1980–82: 1:121). These included Alexandrians (Ausonius the Great, Ausonius, and Neon) and Romans (Firmus, Romulus, and Domnius the Armenian) (SBo 90 = G1 95; Veilleux, 1980–82: 1:123, 362), the former presumably Greek speakers and the latter Latin speakers. Theodore served as their translator. The very need for a house set apart for foreigners in the Pachomian federation underscores the movement's draw and sets it apart from other early Upper Egyptian cenobitic establishments. Later stories in the vita tradition enumerate other Pachomian trips by boat to Alexandria to meet with the archbishop, sell mats, and acquire supplies for the sick (SBo 96, 107, 124, 204; Palladius, *Lausiac History* 32.8, in Butler 1904: 94). One of the accounts includes a reference to three men who boarded the Pachomians' boat so as to return with them to Pbow to become monks (SBo 107; Veilleux, 1980–82: 1:150–51). The trips to Alexandria thus became a source of monastic recruits. One can only imagine that each such recruit further enhanced the federation's ties to Alexandria.

The evidence from the vita tradition clearly indicates that the development of these connections began already in Pachomius's lifetime. The federation's eventual acquisition and use of their own ships to facilitate contact and move supplies between Alexandria and the Thebaid generated knowledge of the federation and its form of monasticism in the city and served as a conduit for recruits from Lower Egypt into the federation. While one suspects that such communication was neither new nor unique to the Pachomians,[7] they appear to have excelled at it, and they wove it into their story. The flow of recruits from Alexandria to the federation continued after Pachomius's death in 346. In 352, during Theodore's tenure as head of the federation, Ammon, a youthful convert and aspiring monk in the Alexandrian church of Pierius, after being warned of heretical anchorites in the city, was steered by his priest to the Pachomians at Pbow (*Epistula Ammonis* 2; Goehring 1986: 124–25, 160). The priest connected Ammon with Theophilus and Kopres, Pachomian monks who had been sent by Theodore to Alexandria to deliver letters to the archbishop. When they left to return to Pbow, Ammon went with them. He was met upon his arrival at the monastery gate by Theodore himself, who ushered him into the monastic life and placed him in the house of foreigners. Ammon described the house as composed of twenty Greek-speaking monks under the leadership of the Alexandrian Theodore and Ausonius, who served as teachers and guides (*Epistula Ammonis* 7; Goehring 1986: 129, 163). One can only guess that the other Greek speakers had likewise come from Lower Egypt. The story indicates that the path for monastic recruits from Alexandria was by this point in the federation's history well worn indeed. Ammon's story, however, does not end here. His path leads back to Alexandria. After three years at Pbow, he expressed a desire to return to Lower Egypt as a result of family concerns. Theodore sent him to the monastic community at Nitria where he dwelt as a monk. He eventually became a priest and bishop in the church. His story, at least so far as it can be believed,[8] underscores not only Alexandria as a source of monastic recruits, but also the later impact of those recruits on the Upper Egyptian federation's relationship with the ecclesiastical authorities in Alexandria, who came as a result of the conduit to include, as Ammon's case suggests, former Pachomian monks.

The draw of Alexandria casts its reflection as well in the almost uninterrupted northward expansion of the federation throughout the course of its history. With the sole exception of the Monastery of Phnoum at Latopolis, each new monastery that entered the federation in Pachomius's lifetime was located farther down the Nile River toward Alexandria from the original settlement at Tabennesi. Pbow lay north of Tabennesi, Sheneset north of Pbow, and Thmoushons north of Sheneset. While the initial three foundations lay within about fourteen kilometers of one another, Thmoushons required a six-hour journey from Pbow (Lefort 1939: 399–400; Veilleux 1980–82: 1:275 [SBo 51n1]). A second northern cluster of four monasteries (Tse, Sne, Tsmine, and Thbew) followed near Panopolis, some ninety kilometers from Pbow as the crow flies. Theodore continued the northward reach of the federation, establishing two monasteries (Kaior and Oui) near Hermopolis Magna (Ashmunayn), some 160 kilometers north of Smin.[9] The pattern seems well set for the federation's eventual establishment of the Monastery of Metanoia on Canopus near Alexandria, and the existence of other federation monasteries between Ashmunayn and Alexandria cannot be ruled out (Goehring 2011: 289–303). The Pachomian federation seems to have been an expansive movement from its beginnings and the pull of that expansion was consistently northward toward Alexandria.

The significance of this phenomenon in the narrative of the Pachomian federation becomes clear when one compares it to the evidence of the somewhat later nearby federation of Shenoute. While the nature of the sources from the two federations differs, it seems clear that Shenoute's federation remained a narrowly local phenomenon in comparison to the Pachomian example (Layton 2014: 21–22). The two monasteries and one nunnery in its federation lay within three kilometers of one another across the Nile from Akhmim (Panopolis) (Coquin and Martin 1991b: 736–37), which stands in stark contrast to the Pachomian federation, whose monasteries ranged from Latopolis in the south to Canopus of Alexandria in the north, a distance of over 650 kilometers as the crow flies. While Shenoute certainly maintained contact with a succession of Alexandrian archbishops and traveled with Cyril to the Council of Ephesus in 441,[10] there is little if any evidence that his connections translated into an influx of monastic recruits from Lower Egypt. While his monasteries followed the Pachomian model of organizing into smaller units called houses, the sources make no mention of a house of foreigners. Likewise, as far as I have been able to determine, there is no evidence of foreign monks or Greek speakers in the Shenoutean sources.[11] While one cannot preclude the existence of such elements in Shenoute's federation, it seems clear that if they did exist, their import paled in comparison to the role they played in the Pachomian federation and the literary tradition it engendered. The difference is significant. It explains the broader contours of Pachomian history, including its preeminent role in the history of monasticism in Egypt and beyond.

As one moves further down through time, one sees that the connections established between the Pachomians and Alexandria in the middle of the fourth century led almost inexorably to the federation's expansion into Lower Egypt by the end of that century, which led in turn to the spread of their narrative story and cenobitic traditions throughout and beyond Egypt.[12] In 391, after the suppression of the local pagan sanctuaries on the island of Canopus, Archbishop Theophilus (d. 412) brought in Pachomian monks to establish a monastery there. According to a late hagiographic account, an initial effort by non-Pachomian monks failed when the local demons proved too much for them. In response, Theophilus turned to the Pachomians, who proved up to the task. They subdued the local supernatural opposition and established the monastery.[13] Initially identified as the Monastery of Canopus, by the time Jerome translated the Pachomian rules into Latin in 404 it had changed its name, given the notorious associations of Canopus, to the Monastery of Metanoia. It became a monastic center in Lower Egypt, which, according to Jerome, attracted numerous Latin speakers in addition to its Greek-speaking majority (Boon 1932: 4; Veilleux 1980–82: 2:141). The appeal to Latin speakers may account in part for Arsenius of Scetis's subsequent sojourn at Metanoia, since he was of Roman senatorial rank, as well as that of the equally ranked Roman virgin whom Archbishop Theophilus sent to him there (*Apophthegmata Patrum*, Arsenius 28). The existence of Latin speakers at Metanoia further parallels their presence in the house of foreigners in the Upper Egyptian Pachomian monastery of Pbow, underscoring once again the diverse and consistent nature of the federation's outreach.

The origin of the Pachomian community of Metanoia under Theophilus's auspices established its close link to the Alexandrian hierarchy from the start, a pattern confirmed in Cyril's reign (412–44) by the homilies he delivered there (CPG 77, 1100–1101; cited by Gascou 1991b: 1609). Cyril's correspondence with Victor, the archimandrite of Pbow, extends the strong ecclesiastical link into the federation's Upper Egyptian core, a fact confirmed by the latter's accompaniment of Cyril and Shenoute to the Council of Ephesus in 431.[14] In this connection, one might note as well a late panegyric attributed to Timothy of Alexandria that links the patriarchate to the building of the great sixth-century basilica at Pbow in the era of the archimandrites Victor and Martyrius (Lantschoot 1934: 13–56;

Schroeder 2007: 122–23; Goehring 2012: 58–59; Goehring 2006: 14–16). While late and suspect with respect to several of its claims, it nonetheless illustrates the extent to which the tradition came to assume a powerful connection between the patriarchate and the Pachomians.[15] None of this seems accidental given the well-worn connections that the federation had with Alexandria by this time, connections that, as the *Letter of Ammon* suggests, included former Pachomian monks in the Lower Egyptian ecclesiastical hierarchy.

In the ensuing years Metanoia's power and influence continued to expand, as did its link to and impact on the Alexandrian patriarchate. In the leadup to and aftermath of the Council of Chalcedon (451), its connection with the emerging Chalcedonian faction seems clear. While one need not conclude that the monastery was uniformly Chalcedonian, the data supports the dominance of the Chalcedonian elements within the community.[16] Evidence from the acts of the Council of Chalcedon indicates that Athanasius, an Alexandrian presbyter, sought refuge at Metanoia from the persecutions of the archbishop Dioscorus, a fact suggestive of the community's early entanglement in the controversies that surrounded the council.[17] In the subsequent struggle over the allegiance of the Coptic Church and its patriarchate, three Chalcedonian (Melchite) patriarchs were drawn from the Tabennesiote monks of Metanoia.[18] The first, Timothy Salofaciolus, was consecrated as the Chalcedonian archbishop of Alexandria in 460 following the banishment of Timothy II Aelurus.[19] His reign from 460 to 482 was briefly interrupted in 476 when Timothy Aelurus returned as a result of changing imperial politics. During this brief period, Timothy Salofaciolus resumed his life as a monk at Metanoia. He eventually returned as patriarch, and when he died in 482,[20] another Tabennesiote monk from Metanoia, John Talaia, assumed the episcopal throne, though he was forced to flee in the same year when Peter Mongus, the non-Chalcedonian successor of Timothy Aelurus, gained the emperor's support (Frend 1972: 174–83; Malaspina 1992: 1:477). Nonetheless, the role played by the federation's Monastery of Metanoia in this period, with its definite Chalcedonian orientation, seems clear.

Later in the sixth century, when the Byzantine emperor Justinian I sought to reestablish the Chalcedonian patriarchal succession in Alexandria after a long period of vacancy,[21] he turned again to the Pachomians at Metanoia for a candidate. Their archimandrite Paul was chosen and served as archbishop from 537 to 539 (Gascou 1991b: 1609). Finally, in the following century (641), when the Chalcedonian archbishop Cyrus sought to meet in secret with Theodore, the imperial commander in Egypt, he chose the church in the Monastery of Metanoia for their rendezvous, suggestive again of the community's abiding Chalcedonian orientation.[22] The overall weight of this evidence, while not precluding the existence of a non-Chalcedonian faction within the monastery, surely supports Metanoia's role as a primarily Chalcedonian establishment. As such it likely offset in this regard the Enaton monastery's equivalent role in the non-Chalcedonian tradition (Gascou 1991a: 956–57).

The power and prestige of Metanoia in this later period gain further support from a series of documentary texts. A papyrus dossier from the sixth century preserves a series of letters addressed by monks to Abba George, the superior of the Monastery of Metanoia. The letters indicate travel by boat between Metanoia and the central Pachomian monastery of Pbow in Upper Egypt, and mention two additional monasteries, Aphrodito and Stratonikos, that were affiliated in some fashion with Metanoia.[23] Their location, however, remains uncertain. While the original editor took them to be daughter monasteries of Metanoia located in the Delta (*P. Fouad* 86–89; Marrou 1939: 175–202), Jean Gascou argues convincingly that they were situated in Middle Egypt, based on the papyri's provenance. He accounts for the two communities' interaction with Abba George by suggesting that by this time the superior general of the Pachomian federation was resident at Canopus.[24] While I am skeptical that the head of the federation as a whole ever relocated to Metanoia, the texts leave little doubt as to the importance of the Monastery of Metanoia within the Pachomian system. I would suggest that the evidence supports the emergence over time of two centers of gravity operating within the federation. The power of the traditional center at Pbow had by the time of the papyrus letters been matched, if not overshadowed in some quarters, by the increasingly influential Monastery of Metanoia. The latter's location fostered its connection to ecclesiastical, political, and economic sources of power in a more immediate and direct way than was available to the more distant Upper Egyptian center at Pbow. Two additional papyrus dossiers of the sixth and early seventh centuries, both fiscal in nature, illustrate as much. They record the Metanoia's involvement in the collection of taxes levied as wheat, which it moved on its own boats down the Nile, and perhaps across the Mediterranean to Constantinople (Remondon 1971: 769–81; Fournet and Gascou 2002: 23–45; Gascou 1991b: 1610). If the latter is true, the reach of the federation, even if dependent on economic demands, was impressive indeed. One has only to compare it with the more parochial federation of Shenoute to fathom the importance of this evidence.

Returning to the efforts of the Byzantine emperor Justinian I to reassert the Chalcedonian ideology in Egypt, it seems clear that the two centers of gravity within the Pachomian federation, Metanoia and Pbow, came into conflict. Justinian's efforts, which centered in the years 536–40, included the appointment of Paul, the archimandrite of Metanoia, as the new Chalcedonian archbishop of Alexandria. It is in this period that Chalcedonian elements within the Pachomian federation, likely centered at Metanoia and perhaps with the support of Paul, sought to impose their position throughout the entire federation. Four monks, led by a certain Pancharis, brought charges against the Upper Egyptian archimandrite of Pbow, Apa Abraham. The fragmentary panegyrics on Abraham report his subsequent arrest and summons to Constantinople, where he appeared before the emperor to answer the charges. When he refused to accept the decrees of Chalcedon, the emperor removed him as archimandrite of Pbow and appointed one of his accusers, Pancharis, in his place. While Abraham was allowed to return to Egypt, he and the other monks who refused to accept Chalcedon were forced to leave Pbow for other monasteries. After a brief sojourn at Shenoute's White Monastery, Abraham established a new monastery in his native village of Farshut. The account suggests an effective purge of at least the more adamant non-Chalcedonian elements within the federation.

While one may quibble over details in the hagiographic accounts, I suspect that the general picture reflects accurately the assertion of Metanoia's power and ecclesiastical ideology into Upper Egypt. The balance of power within the federation, reflected in the dual centers of gravity of Metanoia and Pbow, gave way as a result of the political intrigue recorded in the panegyrics on Abraham. The federation's Upper Egyptian monasteries were brought into alignment with—and, one suspects, under control of—the Chalcedonian faction centered in Metanoia. In the process of gaining control of the federation, however, the Chalcedonian faction effectively sealed its fate in the emerging non-Chalcedonian discourse of Coptic history. While the evidence of Patriarch Cyrus's use of the church in Metanoia as a site for negotiations indicates the monastery's continued existence on the eve of the Arab Conquest, for all practical purposes the later Pachomian federation disappears from the plane of history. Employing the metaphor of a train, one might say that the emerging post-Chalcedonian discourse of Coptic Christian history pulled the switch, so to speak, that sent Pachomian history down an alternate track, aligning its earlier pre-Chalcedonian period with cenobitic institutions that, while not part of the historical Pachomian federation, survived the political controversies of Chalcedon as non-Chalcedonian establishments.[25] The historical elements of the Pachomian federation, on the other hand, as a result of their more thoroughly Chalcedonian orientation, were shunted off down a spur that left them behind, where over time they disappeared from the memory of the Church.

I have argued here for the significance of the Pachomian federation's early link to Alexandria, expressed first in Pachomian travel to the city and the ensuing flow of monastic recruits from the city back to Pbow. The resulting presence of foreigners within the federation, both Greek and Latin speakers, surely impacted it in various ways. One can imagine, for example, that their presence played a role in the early appearance of a vita tradition within the federation. The Pachomian dossier includes a request from Archbishop Theophilus for a copy of the *Life of Pachomius and Theodore*.[26] The establishment and growth of the Monastery of Metanoia in Theophilus's reign (d. 412) likely accounts for the request, as it does for Jerome's translation of the *Rule* into Latin in 404. Jerome apparently translated from a Greek version, the existence of which in turn depended on the "foreign" elements within the federation.[27] One suspects that the original Greek versions that made their way to Alexandria were generated in Upper Egypt to meet a need within the house of foreigners. I do not mean to imply by this that the vita tradition as a whole, or even its first exemplar, came from non-Coptic Pachomian monks, nor do I want to reopen the debate between Chitty and Lefort over the priority of the Coptic or the Greek vita tradition.[28] I certainly do not mean to suggest a divide between learned Greeks and parochial Copts. Rather I would suggest that the federation's close links to Alexandria, and its openness to and integration of Greek and Latin speakers into its ranks, generated broader literary connections and knowledge that inspired the creation of a vita tradition within the Pachomian ranks, whether Coptic or Greek or both, in Upper Egypt. One imagines, for instance, that the monks who traveled to and from Alexandria were conversant in Greek so as to be able to easily communicate, as is indicated in the tradition, with the archbishop. They, together with the monastic recruits that returned with them from Alexandria, who included in their numbers lectors and members of the Alexandrian churches, would have heard of or known the *Life of Antony*, as well as stories and lives of other important religious figures. They would have brought this knowledge back with them to Upper Egypt where they would have shared it with the monks, both within the house of foreigners and more broadly among the native Coptic-speaking elements. Such knowledge would in turn foster imitation, leading to the Pachomian vita tradition and hence the assured place of Pachomius and his cenobitic creation in the history of monasticism. While one can never be certain in such matters, the vita tradition's early appearance, its relative uniqueness, and its powerful impact set the Pachomian movement apart in this regard. Rather than seeing it as an accident of history, I suspect the early outward reach of the movement resulted in a creative backlash, so to speak, of ideas and knowledge that played a seminal role in shaping the movement and the production of its memory of the past.

In closing let me say that for a paper on the Pachomians in Lower Egypt, it may seem that I have spent much of my time on the federation's Upper Egyptian monasteries. I have done so because I do not think one can so easily disengage the elements in Lower Egypt from the federation as a whole. And, as I hope to have shown, neither can one effectively disengage the history and development of the federation in Upper Egypt from its connections to the Delta. While those connections ultimately sealed the fate of the historical Pachomian movement after Chalcedon, they had by that time sealed its place in the history of Egyptian monasticism. They accomplished this in part by helping to develop the movement's literary culture, its *Rules* and *Lives*, which were in turn translated and spread throughout Egypt and beyond.

Notes

1 I suspect, as will become clear below, that the connections to Alexandria played a role in the literary production of the Pachomian story.

2 I use the term 'federation' cautiously to indicate the interconnection of the various individual monasteries within the Pachomian system through their central Monastery of Pbow. Others, notably Armand Veilleux, have preferred to retain the Greek term *koinonia* that was used in the Pachomian sources. While the extent to which the individual monasteries were "regulated" from Pbow remains uncertain, especially in the federation's later years, the vita tradition does report two annual gatherings at Pbow, one of which was for the reckoning of accounts. Furthermore, following problems that arose among the monasteries after Pachomius's death, Theodore instituted a rotation of abbots among the monasteries. While I have no doubt that the individual monasteries understood themselves as a community of monasteries, I also think that the evidence of considerable centralized administrative control indicates some form of federation.

3 I use "post-Pachomian" here to indicate the period after the historical federation linked to Pachomius disappeared from the plane of history.

4 The nature of the sources and their production raises the possibility that the authors of this literature aligned the early connections anachronistically with the federation's later relationship with the Alexandrian church.

5 Sahidic-Bohairic *Life of Pachomius* (SBo) 89 = First Greek *Life of Pachomius* (G1) 94–95. Veilleux 1980–82: 1:119–21 (SBo) and 1:361–62 (G1).

6 The term in the Coptic Bohairic *Life* is *xenikos*, which translates as 'stranger,' 'foreigner,' or 'alien.' Veilleux prefers 'house of strangers.' I have translated 'house of foreigners' to reflect the members' status as non-native, non-Coptic speakers. The Greek *Vita prima* (G1) identifies them as "those who did not understand Egyptian" (τοὺς μὴ ἀκούοντας αἰγυπτιστί). Halkin 1932: 64; translation from Veilleux 1980–82: 1:162; for the Bohairic passage, see Lefort 1925 (1965): 106.

7 SBo 29 (Veilleux, 1980–82: 1:52) reports that a monk who was returning from the north to his monastery near Sne (Latopolis) spent the night at Tabennesi. How far north is not stated.

8 See Chitty/Lefort debate: Goehring 1986: 27–32.

9 G1. 134; Veilleux 1980–82: 1:392–93. Theodore founded a third monastery south of Pbow near Hermonthis, midway between Pbow and Phnoum.

10 The archbishops include Timothy I, Theophilus, Cyril, Dioscorus, and Timothy II Aelurus; see Emmel 2004: 1:8.

11 In addition to my own more limited knowledge of the Shenoutean sources, a query to David Brakke, who in turn checked with Andrew Crislip, led to his observation that "there is, as far as we know, no evidence of 'foreigners' or Greek-speakers in the WM Federation, no stories of people joining from Lower Egypt" (email of January 4, 2015). Shenoute, on the other hand, was apparently bilingual, which one would expect given his contact with important local figures like Caesarius and the various Alexandrian archbishops. See Lucchesi 1981: 201–10; Depuydt 1990: 67–71.

12 While the majority of Coptic texts in the Pachomian dossier depend on Sahidic manuscripts from the White Monastery, the existence of a Bohairic version of the *Life* illustrates the literary spread of the tradition within Egypt. The numerous Greek and Latin versions of the *Life* that were generated outside of Egypt underscore the literary success of the *Life*. On the vita tradition, see Veilleux 1968: 17–107; Veilleux 1980–82: 1:1–21; Goehring 1986: 3–23.

13 Orlandi 1968–70: 2:12–14 (text), 61–62 (translation). The nature of the story underscores the later respect in which the Pachomian tradition was held. For a detailed account of the history of Metanoia, see Gascou 1991b: 1608–11.

14 For the letters, see Cyril's letters 107–109 in McEnerney 1987: 170–75. On Victor at the Council of Ephesus, see Kraatz 1904; Johnson 1980: 415:78.9, 83.9, and 416:60.6, 64.4; van Cauwenbergh 1914: 153–54; Coquin 1991h: 2308.

15 Again it is interesting to compare this tradition with the evidence for the great sixth-century basilica in Shenoute's White Monastery. While Pachomian sources tie support for their basilica's construction to Alexandria, the surviving evidence from the White Monastery connects its basilica's construction to the military governor of Upper Egypt, Caesarius, son of Candidianus. While the latter was

clearly not Egyptian and likely had connections to Lower Egypt, nothing like the panegyric of Timothy of Alexandria emerges to promote the connection. On Caesarius, see Monneret de Villard 1923: 156–62; López 2013: 66.

16 Gascou 1991b: 1609. Gascou supplies the evidence suggestive of diversity within the community of Metanoia.

17 Schwartz 1933: 217; for an English translation, Price and Gaddi 2005: 2:58–61.

18 Schwartz 1933: 217; for an English translation, Price and Gaddi 2005: 2:58–61.

19 It is important to note here Shenoute's link to Timothy II Aelurus, which again sets his federation apart from the emerging post-Chalcedonian direction of the Pachomian movement. Emmel 2004: 1:8; Emmel 2002: 96.

20 On Timothy Salofaciolus, see Frend 1991: 7:2268–69; Frend 1972: 173–77.

21 It had lain dormant since John Talaia.

22 Gascou 1991b: 1609; cf. Butler 1978: 313–14. Butler erroneously takes the reference to the Tabennesiote monastery as a reference to the Upper Egyptian monastery of Tabennesi, which he identifies, again erroneously, as the "centre of the brotherhood of the order of St. Pachomius."

23 Some scholars have suggested a second Pachomian monastery situated within the city of Alexandria, though the evidence is sketchy at best. For a discussion, see Gascou 1991b: 1610–11.

24 Gascou 1976: 157–84; Gascou 1991b: 1609–10. Gascou's suggestion that Abba George served as the general superior for the Pachomians, who was now resident at Canopus, appears to draw on the *History of Dioscorus*, which refers to the fifth-century Pachomian archimandrite Paphnutius as the superior of the Pachomian monks at Canopus (Nau, *Journal asiatique*, 297n1; cited by Johnson 1980: 416:1n3). It is not clear to me, however, that this equation is correct. In the *Panegyric on Macarius* XV.3, for example, the archimandrite Paphnutius stops by the Monastery of Shenoute on his way to Alexandria.

25 The dominant role that Shenoute plays in Coptic history gained strength through this development. While the Pachomian federation tied itself to Chalcedon through Metanoia and the Chalcedonian archbishops it produced, including Timothy Salofaciolus, Shenoute was writing letters to the non-Chalcedonian Timothy II Aelurus (see note 19). See also Goehring 2006: 14–16.

26 Crum 1915: 12–13, 65–66; Lefort 1942: 389–90. Wilhelm Hengstenberg (1922: 238–52) has questioned the authenticity of this text. Whatever the case may be in this regard, it affirms the tradition's belief in the movement of the *Vita* into Lower Egypt at this time.

27 In a similar manner, one might suspect that the presence of Latin speakers in Metanoia encouraged Jerome's translation of the *Rule*. It is from here that one assumes the texts flowed out beyond Egypt, thus impacting the history of monasticism more broadly.

28 For an account of the debate, see Goehring 1986: 3–18.

7 The Relations between the Coptic Church and the Armenian Church from the Time of Muhammad Ali to the Present (1805–2015)

Mary Kupelian

We live in times of increasing sectarianism and intolerance for difference, where diversity is no longer considered a benefit to the whole community, but a threat to its separate parts. Religion, class, and cultural identity have become markers, if not red lines, of social separation, with an inevitable increase in mutual distrust, suspicion, and the politics of certainty.

Bucking this trend in Egypt, the Coptic and Armenian churches (with the exception of Armenian Protestants) share a long history of cooperation and goodwill, and continue to pursue a goal of unity. Egyptian Christians (Copts) and Armenian Orthodox Christians represent the non-Chalcedonian belief in the unity of the nature of Christ (the single nature of Christ) (Sarkissian 1965: 34–35). The majority of Armenian Egyptians are affiliated with the Orthodox Church, but Armenian Catholics, who believe in the dual nature of Christ, also make up part of the Egyptian Armenian community.[1] The Armenian community, as a whole, shows remarkable tolerance and acceptance of other Christian communities, although in recent decades the initiative and commitment to unity has been spearheaded by the Coptic Pope, Shenouda III.

The first Armenians came to Egypt as early as the sixth and seventh centuries. These immigrants were Muslim, but successive waves of Armenian migration to Egypt brought Christian Armenians, starting in the early nineteenth century (Hacikyan, Basmajian, and Franchuk 2005). Egyptian–Armenian ties intensified during the Byzantine rule, continuing to grow during the period of Fatimid rule until they reached their apogee during the reign of Muhammad Ali Pasha (1805–48).

Armenians maintained their separate identity through their religion, social customs, and, especially, the preservation of Armenian as the language of communication and liturgy. During this period, Armenians held prominent positions in the highest administrative ranks in the government, including the Foreign Ministry, the Ministry of Education, and the cabinet (Dadoyan 2013: 65–78; Dadoyan 1997: 81–85, 106–107, 144–54; Immerzeel 2012–13: 41–42; Swanson 2010: 63–64).

Little is known of the Armenian community during the three centuries of Ottoman rule; during this period, the community shrank, leaving few traces, and until now no studies have covered the subject with any depth or detail, nor does the Armenian community host any archives. Our only knowledge of this period comes from private libraries owned by Armenians living in Cairo and Alexandria, and from the records and documents kept in the Coptic Patriarchate Archives in Cairo (Nigosian 1991: 235). In the Centro Francescano Studi Orientali Cristiani, a public library in Cairo's Muski quarter, an Armenian Catholic priest, Father Mansur, spent decades collecting literature on Armenian history and the Armenian diaspora for the library. This library is now mostly managed by Egyptian Christians (an example of Coptic–Armenian integration). However, as with most of the known archives and collections, access is difficult.

Few manuscripts have been preserved from this period. Specifically, the Coptic Patriarchate Archives hold books in Armenian that document the relationships between the two churches in the Ottoman era. However, access to these archives is problematic.

Some indications suggest that during the Ottoman period (1517–1798) the Armenian presence in Egypt was not as strong as it had been in previous eras (Winter 1992: 195–98; Hafiz 1986: 257–72). Armenians worked as craftsmen (jewelers, watchmakers, and tailors) and tradesmen, but they were not involved in commerce (except in a limited role as traders), and their bishops and clergy were poor and modest.

In Ottoman times, significant interaction among Armenians and Egyptian Christians occurred at various levels, and Armenians were particularly influenced by the Coptic culture. On the theological and the church level, the two congregations often shared places of worship, so that Armenians were allowed to pray at the Coptic Harat Zuwayla church (Alboyadjian 1955: 8–9). Historical documents indicate that the leader of the Armenian community oversaw the affairs of this church. He was also referred to as the overseer of the church of Harat Zuwayla (Afifi 1992: 286). The Egyptian historian al-Maqrizi mentions that the Monastery of Mar Mina at Fumm al-Khalig in Old Cairo was originally composed of three adjacent churches:[2] one for the Jacobites, one for the Syrians, and one for Armenians. Generally, the Copts allowed other communities, including Syrian Christians and Armenians, to use their churches for prayer. In a letter to the Armenian patriarch of Jerusalem, the Coptic patriarch, Butrus al-Jawli (1809–52), mentioned the cooperation and support that Copts showed Armenians after that monastery was ruined in a fire (Coptic Patriarchate Library, MS 458/270 Theologica, 34 verso, 35 recto; al-Maqrizi n.d.: 4:376).

It is generally agreed that the Armenian community steadily increased in size until the 1952 revolution of Gamal 'Abd al-Nasser. At that time, Armenian shops and businesses flourished throughout Egypt. With the 1952 revolution, Armenians began to migrate out of Egypt; most of them worked in the private sector, which was threatened by the socialist policies of the new government (Adalian 2010: 275).

Today, the Armenian and the Egyptian Christian communities demonstrate an unusual mutual regard, tolerance, and cooperation: Armenians not only share churches with Copts, they also share neighborhoods, customs, and traditions that have their roots in ancient Egyptian traditions. For example, they visit the tombs of their deceased on the Christmas and Easter feasts. Marriage between Armenians and Copts has become more common, with children gaining the benefits (e.g., school tuition) of membership in both communities. However, this kind of intermarriage may be not be a truly significant marker of Armenian–Coptic unity, but rather a reflection of the lack of choice for marriage partners in the small Armenian community.

Pope Cyril IV (1854–61), known as the "Father of Reform," dreamed of uniting all the Eastern Orthodox churches and creating love and trust among the leaders and communities of all the churches. Putting his dream of unity into practice, Pope Cyril IV invited an Armenian priest, Morkos, to hold Mass in the Coptic church of Archangel Gabriel in Cairo (Mikhail 2012: 112; Tewfik 1913: 141). He further organized the first meeting between the patriarchs of the Orthodox Coptic Church and the Armenian Church, in the Monastery of St. Antony. However, the delegates could not come to an agreement and Pope Cyril's vision of unity was postponed.

During the time of Pope Macarius III (1944–45), the Coptic Church strengthened ties with Vasken, the catholicos of the Armenian Orthodox

Church, with a program of exchange visits with representatives of the Armenian Church. These visits and understanding between the Copts and the Armenians continued during the time of Pope Youssab II (1946–56).

The reign of Pope Shenouda III (1971–2012) was characterized by active cooperation and strong relations between the Coptic and Armenian churches (Sarkissian 1970: 142–44). During his reign, cooperation reached a very high level, as the following examples demonstrate.[3]

1. In 1971, for the first time in history, the Armenian patriarch, head of the church in Lebanon, participated in the enthronement ceremony of the Coptic Pope by sending a delegation of prominent Armenian clergy. Included in this delegation was the late Archbishop Zaven Chinchinian (r. 1969–2001), Metropolitan of the Armenian Orthodox Church in Egypt, Sudan, and Ethiopia. Catholicos[4] Vasken I of Etchmiadzin (Yerevan) and Father Aram Keshishian, who later became Aram I of Cilicia (Lebanon), were also present.[5]
2. In 1972, Pope Shenouda made his first visit to Etchmiadzin in Armenia as head of a high delegation representing both the Church and the Egyptian state (Attyia 2011: 203–204). He met Catholicos Vasken I over four days in what was clearly both a political and a religious meeting (*al-Kiraza* 1973: 63).
3. In 1995, Pope Shenouda, as head of a large delegation, participated in the enthronement of Karekin Sarkissian as Catholicos of the Republic of Armenia.[6]
4. In 1995, Pope Shenouda, as head of a large Coptic delegation that included Anba Abraham, Bishop of Jerusalem and the Near East; Metropolitan and Secretary of the High Council Anba Bishoy of Damietta and Kafr al-Shaykh; and Anba Serabion, later Bishop of Los Angeles, participated in the enthronement ceremony of Aram I Keshishian as Catholicos in Cilicia in Lebanon.
5. In 1996, His Holiness Metropolitan Aram visited Egypt, where he met with Pope Shenouda III and gave a spiritual address to the Coptic congregation, delivered in English and translated into Arabic by Bishop Serabion.
6. In 1996, Pope Shenouda III, Catholicos Aram, head of the Armenian Church in Lebanon, and Pope Ignatius Zakka I, head of the Syrian Church, met to discuss measures for encouraging unity among the three churches over which they presided.[7]

7. In 1998, His Holiness Metropolitan Kraken visited Egypt, where he met Pope Shenouda at the Patriarchate in Cairo. The two men met again at the headquarters of the Armenian Diocese in Cairo, where they both signed a declaration of common faith between the two churches.
8. In 1998, the Coptic Church invited delegations from its two sister churches, the Syriac and the Armenian Catholic churches, to a meeting in Cairo, to formulate an official statement of shared creed. His Holiness, Patriarch of Antioch, Mar Ignatius Zakka I Syriac and His Holiness Aram I led the Syriac and Armenian delegations, respectively. Church officials consider the meeting a significant step forward in bringing the churches together. Unfortunately, the location of the actual text of the statement is not generally known. However, regular subsequent meetings between the sister churches to discuss issues of mutual interest and benefits testify to the positive outcome of this groundbreaking event.

Even outside of Egypt, we find examples of Armenian–Copt cooperation: in 1995, before the official establishment of Coptic communities in Athens and in Romania, Armenians offered the use of their churches to Copts.

Unity was put into practice through agreements concluded between the Coptic and Armenian (both Catholic and Orthodox) churches that allowed for educational exchange. For example, the Egyptian Christian Church has sent one of its teachers, Gerges Saleh, to teach Old Testament at the Armenian Theological Seminary in Antelias, Lebanon, over several years. In return, the Armenian Orthodox church in Antelias sent a group of students and priests to Egypt to complete their higher studies in theology under the personal supervision of Pope Shenouda III.

When Pope Shenouda III died in 2012 at the age of 88, both Karekin II, Catholicos of All Armenians, and Aram I, Catholicos of the Great House of Cilicia, offered condolences on his passing. Both Armenian church leaders sent a delegation to Pope Shenouda's funeral and praised him for his wise leadership and his unequivocal ability to work with all denominations to promote and encourage Christian unity.[8]

The same good relations among the churches continued with the participation of church notables in the enthronement of Pope Shenouda's successor, Pope Tawadros II (2012 to the present). For the first time, Pope Tawadros II, representing the Coptic Church and Egypt, traveled to

Yerevan in Armenia to commemorate the victims of the Armenian genocide at the hands of the Ottomans, in activities held in remembrance of the one-hundredth anniversary of the Armenian genocide, an indirect, but nonetheless important acknowledgment of the genocide on the part of Egypt. While in Armenia, Pope Tawadros II was invited to participate in religious rituals, such as holding a Mass, hitherto reserved for members of the Armenian Church.[9]

In 1990, the Armenians sold their church building in Zagazig, in the Egyptian Delta, to the Coptic Church. The Copts allow the Armenians to celebrate their Feast of the Cross in this church. Moreover, the Armenian decoration of the church has not been changed. Egypt's Armenians established a memorial stone in Port Said, in remembrance of the genocide (Imam 2014: 11–15). This ceremony was attended by the Armenian ambassador to Egypt and the bishop, representing the Coptic Church. Generally, Armenians and Copts attend each other's events, and offer regular prayers for the unity of the churches. Although the Catholic and Orthodox churches differ in their dates of Christmas (Armenians on January 6, Copts on January 7), the two churches regularly exchange delegations to each other's Christmas Masses.

In conclusion, the Armenian Orthodox and Catholic communities and the Egyptian Christian community have demonstrated a remarkable degree of tolerance and interfaith cooperation through the centuries. The history of the interaction among these communities may lack comprehensive documentation, but enough examples survive, in documents, oral histories, and daily life, to serve as inspiration to further efforts to mediate differences across class, religion, and economic boundaries.

Fig. 7.1. Third meeting of the heads of the Oriental Orthodox Churches in the Middle East (2000). Pope Shenouda III, Patriarch Zakka I, and Catholicos Aram I sign a common declaration in Antelias (www.suryoyo-online.org).

Fig. 7.2. His Holiness Karekin II, Supreme Patriarch and Catholicos of All Armenians, welcomes His Holiness Pope Tawadros II, Pope of Alexandria and Patriarch of the See of St. Mark, to Armenia. (http://www.armenianchurch.org/index.jsp?sid=3&nid=2844&y=2015&m=3&d=20&lng=en)

Fig. 7.3. Pope Tawadros II commemorates the victims of the Armenian genocide, Yerevan, Armenia. (http://www.armenianchurch.org/index.sp?sid=3&nid=2844&y=2015&m=3&d=20&lng=en)

Fig. 7.4. His Holiness Aram I and His Holiness Pope Tawadros II of Alexandria meet during the Executive Committee of the Middle East Council of Churches (MECC). (http://www.armenianorthodoxchurch.org/en/)

Fig. 7.5. Armenian ambassador Dr. Armen Melkonian and Bishop Krikor Augustine Koussa meet with Pope Tawadros II. (http://egypt.mfa.am/en/gallery/)

Fig. 7.6. Armenians with Copts in Port Said in commemoration of the genocide (photograph courtesy of Ara Keuhnelian).

Notes

1 Armenian Egyptians are divided into Armenian Apostolic (known also as Orthodox or at times Gregorian), belonging to the Armenian Apostolic Church, and Armenian Catholic communities, belonging to the Armenian Catholic Church. There are also some Egyptian Armenians who are members of Armenian Evangelical churches (Binns 2002: 2–3).

2 Abu Salih al-Armani 1895: 236. He mentions only altars, not separate buildings.
3 Fr. Basilious Sobhy, n.d., "Nabdha Mukhtasara 'an al-'ilaqat al-Qibtiyia al-Armanyia 'abr al-'usur," http://st-takla.org/articles/fr-basilous-sobhy/armenian/ethiopia.html
4 The title Catholicos (Greek 'universal' or 'general') for the supreme head of the Church is used by a number of Eastern churches, such as the Armenian, Georgian, Indian Malabar, and others. The origin of the title Catholicos goes back to the fifth century, when these churches, located in territories east of the borders of the Byzantine Empire, became autonomous from other ecclesiastical centers in the west, due to political developments between Persia and Byzantium.
5 The Cilician Catholicosate, the administrative center of the Church, is located in Antelias, Lebanon.
6 In 1983 Catholicos Khoren I died at Antelias and Karekin II Sarkissian became Catholicos of the Great House of Cilicia. Karekin II of the Great House of Cilicia was elected Karekin I, Catholicos of All Armenians at Etchmiadzin.
7 http://www.suryoyo.uni-goettingen.de/library/3meeting-orientalchurchs.htm
8 http://asbarez.com/101768/karekin-ii-aram-i-offer-condolences-on-coptic-pope%E2%80%99s-death/
9 *Deghadou* 2015: 14; Thabet 2015: 15–16; "Egypt's Pope Tawadros Prays for Armenian Genocide Victims in Lebanon Visit," Ahram Online, July 19, 2015, http://english.ahram.org.eg/NewsContent/1/64/135744/Egypt/Politics-/Aboutus.aspx

8 Saint Barsum the Naked and His Veneration at al-Ma'sara (Dayr Shahran)

Bishop Martyros

The Town of Helwan

In AD 1691, the British orientalist Richard Pocock mentioned that the town of Helwan had a diocese of its own, although the French Coptologist Henri Munier did not mention Helwan among the dioceses of Egypt in his 1943 work (Munier 1943b, as cited by al-Suriany 1972: 23). Nor does the Coptic historian Abu al-Makarim mention it in his book, *The History of Coptic Monasteries and Churches*, in which he describes the churches and monasteries of Egypt in the eleventh century (Samuel 2000). It is known that, in modern history, the first to found a diocese in Helwan was Pope Kyrillos VI, who in 1967 ordained Anba Boulos as bishop for it.

It is possible that the diocese of Helwan may refer to the diocese of Eastern Manf, the region extending from Helwan on the eastern side of the Nile to the area of al-Khandaq, now the area of Anba Ruways, Cairo. History tells us some of the names of the bishops of both Eastern and Western Manf.

The Biography of St. Barsum the Naked

St. Barsum was born in AD 1257 of pious parents and was named Barsuma. His father was called al-Wageh, or 'the preferred one' (Andraous 2012a). He was employed as a scribe for Queen Shagarat al-Durr (Rituals Committee 2012: 2:469).

After the death of Barsuma's father and then his mother a year later, his maternal uncle seized his inheritance. Barsuma did not want to cause any enmity with his uncle, remembering the saying of the wise Solomon, "Vanity, vanity, all is vanity" (Eccl: 1:2). Some of his relatives encouraged him to sue his uncle, but he decisively refused to do so (Malaty 1996: 92).

He left al-Fustat and lived an ascetic life in a cave, perhaps in Mount al-Muqattam or Mount Tura where a number of hermits lived. There he spent five years incessantly praying. He may possibly have been exposed to some dangers in his solitude, as that period was one of the toughest periods of persecution for the Copts.

God guided him to the Church of St. Abu Sayfayn (Mercurius) in Old Cairo,[1] where he lived in a cave beside the northern gate (this cave is still there today). It is said that a large snake was living in that cave when the saint came and that it submitted to him, staying with him in the cave for twenty years.

During the time of St. Barsum the Naked, the Church underwent severe tribulation in the latter part of the sultanate of Khalil ibn Qalawun, when all the churches of Egypt, except in Alexandria, were closed, and Christians were forced to wear blue turbans as a way of distinguishing themselves from the Muslims.

St. Barsum refused to wear a blue turban, and when some people reported this to the governor, the governor ordered his flogging and imprisonment. After he was released, he lived on the roof of the church, continuing to pray that God would forgive the sins of his people and soften the hearts of their rulers.

Once more Barsum was reported to the governor and once more he was flogged and put in jail. After his release, he went to Dayr Shahran at al-Ma'sara, Helwan. There he lived on the roof of the church, leading a life of severe asceticism. Many people used to visit him to ask for his guidance, and he would comfort them.

He continued in his prayers and asceticism, exposing his body to the heat of day and cold of night, until God allowed the ending of this persecution. The churches were allowed to open again, but he remained on the roof of the church, leading his life of prayer.

After a long struggle, St. Barsum died at the age of sixty on 5 Nasi AM 1033, corresponding to August 28 AD 1317 (Rituals Committee 2012: 2:469). The priest Yuhanna ibn al-Shaykh (perhaps the abbot of the monastery at that time) was present at St. Barsum's death (Andraous 2012b).

Historians say that Pope John VIII (known as Ibn al-Qiddis), the eightieth patriarch of the Coptic Church, himself headed the funerary prayers for the saint.

After the funeral, St. Barsum was buried with honor in the graveyard southwest of the monastery church, beside the abbot of the monastery known as Hegumen Ishaq ibn Qarkura (Andraous 2012b). Later, that section of the cemetery was annexed to the church in the monastery (Mansi 1983: 433).

The grave of the saint can still be found today at Dayr Shahran and many visitors still come to receive the blessings of the beloved St. Barsum, seeking his intercessions and prayers.

The Nicknames of the Saint

St. Barsum had several nicknames, corresponding to various personal characteristics.

1. "The Naked": Because St. Barsum had only one worn-out woolen garment and a white turban, he was nicknamed "the naked" (Mattaos 1985: 632–34). It was also said that he was nicknamed this because he used to wear a belt made from goats' hide around his waist. There is yet another explanation for this nickname: in the church of Abu Sayfayn in Old Cairo, an ancient icon of the saint was found, at the bottom of which was written, "S. Ava Barsum who is naked of vices and clothed with virtues" (Andraous 2012b).
2. "Ibn al-Tebban" (the son of al-Tebban): al-Tebban was the family name of his mother (al-Suriany 1972: 34).
3. "The Son of Fasting": Barsum is a Syriac word meaning 'the son of fasting.' His name is written in Coptic Abba Parsōma.

An Ancient Manuscript that Mentions St. Barsum

There is a manuscript concerning St. Barsum that was written in the sixteenth century, now in the Cairo Patriarchal Library No. Hist.15 (al-Suriany 1972: 43). This manuscript also includes the biography of Pope John VIII.

The Monastery of St. Mercurius (Abu Markora Martyr)

It was said that this monastery was established during the patriarchate of Pope Simon II, the fifty-second patriarch of Alexandria. He was enthroned in AD 830 and his patriarchate lasted for only about seven months. The governor of Egypt at that time, 'Abd al-'Aziz ibn Marwan the Ummayad, gave his permission to build two churches in Helwan (al-Masri 1998: 287). Anba Gregorios of al-Qeis was commissioned to perform this task.

Anba Gregorios built a large church under the name of the Holy Virgin; it was known as "the Church of the Servants." Its construction expenses were paid by a Coptic servant in the palace of the governor. Anba Gregorios also built a large monastery under the name St. Mercurius the Martyr (Abu Sayfayn), the ruins of which can be easily identified in the area known as Qarkura. It is mentioned that the governor ʻAbd al-ʻAziz ibn Marwan stayed for a while in a place called Abu Qarkura in Helwan, for fear of an epidemic (al-Suriany 1972: 16).

The Reconstruction of the Monastery and the Role of Monk Beymen

It is difficult to know the history of the monastery once known as the Monastery of St. Mercurius the Martyr, before its overall renovation by a monk named Beymen, who was forced to convert to Islam during the reign of al-Hakim bi-Amr Illah (Isidorus 2002b: 218). The historian Abu al-Makarim says, "The monastery known as Deir Shahran was renovated by the monk Beymen . . . after succeeding in making friends with the caliph" (Samuel 2000: 58), "who visited the monastery from time to time, holding talks with the monks and sharing in their meals" (Isidorus 2002b: 323).

The Origin of the Name "Dayr Shahran"

Shahran was the Coptic name of a village about which the twelfth-century historian Abu al-Makarim wrote (Samuel 2000: 58). He said that it was a vast village located south of the area of Tura on the eastern bank of the Nile. It is said that there was a wine press there, and so it was called "the village of the press" (al-Maʻsara) (Malaty 1996: 8). He describes the monastery as follows: "In this monastery there is a palace . . . and it has a garden, its area is 6 feddans, and in it fruitful palms and agriculture lands. The caliph used to retire in this monastery and go out to the mountains and roam the wilderness" (Samuel 2000: 59).

The Arabic historian al-Maqrizi (1364–1442) wrote,

> This monastery is near the area of Tura. It is built of mud bricks. There are palm trees and a number of monks in it. It is said that the man Shahran for whom the village was named was a Christian wise man and it is said that he was a king. This monastery was known in

> the past as Marcorius, who was also called Marcora and Abu Marcora. When Barsuma ibn al-Tebban lived there, it was known as the Monastery of Barsuma, and he has a feast celebrated on the fifth week of Lent, which is attended by the patriarch and the Christian notables. And a great deal of money is spent in it. Mercurius was among those killed by Diocletian on the 19th of Tamouz (July), the 15th of Abib and he was a soldier. (al-Maqrizi 1998a: 788)

Inside this monastery was a church (al-Suriany 1972: 73). The date of its construction is unknown but it was certainly after the death of St. Barsum the Naked (1317), but before 1426, the year when the priest Mikhael al-Maarigy was ordained. This priest composed a hymn venerating St. Barsum the Naked, which is found in the manuscript Paris Copte 32 (=P. Copt.32), in the National Library of Paris.

Certainly the monastery was built before al-Maqrizi wrote his book, in which he described the celebration of the feast of St. Barsum the Naked. This means that the church was built in the century following his death.

However, it was also said that this church was the church known as St. Mercurius Abu Sayfayn, which was renovated in different eras and was better known as the Church of St. Barsum the Naked (al-Suriany 1972: 90). The oldest buildings there are the three sanctuaries, the choir area in front of them, which is covered by domes (Andraous 2012b), and the grave of St. Barsum the Naked, which is found in a domed room beside the southern wall of the church.

In the 1970s, an ancient well was discovered northeast of the Church of St. Barsum the Naked. This well has a mouth made from red granite (al-Suriany 1972: 74).

The Monastery Escapes Destruction

During the patriarchate of Pope John VIII, the eightieth patriarch of the Coptic Church, it happened that the churches of Cairo were closed down for a short time. The monasteries in the suburbs of Cairo, as well as the churches in the provinces of Egypt, remained unharmed.

In Alexandria, the churches and houses of the Copts were exposed to demolition because of an incitement addressed to the ruler Baybars al-Jashnakir against the Copts (Nakhla 2011: 160), made by a Moroccan high official during his passage through Egypt on his way to the pilgrimage in Arabia.

On another occasion some malcontents complained to Sultan Barquq (r. 1382–98) against the monks of Dayr Shahran, accusing them of injuring their honor and asking for the expulsion of the monks and demolition of the monastery. The sultan allowed this. When Pope Matthew I, the eighty-seventh pope of Alexandria (r. 1378–1408), heard of it, he hurried to the monastery to reason with those who wanted to destroy it, but to no avail.

The pope then hurried to defend the monastery and its monks before the sultan, who became convinced of their innocence and sent a military force to prevent the demolition of the monastery. As a result, those evil people fled and the monastery escaped destruction.

The Annual Celebration of the Feast of St. Barsum the Naked

The monastery in Helwan was made famous over the years by a number of events: its renovation by the monk Beyman (Poemen); visits from Sultan al-Hakim bi-Amr Illah; the selection of three patriarchs from the monastery; St. Barsum the Naked's residence in it; the many people who came to ask for his prayers; and the saint's death and burial there. The monastery's proximity to Cairo, on the eastern bank of the Nile, makes it easy for the Copts to visit it to celebrate the anniversary of the saint's death on his feast day, 5 Nasi.

The Coptic Church also used to celebrate the fifth Sunday of Lent every year at the monastery. The pope, along with a number of bishops, priests, and deacons, would celebrate the liturgy there on that Sunday. This celebration was mentioned by the historian al-Maqrizi (al-Maqrizi 1998a: 409).

A Hymn for the Veneration of St. Barsum the Naked

In the fifteenth century, Fr. Mikhael al-Maarigy composed a Coptic hymn for venerating St. Barsum the Naked (P.Copt.32, f. 12). The composer was ordained a priest before 1426, and was later ordained bishop for the diocese of Samannud with the name Anba Mikhael al-Maarigy.[2] He composed this well-known hymn while he was still a priest, before his episcopal ordination. It is titled "Apekran," or "Your Name." The scribe of the manuscript says, "Hail to your grave, which is full of grace. Hail to your holy body . . . ."

Patriarchs Selected from Dayr Shahran

Pope John VIII

This fourteenth-century patriarch was born in Minyat Bani Khosaim. His original name was Yuhanna ibn Ibsal but he was known as al-Mu'ataman ibn al-Qiddis. He became a monk at the Monastery of Shahran and was ordained pope under the name of John VIII, as the eightieth pope of Alexandria (1300–20).

John VIII was contemporary with three Mamluk sultans: al-Nasir Muhammad ibn Qalawun, al-Nasir, and al-Muzzafar. Under the rule of these sultans, severe persecutions befell the Copts. Heavy taxes were imposed on them and they were ill-treated. Among the persecutors was a Moroccan senior official who passed through Egypt on his way to the pilgrimage. It did not please him that the Copts were in charge of the financial matters of Egypt, so he began inciting the sultan against them and humiliating them in every way. During these days the churches of Cairo were closed down for some days, but the churches and monasteries in the provinces remained open. In Alexandria, the churches and the houses of the Christians were demolished.

Pope John VIII died on May 29, 1320, during the reign of Sultan Muhammad ibn Qalawun II, and was buried in Dayr Shahran.

Pope Peter V

This patriarch began his religious life as a monk in the Monastery of St. Macarius. His original name was Butrus ibn Dawud. He was chosen as abbot for Dayr Shahran (al-Masri 1998: 274). Due to his great virtues he was chosen as the eighty-third patriarch of Alexandria (r. 1340–48), under the name of Peter. He was contemporary with three Mamluk sultans: Abu Bakr al-Mansur, 'Ala' al-Din al-Ashraf, and Hassan ibn Qalawun. The Copts were also severely persecuted by these sultans. Pope Peter V was buried in Old Cairo (Nakhla 2011: 92).

Pope Mark IV

Pope Mark IV was the eighty-fourth patriarch of Alexandria (1348–63). His original name was al-As'ad Faragalla. He was from Qalyub and his father was a priest at al-Mu'allaqa Church in Old Cairo. He became a monk at Dayr Shahran, and then was ordained priest under the name of Ghobrial. He was chosen as patriarch under the name Mark IV. He was contemporary with three sultans: Sha'ban, Haji, and Hassan.

Once again the Copts were persecuted under the rule of these sultans so severely that the pope was arrested and tortured. He was released only when the Nubian king intervened (Mansi 1983: 443). He was buried at Dayr Shahran.

The Abbots of the Monastery of Dayr Shahran

1. Butrus ibn Dawud, who later became Pope Peter V.
2. Hegumen Ishaq ibn Qarkura: It is recorded that when St. Barsum the Naked died in 1317, he was buried beside Hegumen Ishaq ibn Qarkura, the abbot of the monastery (Isidorus 2002b: 402).
3. Fr. Yuhanna ibn al-Shaykh: He was present at the death of St. Barsum the Naked, and may even have been the abbot of the monastery at that time (Andraous 2012b).
4. Fr. Mina: He was the abbot of the monastery at the time of Pope Mikhail VI, the ninety-second patriarch of Alexandra (1477–78). He opposed the bishop of Manf, who wanted to annex the monastery to his diocese (al-Suriany 1972: 72).

The Popes Buried at the Monastery of Dayr Shahran and Their Graves

Three patriarchs were buried together with St. Barsum the Naked and Hegumen Ishaq ibn Qarkura, the abovementioned abbot of the monastery, in the same graveyard (Yusab 1994: 183), which was located southwest of the church. Later this graveyard was annexed to the church and became part of it. These popes were John VIII (1300–20) (known as Ibn al-Qiddis), Benjamin II (1327–39), and Mark IV (1348–63) (Nakhla 1943: 92–93).

Ancient Icons of St. Barsum the Naked

The church in Dayr Shahran

This icon (fig. 8.1) dates to around the eighteenth century, and is written by the famous iconographer of that period, Yuhanna al-Armani. St. Barsum is depicted as old and thin, and is facing slightly to the left. His arms are stretching in front of him, and his hands are open. He is semi-nude and barefooted. A piece of black cloth is wrapped around his waist.

The saint is standing on a huge snake which is submissive to him, according to one of the traditional stories in his biography. He has a long white beard. His hair, which dangles down his back, is long, white, and parted in the middle.

His eyes are wide and his brows are arched. His nose is small. Around his head is a wide brown halo. His body is outlined in black. To his right is a pot containing fruits, and to his left is the cave in which he lived.

In the background, there are architectural elements representing the buildings of the monastery, which are provided with windows. There are

Fig. 8.1. An eighteenth-century icon of St. Barsum the Naked, by Yuhanna al-Armani.

also conical domes and steeples over these buildings. There is a large cross to the right over these buildings, which are surrounded by a high wall with buttresses at the top.

The background is light brown. There are Coptic and Arabic words at the top left. At the bottom of the icon there is a blue strip on which is written in Arabic, "St. Ava Barsum the Naked of vices and clothed with virtues" (Andraous 2012a).

Sts. Abakir and Yuhanna (Atalla 1998: 131)

The icon of St. Barsum in the church of Sts. Abakir and Yuhanna, in the district of Old Cairo, is distinguished by its simplicity. The artist is unknown. With simple outlines, he shows St. Barsum standing naked, with a huge snake with a red tongue and big teeth under his feet. He is stretching out his hands in prayer. He is holding a cross in his left hand and there is a golden halo around his head. His beard is small. His head is facing slightly to the left, but his eyes are looking at the viewer. Around his waist is a piece of red clothing.

The background is light brown but the rest of the icon is blue. In the upper part of the icon there are three stars, and there are three candles on either side of the saint. The writing on the icon consists of the words Pi-Agios in white, and under them the name of the saint in Coptic in black, and then his name in Arabic. The icon was made in the nineteenth century and it is placed in a wooden frame.

St. Mercurius, Old Cairo

The icon in the Church of St. Mercurius dates to the eighteenth century, and the artist is again Yuhanna al-Armani. The saint is shown standing naked, with only a piece of clothing with many folds covering his waist. He is holding a cross in his right hand and a scroll in his left. His hair is shown with a yellow halo around his head. He has a moustache and a short beard.

The background is green in the upper part of the icon and golden in the lower part. There is a tree on either side of the saint, a distinguishing characteristic of the works of Yuhanna al-Armani.

Another icon in St. Mercurius (Salib 2002: 21)

Another icon of St. Barsum in the Church of St. Mercurius in Old Cairo is found in the trilateral enclosure of the church. St. Barsum is shown standing on a snake and his head is facing to the right. He is naked except for a piece of clothing around his waist. He is holding a cross in his right hand and a book in his left. There is a halo around his head and his hair is dangling on his shoulders. He has a moustache and a short beard. The background is red in the upper part of the icon and golden in the lower part, and it contains architectural elements that may refer to his monastery in Shahran. Again, the trees in the background are characteristic of the work of Yuhanna al-Armani.

Conclusion

The Monastery of Anba Barsum the Naked, now known as Dayr Shahran in al-Ma'sara, Helwan, originally called the Monastery of St. Mercurius, was established during the patriarchate of Pope Simon I (693–700). Dayr Shahran and its monks acquired a prestigious status in the fourteenth century, as three patriarchs were chosen from this monastery in that century.

The buildings of the old monastery developed over the ages. The current bishop of Helwan, His Grace Anba Basanti, has renovated several of the older small churches and buildings and also added new ones. A large cathedral in the name of Anba Barsum the Naked is to the west of the monastery.

This beloved saint, who was willing to give up all worldly goods and devote his life to God, praying for the well-being and justice of all of Egypt and its people, is still venerated to this day. He provides an important example in today's world for perseverance, nonviolent protest against injustice, praying for peace, and an abiding faith in God.

Notes

1 This historically and artistically important church was probably built in the sixth century and was later demolished. It was completely renovated by Pope Abraam al-Suriany during the reign of the Fatimid al-Mu'izz li-Din Illah. It remained steadfast in the face of challenges until it was burned in 1168 during the burning of al-Fustat. It remained a ruin until it was restored by archon Abu al-Barakat in 1176, when he replaced the marble pillars supporting the ceiling with pillars of bricks and built the domes over the sanctuaries.

2 Fr. Basilious Sobhy, "al-Anba Mikhail al-Maarigy—al-Qumus Girgis al-Hakim," http://st-takla.org/articles/fr-basilous-sobhy/characters/maarigy-intro.html

9 The Traditions of the Holy Family and the Development of Christianity in the Nile Delta

Ashraf Alexandre Sadek

AFTER TRAVELING THROUGH the Sinai, the Holy Family, according to tradition, walked from east to west through the Nile Delta. Pope Tawadros II declared that their trip "drew a cross over Egypt":[1] the Delta would be the upper, transverse part of this cross, the Nile Valley being the vertical part.

The various written and oral traditions mention eight place names associated with this journey in the Delta: Tell Basta, Musturud/Mahamma, Bilbeis, Daqadus, Samannud, Burullus (St. Damiana), Sakha (Bikha Issous), and Wadi al-Natrun. This chapter will examine whether the memory of the coming of the Holy Family has had an impact on the development of Christian life in the Nile Delta. To this end, we shall draw for each site a parallel between the traditions of the Holy Family and the history of Christian communities on this site; this should enable us to measure, to some extent, the impact of the Holy Family traditions on the history of the Christian Church in the Nile Delta.

Tell Basta (Bubastis)

This place, situated in the eastern Delta two kilometers from Zagazig, is already mentioned in the Old Testament, Ezekiel 30:17: "The young people of On (Heliopolis) and Pi-Bastet (Bubastis) will fall under the sword, and the cities will be taken away in captivity."[2]

This city is mentioned in connection with the Holy Family in four important Coptic sources: the *Vision of Theophilus* (Sadek and Sadek 2011: 107–11, 241–53), the *Homily on the Rock* (Boud'hors and Boutros 2001: 119), the Synaxarium (Basset 1989: 4:407–10 [24 Bashans]), and the *Homily of Zacharias* (Sadek and Sadek 2011: 259). In these sources, several events are associated with this important place, as can be seen in the following table.

Text	**Events**				
	Meeting with the robbers	Falling of idols	The Holy Family is rejected by the inhabitants	Creation of a well	Sojourn at Qolum's home
Vision of Theophilus	X	X	X	X	
Homily on the Rock			X		
Synaxarium			X	X	
Homily of Zacharias		X	X	X	X

In the tenth century BC, this city honored the goddess Bastet, represented by the cat—a late form of the lion goddess Sekhmet. During the Twenty-first Dynasty (1089–1063 BC) it became the capital of Egypt, a powerful political center. Ancient Egyptian theology and cults were usually close to monotheism and popular religion shows a high level of spirituality (Sadek 1987; Sadek 2005: 279–86). However, during the Late Period (1089–332 BC), while the city was the capital of the eighteenth nome of Lower Egypt, the cult of Bastet in the form of the cat degenerated into exaggerated worship; Herodotus in the fifth century BC described the excesses of the behaviors of the pilgrims (Book II, 60). Consequently, because of this cult and the way it degenerated in the Late Period, this city was considered by the early Christians as a symbol of idolatry. The destruction of idols described by the *Vision of Theophilus* is thus viewed as a logical sign of the new worship introduced by Christ.

Indeed, Bubastis is attested as a Christian center and a bishopric as early as the third century AD (Stewart 1991b: 360–61). It offered many martyrs to the Church. The *History of the Patriarchs* (eleventh century AD) mentions it in its list of the places visited by the Holy Family. In 1991, Mohamed Mahmoud Omar, a professor of archaeology at the University of Zagazig, discovered among the ruins of the temple of Bastet a well that he dated to the first century. This well is, of course, considered by the Copts as the well created by Jesus. Besides, an oral tradition relates the Church of St. George to an ancient church that would have been built on Qolum's house, where the Holy Family is supposed to have rested during their sojourn in this place.

Until the present day, in spite of the fact that no pilgrimage is officially held in Tell Basta, the inhabitants of Zagazig have not forgotten the memory of the Holy Family, which remains an important link between this place and the Christian faith (Hulsman 2001: 38).

Musturud/Mahamma

Musturud,[3] also called al-Mahamma, which means 'the bath,' is now part of the greater Cairo metropolis; in the first century AD, it was probably a tiny village in the eastern Delta.

The *Vision of Theophilus* and the *Homily of Zacharias* mention that the Holy Family went through Musturud on their way to the south; the Synaxarium and the Difnar mention it on their way back. According to these documents, Jesus created a spring in which the Holy Virgin bathed him and washed his clothes (Sadek and Sadek 2011: 259). Since then, this water has been considered miraculous (*Difnar* 1985: 484).

According to various manuscripts, a church dedicated to the Holy Virgin existed at an early date on this site; Amélineau mentions it in his *Géographie* (Amélineau 1893: 261 and n1). Mark III, seventy-third patriarch of Alexandria, consecrated the present church in 1185 (Viaud 1979: 33–34; Viaud 1991: 1970).

Vansleb visited this place in July 1671 and mentioned, among its "spiritual treasures," a miraculous icon of the Virgin (Viaud 1979: 33n2; Vansleb 1677b: 236). Until 1925, this church and the whole place were affiliated with the See of Jerusalem because many pilgrims used to visit it at the end of their pilgrimage to the Holy Land (Meinardus 1977: 152, 155, 252, 253, 647; Meinardus 1992a: 65).

Up to the present time, this church continues to be a place of pilgrimage for the memory of the coming of the Holy Family. This pilgrimage takes place on June 14 and 15 (7 and 8 Ba'una); during the liturgy, the Synaxarium mentioning the stopping of the Holy Family in this place, Mahamma, is read (Basset 1924: 5:544–45; Sadek and Sadek 2011: text IV, 6c, 142). This pilgrimage of 8 Ba'una is ancient, as is attested by travelers (Jullien 1891: 210). It was at some periods linked to the tree of Matariya. Another important pilgrimage takes place on the feast of the Assumption on August 22.

It seems clear, in the case of Musturud, that the traditions of the Holy Family's sojourn there were an element of the development of Christian faith and pilgrimage to this place.

Bilbeis

Bilbeis (Belbeis, Belbays, Bilbays), situated forty-eight kilometers northeast of Cairo, is mentioned in the *Homily of Zacharias*, which states that, on their arrival, the Holy Family met a burial procession for a widow's son. Deeply moved by the mother's sorrow, Jesus raised the dead man (Sadek and Sadek 2011:260).

A non-Coptic apocryphal text, the *Armenian Book of Childhood*, also mentions a "long sojourn" in a city called Polpay, which the scholar Paul Peeters has identified as Bilbeis (Peeters 1914: 162–63).[4]

A local oral tradition mentions that the Holy Family stopped again in Bilbeis on their way back to the land of Israel (al-Syriani 1999: 3). According to another oral tradition reported by medieval pilgrims, the Virgin sat at the foot of a tree which became an object of great veneration for Christians and also for Muslims, who used to bury their saints in this place. This tree was burned during the nineteenth century (Jullien 1891: 246).

Bilbeis was an early bishopric, prior to the seventh century (Munier 1943a: 47, 54, 63). The Crusaders took the city in 1168; however, in the fourteenth century the city was again a Coptic bishopric and the site of a theological school (Stewart 1991b: 391). As we have mentioned, this place was on the pilgrimage route to and from the Holy Land, and was visited by pilgrims who came to pray at the tree of the Holy Family, thus encouraging Christianity in this area.

Nowadays, the Christian community is small yet very much attached to their traditions; they pray in a church built in 1932 over an old church which, according to the local tradition, was built in the fourth century.

Daqadus

No ancient written text mentions the village of Daqadus in the itinerary of the Holy Family. Yet, according to Father Gérard Viaud, there is a tradition mentioning the passage of the Holy Family through Daqadus (Viaud 1991: 1970–71; Stewart 1991d: 692), between Bilbeis and Samannud; a local tradition says that the population of the village welcomed them and Jesus blessed the water of the well (Hulsman 2001: 42–44).

Daqadus is mentioned in a medieval list of Egyptian churches (manuscript Arabe 174 of the Bibliothèque nationale of Paris), which speaks of a "church of the Virgin" called *ti theotokos athotokos* 'The Mother of God of Daqadus' (Viaud 1979: 24).

In the twelfth century, a man from Daqadus became patriarch of Alexandria: Anba Michael V (r. 1145–46).

The present church, built in 1888, possesses a manuscript (Nr 27) dated AD 1332. It is probably built on a medieval church (1239), itself built on an ancient fourth-century church built by Empress Helena, mother of Emperor Constantine. In 1970, excavations confirmed the existence of a medieval sanctuary under the choir of the modern church (Viaud 1979: 24). Ancient columns were reused in the church porch; a medieval crypt has several early archaeological elements.

A *mulid* is held at the end of August for the "Virgin of Daqadus."

Samannud (Minyat Samannud/Minyat Ganah)

Samannud,[5] situated on the Nile in the center of the Delta, is mentioned as a Holy Family site in the *Vision of Theophilus*, the *Homily of Zacharias*, and both the Coptic and Ethiopian Synaxaria on 24 Bashans. According to these texts, the Holy Family blessed the city and its inhabitants (*al-Laali' al-saniya* 1936: 65). Local tradition claims that they stayed in Samannud for a couple of weeks, that Jesus blessed the well, and that Mary prepared bread in a special granite *gurn* that is still visible and venerated in the churchyard (Hulsman 2001: 46).

Samannud is one of the oldest towns in Lower Egypt; it was an important center in pharaonic times. During the Ptolemaic Period (beginning in the fourth century BC) it was the center of a cult of Osiris. The Egyptian historian Manetho came from Samannud (300 BC).

The Christian church in Samannud is attested in AD 325 by Athanasius the Great, who mentions in a letter the name of a bishop of Samannud (Munier 1943a: 3). This town also produced three patriarchs of Alexandria for the Coptic Church: John III in the seventh century, Mina I in the eighth century, and Cosmas in the ninth century. In the thirteenth century (1235–57) a bishop of Samannud, John, became famous for his writings on grammar, his composition of hymns, and his copying of manuscripts (Stewart 1991g: 2090).

Roman persecutions were particularly severe in Samannud. Among the long list of martyrs is the famous child saint Abanub, who is still admired and venerated all over Egypt.

According to tradition, like the sites previously discussed, the present church, dedicated to Saint Abanub, is built on former sanctuaries built on the house where the Holy Family dwelt. Ancient columns have been used in the entry. In the yard is a well blessed by Jesus, the *gurn* used by Mary, and a beautiful ancient baptistery carved in the rock.

Few Christians live nowadays in Samannud, but the *mulid* for Abanub attracts thousands of people on May 30 and July 31 (Viaud 1979: 26–27; Meinardus 1977: 620–21). The water of the well is famous for producing miracles, especially for healing children.

In this city, the cult related to the Holy Family is associated with the cult of Saint Abanub: the child Jesus and the young martyr are united in common praise and veneration.

Burullus (St. Damiana's Monastery)

Three ancient texts document the passage of the Holy Family in the Burullus area, between the two branches of the Nile: the *Vision of Theophilus*, the *Homily of Zacharias*, and the Synaxarium. In the *Homily of Zacharias*, Jesus makes a prediction according to which there would be holy churches in this place (*al-Laali' al-saniya* 1936: 75; Sadek and Sadek 2011: 260).

This location has been blessed with monastic life. Some documents, such as the *History of the Patriarchs*, mention the existence of a monastery near Lake Burullus (Dayr al-Mightas or al-Maghtis), where the Virgin Mary was honored in memory of the passage of the Holy Family (Viaud 1979: 10, after Leroy 1908: 197). In this monastery was kept the stone bearing the print of Jesus's foot, as related in the *Homily of Zacharias*. This stone is now kept in Sakha; it is in this monastery that St. Damiana was baptized. This monastery was important until it was burned in 1438 (Coquin 1991b: 818–19). Oral traditions report also that before its destruction, one of the monks took the stone bearing Jesus's footprint and buried it under the vestige of a column in order to be able to find it again easily (Hulsman 2001: 50).

The Ethiopian Book of the Miracles of Mary, a fifteenth-century compilation of legends concerning Mary, is an important liturgical book in Ethiopia; it records about ten miracles taking place at Dayr al-Mightas, called in Ethiopia "Dabra Metmaq." "Miracle 82" tells how the monastery was destroyed by a group of Muslims eager to remove an important Christian center where visions of Mary used to bring many Muslims to the Christian faith (Colin 2004: 193–227).

There were also in this area three other monasteries: al-Asqar and al-Mayma, which have both disappeared, and St. Damiana,[6] which is presently one of the biggest female convents in Egypt. A tradition which may be rather recent says that the Holy Family blessed the exact place where this monastery has stood since the fourth century. It was built at the end of the third century by Mark, a Christian governor of this area, for his daughter Damiana, who settled there with forty other virgins. All of them were martyred by order of Diocletian. A manuscript reports that St. Helena herself came on May 20, 325 or 326, to participate in the consecration of the martyrium by Patriarch Alexander I (r. 303–26) (Viaud 1979: 21–22). The tradition of the pilgrimage to St. Damiana, on January 21 and August 5–22, dates from this time.[7]

Three types of blessings are associated with this site: the visit of the Holy Family, monastic life, and martyrdom.

Sakha (Bikha Issous)

After crossing the Burullus area and before crossing the desert of Scete, the Holy Family went to the small town of Sakha,[8] in the western Delta. Sakha is the place where the stone with Jesus's footprint is now kept (the story of this miracle is reported in the Synaxarium). This city has been identified by Murad Kamil with "Bikha Issous" (Meinardus 1977: 621), a place mentioned in the *Homily of Zacharias* and the Synaxarium (Sadek and Sadek 2011: 116, 139, 260).

From the early Middle Ages, Sakha shared with Alexandria the title of "the city beloved of God" (Amélineau 1893: 410): it was a bishopric prior to the fourth century, as confirmed by a letter from St. Athanasius (Munier 1943a). Several bishops from Sakha are mentioned in the Synaxarium. It is also there that St. Severus of Antioch was exiled and died in 538. St. Agathon the Stylite (seventh century) stayed on a pillar near this city for fifty years. St. Zacharias was bishop of Sakha in the eighth century. A *Homily* on the Flight into Egypt is attributed to him (Detlef and Müller 1991: 2368–69). In the thirteenth century, Abu al-Makarim mentioned five churches in Sakha (Samuel 1992: 72–73).

According to Viaud, pilgrims came to this church and venerated an old icon of the Holy Family in Egypt (Viaud 1979: 29). This icon can still be seen in the church. However, since its rediscovery in 1984, the main object of veneration is the stone with Jesus's footprint (Hulsman 2001: 50).[9] Pope Shenouda III officially recognized the authenticity of the stone. Some miracles are attributed to it.

In 1994, the Egyptian government gave permission to renovate the church. The excavations produced some very ancient architectural elements, exhibited at the entrance of the church: a fragment of a chancel (barrier between the nave and the choir of the church, used before the introduction of the iconostasis in the fifth century); a large capital in white marble with three registers of acanthus flowers; broken parts of columns. All these elements point to the existence of a very ancient church at the same spot as the present one.

Within the church, other elements are visible: an old baptistery, the fragment of a column foot under which was found the stone bearing the footprint of Jesus, two beautiful ancient 'thrones' *(corsi)*, a *gurn (jorn; majour)* supposedly used by Mary, several liturgical instruments, and of course the famous stone with Jesus's footprint. On June 1, feast of the Entry of Christ into Egypt, the stone is carried in procession through the church and anointed with holy oil. This pilgrimage is still held, and each year it attracts an increasing number of people.

Wadi al-Natrun

Although this place is not part of the subject matter of this volume, it needs to be included in the Delta places blessed by the Holy Family, according to the *Vision of Theophilus*, the *Homily of Zacharias*, and the Synaxarium. As we know, the area developed a strong monastic tradition, produced many saints, and remains a high point for pilgrimages.

Conclusion

The following table presents the traces left by the Holy Family (traditions on wells, objects, pilgrimages), and the development from the early centuries of a Christian community (ancient church, ancient bishopric).

In six of the eight places studied, traces or memory of an ancient church, probably dedicated to the Virgin because of her presence here, are to be found. Four of these sites were early bishoprics. Two have been important monastic areas since the early centuries. Three still possess a well whose water is considered to have been blessed by Jesus. Two of them have visible ancient objects (*jorns* or *gurns*, footprint) venerated as having a strong link with the coming of the Holy Family. Seven are places of pilgrimage. One shows broken idols. These details clearly show that on these spots, the growth of the Church was strengthened by the memory of the coming of Christ and his Mother and the blessings left by this event. Even today,

	Traces or traditions concerning an ancient church in honor of the Holy Family	*Early bishopric*	*Famous bishops, saints, martyrs*	*Monasteries*	*Well or spring of the Holy Family still used*	*Other objects venerated*	*Pilgrimage*	*Broken idols*
Tell Basta	X	X (3rd c.)			X			X
Musturud/ Mahamma	X				X		X	
Bilbeis	X	X (before 7th c.) and theological school				X tree	X	
Daqadus	X		X				X	
Samannud	X	X (4th c.)	X		X	X *gurn*	X	
Burullus			X	X (4 ancient monasteries)			X	
Sakha	X	X (5th c.)	X			X stone with Jesus's footprint *Gurn*/ icon	X	
Wadi al-Natrun			X	X			X	

the local Christian communities rely on these elements to strengthen their faith and their roots in the land of Egypt.

Of course a study of this kind has its limits: it should be expanded to cover all the other places visited by the Holy Family. They could then be compared with other Christian sites that were *not* visited by them. For the time being, it is reasonable to suggest that the Holy Family traditions have helped Christianity to settle and grow in the Delta, and that they are still a reason and a means for Christians to maintain their faith in spite of all the difficulties.

Notes

1 Speech to Francis I, Pope of Rome, Vatican, May 10, 2013.

2 Ancient Egyptian names: Pi-Bésèt, Pi-Beseth, Per-Bastet; Greek: Bubastis; Coptic: Bouasti or Pouasti; biblical name: Pi-Beseth (Ezekiel 30:17–18). Concerning Tell Basta, see Amélineau 1893: 89; Abu al-Makarim 1895: 9.

3 Also called, since the Ottoman period, Mostrod; Coptic names: Mît Sorad, Menyet Serd, or Mynet Serd.

4 *Livre arménien de l'Enfance*, ms B, ch. XV. See the discussion on Bilbeis in Amélineau 1893: 334–35.

5 Deb-nuter of ancient Egypt; Sebennytos in Greek; Djemnouti in Coptic; cf. Amélineau 1893: 411–12; Montet 1957: 104.

6 Other names: Dimiana, Sitt Guimyanah, Monastery al-Barari, Zafaran, Wadi al-Sisiban (Viaud 1979: 21–22).

7 See also Coquin 1991d: 837–38; Coquin and Martin 1991c: 783–84; Coquin 1991c: 870–72; Grossmann 1991b: 872; Meinardus 1965: 58, 171–74; Van Doorn-Harder 1995: 36–37, 48–49.

8 *Xois* in Greek; *Sekoou* in Coptic. This city is 150 kilometers north of Cairo.

9 The metropolitan of Damietta, Anba Bishoy, played an important part in this discovery; cf. Perry 2003: 24–33.

10 Anba Ruways and the Cathedral of St. Mark

Adel F. Sadek

Area History

The name of Dayr al-Khandaq, or 'Monastery of the Moat,' appeared first in Islamic references when Jawhar al-Siqilli, commander of the Fatimid armies, founded the city of Cairo in AD 969. He built a palace for the caliph in the area known as al-Rukn al-Mukhallaq (Grossmann 1991a: 810) near al-Aqmar Mosque located on the north of Mu'izz Street, in the vicinity of an old monastery known as Dayr al-'Izam ('Monastery of the Bones') or Bir al-'Izam ('Well of the Bones').[1] That monastery was dedicated to St. George, or possibly to St. John the Baptist (Abu al-Makarim 1984b: fol. 14b; Coquin and Martin 1991a: 814; Stewart 1991e: 1413). A general description of the area is provided in Abu al-Makarim's *History of Churches and Monasteries*.[2] Jawhar removed the monastery because of its proximity to the new palace, but the well existed until the fifteenth century with the name of Bir al-'Izam. He compensated the Copts with an area called al-Khandaq, where the Coptic Orthodox Patriarchate in 'Abbasiya is currently located. He then ordered the bones and corpses to be moved to the new place (Ibn 'Abd al-Zaher 1996: 15–16; Ibn Taghri Birdi 1992: 36; al-Maqrizi 1853: 507).

Cairo at the end of the Mamluk period was a long strip stretching between al-Fustat to the south and Raydaniya (now 'Abbasiya) in the north. The Khalig (canal) formed the city's boundary. The west bank of the Khalig retained a suburban character. During the reign of the Fatimid caliph al-Hakim bi-Amr Illah (r. 996–1021), the Khalig was restored, and renamed al-Khalig al-Misri or simply al-Khalig. The area known as al-Maqs was then a Nile port, receiving grain and goods from Lower Egypt as well as from across the Mediterranean. The name al-Maqs is derived from the Arabic word for customs taxes. It was a village that existed before the Arab conquest of Egypt, by the name of Tandunias. In early Arabic sources it was called Umm Dunayn, but later sources and Ottoman documents more often used the name al-Maqs. Throughout its history, al-Maqs, now known as al-Azbakiya, retained a predominantly Christian population (Behrens-Abouseif 1985: 4–5). In his antipathy against the *dhimmi* or non-Muslims, al-Hakim bi-Amr Illah destroyed some churches in the area. However, it has remained a Christian quarter until the present day, and it was the site of the Coptic Patriarchate until the cathedral at ʻAbbasiya was built (Behrens-Abouseif 1986: 122).

The Khandaq was therefore considered the least inhabited place of the Old Cairo area. The moat itself was on the site of an old village known by the name Minyat al-Asbagh, named for Abu Rayan Asbagh ibn ʻAbd al-ʻAziz ibn Marwan ibn ʻAbd al-Hakam. His father, ʻAbd al-ʻAziz ibn Marwan, was the governor of Egypt during the Umayyad era (685–705), and he constructed this village on the Egyptian canal (al-Khalig al-Misri) in the late seventh century. It kept this name for about three hundred years, up to the late tenth century. On Saturday 11 Shaʻban AH 360 (June 10, AD 971), the Fatimid general Jawhar commanded that a moat be dug, starting from the mountain, to "al-Eblize," that is, the Nile, north of Cairo, following the route into Egypt from Syria. The moat was dug adjacent to Minyat al-Asbagh to ward off the attacks of the Carmathians. From that time on it became known by the name Khandaq ('moat'), as recorded in *waqf* (endowment) lists, colophons of manuscripts, and history books. In the year AH 806 (AD 1403/4), al-Khandaq was destroyed and its inhabitants abandoned it, as reported by al-Maqrizi: "I saw al-Khandaq, a small nice village, where people walked up from Cairo for excursion in the days of the Nile and spring seasons .... But with the mishaps and hardships occurring from the year 806 Hijra [AD 1403/4], al-Khandaq was destroyed and its inhabitants left it" (al-Maqrizi 1853: 510). Al-Khandaq then stretched from Hasanat Durra to Kom al-Rish. Al-Maqrizi wrote further: "Two churches were added to al-Khandaq outside Cairo: one named after Angel Gabriel and the other one after Mercurius, known as Ruways" (al-Maqrizi 1853: 511). The correct name is actually Archangel Michael Church, known by the name Dayr al-Malak al-Bahari, the Northern Angel Michael Monastery. Another name for it is Dayr al-Malak Michael of Hadayiq al-Qubba. The second monastery is the Monastery and Church of Anba Ruways (al-Khandaq), now on Ramses Street (Amélineau 1893: 220; Casanova 1901: 167).

The village of Kom al-Rish was near al-Khandaq on the western side of the Khalig al-Misri. It is now known as al-Zawya al-Hamra district, west of al-Demerdash Metro station, which is one kilometer away. Al-Khandaq is thus the area comprising Dayr al-Malak al-Bahari, between al-Demerdash station and al-Zawya al-Hamra district. The outer Khandaq starts from al-Gabal al-Ahmar (the Red Mount) and continues northwest through al-Sikka al-Bayda to its western end, then to the area of the present Faculty of Science of Ain Shams University, and again to the west until it intersects with the present Misr wa Sudan Street, encompassing al-Zawya al-Hamra. In the fifteenth and sixteenth centuries a new addition was made to the geographic name of al-Khandaq, dividing the name into Upper al-Khandaq, referring to the area of Dayr al-Malak al-Bahari and its church, and Lower al-Khandaq, which is Anba Ruways Monastery. The purpose of this division was to distinguish between them in manuscripts and *waqf* lists. This is recorded in MS Ritual 286 of the Patriarchal Library, History of Myron (chrism), dating back to 1461. Other manuscripts kept in al-Malak al-Bahari Church in the neighboring area include Liturgy 103 for making the *myron*, dating from 1703, in the days of Pope Yuhanna XVI, the 103rd patriarch (Daowd 2003: 14).[3] A railway line separated them at the beginning of the twentieth century, which turned into a metro line. Near Dayr al-Khandaq lies the shrine of a Muslim shaykh named al-Dimirdash, a name that was later given to the underground metro station near the cathedral.

Abu al-Makarim described the area as the length of territory known by the name Ras al-Tabia and Saqyat Raydan, a land that was governed by a servant of al-Hakim bi-Amr Illah whose name was Raydan al-Soklobi, now known as al-Raydaniya or 'Abbasiya. In the twelfth century, Abu al-Makarim describes the monastery as surrounded by a fence or a wall, with one door with a dome over it and a long upper room with a stone door. The monastery at that time comprised a number of churches, the largest of which was Mar Girgis the Martyr or St. George Church (Abu al-Makarim 1984b: fol. 15a). It was called the catholica, meaning the large church. It seems to have been quite luxurious, containing a marble ambo for preaching and a marble cathedra (bishop's seat), as this area had been a diocese since the mid-eleventh century. It is known that its Bishop George attended a council in the days of Pope Christodoulus, the sixty-sixth patriarch (r. 1047–77) (Labib 1991b: 545; Stewart 1991e: 1413).

Above Mar Girgis (St. George) Church there exists another church dedicated to the Three Holy Youths. It is made of wood and was renovated by Shaykh Amin al-Malik Abi Sa'id, the son of Shaykh al-Sa'id Abi al-Makarim, who replaced the original gabled wood ceiling with an ordinary ceiling. Then he drew inside the dome (the *ashkenah*) portraits of his father and two others: Shaykh Sani'att al-Khelafa al-Akram, known by the name al-Akram, a highly placed government official, and Shams al-Riassah, the brother of al-Akram. Probably both of these men were killed during the caliphate of al-Hafiz and were buried in a place called Khazanit al-Binud, the weapons storehouse of the army (Abu al-Makarim 1984b: fol. 14b). Since Shaykh Amin al-Malik did not have them buried in the monastery tombs, he put portraits of them there. This renovation was finished in the days of Caliph al-Zafir (r. 1149–53). Adjacent to this church is the house of the hegumen or steward of the church.

The same church was once again renovated by a priest named Mansur, who painted it and tiled the floor of the upper church, which was named after the Three Holy Youths. He had wall paintings inside the sanctuaries, and it was consecrated on the second Sunday of the Coptic month of Amshir, AM 901 (AD 1184). This church was distinguished by its magnificence, for it contained part of the marble seat of the bishop and a splendid baptistery, described by Abu al-Makarim as being cone-shaped, and carved of white marble in the form of a cup. The Fatimid vizier Abu al-Qasim Shahenshah al-Afdal ibn Badr al-Gamali, upon taking charge in Cairo in AD 1094, heard of the baptistery and asked to have it brought out. But at the door of the church it fell from the hands of the porters and was completely destroyed (Abu al-Makarim 1984b: fol. 15a).

Above this church there existed a story inhabited by a monk called Nagah, who was in charge of many affairs in the days of the Fatimid caliph al-'Amer (r. 1102–21) and had unjustly taxed his subjects (al-Maqrizi 1996: 125–27). This floor had a separate stone staircase. It is known that the Nubian king at this time, Solomon, abdicated his throne to a nephew and retired to Egypt to worship in its sacred wilderness. Although Solomon was later seized by Fatimid agents and taken to Cairo, Badr al-Gamali, the military commander (Labib 1991a: 324–26), treated him with deference, as a guest rather than a prisoner, and placed him in one of the state palaces.

When he died shortly afterward, he was buried in St. George Monastery at al-Khandaq with full Coptic funerary honors (Labib 1991d: 675–77).

In front of Mar Girgis Church there is a two-story fortress accessible from the church. The lower story is a residence for the bishops (Abu al-Makarim 1984b: fol. 15b), indicating that the monastery was a residence for visiting bishops. There is also a tomb for any visiting bishop who might die in Cairo, as it was difficult to transport the deceased for burial in his diocese, as will be mentioned later. This is where Anba Zakharios ibn Arnon, Bishop of Atripe, was buried when he died in Cairo, in one of the churches of al-Khandaq. This fortress looks onto al-Gabal al-Ahmar (the Red Mount) and other areas owned by the caliph, such as al-Bustan al-Kabir (the Big Garden), Khandaq al-Mawali al-Qasriya (probably the residence of the sister of the ruler), and al-Bustan (the Garden), known by the name 'al-Mokhtass.'

Abu al-Makarim goes on to describe the other churches in the monastery, mentioning various churches to the left of the main entrance. They include:

- An Armenian church built by an Armenian called Sarkis, who worked as superintendent of the camel stables belonging to the caliph al-Zafir (r. 1149–53).
- Abu Maqar Church, which the Armenians took for themselves. When Gregory, the patriarch of Armenia, arrived in Cairo and knew that this church had not been in use for prayer, he asked the army commander Badr al-Gamali, who was of Armenian origin, to give them this church. So Badr, having made sure that it was not used for prayer, commanded that it be given to the Armenians. They called it St. George (Sawirus ibn al-Muqaffa' 1959: 225 [text], 355–56 [trans.]). This took place in the days of Pope Kyrillos II, the sixty-seventh Coptic patriarch (r. 1078–92). In front of the church there is an oven for bread and for the Host, with a dome above it.
- Martyr Abali ibn Yostos Church (Abu al-Makarim 1984b: fol. 16a; Khalil 1991: 2305–2308), commemorated on 27 Barmuda. It is adjacent to the fortress, but his relics are kept in St. George Church in a wooden coffin. Probably the relics of this martyr were carried from there because the Syrians came to use the church during the caliphate of al-Mustansir (r. 1063–94), who commanded the Syrians to move away from the Husayniya

neighborhood near al-Azhar. A Syrian named al-Taweel came with a number of other Syrians and stayed in this church. The church witnessed a series of renovations and extensions after an area from the adjacent tombs was annexed to it. It was then consecrated as a church in the name of St. Bimen in the presence of Anba Mikhail, the bishop of al-Khandaq, in the year AM 901 (AD 1184). Later, when an archon of the church named Abu al-Yaman ibn Abi al-Farag ibn Zanbur died, he was buried there. He had renovated the church, enlarged it, and then built a new church over it. This new church was consecrated at the beginning of the pontificate of Pope John VI, the seventy-fourth patriarch (1189–1216), on the feast day of the martyr Abali ibn Yostos (Galtier 1905: 127–40), in the presence of the senior scribe Abu al-Makarim (Abu al-Makarim 1984b: fol. 16a).

- The Church of Virgin Marti Mariam (St. Mary) had been built by Shaykh Abu al-Fadl, the son of the bishop of Atripe and the manager of al-Afdal Divan during the caliphate of the Fatimid al-'Amer (r. 1101–30). He built a burial place for himself and his family under the church. He decorated it with portraits of himself and of his son, Abi al-Sorour, below the dome, each wearing a white head cover (pallium) in an *orans* posture. He also built a garden with a door facing the church. A person named 'Izz al-Kofah Abi al-Makarim, the son of Mustafa al-Malik Abi Yusuf, attempted to build another church over this church, named for the Apostles, because his father was buried under one of the sections of the church and his portrait was depicted on the walls of his tomb. However, this church was not completed (Abu al-Makarim 1984b: fol. 16a).
- Martyr Mercurius Church, in front of the fortress, constructed by Abu al-'Ala' Fahd ibn Ibrahim. He first served as Coptic secretary to Barjawan, tutor of the young caliph al-Hakim. Barjawan at that time was at the zenith of his power (AH 387/AD 997). Abu al-'Ala' was buried in this church beneath the southern altar, which became a burial place for his family as well. Anba Simon the Bishop added two churches above it in AH 549 (AD 1153), one in the name of St. Abu Buqtur, and the other in the name of St. Philotheus (Abu al-Makarim 1984b: fol. 18a). When the buildings of the church became old, its sanctuaries were renovated

> by Anba Mikhail, the bishop of Basta (Timm 1984–92: 362–65; Fedalto 1984: 282), and Abu Bishr the brother of Abu Sulayman, the governor of al-Matariya, in AH 562 (AD 1166). A lady named Sitt al-Ahl took care of the St. Philotheus church. Her husband, Muhazzab al-Sayrafi, renovated it once more after his wife had been buried in it and the sanctuaries began to collapse. In front of the church there was a well whose water had healing powers. In the same church Bishop Zakharios, the son of Arnon the bishop of Atripe, was buried, and his portrait was depicted in his tomb. This reveals that the area was a cemetery for the bishops who died in Cairo away from their dioceses (Youssef 2012: 5).

Al-Khandaq Monastery had a waterwheel for irrigating its gardens, and a baptistery with a dome over it. As Abu al-Makarim wrote, "Water ran into it in the evening of the holy purification," referring to the evening of the Epiphany feast. It seems that the whole area was a location for an older Coptic monastery. When a state official named Sayf al-Dawla ('Sword of the State') purchased a plot of land to cultivate near the monastery in the days of Caliph al-Hafiz (r. AD 1130–49), he found the relics of a bishop and his cross, so he filled up the tomb again. Abu al-Makarim, who lived at the end of the twelfth century, finished his chapter about al-Khandaq believing that the place had been previously a monastery and a church. Al-Khandaq Monastery was destroyed on 14 Shawwal AH 678/February 17, AD 1289 during the reign of the Bahari Mamluk al-Mansur Qalawun, and was later renovated (al-Maqrizi 1853: 511).

From all of the above it is clear that the land of al-Khandaq Monastery was a cemetery for the Copts, where many churches had been built or renovated by the Coptic elites and adorned with gardens. Inside they found space for expressing their beliefs by adorning these churches with portraits, and even putting their own portraits on or inside the tombs in the *orans* posture. This was a tradition either unknown or not in favor in the culture of the Egyptians during that period. The relative seclusion of al-Khandaq from the inhabited areas of Old Cairo, like al-Fustat, Harat Zuwayla, Harat al-Rum, and the old patriarchal residences, all of which suffered destruction, helped to keep these churches in existence and permitted innovations to them. Moreover, the area was a beautiful place outside Cairo where people used to go for a walk, as the Muslim historian al-Maqrizi wrote.

The Cathedral Area in the Modern Age

The modern historian Ali Pasha Mubarak (Mubarak 1987: 229) says that after the destruction that took place in the days of Qalawun (AH 678/AD 1280), five churches were built. The same is stated in Abu al-Makarim (1984b: 18f.). These churches are the Virgin's Church, St. George Church, St. Prince Tadros Church, St. Mercurius Church, and Martyr Abali Church. However, the only churches that still remained in 1888, when Mubarak was writing, were a church in the name of the Virgin and a church in the name of Anba Ruways. The latter was built in the fourth century in the name of St. Mercurius; after St. Anba Ruways was buried in it in AD 1404, the church came to be known by his name (fig. 10.1).[4]

The shrine of the saint lies under the church altar, and to the right of the shrine, on the south, four patriarchs are buried: Pope Mattaeus I (eighty-seventh), who was a contemporary of the saint; Pope Yuhanna XI (eighty-ninth); Pope Mattaeus II (ninetieth); and Pope Ghobrial VI (ninety-first). Downstairs

Fig. 10.1. The church of Anba Ruways, interior view featuring the entrance and wooden screen of the sanctuaries (Gabra, Van Loon, and Sonbol 2012: 184).

lie the relics of the disciple of Anba Ruways named Sulayman, and the relics of St. Abali ibn Yostos (1 Misra) in a closed chamber.

Mubarak also mentions that many of the Coptic elites who served under Muhammad Ali and his sons were buried in this monastery. They built splendid tombs with places to stay overnight on the days when memorial masses were offered for the deceased. He also included a detailed description of the funerals of some Coptic statesmen, as well as the traditions and habits of mourning over the deceased in those days, such as distributing alms to the needy, eulogizing the deceased, and many others (Mubarak 1987: 230–35). On July 10, 1929, the minister of health issued a decree that the area was considered a cemetery and that no further burials should be done there, since cemeteries are allowed only outside of urban areas. A dispute then arose concerning the ownership of the land. The State Judiciary Department issued a legal opinion that the cemeteries are a public utility, and once they cease to be used for that purpose, the ownership is transferred to the state. Thereupon a Coptic lawyer with the Coptic Lay Council instituted a lawsuit to protect the Church's rights. An earlier legal opinion had been issued in AD 1738, when some of the local inhabitants complained that the area of the Khandaq land had originally been one acre, but that the Copts had unlawfully seized the surrounding lands until the area became nine acres, sixteen *kirats*, and ten *sahms*.[5] The judge appointed a committee to examine the complaint. Eventually the judge's opinion affirmed the invalidity of the complaint and the validity of the ownership of the Copts—a process that lasted from 1929 to 1946. At the end the right of the Copts was established, provided that they construct public institutions such as churches, Sunday schools, an institute of Coptic studies, a nursery, or a youth social club. On February 1, 1953, there was an attempt by a Ministry of Health official to usurp part of the land, so on February 5, Pope Youssab II (the 115th patriarch) ordered the seminary to move immediately from the Mahmasha area, adjacent to Anba Ruways, to its present location in the cathedral. It became the first and the most important ecclesiastical institution constructed on the location (Habib 1996: 169–71).

The Present Cathedral

On July 24, 1965, during the celebrations of the thirteenth anniversary of the July 1952 Revolution, a celebration was held in a large tent on Anba Ruways land for the groundbreaking of the largest cathedral in the Middle East, to be named for St. Mark the Apostle. The celebration was attended by President Gamal 'Abd al-Nasser (fig. 10.2).

Fig. 10.2. Laying of the foundation stone of St. Mark Cathedral by His Holiness Pope Kyrillos VI and President Gamal 'Abd al-Nasser (Habib, n.d.)

On May 8, 1967 (30 Barmuda), the Feast of the Martyrdom of St. Mark, His Holiness Pope Kyrillos VI held a blessing prayer on the construction site and sprinkled blessed water to start the building work on the cathedral (Atta and Roufaeel 1981: 84). During this celebration, His Holiness Pope Kyrillos VI mentioned that in the following year, 1968, the church was going to celebrate the nineteen-hundredth anniversary of the martyrdom of St. Mark. President Gamal 'Abd al-Nasser spoke about the state's policy for the citizens, relying on justice, for the structure of the state is based on the love uniting the two constituents of the nation (Hakim and Mansour 1969: 145). Work began in August of the same year with great enthusiasm and speed, so that it would be finished in the ten months remaining before the anniversary date. President 'Abd al-Nasser donated a hundred thousand pounds from the state at the beginning of the project, then another fifty thousand pounds on its completion. The cathedral is one of the largest churches in Africa, measuring one hundred meters in length and thirty-six meters in width. The central dome has a height of fifty-five meters. The two bell towers are eighty-five meters high. The seating capacity is five thousand people (fig. 10.3).

Fig. 10.3. St. Mark Cathedral interior looking east (Gabra, Van Loon, and Sonbol 2012: 180).

The upper church has three *haykals* (sanctuaries), dedicated to St. Mina, St. Mark, and the Holy Virgin. The center altar is a gift from the Russian Orthodox Church. Pope Kyrillos VI had sent a message to His Holiness Pope Paul VI of Rome asking him to return part of the relics of St. Mark the Apostle. The Roman pope responded favorably to the request. A delegation

Fig. 10.4. Arrival of the relics of St. Mark in Cairo (Habib, n.d.)

of seventy-five persons, made up of metropolitans, bishops, and many of the Coptic elites, traveled to Rome in a private plane offered by the Egyptian airlines company (Hakim and Mansour 1969: 148; Meinardus 1999: 198–200).

The Coptic delegation and the Vatican delegation, carrying the body of St. Mark, arrived at Cairo International Airport at 11:00 p.m. on Wednesday, June 24, 1968. They were received by over thirty thousand people who congregated at the airport, including His Holiness Pope Kyrillos and a number of church delegates from abroad who had come to take part in this celebration. When the plane landed, the Pope accompanied the deacons in singing hymns. He received the relics of St. Mark and carried them in his car to the new cathedral in 'Abbasiya (fig. 10.4).

The body was carried around the cathedral in a glorious procession. His Holiness prayed a glorification service to the martyr saint and put his body in a special chamber. On the morning of the following day, June 25, 1968, the official celebration for inaugurating the new St. Mark Cathedral was held at Anba Ruways Monastery in the presence of President Gamal 'Abd al-Nasser, Emperor Haile Selassie of Ethiopia, and 272 representatives of churches worldwide. On Wednesday morning, June 26, the first liturgy was celebrated on the new cathedral altar, in the presence of the Ethiopian emperor and the delegations of the Oriental Orthodox Churches. At the end of the service, the pope carried the body of Martyr St. Mark to its special chamber below the grand altar at the eastern end of the cathedral (fig. 10.5).

Fig. 10.5. The Shrine of St. Mark. Top: Pantocrator. Bottom: Martyrdom of St. Mark and the translation of his relics (Gabra, Van Loon, and Sonbol 2012: 185).

Pope Kyrillos VI approved the annual feasts of St. Mark officially in the church Synaxarium as follows:

- Receiving the relics of St. Mark in Rome (15 Ba'una)
- Return of the relics of St. Mark to Cairo (17 Ba'una)
- Opening of the new St. Mark Cathedral at Anba Ruways Monastery (18 Ba'una)
- The first liturgy celebrated by the Pope in the new St. Mark Cathedral at Anba Ruways Monastery (19 Ba'una)

A papal residence was prepared for His Holiness Pope Shenouda III in November 1971 at the cathedral. St. Mark Cathedral at Anba Ruways thus became the central location for the activities of the Coptic Church. Its construction had been preceded by the establishment of the Institute of Coptic Studies on January 21, 1954,[6] for the study of the Coptic language, art, archaeology, and music. In 1962, the Coptic Orthodox Church founded the Bishopric of Public, Ecumenical, and Social Services (BLESS) to be the leading church institution in serving the poor and disadvantaged communities with a pioneering concept, shifting from charity to a development approach.[7] A general bishop for youth, His Grace Bishop Moussa, was ordained by His Holiness Pope Shenouda III to oversee the youth and their activities, and a bishopric for youth was established at the cathedral. This bishopric carries out a number of activities including publications, big festivals, exhibitions, and consecration of youths for service in the Church.

One of the most important projects accomplished by Pope Shenouda III within the cathedral is the Coptic Cultural Center. It was officially opened on November 14, 2008, when the St. Mark Public Library was also opened. The center is directed by His Grace General Bishop Ermia. Its activities include the public library, Manuscript Museum, Patriarchal Museum, and Coptic Panorama.

The space below the cathedral contains two other newly constructed churches: the Virgin and Anba Ruways Church, and the Virgin and Anba Bishoy Church. The latter was consecrated by His Holiness Pope Shenouda III. Its iconostasis is that of the old Virgin Mary's Church, which had been adjacent to Anba Ruways Church but was demolished in 1968 to allow the cathedral staircase to be built. Between these churches there is a tomb containing the relics of Anba Samuel, the bishop of public relations and social services, who was martyred during the military show in which President

Anwar al-Sadat was also killed by extremists. Here also are the remains of Hegumen Mikhail Ibrahim, the spiritual father of His Holiness Pope Shenouda III, and of Anba Gregorios, the bishop of higher education, Coptic culture, and scholarly research. The relics of St. Athanasius the Apostolic, the twentieth pope, are also there; they were obtained from Rome during the visit of Pope Shenouda there and arrived in Cairo on May 15, 1973.

Other churches within the cathedral area are St. Maurice and St. Verena Church, located in the social-services bishopric, and St. Antonius Church inside the papal residence.

Notes

1 The name probably was due to the use of the area as cemetery and the presence of a well, where the caravans used to get their water.

2 In Abu al-Makarim 1984, the editor corrected the previous false attribution of this work to Abu Saleh al-Armani.

3 Nabih Kamel Daowd was the former librarian of the patriarchal manuscript library. He cataloged most of the manuscripts that were not included in the 1942 published catalog (Simaika and 'Abd al-Masih 1942). His papers are kept now at the Coptic Orthodox Cultural Center, in accordance with his will.

4 A biography of St. Ruways and his miracles may be found in Troupeau 1972: no. 282, 82v–151.

5 A *kirat* is 1/24th of a feddan; a *sahm* is 1/24th of a *kirat*.

6 Founded by many Coptic scholars, among them its first president, Aziz S. Attiya, and two vice presidents, Murad Kamil and Sami Gabra. They in turn recruited volunteers from among noted scholars and specialists to serve as a teaching body and to constitute the Institute's board.

7 Pope Kyrillos VI ordained Father Makari al-Suryani as bishop of public, social, and ecumenical services. In this capacity, he fostered the Diaconate of Rural Areas and sponsored social and educational movements in the Church, notably the Sunday School movement and the creation of centers for the training of young men and women in technical handicrafts. He played an important part in the completion of the huge edifice of the new St. Mark Cathedral on the grounds of Anba Ruways.

11 The Perception of St. Athanasius of Alexandria in Later Coptic Literature

Ibrahim Saweros

As far as bibliographies can tell us, not many scholars took the trouble to study the image of St. Athanasius of Alexandria among Copts after his death. Although there is a general awareness of the existence of a large corpus of texts attributed to him, in both Coptic and Arabic, scholarly publications about this corpus are not numerous. Tito Orlandi started work on this issue a few decades ago (Orlandi 1968; Orlandi 1970a: 75–78; Orlandi 1981: 47–70). Recently, David Gwynn has drawn attention to Athanasius in the oriental traditions.[1] He depended on only two sources in his research, unfortunately. Gwynn used the famous *History of the Patriarchs of the Egyptian Church* attributed to Sawirus of al-Ashmunayn and the *Chronicles of John of Nikiou*[2] and compared Athanasius's *Vita* in both of them with what the Greek ecclesiastical historians reported about him.

He concluded that Athanasius, who dominates Coptic historiography and whose works were traditionally valued, was not a controversialist, but an ascetic and a pastoral leader spiritually guiding and protecting his flock. I do agree with this conclusion, but the question is, why is Athanasius seen like this? Gwynn answers that the writings of Athanasius that dominate our Coptic evidence either do not survive in Greek, or were texts that Greek ecclesiastical historians ignored (Gwynn 2011: 55).

This chapter will present the results of an examination of a set of four Sahidic homilies attributed to Athanasius of Alexandria to explain how

Athanasius was seen among Copts after his death, and why he was seen in this particular way.[3] The manuscripts which contain these sermons belong to the famous find of al-Hamuli and are now kept at the Pierpont Morgan Library and Museum in New York.[4] The first homily is entitled "On Michael and Gabriel" (CPG 2197; CPC 0059). In this homily, Athanasius begins with warnings to his congregation against fornication. He gives many biblical quotations about the punishment of adulterers (f. 91r.a–91v.a).[5] Then he moves to the most attractive part of the homily, in which he narrates five nice stories that convey the same spiritual message against fornication. Athanasius starts with himself, telling about his conflict with George, who was a follower of Arius and who tried to usurp Athanasius's episcopate (f. 92v.b–93r.b). In this story Athanasius confesses that God helped him to overcome this crisis, and the audience is made to understand that God, through his two archangels, Michael and Gabriel, supports the innocent bishop, who believes in the true Orthodox faith.

Here, as in most Coptic homilies, the author is not interested in theology at all. He mentions nothing about Arius and his heresy, and why George is against Athanasius. He just stresses the idea that God is with us—that is, with Athanasius. The author continues his homily with four more stories; each one is conveying more or less the same spiritual message. Athanasius recounts to his listeners a story about a rich man from Pentapolis who tried to take a large amount of money from a boy by fraud. In this story, the archangels save the boy and his money (f. 93r.b–95r.a). In the next story, Athanasius tells about a pagan boy who dreamed of seeing Christ. This boy came to a church and when he saw Jesus Christ depicted on the walls, he became very happy and made some noise. A deacon came and asked him to leave the church. Jesus himself prevented the deacon from dismissing the child and appeared to him. As a result, the pagan boy and all his family members were baptized (f. 95r.a–96v.b).

Then the author tells about a man who fell down in the church and could not speak until he confessed all his sins. The audience later hears that he had committed adultery and yet dared to come to share in the Eucharist (f. 96v.b–97v.b). In the last story, Athanasius presents to his audience the importance of going to church by telling about a pious builder who used to come to the church daily to light a candle and to pray. For some reason, the builder was not able to come to the church once, and on the same day he was seized by a demon (f. 97v.b–98r.b). Then Athanasius speaks about the role of the two archangels Michael and Gabriel and finishes his sermon.

The core of the stories conveys the message that Michael and Gabriel are tools of God. God sends them to protect the pure, innocent ones, including Athanasius himself, as in the first story.[6] Athanasius himself appears as a good preacher who guides his flock, instructs them against sins, persuades them, and attracts their attention through a series of stories from the Bible and from their modern life. The image of the theologian Athanasius of the fourth century is totally missing. Athanasius appears here as a preacher with a limited cultural background.[7]

The second homily is entitled "On Murder and Greed and on Michael, the Archangel."[8] The homily starts with a short introduction about St. Michael's feast; then the author advises his congregation not to transgress God's commandments (f. 99v.a–100v.b).[9] The largest part of the homily is occupied by the stories that Athanasius recounts about St. Pachomius, the archimandrite of Upper Egypt. Athanasius starts with a short description of the welcome of Pachomius when he came to Alexandria to visit the archbishop and to return the visit that the archbishop made to Upper Egypt earlier.[10] Athanasius and the deacons went to the harbor to receive Pachomius, singing hymns in front of him until he reached the main church of Alexandria. Athanasius reminds his listeners that Pachomius had no rank in the ecclesiastical hierarchy, so he stood at a distance while Athanasius celebrated Mass.[11] While the holy sacraments were being offered to the deacons of the church, God revealed to Pachomius that one of the deacons was unworthy to receive the holy Body and Blood of Christ.

Later, Pachomius tells his vision to Athanasius. The latter summons all the deacons of Alexandria in front of Pachomius to identify the sinner. They find out that the deacon is a murderer, and the highest authority of the city, the *augustalis*, arrests him to punish him (f. 102v.a–106v.b). Athanasius praises Pachomius as a holy man to whom God reveals what the archbishop of Alexandria himself is not pure enough to see. Athanasius continues his narrative about the graces and abilities of Pachomius. He says that when he asked Pachomius whether the sinful Christians will be tortured in hell like the pagans, Pachomius answered that he is not a man of grace to know such eschatological issues. He recounts a revelation that God gave to a holy monk from his community. The vision of this holy monk gives a direct answer to Athanasius's question: yes, the Christian who is a murderer will be punished in hell just like the heathen (f. 106v.b–107v.a).

After this revelation, Athanasius addresses the audience, saying that the humble St. Pachomius himself is the one who saw the vision, but he said that it was another monk from his community in order not to be glorified. This type of direct speech about the marvelous man Pachomius has its origins in the lives of Pachomius, where he is recognized in the local synod of Latopolis as having the gift of clairvoyance.[12] The author here is building upon this type of popular story about Pachomius in order to deliver a double message: Athanasius is a supporter of monasticism, and the monastic leaders are supporting the archbishop in his struggle against heretics.[13]

In this homily, and by his own tongue, Athanasius confesses that God did not grant him the abilities and graces which he granted to Pachomius, although they are very good friends and one supports the other. Here, one can see Athanasius as a representative of the official Church, the hierarchs and the clergy, while Pachomius is a representative of the men of the desert who support the official Church with their prayers and physical presence. The message here is that both are in the same army against heresies, even though the author never speaks about any heresy in specific.

The homily continues with another interesting story in which Athanasius recounts his personal relationship with the angelic figures. While Athanasius was exiled from his see, in Upper Egypt, working as a poor dyer, St. Michael the Archangel revealed himself to him. Michael tells Athanasius that his time to return to his throne has come and his difficult days have come to an end (f. 109r.a–110v.b). The vision in which Michael appears to a bishop in trial is well known in Eastern Christian literature (Youssef 2007: 645–56). This revelation follows upon the visions of Pachomius to give the impression that it is not only Pachomius who has marvelous abilities, but Athanasius too. The message here is clear enough: the archbishop, who is tortured for defending the Orthodox faith, is supported by heaven. Actually, the faith itself satisfies heaven. Athanasius here is praising himself indirectly, attracting the audience's attention by recounting a marvel in which an angelic figure is involved. He gives a full description of the angelic figure to arouse the imagination of his audience. The homily ends with final words of praise to St. Michael, who is so helpful to humanity (f. 109r.a–110v.b).

In a third homily belonging to the same type of pseudo-Athanasian writings, entitled "On Luke 11:5–9" (Hyvernat 1922a: 53:70–98 = M 577: f. 35v–49v),[14] Athanasius appears as an interpreter of the Bible, and he does so within the church and directly in front of his flock. The homily starts with basic comments on the parable of the midnight friend (f. 36r.a–38v.a), and then he proceeds to offer a complex spiritual interpretation of the parable (f. 38v.a–42r.b). It looks as if his interpretation and the Bohairic catenae came from a common source, as the influence of the Bohairic catenae is clear in his interpretation (de Lagarde 1886: 143–45). Athanasius then narrates the story of Bishop Phoibammon, who started his life as an evil rich man, living in Upper Egypt. Phoibammon is famous as a greedy man who mistreats his servants and cuts the wages of his workmen. The workmen used to come to St. Pachomius to complain against this unfair treatment. It happens that Phoibammon comes to attend Mass in the church where Pachomius prays and leads his monastic community. The workmen start to shout against Phoibammon. Pachomius becomes angry because of the lack of respect for the church and the holy sacraments, and starts to ask God to execute justice and to do something against Phoibammon. Immediately, Phoibammon becomes speechless and unable to move, like a piece of stone.

Phoibammon then gestures that he wants to write something. He writes that he will not only give one-third of his wealth to the poor, one-third to his family, and one-third to the monastic community of St. Pachomius, but also he will give all his properties away and join the Pachomian community. As expected, in a few seconds, God grants Phoibammon healing. He then becomes a notable monk and a famous hermit, and is finally consecrated as a bishop (f. 42r.b–45v.a). Again, through this episode, Athanasius stresses his own relationship with the monastic communities in the far south of Egypt. He shows his knowledge about all the events that take place there, not only in order to speak about their angelic life and holiness, but also to show his own authority over the whole of Egypt and that all those holy men are on his side in his conflict with the Arians.

Athanasius then recalls the friendship between Jonathan and David to give an example of true friendship, which he felt was disappearing in his age (f. 45v.a–46v.b). Athanasius then speaks about himself, narrating a marvel that he saw when he was a young deacon who was fortunate enough to attend the Council of Nicaea. He describes the council as a place where the bishops are sitting in humility in the presence of the emperor, Constantine, who is sitting on his throne in greatness, listening to the different points of view about the nature of Christ. A certain heretic called Carpocratius,[15] who apparently represents the Arians in this story, thinks that Christ spent only seven months in the Virgin's womb and says that this is what the Church used to believe for ages. Then Alexander (either of Alexandria or of Constantinople) presents his point of view, with which all the bishops at the council agree, as Athanasius reports. The righteous emperor Constantine cannot judge which opinion is true. He asks one of his servants to collect the cloaks of Carpocratius and Alexander, and to throw them into the fire. The fire burns only Carpocratius's cloak. For Constantine, Athanasius, and the bishops from all over the world, this is the heavenly evidence that Alexander is defending the true faith of Jesus Christ. The 318 bishops then start to recite the creed, according to Athanasius (f. 46v.b–48v.b).

What is really astonishing here is that Athanasius does not attribute any heroic achievement to himself at Nicaea. He speaks about his predecessor Alexander with much respect to show his gratitude to him.[16] The *History of the Patriarchs of the Egyptian Church* tells a story similar to that of the burned mantle of Carpocratius/Arius. It recounts that St. Peter of Alexandria saw Christ in a rent garment in a revelation, which put him on guard against Arius (Evetts 1907b: 405–406). Athanasius, even in his genuine writings, does not mention any role that he played at Nicaea, nor do the Greek ecclesiastical historians attribute any great achievement to Athanasius at this council (Gwynn 2011: 49n29).

Athanasius uses a miracle to prove the correctness of his faith. This is a literary technique which is well attested in the Coptic literature (Sheridan 2007: 27). On the other hand, Athanasius is seen in this story as merely a witness, who did nothing to defend the faith. I think this is intended by the original author to complete the spiritual image of Athanasius. Athanasius is made to speak about the miracles of Pachomius and Alexander as an eyewitness, not as a miracle-worker himself. The author draws the image of the humble Athanasius, whom one does not expect to speak about himself while preaching. On the contrary, he preaches by citing instances from the lives of other heroes of the faith whom he knows personally. The homily ends with a short epilogue about receiving Communion (f. 48v.b–49v.b).

The last homily is entitled "On Pentecost" (CPG 2192; CPC 0052; Hyvernat 1922a: 43:238–82 = M 595: f. 118v–140v). This homily is quite different. Athanasius appears not as a narrator but as a real preacher. The storytelling is almost absent from this homily. Athanasius starts this homily with warnings against sins; this is a usual prologue in this type of pseudo-Athanasian writings (f. 118v.b–121v.a). The author then moves on to some instructions about the Christian household. In these instructions he concentrates on the man as the one who fulfills the major roles within the family. Athanasius, as seen in this homily, is adopting a polemical position against the Jews. He advises the Christian woman not to dress or behave like a Jewish woman. He spends a large part of the homily describing how the Jewish woman decorates herself in order to seduce a man, arguing that this is not suitable for Christians (f. 121v.a–127v.a).

In the same homily, Athanasius addresses the theme of poverty and wealth in order to assure his audience that they are able to go to heaven whatever the wealth they have. It depends on how they use it (f. 127v.a–137r.a). Then Athanasius addresses the bishops who are supposedly listening to his sermon, and gives instructions about being active in their service. Finally the author warns unworthy people not to share in the Eucharist (f. 137r.a–140v.b). In this homily, we see a major side of the personality of the *Coptic* Athanasius. We see him as a man of virtues. He is a perfect man who gives advice about everything and to everyone: married people and singles, laymen and clergy, male and female. He appears as an expert in life, giving to all exactly what they are lacking.

The first three homilies mentioned above were copied more than once during the ninth and tenth centuries in two of the most influential scriptoria of Christian Egypt, St. Michael Monastery at al-Hamuli, Fayoum, and the White Monastery, near Sohag.[17] The texts themselves are much older. All of them belong to the so-called Athanasian cycle, the term that scholars started to use after Tito Orlandi to describe the texts falsely ascribed to the Church Fathers and that were composed based on some well-known events of their lives (Orlandi 1991: 666–68). There is a strong possibility that these texts are derived from a missing Greek original and found their way into Arabic, at least partly.[18] These homilies were written for the sake of pious Copts. The image drawn of Athanasius in these homilies is exactly what this pious congregation needs. Athanasius is presented as a good, active shepherd, as any bishop should be. He is an influential preacher and he addresses every type of person with the exactly suitable speech.

Athanasius is not a normal archbishop. He has an unusual history. Part of this history is defeating Arius, the evil heretic, although not a word is mentioned about what exactly are the beliefs of Athanasius and Arius. One cannot ignore the confidence with which the authors of these homilies write. It is clear that they are sure that their listeners will believe in their words, that they do not need to explain anything or go into a theological debate to persuade anybody. They only need to seal their words with the name of Athanasius. Athanasius is the marker that points to the right direction. In this way, the authors also urge their audience to be closer to their

Church. They are saying indirectly that heretics will try to cheat you, to take you the wrong way that leads to hell, but the Church and its leaders are guiding you to heaven.

Athanasius is also represented as a friend of the monastic leaders. Pachomius comes to visit him in Alexandria because Athanasius visited him earlier. Many messages are given through stories that Athanasius tells about Pachomius. On the one hand, they want to say that all the Christians of Egypt, including the hermits, the inhabitants of the cells in the deserts, and their leaders, are supporting Athanasius in his fight against Arius and his followers. It also refers to the awareness of the monastic leaders of what is going on within the universal Church and the Arian crisis. On the other hand, they emphasize that the archbishop, who was a normal layman before, was a friend of the most famous hermit in Upper Egypt.

Athanasius is also presented as a man of God. He has contact with the angelic figures. When he is exiled, Michael comes to console him. He is able to describe what Michael looks like, and how a dialogue between a human and an angel might take place. He tells his people what everybody wishes to see and experience. The authors of these homilies are presenting to us a perfect, exceptional man, of whom one should believe every word that he utters. There is no need to mention that he is a controversialist and one of the best theologians who has ever existed, as this is not a point of interest for the audience of these homilies. Similarly, in the one rare case when a writer—the composer of Athanasius's *Vita* in the *History of the Patriarchs of the Egyptian Church*—refers to Athanasius's writings, he refers to the life of St. Antony, the *Festal Letters*, and a homily on virginity, leaving aside any polemic or apologetic works (Seybold 1912: 57–66).

It is striking that the corpus of pseudo-Athanasian writings is well connected with Pachomius, but not with St. Antony, whose life was written by Athanasius, nor with any other monastic figure of the period (Garitte 1949). The corpus shows a strong moralizing element, such as the excellent warnings against sins, showing a focus on family in a monastic milieu, and telling stories about crime and punishment. The Byzantine civic life in Alexandria is still intact and is reflected in the stories, which may suggest that the writers of these homilies lived in the neighborhood of Alexandria sometime before the eighth century, perhaps in a milieu where Pachomius was considered the major figure of fourth-century monasticism.

The corpus of texts that is attributed to Athanasius in both Coptic and Arabic is too large to be summarized here. It is a witness of the past that deserves much more attention from scholars. This chapter presents just four pieces out of the big puzzle. The image of Athanasius, as it is still alive among Copts today and as it appears in the Coptic historical resources, surely has its roots somewhere in the pseudo-Athanasian writings.

Notes

1 The core of his research has appeared three times: Gwynn 2011: 43–58; Gwynn 2012: 187–93; Gwynn 2013: 43–54.
2 Concerning the two books, their contents, and transmission, see Moawad 2014b: 11–13.
3 The four sermons are the subject of my PhD dissertation, defended at Leiden University in 2016. For descriptions of the manuscripts, their contents, and previous scholarly work on them, see Depuydt 1993: nos. 116.6–7, 170.9, 172.4. For editions, English translations, and commentaries, see Saweros (forthcoming).
4 For more about this collection, see Emmel 2005: 63–70.
5 Hereafter I give the folio and column numbers according to the facsimile edition of al-Hamuli collection. Hyvernat 1922a: 25:179–97 = M 602: f. 89r–99r.
6 On Michael and Gabriel in Coptic literature, see Müller 1959: 8–47.
7 A parallel fragment to this homily came to the British Library from the Syrian Monastery: Layton 1987: 215–16. The validity and spread of this homily is discussed in Saweros (forthcoming).
8 CPG 2191; CPC 0048. Italian translations appear in Orlandi 1981: 59–70.
9 Hyvernat 1922a: 25:198–222 = M 602: f. 99v–111v.
10 The welcoming of Pachomius in Alexandria, according to this homily, looks like the welcoming that Athanasius received in Thebes, according to the First Greek and Bohairic lives of Pachomius. See Veilleux 1980–82: 1:51–52, 317–18.
11 The same is known from the lives of Pachomius; see previous note.
12 It occurs only in the first Greek life of Pachomius: Veilleux 1980–82: 1:357–77.
13 On the historical relationship between Athanasius and Pachomius, see Brakke 1995: 111–20.
14 CPG 2194; CPC 0057. Italian translations appear in Orlandi 1981: 47–57.
15 Carpocratius was an Alexandrian Gnostic teacher who lived in the first half of the second century. His followers, the Carpocratians, survived until the fourth century. Traces of his teachings can be found in Irenaeus, *Against Heresies* I, 25; Hippolytus, *Refutation of All Heresies* 7, 32; and Clement, *Stromata* 3, 2–6. See also Wace 1877: 407–409; Griggs 1991: 461; Cross 1997: 291–92. For Carpocratius in Coptic literature, see van den Broek 1996: 142–56.
16 Alexander is mentioned once in this homily, as Alexander of Constantinople. For further discussion of this point, see Saweros (forthcoming).
17 For the parallel fragments of the second homily, see Suciu 2012: 87–90.
18 See, for example, MSS: Paris. ar. 143: f. 116v–122r and Coptic Museum Theo. 395 f: 200r–211r. A full account of possible Arabic versions will appear in Saweros (forthcoming).

12 The Discovery of the Papyri from Tura at Dayr al-Qusayr (Dayr Arsaniyus) and Its Legacy

Caroline T. Schroeder

IN 1941, EIGHT CODICES' worth of Greek manuscripts were discovered in the ruins of Dayr al-Qusayr, an abandoned monastery.[1] Dayr al-Qusayr was associated with Abba Arsenius of Scetis, known to us primarily from the *Apophthegmata Patrum*, or *Sayings of the Desert Fathers*. According to tradition, Abba Arsenius supposedly died there, and his student, Arcadius, built a monastery at the site of his tomb (Coquin, Martin, and Grossman 1991: 853b). Though the historically definitive account of Dayr al-Qusayr's origins remains uncertain, we do know that the monastery was active in the medieval period until 1010, when it was destroyed and burned. It was later reactivated and inhabited until the fourteenth century, when it was abandoned for the final time.[2] Records about the monastery's active periods indicate it was a Melkite, or Greek, monastery, not Coptic Orthodox (Coquin, Martin, and Grossmann 1991).

According to the standard, accepted account of the Tura papyri's origins, the British military discovered the documents when cleaning out old limestone quarries during the Second World War. Many of the papyri were confiscated by authorities before they could be sold on the antiquities market, while others were quickly purchased from dealers through a program endorsed by King Farouk I. Still others were sold and now can be found in collections in the United States, Germany, England, France, Switzerland, South Africa, and Australia (Coquin, Martin, and Grossmann

1991: 854a; Doutreleau 1955; Doutreleau and Koenen 1967; Guéraud and Nautin 1979: ch. 1; Krause 1991b: 1898b–1899a; Layton 2004: 2–4).

The manuscripts—papyri, not parchment—date to the sixth or possibly seventh century. Many of them are unbound, and many are palimpsests: pieces of papyri that bore writing and were later scraped clean and reused for another text.[3] Some pages consist of stitched-together papyrus scraps. The top layer of writing bears witness to the writings of the church fathers Origen and Didymus the Blind. Origen was a teacher and theologian in Alexandria during the late second and early third centuries. Didymus was a teacher and theologian in Alexandria during the fourth century, 313–98; despite being blind from childhood, he was a prodigious writer and exegete.

The current scholarly consensus is that the Tura papyri show signs of deliberate damage and may even have been deliberately hidden. They date to the same period in which theological ideas attributed to Origen (known as Origenism) were condemned as heresy by the Second Ecumenical Council of Constantinople in 553. Didymus's theology was also condemned as heresy for being Origenist (Coquin, Martin, and Grossmann 1991: 854a; Doutreleau 1955; Doutreleau and Koenen 1967; Guéraud and Nautin 1979: ch. 1; Krause 1991b: 1898b–1899a.)[4] The surviving codices contain the following texts, all in Greek: Origen's *Dialogue with Heraclides*, *Commentary on Romans* (partial), *Against Celsus* (partial), *Sermon on the Witch of Endor* (partial); Didymus's *Commentary on Ecclesiastes*, *Commentary on Genesis*, *Commentary on the Psalms*, *Commentary on Zechariah*, *Commentary on Job*; and Commentaries on Psalms 125, 129, 131–33, and John 6:3–28 by an unknown author. The Tura papyri inform several important areas of research on early Christianity in Egypt: understanding Didymus, understanding Origen, biblical exegesis and commentary generally, and understanding the reading and writing practices of the community at Tura. Much of this chapter is devoted to Didymus, since that area has produced significant new scholarship.[5]

The Significance of the Tura Papyri for Understanding Didymus the Blind

Didymus has rarely received the scholarly attention one would expect for someone with such a high reputation in antiquity and with such a prodigious output of texts to study. His legacy in historiography has been affected by the perception that he is either an unoriginal thinker or a heretic. According to Richard Layton, in the early twentieth century, scholars such as Johannes

Leipoldt deemed Didymus a "derivative thinker" when it came to Trinitarian theology, and thus of less importance for study. The contents of the Tura papyri *should* have changed this assessment of his significance, but they were eclipsed by the Nag' Hammadi find in 1945. And in subsequent decades, even those who worked through his commentaries concluded that he was more of a teacher than an innovative scholar (Layton 2004: 4–5). In the late twentieth and early twenty-first centuries, much scholarship about Didymus has overlooked his theological sophistication; in the words of Mark DelCogliano, "The Tura discovery changed Didymus from a Theologian to an Exegete in scholarship."[6] I have traced three threads in Didymus scholarship: theology, exegesis and text criticism, and ancient education. All of the Tura texts by Didymus are biblical commentaries, which is why Didymus as exegete and text critic and Didymus the teacher eclipsed Didymus the theologian in the late twentieth and early twenty-first centuries. The early evaluation of Didymus as an unoriginal theologian comes from scholarship based on the very few texts of his that survived outside of the Tura find: most notably, a short text against the Manichaeans and a treatise *On the Holy Spirit*. The latter survives only in Jerome's Latin translation. (Scholars debate the authorship of a text *On the Trinity* which has been attributed to Didymus; likewise, claims to Didymus's authorship of sections IV–V of Pseudo-Basil's *Against Eunomius* are contested.)

Some of the most notable scholarship on Didymus as exegete has focused not just on his interpretations of the biblical text but also on the *content* of the New Testament texts he quotes in his commentaries. Bart Ehrman's book, *Didymus the Blind and the Text of the New Testament Gospels*, is the most significant example of this approach. Ehrman culls from Didymus's commentaries "every gospel quotation and allusion found in Didymus's writings, and a critical apparatus which supplies full collations of representative textual witnesses at every point" (Ehrman 1986: 2). Ehrman's work has influenced text-critical study of the New Testament in the Greek patristic writers since its publication in 1986. His methods have been adapted by other text critics, and he questioned the established narrative about the text of the New Testament that was read and circulated in Alexandria in the fourth century.

Didymus's exegetical style is usually characterized as allegorical and symbolic, reflecting Origen's influence. As Blossom Stefaniw writes about his *Commentary on the Psalms* in her book, *Mind, Text, and Commentary*, "Didymus the Blind's conviction of the revelatory content of Scripture is so strong that he is able to find mysteries in the subtitles of Psalms" (Stefaniw 2010: 90). Stefaniw's work also proves an exception to the trend in Didymus scholarship to favor his exegesis over his theology: Stefaniw's work illuminates a Didymus who regards exegesis *as* theology (Stefaniw 2010: 83–84). The objective of exegesis and scriptural reading for Didymus is theological and spiritual, something he takes from Origen. Regarding Didymus's work on the Psalms and Zechariah, Stefaniw writes,

> Didymus, not just in his comment on this verse, but also in his work as a teacher, is interested in "the goal" taken as the goal of the spiritual life, so that those who are in view of it are those who have already been transformed and who have insight. In Didymus' *Commentary on Zechariah*, we hear echoes of the same rhetorical certainty that the revelatory nature of the text is obvious and indisputable to any right-thinking person which we found in Origen. (Stefaniw 2010: 91)

Some of Didymus's other theological work, including his heresiology, was known prior to the Tura find. His treatise on the Holy Spirit has been translated into English (DelCogliano, Radde-Gallwitz, and Ayres 2011). In contrast to the early twentieth-century characterizations of Didymus as derivative, Lewis Ayres's essay on *On the Holy Spirit* argues that Didymus adapted concepts from Philo and Neoplatonism into his theology. Ayres also dates the text to an earlier period than prior scholars did, and posits that Didymus's pneumatology went on to influence fourth-century theology, including that of the Cappadocian father Basil (Ayres 2010).

In both his commentaries and his treatises, Didymus defends Christianity and his definition of orthodoxy in debates with pagan philosophers and 'heretics.' (Twenty-twenty hindsight makes this somewhat ironic, of course, since his ideas were condemned as heresy in 553 and he himself was condemned in the Sixth Ecumenical Council; his ideas—along with Origen's and Evagrius's—were anathematized and characterized as "fables" in the Seventh Ecumenical Council.)[7] Byard Bennett edited and translated into English Didymus's *Against the Manichaeans*, a text known to us before the Tura discovery. Bennett's analysis of Didymus's anti-Manichaean rhetoric in subsequent work, especially his article "Didymus the Blind's Knowledge of Manichaeism" in a volume on Manichaeism edited by Paul Mirecki and Jason BeDuhn, includes the commentaries found at Tura, as well, in order to provide a fuller representation of Didymus's views (Mirecki and BeDuhn 2001). Bennett discovers that Didymus understood some core Manichaean beliefs, including their rejection of the Old Testament and their views on the flesh, but in other respects attributed to Manichaeism (inaccurately) beliefs we see in Christian anti-Manichaean polemic, not Manichaean writings themselves (such as on the origin of evil). Didymus seems to know none of the names of any Manichaean "mythological figures," either. Bennett concludes that Didymus had not actually "read any Manichaean literature or any anti-Manichaean work which contained a detailed account of Manichaean beliefs" (Bennett 2001: 48). In addition, Didymus wrote against other 'heretics' such as Arians (though his authorship of a specific text against the Arians attributed to him is in dispute).

Didymus also debates the pagan philosopher Porphyry, even naming him in his writings. The theologian and exegete engages with the details of Porphyry's critique of Christianity and defends the faith. Both Blossom Stefaniw's book on noetic exegesis and Philip Sellew's article "Achilles or Christ?" explore this debate in more detail (Sellew 1989; Stefaniw 2010: 83–84). The dispute centers on the use of allegorical exegesis to interpret scripture. Some of this argument is embedded in Didymus's commentary on Ecclesiastes, which was discovered at Tura.

As we can see from his writings, Didymus regarded himself as a defender of 'Christianity' during his lifetime. And yet the ideas he developed in defending Christianity (such as allegorical exegesis) were the very things by which his ideas were judged heresy after his death by the Greek and Roman churches. Although Martiniano P. Roncaglia, the author of the *Coptic Encyclopedia* entry on Didymus, states that "the orthodoxy of Didymus is entirely above reproach" (Roncaglia 1991), the ancient author's scriptural interpretation and views on the preexistence of souls were influenced by Origen. Stefaniw's and Layton's books both discuss Didymus's 'Origenism' and whether this label is warranted; the issue is complex, because during his lifetime there wasn't really a concept of an 'Origenist' theology or group of theologians, yet there would, soon after his death, come to be such an association. Didymus was clearly influenced by Origen; whether this makes him an 'Origenist' is a thornier question. The Coptic Orthodox Church venerates Didymus as a saint, and an important institute for the blind is named after him (Moftah and Roy 1991).

The Tura papyri are especially important for learning about Didymus as a teacher. Didymus is traditionally regarded as one in a line of leaders of the Alexandrian 'catechetical school.' The concept of such a 'catechetical school' has come under scrutiny in recent years. Was there an official 'school' for catechumens; were the teachers appointed in a line of succession? Were they appointed by the bishop? The Tura papyri do not answer these questions, unfortunately. But they do tell us about Didymus the teacher.

Some of the commentaries discovered at Tura contain questions from students about the scriptural passages, followed by explanations from Didymus. He then returns to quoting scripture, with more questions, and more exegesis in response to questions. Both Richard Layton, in his book *Didymus the Blind and His Circle in Late-Antique Alexandria*, and Blossom Stefaniw, in a recent conference paper that should soon be published, examine how these texts reflect ancient educational practices (Layton 2004; Stefaniw [forthcoming]). Layton argues that Didymus was the leader of an ascetical circle of Christians, not necessarily catechists. Through their interpretation of scripture they were developing a scholastic, ascetic Christian identity in an Alexandrian environment. Stefaniw argues that Didymus's methods show that he is a grammarian in the classical sense. In the traditional Greek and Roman educational system, the grammarian taught a level of education beyond basic literacy but below philosophy and more sophisticated rhetoric. Grammatical education was an important phase in the socialization of the Roman elite, learning the classical texts and their literary analysis (Stefaniw [forthcoming]). Didymus, argues Stefaniw, is both "connecting young people to their cultural heritage" and "lobbing Christian scriptures into the position of the cultural patrimony, thereby also validating Christian young people in participating in the mainstream of privileged society" (Stefaniw [forthcoming]). Didymus, in other words, was a teacher like any other in Alexandria, and yet also not like any other, in his adaptation of scriptural exegesis for education. Neither Layton nor Stefaniw subscribes to the view that Didymus was the leader of an official catechetical school.

The Significance of the Tura Papyri for Understanding Origen

Due to limited space, only a few of the documents written by Origen and found at Tura will be addressed here. Some of the texts by Origen in the Tura find were known before, but others are new. Moreover, some of them provide interesting witnesses to known texts. For example, in Codex II survives a partial copy of *Against Celsus*. Origen wrote this work to defend Christianity against various arguments by a pagan named Celsus, who posited that Christianity was a superstition, or inauthentic tradition. The text survives primarily in Latin translation, and this find at Tura of part of the treatise in Greek gives us an important witness in the original language. Codex I brings us two texts of Origen's that had not survived elsewhere: a sermon *On the Passover* and his *Dialogue with Heraclides*. These have both been published in Greek as well as in an English translation by Richard Daly (Daly 1992). *On the Passover*, according to Daly, "follows a radically different line of interpretation than most of the other early Passover homilies or treatises known to us" (Daly 1992: 2). The *Dialogue with Heraclides* is "the only surviving dialogue of Origen" (Daly 1992: 21). The dialogue is a classical genre of writing dating back to ancient Greek rhetoric and philosophy, and a number of early Christian authors adapted it as a genre to explain Christian history and theology. Another notable dialogue is Justin Martyr's *Dialogue with Trypho the Jew*. Origen's is constructed, in Daly's words, as "a stenographic record of a synod-like meeting of bishops, theologians, and lay-people assembled to discuss and decide on important matters of belief and worship." These "stenographic"-type passages contain discourses by Origen on theology, in which he convinces others of certain views (Daly 1992). These texts give us crucial insight into Origen's works, especially in Greek, that we did not have before the discovery at Tura.

The Electronic Study of the Papyri Manuscripts

One of the pieces of the Tura papyri is currently located at Brigham Young University (BYU), and a team there are studying the documents for what they can tell us about the scribal practices and reading practices at Dayr al-Qusayr. There are a number of approaches to studying the scribal practices. For example, Greg Schwendner is looking at markings on the texts and the different writing styles in Didymus's *Commentary on the Psalms* to see whether the scribe used grouped parts of the text in ways that correspond to Didymus's lecturing style, and whether this stylistics in transcribing the text is linked to the scribe's use of memory to remember the text as he is transcribing it (Schwendner 2014).

Computer technology can tell us even more about the papyri than the text we can read. Roger Macfarlane is conducting a study of Tura Codex 5, both to reconstruct the pieces as a final codex and also to use spectral imaging to study what is under the text of Didymus on the palimpsest. So far he has identified different pages with similar hands underneath. He has also found a documentary text (Macfarlane 2014). His work will tell us more about what kinds of texts were in circulation and were read at the monastery. A piece of Codex 5 is at BYU in Utah, but others are housed in other collections. Macfarlane plans to conduct spectral imaging campaigns at various collections where the codex fragments are held. Not all the Tura papyri are palimpsests, but many are. Since some of them consist of fragments sewn together, we have pages with multiple different texts underneath, sometimes with the handwriting running in different directions.

Conclusion: Future Directions

There has been some research capitalizing on the Tura find. But in English scholarship especially, more can be done. Didymus is still not fully integrated into the scholarly landscape of fourth-century theology. And although Layton, Stefaniw, and Edward Watts have studied the commentaries as educational texts, much more needs to be done (Watts 2006). Notably, English translations of many of the commentaries would be desirable. Macfarlane's spectral imaging will open up many avenues for studying scribal practices as well as the reading materials of the monks at Dayr al-Qusayr.

Finally, I would like to see a thorough revisiting of the origin story of the find. While I do not doubt the veracity of the general report about conditions leading to the find, any more information about the discovery and provenance of the texts—and therefore also the location of any more papyri fragments from the find—would be useful. Furthermore, very little has been written about the monastery itself. Many more discoveries about the Tura find await us in future scholarship.

Notes

1 Thank you to the organizers of the symposium, especially Gawdat Gabra and Fawzy Estafanous; the monks of the Monastery of St. Mina, who hosted the conference; and also to Hany Takla of the St. Shenouda Society. I also wish to thank Dr. Blossom Stefaniw for sharing with me her work in progress, and Dr. Mark DelCogliano for some bibliography.

2 A full history of the monastery is beyond the scope of this chapter. See Coquin, Martin, and Grossmann 1991; Layton 2004: 2–4.

3 Layton writes that all the manuscripts are palimpsests (Layton 2004). Macfarlane, however, in a presentation at the 2014 annual meeting of the Society of Biblical Literature, observed that not all are palimpsests (Macfarlane 2014).

4 The previous two paragraphs summarize information in Layton 2004: 2–4.

5 A more extensive bibliography can be found online at https://www.zotero.org/groups/tura_papyri. It contains the most significant recent publications in the areas of editions and translations, encyclopedia articles, online resources, and studies.

6 "@ctschroeder The Tura Discovery Changed Didymus from a Theologian to an Exegete in Scholarship, and No One Has Really Tried to Synthesize +" @MarkDelCogliano, January 29, 2015, https://twitter.com/MarkDelCogliano/status/560912032300806146

7 See the collection of references to the condemnations of Didymus's teachings in Kalvesmaki 2014; Percival 1892.

13 Nitria

Mark Sheridan

The Principal Ancient Sources

The principal literary sources for the monastic settlement of Nitria include Rufinus's continuation of Eusebius's *Ecclesiastical History (HE)* up to the death of Theodosius (401–403), the *Historia monachorum in Aegypto* (395?) in Greek and Rufinus's Latin translation of the same work (404), and the *Lausiac History (HL)* of Palladius some twenty years later (420?). There are earlier briefer notices, such as Antony's vision of the death of Ammoun recorded in the *Life of Antony (VA)*, ch. 60 (357?) and Jerome's mention of Macarius, Isidore, and Pambo in his *Letter 22* written in 384. There are also some later reports, such as the historians Socrates and Sozomen and *Apophthegm Antony* 34. These reports are not necessarily independent of one another and the information they offer needs to be assessed in detail.[1]

What can we learn from these sources? Although Rufinus produced his translation and continuation of Eusebius's *Ecclesiastical History* early in the fifth century, the events he reports took place thirty years earlier and he claims to have been in Egypt at the time, about 373–74, shortly after the death of Athanasius. Rufinus narrates that, after the death of Athanasius (373), the Arian bishop Lucius began a persecution of the monks. He mentions in particular Macarius, an Isidore, the other Macarius, Heraclides, and Pambo, saying that they were disciples of Antony and lived in Egypt, especially in Nitria. Rufinus states that he is speaking of things that he saw personally and that he was a companion of their sufferings. Macarius the Great was not resident in Nitria but in Scetis, as Rufinus makes clear a little later (ch. 8). What can Rufinus have meant by the assertion that they were disciples of Antony? It seems likely that Rufinus had heard of the development of monasticism in Egypt before his arrival in 373 and that he may have been acquainted with Athanasius's *Life of Antony* also (Fedalto 1990: 58–65). Did the monks he met in Nitria and elsewhere in the Delta profess themselves to be disciples of Antony in a broad sense?[2] Unfortunately we can only speculate. Perhaps it means no more than that they were imitators of Antony, "the first desert dweller" (Rufinus, *HE* I,8).[3] One thing is clear: they were not Arians and the miracles they worked (in the Eusebian tradition of historiography) served to legitimate them as orthodox. In this context Rufinus inserts also a lengthy description of Didymus of Alexandria, who received a visit from Antony, when the latter came to Alexandria to support Athanasius against the Arians in 338 (*HE* II, ch. 7 = Vogüé, *HL* 3:304n451). From this work we learn little about the monasticism at Nitria other than some names associated with Nitria and that their faith was orthodox.[4]

Shortly after completing the extension of Eusebius's *Ecclesiastical History*, Rufinus undertook the translation of the Greek work known as the *Historia monachorum in Aegypto (HM)*, which contains a chapter on Nitria as well as material on Macarius of Alexandria associated with Nitria and a chapter on Ammoun the founder of Nitria (Schulz-Flügel 1990). The Latin version differs notably from the printed Greek version, to such an extent that it seems more likely that Rufinus was translating a different Greek text from the one edited by Festugière rather than that he made additions, as has sometimes been assumed.[5] In the Latin version the account states: "Then we came to Nitria, the best-known *(famosissimum)* of all the monasteries *(monasteriis)* of Egypt, about forty miles from Alexandria." The account states that there are about fifty dwellings *(tabernacula)* there, located near one another and under one father. In some there are many living together, in some only a few, and in others some living alone. The author singles out the ardent or enthusiastic hospitality of these monks as one of the salient features of the place, noting in particular the custom of washing the feet of the guests, which is described as "this traditional mystery."[6] The glowing account of the monks' humanity, courtesy, and love concludes with a significant observation: "nowhere have I seen such meditation upon Holy Scripture, or a better understanding of it, or such discipline of sacred learning. You might think that each of them was an expert in the wisdom of God." This is also missing from the extant Greek version and may be a significant clue to the nature of Nitrian monasticism and the reasons for the revision of the Greek text. In the Greek version the description of Kellia forms part of the chapter on Nitria without a clear indication that it is a separate place. In it Ammonius and Evagrius are mentioned. In Rufinus's version, on the other hand, there is a longer decription of Kellia as a distinct place, "about ten miles away," and a separate section on Ammonius (located at Kellia), whose brothers, Eusebius, Euthymius, and Dioscorus (the "Tall Brothers"), are also mentioned. A separate section is devoted to Evagrius. After a section devoted to Macarius (or the two Macarii), notably different in the Greek and Latin versions, there is a section (ch. 22) describing the founder of Nitria, Ammoun.[7] The section contains a reference to the *Life of Antony*, ch. 60, where Antony saw his soul "borne up to heaven." Ammoun is said to have persuaded his bride that they should preserve their virginity and he departed a few days later for Nitria. His wife "exhorted all her servants to adopt a celibate life and converted her house into a monastery" (Russell 1981: 111).

Almost twenty-five years after the original Greek version of the *Historia monachorum*, Palladius, according to his own indications, wrote the *Lausiac History* (about 419–20).[8] Palladius arrived in Egypt in 388 after having spent about three years on the Mount of Olives under the guidance of a monk named Innocent. There he had also become acquainted with Melania the Elder and Rufinus. After a few (two?) years in Alexandria under the guidance of Isidore, the Hospitaler (guestmaster—*xenodochos*) of the Church in Alexandria, he went to Nitria where he met Ammonius, one of the Tall Brothers and an acquaintance of both Isidore and Melania. Palladius states that around Alexandria there were about two thousand men living in the monasteries, but seemingly by way of contrast on the "mountain" of Nitria there were five thousand.[9] They had different styles of life *(politeia)*: everyone did what he was able or wished to do, living alone or in the company of another or of many, a description which seems to echo the description of the *Historia monachorum*. He states that he remained a year at Nitria, during which time he was helped by Arsenius and several others, and then he went further into the desert (Kellia).

Palladius, however, offers much more detailed information about the conditions of life at Nitria. There were seven ovens (bakeries) to produce bread for those at Nitria and the six hundred anchorites who lived in the desert (Kellia).[10] There was a large church in which there were three palm trees, each with a whip attached for the punishment of those who committed sins: for monks, thieves, and others respectively. After receiving strokes of the lash, they were absolved. Beside the church there was a guest house for strangers where they could stay as long as they wished, but after a week of rest they were required to do some form of work, in the garden or the bakery or the kitchen. Those considered worthy were given a book with the prohibition of speaking until the established hour. There were also physicians and pastry cooks on the "mountain" and wine was both used and sold. All were engaged in producing linen so as to be independent.

Toward the ninth hour, says Palladius, one could hear the chanting of psalms from all the dwellings. The monks assembled in the church only on Saturday and Sunday. There were eight priests (presbyters), but only the senior celebrated or preached or judged and all the others assisted silently while seated. Palladius says that Arsisius and other older monks were contemporaries of Antony *(sunchronoi)*, which suggests at least that they were monks before Antony's death in 356, and some recounted having known the founder of Nitria, Ammoun, with an explicit allusion to the *Life of Antony* ch. 60, where Antony is recorded as having witnessed the soul of Ammoun being taken to heaven by angels. The fact that this chapter follows on the description of Nitria as in the *Historia monachorum* and that the same reference to the *Life of Antony* is present cannot help but suggest that Palladius was acquainted with the *Historia monachorum*. However, the story is considerably embellished by Palladius, who presents it as having been told by Arsenius at Nitria (*HL* 8.1). In this version Ammoun, after persuading his spouse not to consummate the marriage by reading to her from the Scriptures[11] and convincing her of the desirability of virginity, does not depart at once for the mountain of Nitria, but remains, at her insistence, for eighteen years in the same house working at the production of balsam. Both achieved *apatheia*, says Palladius, and finally the woman suggests that they live apart. Then Ammoun goes to Nitria where he builds two little cells *(tholoi)* and lives for twenty-two years, visiting his wife twice a year. Palladius concludes the account (no longer being related by Arsenius, but his own addition) with another reference to the *Life of Antony*, ch. 60, where the miraculous crossing of the river Lycos by Ammoun is told. He adds that he himself had crossed this branch of the Nile in a boat.[12]

Palladius also includes the stories of several prominent monks of Nitria, including Or, Pambo, Ammonius, Benjamin, Apollonius, Paesio and Isaiah, Macarius and Nathanael, some of whom were deceased before he arrived at Nitria. Although he insists that the whole community of brothers bore witness to the virtue of Or, he also mentions that he had heard of him from Melania, and in the account of Pambo he states clearly that his information came from Melania. In the relatively long story of Pambo (ch. 10), who is described as the teacher of the Tall Brothers, Dioscorus, Ammonius, Eusebius, and Euthymius, Melania is quoted at length regarding her atttempt to give a large sum of money to Pambo. He in turn presented her with the last basket he wove. She was also present at his death and prepared his corpse for burial. This must have been in 373, for Melania left Egypt for Palestine with the monks persecuted by Lucius. However, in ch. 46, dedicated to Melania, Palladius writes that Pambo was among those sent into exile by the prefect of Alexandria and that Melania followed them, aiding them with her own possessions. She had spent the preceding six months at Nitria and the desert visiting "all the saints."

Among the others mentioned as disciples of Pambo, the most interesting notice concerns Ammonius, who cut off his ear in an effort to escape being ordained a bishop. Timothy is mentioned as the bishop of Alexandria, which would place the incident about 381–84. The reason why Ammonius was sought as bishop was because of his extraordinary knowledge of the Scriptures *(philologos)*. Palladius states that he had learned by memory the Old and the New Testaments and had read six hundred myriad lines of famous authors such as Origen, Didymus, Pierius, and Stephen. The last two are mentioned again in ch. 55,3,24 in connection with Melania, who is praised for her love of Scripture and her knowledge of the "ancient" *(archaion)* commentators including Origen, Gregory (which?), Stephen, Pierius, Basil, and others.

Other Ancient Sources

The Greek alphabetical collection of the *Apophthegmata* contains a story (Antony 34) in which Antony visits Ammoun at Nitria. Ammoun informs him that some of the brethren wish for greater peace. So they eat at the ninth hour and then walk in the desert until sunset. Antony proposes that they plant a cross on the spot so that those who wish may settle there, but the distance from Nitria will not be too great to allow communication. The distance is said to have been twelve miles. Another apophthegm records a visit of Ammoun to Antony (Ammoun 1).

The historian Socrates (*HE* 4,23) offers a slightly different version of the story of Ammoun. Both Ammoun and his wife retired to the mountain of Nitria and lived together for a short time in a hut with an oratory attached. Then they separated and lived apart. Sozomen follows Palladius more closely.[13] Both these historians are writing in the mid-fifth century, long after the events, and obviously relied on earlier sources. Attempts to date the story of Ammoun and development of the monastic settlement at Nitria have varied considerably. Tillemont (1732: 7:158) suggests that he died between AD 340 and 345. He certainly died before Antony (356) if the story of Antony seeing his soul carried to heaven is accepted. Evelyn-White, on the basis of a notice in the *Menologium Sirletianum*, dates Ammoun's birth in 275, his marriage in 297, his retirement to the Mount of Nitria in 315, and his death in 337.

From what has been said so far it should be obvious that we really know very little about the early development of Nitria beyond the legendary story of its founding. The tradition records contacts between Ammoun and Antony; Athanasius, writing about 457, obviously knew about Ammoun. It is only when "the world breaks in" (to use the expression of Chitty) with the visits of Rufinus and Melania and later that we have more information. But that is already thirty-five years at least after the death of Ammoun. By then the settlement was populous and famous, and the disciples of Ammoun such as Pambo were renowned.[14] At the time of the Arian persecution under Lucius, Nitria was obviously a center of orthodox resistance, and later in the century played a prominent role in the Origenist dispute, to which we shall return. From the fifth and sixth century we hear very little about Nitria. There is only one brief mention of the situation there after the Council of Chalcedon, by Cyril of Scythopolis (writing about the middle of the sixth century), who states that because of disturbances caused by Timothy Aelurus (after 457), the pro-Chalcedonian monks Martyrius and Elias left Nitria and retired to Palestine (Evelyn-White, Hauser, and Lythgoe 1932: 222). At Kellia, according to an apophthegm of Phocas (1), there were two churches, "one for the Orthodox and one for the Schismatics."[15]

In the seventh century the patriarch Benjamin is said to have visited Gabal Barnug on his way from Alexandria to the Wadi al-Natrun (*Patrologia Orientalis*, 242).[16] The excavations at Kellia have indicated that the hermitages there were still in use in the second quarter of the eighth century (Bonnet 1986: 293). Since Kellia was originally conceived of as an appendage of Nitria, that may be an indication that Nitria was still in existence as a monastic settlement, but this is highly uncertain because there is no archaeological evidence as there is for Kellia.

Nitria and Origen

The events of the Origenist controversy of the year 400 have been investigated extensively in recent times, beginning with Evelyn-White's *History of the Monasteries of Nitria and Scetis*, then more recently in the publications of Dechow, Clark, and above all Guillaumont. There is no doubt that certain prominent monks from Nitria were involved and were opponents of Patriarch Theophilos. These included above all the Tall Brothers and Palladius, who had lived earlier at Nitria and the Cells. There seems little point in recounting these events again, which are in fact rather complicated and to which justice can hardly be done in a limited space.

What has received less extensive coverage is the background of the study of Scripture in Nitria and in other monasteries of the period. Two of the principal interpreters of Scripture from this period were associated with Nitria and the Cells, Didymus the Blind[17] and Evagrius, both of whom were dead before the outbreak of the Origenist controversy. Only later did their names come to be associated with it. Both Rufinus and Palladius, as we have seen, stressed this aspect of the monastic culture of Nitria, the reading and interpretation of the Scriptures. For Palladius, Ammonius was a particularly noteworthy example. Since the presuppositions and the rules governing the interpretation of the Scriptures in antiquity differ notably from modern ones, it may be useful to give a brief summary of these.

First, however, it needs to be stressed that reading the Scriptures was a basic exercise of monastic life as far back as we can trace it. Antony is said by Athanasius to have imitated the practice of studying the Scriptures *(philologounti)* from an older monk in his vicinity (*VA* 4.1).[18] He also memorized the Scriptures so that his memory served him as a book. Palladius uses the same word to describe Ammonius as learned in Scripture *(philologos)*. The prodigious number of scriptural citations and allusions, even to the most obscure passages, in all of the early monastic literature bears witness to the role of Scripture in the life of the monks.[19] The rules of the Pachomian community suggest that the monks should memorize at least the New Testament and the Psalter (Sheridan 2002: 49).[20] The relative degree of literacy in the monasteries appears to have been high, but knowledge of the Scriptures was not limited to the actual reading of books, as can be seen from the examples of Antony and Didymus. It could also be derived from listening.

For those like Didymus and Ammonius, who had access to books or even to a library, the works of Origen were the obvious tool for seeking to understand the Scriptures. Origen had been the first to comment extensively book by book on the Scriptures and had left a formidable literary heritage. However, the Alexandrian tradition of interpretation is not limited to Origen and did not originate with him, but had its roots in the rich Hellenistic Jewish tradition represented above all by Philo of Alexandria. Both Origen and Didymus made extensive use of Philo's commentaries on the Law of Moses. Indeed, most Christian commentators (Eusebius, Athanasius, Basil, and others) made use of both Philo and Origen in producing their own commentaries. However, Christian commentators faced challenges that Philo had not had to face, since 'Scripture' for him was limited to the Pentateuch. The Christian Scriptures comprised a much larger and more heterogeneous collection that included not only the Law of Moses, but the historical books, the prophets, the wisdom literature, and the New Testament. The task of interpreting this vast collection from a Christian perspective had been begun in the New Testament, but very selectively. As Origen saw it, Paul especially had offered rules and examples of how to do it, but the task was far from finished. Origen believed that the Scriptures wrongly interpreted could be dangerous and harmful to the spiritual life.

In the ancient world the idea was widespread, if not indeed universal, that sacred texts had hidden meaning. An indication of this belief can be seen in the widespread use of the phrase 'sacred oracles' to refer to the Scriptures in antiquity, a practice that seems strange to modern ears. Oracles are by their nature obscure and require explanation. Clement of Alexandria had developed an extensive theory about hidden meaning in all sacred texts. Origen's search for the 'spiritual meaning' of the Scriptures in his commentaries was not a radical new departure, but the development of a long tradition. Clement and Origen as well as many others made use of a rule of interpretation already found in Philo, that the meaning of a text must be "worthy of God" or "fitting to God," who is considered the divine author. This principle made it necessary to seek a 'spiritual' sense for many passages describing things that could hardly be considered "worthy of God" or of the divine majesty, especially those attributing human emotions or behavior to God. The concept of God thus becomes the controlling principle of interpretation (Sheridan 2015). Another principle that Origen developed and used extensively, based on the assertion in 2 Timothy 3:16 that all Scripture is divinely inspired and useful, is that it must be useful for us (Sheridan 2006). The real meaning must provide moral and spiritual nourishment.

Using these principles, Origen, Didymus, and Evagrius were able to interpret many passages of Scripture in such a way as to provide spiritual nourishment within the perspective of spiritual progress. Examples of such interpretation include the following: the seven nations that the Israelites are commanded to destroy (Deut 9:4–5) become the seven carnal vices to be uprooted in the quest for spiritual progress; the land to be conquered in Joshua becomes a spiritual territory; and the command to smash the heads of the Babylonian children against the rock in Ps 36:9 becomes a counsel to resist beginnings of temptations while they are still young (*propatheiai* in Stoic terms). Interpreted in this way, such passages become not only acceptable but useful to Christian and monastic readers. Allegory was never an end in itself for these interpreters, but a means to find the hidden meaning, worthy of God and useful to the reader, that they were convinced must be there because the Scriptures were divine. Paul had shown the way by offering examples of allegorical interpretation, especially in 1 Corinthians and Galatians.

These basic principles and presuppositions were never understood by Epiphanius of Salamis, who conducted an unrelenting campaign against Origen and against the monks of Egypt for almost forty years, which ended in the Origenist controversy of the year 400 and probably greatly harmed the monastic community of Nitria and Kellia. He railed against allegorical interpretation but had no appreciation of the theological sophistication that lay behind it.

Notes

1 Rufinus translated the *Ecclesiastical History* into Latin in 404. The Greek original may have been used by the historians Socrates and Sozomen. See Thelamon 1981.

2 Tillemont says judiciously, "On dit generalemont de ces Saints qu'ils estoient disciples de Saint Antoine, quoique cela puisse suffrir quelque exception" (1732: 8:309); Vogüé notes the dominant and persistent influence of the "grand initiateur célébré par Athanase" (1996: 1, 3:309).

3 This phrase derives probably from the mention in the *Life of Antony* (ch. 3) that "no one even knew the great desert."

4 Although Rufinus says that he was in Egypt at this time, he does not mention Melania the Elder in this context, who, according to Palladius, visited the monks at Nitria and helped them when they were expelled or fled to Palestine. Rufinus relates that Lucius deported the heads of the monasteries to a swampy island (*HE* II,4). Because of the fame of the miracles they worked, Lucius relented and allowed them to return. We do not know when Rufinus became acquainted with Melania, whether earlier in Rome, or in Egypt, or later on the Mount of Olives.

5 See Vogüé *HL* 3:364; Bammel 1996: 92–104. There are good reasons to believe that the Greek version has been revised and shortened in the wake of the Origenist controversy of 400: Russell 1981.

6 *Mysticis traditionibus abluentes*. See Ambrose, *On the Mysteries* 6.31; *On the Sacraments*, Catechesis 3, 1.4 (Johnson 2009: 976–78; 1056–57). See also Augustine (Johnson 2009: 2625).

7 In the Greek version the story of Ammoun is preceded by the story of Macarius the Egyptian, which interrupts the geographical continuity, since this Macarius was always associated with Scetis.

8 *HL* Prologue says this was his thirty-third year of monastic life, his twentieth year as a bishop, and the fifty-sixth year of his life: Katos 2011: 99; Butler 1898–1904: 1, 3:179–81. There has been much speculation about an earlier version of this work that would have been produced while Palladius was still in Egypt. See Katos 2011: 102–103.

9 Wipszycka (2009: 408) doubts the figure, saying the space was too small. Palladius knew the number was large.

10 For the question of the reliability of the number, see Wipszycka (2009: 411), who seems to think it exagggerated.

11 *HL* 8.2. See Bartelink 1994: 321, who says it was probably the Acts of Thomas, but Socrates in *HE* 4.23 says it was 1 Corinthians.

12 The *HM* 22,7 also contains an account of this miracle, but without the mention of Theodore, who is mentioned in the *VA* and the *HL*. The story relates instead that Antony had sent some monks to bring Ammoun to him.

13 Evelyn-White, Hauser, and Lythgoe 1932: 46. Sozomen, *HE* 1,14,1f.

14 The later notices in the Coptic sources do not provide substantially more information. See Timm 1985: 980–81.

15 Ward 1975b: 201 has "Monophysites" instead of "schismatics."

16 This has also been interpreted to mean that there were no longer monks at Nitria.

17 Palladius (*HL* 4.1.3) seems to indicate that Didymus had a cell at Nitria, but does not say so explicitly. He indicates that he had four meetings with him. His teaching activity obviously took place in Alexandria (Rufinus, *HE* 11.7 [GCS 9.21012–13]). Palladius indicates that Antony met with him also (*HL* 4.3).

18 SC400: 141. Bartelink (love of study/*amour de l'étude*) gives a reference to Girardet (in bibliography).

19 That this was true not just of the Greek-speaking ambience but of the Coptic one as well can be seen from the works of Paul of Tamma and the Catechesis attributed to Pachomius, both of which are filled with allusions and allegorical interpretations drawn from the Alexandrian tradition.

20 For the question of literacy among the monks in general see Wipszycka 2009: 361–65.

14 Yuhanna al-Samannudi, the Founder of National Coptic Philology in the Middle Ages

Adel Sidarus

We know nothing definite about this bishop of Samannud before his consecration by Patriarch Kyrillos III Ibn Laqlaq (no. 75, r. 1235–43) on June 29, 1235, at St. Mercurius/Abu Sayfayn Church in Old Cairo, together with the four first bishops ordained shortly after Kyrillos's enthronement.[1]

Graf claims without reference that Yuhanna's original name was al-As'ad ibn al-Duhayri.[2] No information on this point has been found in the historical sources or the manuscripts related to him. Actually—as stated by Graf himself (1947: 378)—this was an alternative name for Yuhanna's contemporary fellow bishop al-Thiqa ibn al-Duhayri, later Metropolitan Christodoulus of Damietta.[3] On the other hand, in all the events in which both prelates were involved, according to the accounts related in the national *History of the Patriarchs*, no allusion is made to any kinship between them.

Considering the crystallized form "Yuhanna al-Samannudi"—or simply "al-Samannudi"[4]—which prevailed among his contemporary and coreligionist writers and philologists, we may assume he had published his grammar known as *al-Muqaddima al-samannudiya*, together with his *Sullam kana'si*, sometimes named *al-Sullam al-samannudi*, before his consecration as bishop. Hence, Samannud should likely be his native town and Yuhanna his original proper name, later modified to "Yu'annis" (Coptic *Ioannes*) in ecclesiastical documentation as well as in some manuscripts.[5] In any case, in Arabic anthroponomy the *nisba*, or origin marker, indicates the geographic, ethnic, tribal, or family origin and never—so far we know—the see of a bishop.[6]

As a matter of fact we meet the same occurrence with Patriarch John III, the Merciful (no. 40, r. 677–89), as he is referred to in the *History of the Patriarchs* under the name of Yuhanna al-Samannudi.[7]

Located in al-Gharbiya District on the Damietta branch of the Nile in the Central Delta, not far from Mahalla al-Kubra, Samannud was an important town and bishopric in the beginnings of Christianity in Egypt under the Greek name of Sebennytos—Coptic Djebenoute or Djemnouti, from Old Egyptian Tjebnutjer.[8] There is much to say on the city and its bishopric, which is attested before the end of the fourth century. It suffices here to point out some data in direct relation with our bishop from the thirteenth century.

Our bishop must be John II or III of Samannud, as a former bishop with the same name is attested in the second half of the fifth century (Timm 1984–92: 2255 top). Later, in the time of Patriarch John V (no. 72, r. 1147–67), originally from Samannud itself, one Yuhanna ibn Qadran was consecrated bishop for the diocese but he never took possession of his see, remaining in his monastery; instead, it was Macarius, a nephew of the patriarch, who acted as bishop (Timm 1984–92: 2258). Finally, a later Bishop John (III or IV) of Samannud is attested in 1320 and 1330 as being present at both ceremonies for the ritual preparation of the Holy Myron.[9]

Among the local martyrs is one John who suffered with his companion Simeon in the time of Emperor Diocletian and the Alexandrian governor Armenios. Their tomb lies in Shurmoulos/Chenemoulos in the nomos of Samannud[10] and they are celebrated in the Coptic *Synaxar* on 11 Abib. They have also a bilingual *vita* or *passio* in which our Bishop Yuhanna had some literary involvement, as explained below in the section "Life and Martyrdom of John and Simeon."

Later in the Middle Ages, Samannud gave to the Coptic Church three patriarchs, two of whom were named John: John III and John V, who were mentioned above; the third one was Cosmas II (no. 54, r. 851–58).[11]

The city strongly resisted the Arab invasion in 639 and was the home of a few revolts against the government in the first half of the eighth century. The fourth, in 750, was championed by one . . . Yuhanna al-Samannudi.[12]

Status and Role in Church Life

Bishop John was the dean of the Coptic bishops (and metropolitans) of his time and was very active and influential in Church affairs.

In a protocol that deals with the rank of the bishops, dated to 1240, we find him as the first subscriber with the full designation: *Yu'annis al-kabir usquf Samannud* ('John, the Elder, Bishop of Samannud').[13] A few years later, when some notables and bishops tried to choose a successor for Pope Kyrillos, Bishop John of Samannud is labeled precisely *Kabir al-asaqifa* ('the dean of the bishops'), because—as the document explains—he belongs to the first group of bishops consecrated *(awwal takriz asaqifa)* by this very pope.[14]

Exactly one year after the patriarchal enthronement and his own ordination as bishop, on the occasion of the ritual preparation of the *myron* at the Monastery of St. Macarius, during Holy Week of 1236, the monks appealed to him with the aim of resolving a serious clash with the patriarch. Although they could not obtain his direct support against Pope Kyrillos, he worked together with Anba Yusuf/Yusab—later Bishop of Fuwwa but then still the abbot of the neighboring Monastery of St. John the Little—in order to resolve the conflict.[15]

Two years later, in March 1238, he is one of the signatories of a double canonical document issued after a synod of the bishops from Lower Egypt, who gathered in order to protest the behavior of Patriarch Kyrillos, to put limitations to his authority, and to clarify certain aspects of Church life.[16]

After Kyrillos's death, our bishop joined Bishop Yusab of Fuwwa and the venerated rector of the Church of St. Sergius/Abu Sarja, Anba Butrus al-Rahib (formerly al-Sana' Abu al-Majd), to name a successor. Their choice fell on Bulus ibn Kalil, a monk from St. Antony who was descended, through his mother, from the prestigious family *(bayt)* of the Banu al-'Amid (Sidarus 2013b: 193). Once more, the struggle between the different factions left the Coptic community without a leader for seven years. Monk Paul did not reach the patriarchal throne as Athanasius III until 1250.[17]

In 1255/6 Bishop John is believed to have stayed for a while in the Monastery of St. Macarius, since he left there as *waqf* a precious Coptic codex with hagiographical texts, now held in the Vatican Library. It had possibly served for his translation into Arabic of one of these accounts which is related to the Samannudian martyrs, as discussed below in the section "Life and Martyrdom of John and Simeon."

The last documented evidence for this bishop is his participation in another occasion of preparing the *myron*, also at St. Macarius Monastery in 1257, during the patriarchate of Athanasius III (r. 1250–61) (Munier 1943b: 34; Muyser 1944: 155–56). However, Bishop John is still mentioned with high praise and veneration as a living person in the beginning of the 1260s by Abu al-Mu'taman ibn al-'Assal in the introduction to his *Sullam muqaffa'*. This work provides a 'rhymed' reworking of Samannudi's *Scala Ecclesiastica*, which we will examine below in the section on John's philological works.

Intellectual Profile and Literary Output

Yuhanna al-Samannudi was celebrated by his contemporaries first of all because of his pioneering work in the field of Coptic language. His grammar and vocabulary proved to be seminal for posterity far beyond this specific field, insofar as the linguistic movement of his time constitutes the foundation of the renaissance in which the Copts were engaged in the thirteenth century.[18]

Due to the complexity of this writing and its textual transmission, let us first put forward the scholar's other works, which are not much acknowledged. Few of them could have predated his philological output; they build, to a certain degree, its general intellectual and literary frame.

Translation from Coptic into Arabic of the *Life and Maxims* of the Sophist philosopher Secundus the Silent (first half of the second century)[19]

There are almost twenty Arabic manuscripts which preserve this 'didactic novel' from Late Antiquity, almost all of Coptic origin. The Greek original was actually translated into many languages, but the Geez–Ethiopian version is based on Samannudi's Coptic Arabic text.[20]

While Graf does not refer to the translation from Coptic and its author, Heide hesitates to assert the fact because only two of the ten manuscripts he knew of (nos. 1–2 below) mention it, one of them in an ambivalent way. Besides, there is no trace of such a Coptic version. Actually, the heading of the Paris MS 275 (no. 2) states: "Questions and maxims put down by . . ." (*Masa'il wa-ahkam wada'aha . . .*). As the Arabic version, compared to the original Greek text, has a long additional chapter with a set of maxims others than the ones following the *Vita* and with a clear theological drift, Heide (2014: 11–12) suggests that the work of the Bishop of Samannud should relate precisely to this 'appendix' and not so much to the translation from Coptic. However, we have pointed out in an earlier study (Sidarus 1990: 359) that the Greco-Coptic vocabulary from the last decades of the sixth century, the so-called *Glossary of Dioscorus*, ends with a few sentences of Secundus (Bell and Crum 1925: 118–19). On the other hand, in addition to the Paris MS 309 (no. 1) there are two further manuscript witnesses (nos. 3–4), overlooked by Heide (along with Graf and the other scholars), which identify the translation as done from Coptic by "Anba Yu'annis, Bishop of Samannud."

- 1–2. Paris, Bibliothèque nationale de France (BnF), arabe 309 (first half of fifteenth century), fol. 54v–104r (piece no. 2) and 275 (y. 1685), fol. 4r–34r (piece no. 1).[21]
- 3. Maadi, Coptic Catholic Theological Institute, KM 14 (seventeenth–nineteenth centuries), fol. 4–64 (piece no. 1).[22]
- 4. Wadi al-ʿAraba, Monastery of St. Antony, History 193 (w/d.), fol. 1–68 (piece no. 1).[23]

Previous to Heide's edition and translation,[24] Perry offered, as a complement to the edition and study of the Greek original, a kind of diplomatic edition, with English translation, of one Paris manuscript (no. 6 below) with the collation of other copies in the footnotes.[25]

As to the whole set of available copies, besides the four mentioned above, we must correct and complete the listings given by Graf and Heide as follows.[26]

According to the information in the respective catalogs, the following Paris copies show an identical text:[27]

- 5–7. Paris, BnF, arabe 49 (fifteenth century), fol. 217v–284v (last piece no. 7); 150 (sixteenth–seventeenth centuries), fol. 300r–333r (piece no. 3);[28] 310 (seventeenth century), fol. 61r–108r (piece no. 2).[29]

We know personally of three further manuscripts from St. Antony, completely unknown to Heide and Graf, along with the aforementioned MS no. 4:

- 8–10. Wadi al-ʿAraba, Monastery of St. Antony, History 190 (y. 1744), 137 ff. (alone); 192 (w/d.), 46 ff. (alone); 21 (w/d.), fol. 270r–284r (last piece no. 3; vita only?).

In their listing of the manuscripts Graf and Heide mention only one from the Coptic Patriarchate at Cairo (below, no. 11). Actually they are four in total, in addition to one in the Coptic Museum, as follows:

- 11–14. Cairo, Coptic Patriarchate (CopPatr.), History 46 (Simaika 677/Graf 477, nineteenth century), 65 ff. (alone);[30] 31 (651/491, y. 1737), fol. 21v–23v (piece no. 3); 60 (661/456, in-4° MS, eighteenth century), piece no. 6; 87 (Simaika 682, w/d.), piece no. 2.[31]
- 15. Cairo, Coptic Museum (CopMus.), History 468 (Simaika 125/Macomber 1995: B-12.15-m, nineteenth century), fol. 80r–92r (last piece no. 12).[32]

Finally, there are the following manuscripts:

- 16. Oxford, Bodleian Library, 183 (y. 1607), fol. 118v–198v.[33]
- 17. Aleppo, Fondation Georges and Mathilde Salem, Arabic 202 (Sbath 1004; seventeenth century), fol. 1r–62r (piece no. 1).[34]
- 18. St. Petersburg, Institute for Oriental MSS, Russian Academy of Sciences, B 1229 (Kračkovskij 31; nineteenth century), fol. 202v–230v.[35]

Translation of a catechetical work

The work in question is a translation allegedly from Greek into Arabic—more credibly, through an intermediate Coptic version—of a catechetical work of the *Erotapokrisis* ('Questions and Answers') type.[36] The only witness we know of, namely MS Cairo, CopPatr. Theology 91 (Simaika 268/Graf 371/Macomber 1997: A-25.13, eighteenth century), fol. 223r–284r (piece no. 2), gives the uninformative title: *Kitab yusamma Nur al-majalis / wa-Nuzhat al-sadiq wa-l-mu'anis (wa-yusamma K. al-Zahr wal-ghiyad / wa-Baha' min 'arus tajalla fi-l-bayad, wa-yusamma K. al-Jawhar al-multaqat).*[37]

These alternative, somehow poetic titles do not help us to guess the real content of the work. According to the description given by Graf, it presents successively, in the form of commentaries, the Christian Credo, the Lord's Prayer, the Ten Commandments, and the Seven Sacraments. In his short description of the manuscript Simaika points out that it is suggested *(yuqal)* in the text that the 'Master' is Peter the Apostle, and the 'Disciple' Clement. Consequently, the work should be the one edited under the title *al-Mu'allim wa-l-tilmidh min qawl Butrus al-Rasul*, by Bishara Bistawrus (Cairo, 1948).[38]

Life and Martyrdom of John and Simeon

This work is a composition or translation into Arabic of the *Life and*

Martyrdom of John and Simeon from Shurmoulos (Coptic Chenemoulos), in the Samannudian territory,[39] possibly after having copied the Bohairic Coptic prototype inserted in a hagiographical collection.

According to Sbath Fihrist 2707, an undated MS from the private collection of one Jirjis 'Abd al-Masih from Cairo, the whereabouts of which are today unknown, al-Samannudi should be the author of some accounts of martyrs from Samannud. We made mention of such saints above, and we may assume that they are a translation or adaptation of the existing Bohairic text we know of, as discussed below.

There are several accounts in Arabic related to these Samannudian saints. How far do they mirror the writing or translation of our bishop? And what are the relations among them all, including the text transmitted in the *Synaxar* for 11 Abib?

The general feature of these Arabic text witnesses is that they are set out in two or three sections: the short *vita* plus the *passio* or dramatic account of the martyrdom, mostly embedded in a homily or ritual discourse *(maymar/mimar)*, then the miracles (six or seven), and finally the translation of the body, passing through a few neighboring localities. One particular detail of the story is that Simeon (Sim'an) was the paternal cousin *(ibn 'amm)* of John *(Yuhanna/Hanna)*, and not his companion or partner as stated in Coptic: *shphêri*.

The following is a list of the manuscript witnesses we were able to assemble, sorted according to their age. The lives of our saints often form parts of collections which deserve a comparative examination in order to elucidate the exact origin of the text in question.

1. Cairo, CopMus., History 470 (Simaika 97/Graf 713/Macomber 1995: A-11.1, y. 1365/6), ff. 101v–108v (Graf = piece no. 9) or 96v–103v (Macomber = piece no. k). A restored MS with some original folios missing. A collection of hagiographical accounts as parallel reading of the *Synaxar*, as the saints here gathered are celebrated in the month of Abib. The former MS 469, from 1363 and copied by the same scribe, was for Ba'una. Macomber states our MS "is made of sections derived from at least three different original MSS, all of the 14th century."
2. Wadi al-'Araba, Monastery of St. Antony, History 86 (y. 1375), fol. 45–67 (piece no. 2).
3. Paris, BnF, arabe 277 (y. 1524), ff. 74v–115v (piece no. 3): martyrdom + miracles (6) + translation of the relics to Balya, al-Bandara,

and al-Qurashiya (here, together with those of St. Paphnutius = Abinuda/Babnuda).[40]

4. Cairo, CopPatr., History 40 (Simaika 608/Graf 478, y. 1558), fol. 24r–49r (piece no. 2 in Graf, corresponding to nos. 2–4 in Simaika): same content, but with seven miracles.
5. Paris, BnF, arabe 4777 (nineteenth century), fol. 24–40 + 71–81 (piece no. 2): contents as in MS no. 3.
6. Wadi al-Natrun, Monastery of St. Macarius, Tafasir 26. A dubious fragment of two folios pasted to the binding (fourteenth century).[41]

In respect to the potential Coptic original, there is a Bohairic version (CPC 0279; BHO 0525)[42] in one copy in the Vatican Library originating from the Monastery of St. Macarius, to which library precisely our Bishop John dedicated the codex in 971/1254–55. Hence the codex as a whole belonged originally to him, if it was not copied by him.

MS Vatican copt. 60 (twelfth–thirteenth centuries), fol. 61r–85v (piece no. 2) seems an artificial amalgamation of two or three MSS of the same age and copied by the same scribe, with some folios and lacunae in their actual state (in total: 126 ff.). It offers a small hagiographical collection of four pieces, with some decorations and two illustrations by a certain "David, the painter" (Coptic *pi-zôgraphos*), on fol. 22r and 60v, the latter giving a portrait of both our saints.[43] The dedication deed appears in Arabic on the verso of the final page of the fourth piece (fol. 125), that is, at the end of the codex, inscribed by the "poor Yu'annis, the servant of the see of Samannud."[44]

Consequently we may state that the Coptic text that Yuhanna has possibly translated into Arabic is the Bohairic version preserved in this manuscript[45]—even if the existing Arabic witnesses that reached us, or some of them, were later enriched or modified. It has similar composition: announcement of a marvelous birth; holy way of life; miracles (four or five of them); martyrdom; translation of mortal remains; building of a topos.

Coptic–Arabic New Testament

This work is a manuscript copy, possibly illuminated and illustrated, and with a new translation into Arabic.

As stated in inscriptions inserted in two manuscripts from Cairo identified below (nos. 2–3), a copy by John (Yuhanna), Bishop of Samannud, served as the prototype for a codex copied (and painted?) by the monk and priest Gabriel, the future Patriarch Gabriel III (no. 78, r. 1268–71).[46] This luxurious codex, executed on behalf of Archon Nushu' al-Khilafa Abu Shakir ibn al-Sanaa Butrus al-Rahib ibn al-Muhadhdhab in 1249,[47] is preserved today in two partial manuscripts: the Tetraevangelion in Paris and the Praxapostolos in Cairo (nos. 1–2 below). Both parts served in turn for further copies: the Praxapostolos of the Coptic Patriarchate, where the same information about the Samannudian archetype is corroborated, and the Tetraevangelion of the British Library (below, nos. 3–4), and so on.

That both MSS (nos. 1–2) were originally part of one codex is not only clear from a range of internal evidence, but it is asserted explicitly in two notes inserted in the Patriarchate's copy just mentioned (no. 3), as discussed below.

The question arises as to whether the available information concerning the original codex produced by Bishop John refers to the bilingual text or to the whole codicological framework, including illumination and illustration, or at least the bulk of them. Considering the similar achievement of Michael, the metropolitan of Damietta, dated to around 1180,[48] and the established tradition attested in a few more New Testament codices from the same epoch executed in Lower Egypt,[49] the supposition is compelling. As in the case of his older colleague, John could have actually written down the codex and let artists and painters do the rest under his patronage. We saw a similar situation in the aforementioned Vatican Codex Copticus 60 on the martyrs of Samannud.

In any case, there is more to the literary component of the question. The Arabic text is not the so-called vulgate, of Syriac origin or influence, but rather a translation from Bohairic Coptic. Similar to three of his contemporaries who simultaneously wrote Coptic grammars and undertook 'critical' translations in Arabic of a segment of New Testament books,[50] he could have broken new ground in that field in connection with his pioneering philological enterprise, chiefly his *Scala ecclesiastica*, which we will examine below. As noted elsewhere, in the literary movement of the Copto-Arabic renaissance in the thirteenth century, most of the philologists were simultaneously biblicists.[51]

These are the manuscripts mentioned, along with some others. All are bilingual in two columns: Coptic Bohairic and Arabic.

1. Paris, Institut Catholique, copte-arabe 1 (y. 1249, 235 ff.). Tetraevangelion copied by Priest Gabriel, the Monk [on behalf of Archon Abu Shakir ibn al-Rahib . . .], in 1249 (fol. 225).[52]
2. Cairo, CopMus., Biblical 94 (Simaika 4/Graf 151/Macomber 1995: A-20.6, y. 1249, 223 ff.). Praxapostolos. Same copyist and sponsor (fol. 130r + 217v–218r). From a copy by Anba Yu'annis, Bishop of Samannud, for the Pauline Epistles (fol. 130r) and from another by Jirja ibn SKSYK/KSYK (*Sarkis*?), the famous scribe *(al-nasikh al-mashhur)*, for the rest (fol. 217v).[53]
3. London, British Library (BrLibr.), oriental 425 (y. 1308, 162 ff.). Complete New Testament copied from both former manuscripts before their division, without the illustrations and the rich decoration.[54]
4. Cairo, CopPatr., Biblical 143 (Simaika 180/Graf 291/Macomber 1997: A-12.7, y. 1853, 210 ff.). Pauline Epistles, of which the (alleged) prototype MS "was copied, collated and improved" by the same Gabriel in 1249, on the basis of a copy in the handwriting *(bi-khatt)* of Anba Yuhanna, Bishop of Samannud, which thereafter served as archetype MS ('Urvorlage'; see fol. 158r + 210r).[55]

In her first appraisal of some manuscripts of this type held in the Coptic Museum, Hunt says that "an integral approach to the manuscripts' texts, inscriptions and illustrations shows how scribes and artists worked during the 12th–14th centuries to promote Christian Arabic texts."[56] In this line, it should be most relevant for a correct evaluation of the aforementioned set of manuscripts to study accurately the textual relations between them, as well as with the three aforementioned Bohairic Coptic–Arabic copies from approximately the same epoch and described by Leroy, together with Michael of Damietta's copy, in addition to the following:

- Cairo, CopMus., Biblical 93 (Simaika 5/Graf 153/Macomber 1995: A-1.3, y. 1257, 357 ff.). Tetraevangelion with moderate decoration, except a rich illuminated frontispiece at the beginning of Luke's Gospel (157r) and a dislocated portrait of St. Mark (fol. 1b). Copied by Gabriel, in the household of Archon al-Amjad ibn al-'Assal and on his behalf (bilingual colophon: in Coptic on fol. 345r and in Arabic on fol. 346v).[57]
- Cairo, CopMus., Biblical 92 (Simaika 6/Graf 152/Macomber 1995: A-12.4, y. 1272, 327 ff.). Tetraevangelion illuminated but

not illustrated, copied by Priest Sim'an ibn Abi Nasr al-Tamada'i on behalf of al-Shaykh al-Amjad Abu al-Majd ibn al-Shaykh Abu al-Mufaddal ibn al-Shaykh [al-Mu'taman], for the patriarchal church al-Mu'allaqa in Old Cairo (fol. 327v).[58]

- Cairo, CopMus., Biblical 95 (Simaika 3/Graf 162/Macomber 1995: A-14.7, y. 1226, 354 ff.). Tetraevangelion restored in 1767 by the scribe Ibrahim Sim'an from Harat al-Rum, in Old Cairo (fol. 354r–v). Copied, collated, and corrected, for the Coptic and the Arabic, in 1226 (fol. 105r + 168r + 354r–v). An icon of St. John on fol. 219v.
- Wadi al-Natrun, Monastery of St. Macarius, Biblical 17 (Tetraevangelion, Bohairic Coptic–Arabic, with rich illumination and decoration, from the fourteenth century) and Biblical 36 (Arabic Praxapostolos from 1246, collated with Greek and Coptic texts and five Arabic MSS, one of which goes back to the celebrated Severus of Ashmunayn, alias Sawirus ibn al-Muqaffa').[59]
- Wadi al-Natrun, Dayr al-Suryan, Liturgy 383 and Biblical 11.[60]

The Philological Achievement

As previously stated, Yuhanna al-Samannudi was renowned among his contemporaries as the founder of Coptic–Arabic philology. In fact, this was chiefly in the field of grammar, as no one before him had engaged in describing the Coptic idiom in any language at all. Being Arabized on both the oral and written levels, he naturally had recourse to the Arabic linguistic tradition, whose masters, at that time, happened to be flourishing in Egypt. Thus, the merit of Samannudi's pioneering work lies in having applied the tools worked out for a Semitic language to describe a non-Semitic one. In addition, Coptic presents itself, in many aspects, as an agglutinative language, which separates it widely from the internal flexion system that characterizes the Arabic language.[61]

In point of fact, our Coptic author did not intend to compose a real grammar. In the form of a "concise introduction *(muqaddima)* to the parts of Coptic speech," he merely intended to provide the readers of his 'glossary' (see below) with the basic rudiments that permit the making of "the feminine out of the masculine, the plural out of the singular, the past out of the future, the first or second person out of the third, according to the context." This is the core of the grammatical writing. In fact, the *Scala ecclesiastica* contains the words or lexical units in the grammatical form they take in the first passage of the compiled corpus (biblical and liturgical texts), avoiding as a rule the repetition of similar or analogous forms. So the 'introduction' gives clues to the understanding of alternative occurrences. A second part, ill-assorted and not very learned, showing some recasts and later additions, lists other items considered as peculiar to the Coptic language: orthographic, morphologic, syntactic, and even lexical—including a chapter on homonyms, which will be discussed below.

It is only later that the pioneering endeavor of al-Samannudi was restarted, deepened, and improved by other writers in order to establish a real grammar of Coptic. The literary transmission took account in some way of this continuous chain of more or less homogenous attempts. Approximately one-quarter of the hundred or more Coptic–Arabic philological manuscripts provide a kind of a *Corpus grammaticarum*, occasionally entitled *al-Muqaddimat al-khams* ('The Five Prefaces/Grammars').[62] It generally introduces the vocabularies of al-Mu'taman ibn al-'Assal, Abu al-Barakat ibn Kabar, or both, occasionally that of al-Samannudi.[63]

Obviously, John of Samannud's grammar concerns Bohairic. However, one century later, still before Bishop Athanasius of Qus wrote his Sahidic grammar, it was adapted to the dialect of Upper Egypt. This version shows some modifications and divergences, and attaches more systemically than some Bohairic versions a portion from Ibn al-'Assal's grammar without any formal transition, so that the catalogs' authors and the editors have not noticed this kind of appendix.[64] One very original output is a mixed, comparative-like version of Bohairic and Sahidic which is attested in one old manuscript in Paris, as indicated below (MS no. 5).

Unfortunately there is not yet a critical edition of this pioneering *Muqaddima* of Samannudi, although this is an absolute priority from all points of view. The longer Bohairic version knew three editions, two of them based on one Vatican manuscript from 1319 (below, no. 1), and the third, containing the main part only, on a manuscript in Montpellier dated to 1634 (no. 2). The oldest witness of the grammar, preceding the vocabulary as in the original enterprise, is in a manuscript from 1263 held in Paris (no. 3), and which is worthy of edition or at least collation.[65] The Sahidic version, curiously enough following the vocabulary, was twice edited on the basis of another Paris manuscript from 1389 (no. 4), though not the oldest (no. 5).

1. Vatican, Biblioteca Apostolica Vaticana, copt. 71 (y. 1319), fol. 3r–11r: First piece, starting the aforementioned *Corpus* of

grammars (Hebbelynck and Lantschoot 1937b: 531–37; Sidarus 2012), *editio princeps* with a rather feeble Latin translation by the Jesuit Orientalist Athanasius Kircher (1643: fol. 1v–20r, sic). An earlier, better attempt, but published much later, was made by the Franciscan Thomas Obicini.[66]

2. Montpellier, Faculté de Médecine, H 199 (y. 1634), fol. 1r–26v (preceding the *Scala*). Partially edited and translated by Dulaurier 1949.
3. Paris, BnF, copte 46-I (y. 1263), 137 ff. Samannudi's *muqaddima* preceding the *sullam*. Originally an autonomous MS joined artificially to others in Sahidic.[67]
4. Paris, BnF, copte 44 (y. 1389), fol. 23v–30v: Diplomatic edition by Munier (1930: 47–54a). Second edition with French translation and annotations by Khouzam (2002: 98–127).[68]
5. Paris, BnF, copte 43-I (y. 1310). Originally an autonomous MS from Akhmim, gathered artificially with other Sahidic MSS. The whole volume was entirely restored in 1993 and the folios rearranged and newly foliated according to the meticulous analysis undertaken then by Sidarus (Sidarus 1997). The texts related to Yuhanna al-Samannudi are: a) Sahidic vocabulary, acephalic with other lacunae, on fol. 12r–55r; b) Bohairic–Sahidic 'mixed' grammar unique in its genre, on fol. 55v–69v; c) Bohairic vocabulary, shortened version, on fol. 75r–108v.[69]

As to the vocabulary as such, the *Sullam kana'si* ('Ecclesiastical Vocabulary'), it is but a set of glossaries to the books of the New Testament, to a few from the Old Testament (Psalms, Song of Songs, and extracts from the Wisdom Books), and to some liturgical texts. Aware of the limitations of this endeavor, the half-brother of al-As'ad, whom we met earlier as the author of one of the grammars composed in the wake of *al-Muqaddima al-samannudiya*, made use of *al-Sullam al-samannudi* to make up his own *Scala rimata (al-Sullam al-muqaffa')*, with the purpose of finding the words out of context and also to help compose liturgical hymns (*psalis* and doxologies).[70] On the other hand, Samannudi's Bohairic 'Church glossary' was rendered in Sahidic together with his grammar, and a contemporary reworking of the original Sahidic *Daraj al-sullam (Liber graduum)* tried to fill the lack of the main books of the Old Testament by adding a specific (short) chapter on this matter.[71]

Only the Sahidic version was edited in the same circumstances as the grammar—that is, successively by Munier and Khouzam.[72] For the original Bohairic version, the same comments given above about MS Paris copte 46-I (no. 3) apply equally to it.

It should be emphasized that John of Samannud created another lexical document in the second, longer version of his grammar. It is a glossary of homonymous words which covers homographs, homophones, and even paronyms, as in similar Bohairic works. It reveals some recasts and later additions, as well as some discrepancies with the original version. The Sahidic version must have given origin to the specific corresponding work, now lost, composed in the form of a didactic poem *(urjuza)* by Athanasius of Qus entitled *Bulghat al-talibin . . . fi tajanus al-alfaz al-qibtiyya* ('Fulfillment of the researcher . . . in the matter of Coptic homonyms') (Sidarus 2000a, §4.4; Sidarus 2012: 89–90).

The textual transmission of both grammar and vocabulary poses problems. Out of the huge number of some eighty manuscripts, only a dozen preserve the original double work together. Otherwise, *muqaddima* and *sullam* are conveyed separately, mainly within a set of grammars, as seen above, or together with the two vocabularies of Ibn al-'Assal and Ibn Kabar, often with misleading titles and even with alien prologues. Furthermore, only a small number of the textual witnesses are from the thirteenth and fourteenth centuries; the majority are as late as the eighteenth and nineteenth centuries. Any attempt to gauge the value of any text or to reconstruct family affinities must take all these points into consideration.

It would be redundant to repeat here the extensive listing of manuscripts of both works included in Graf's and Athanasiyus's reference works. Generally speaking, in the inventory undertaken by Graf there is much incongruence and confusion. Athanasiyus's inventory is mainly based on Graf, adding some witnesses from the monasteries in Egypt.[73] A more complete and detailed listing of these manuscripts in particular is given by Sidarus (Sidarus 2001: 75–77). The same applies for two additional London manuscripts largely unknown before Layton's catalog—and to Athanasiyus as well.[74]

On the three Bohairic manuscripts of Munich—Bayerische Staatsbibliothek, copt. 14, 15, and 16—some critical observations were made by Sidarus.[75] Further, Sidarus (2004: 16–18) gives some details and displays the intertwined relationships among a set of some ten manuscripts with Bohairic philological miscellanea from different libraries in Europe and Egypt, where Samannudi's works can be mostly found.

Two further manuscripts with the works of al-Samannudi have appeared recently in the catalog of the Franciscan Center at Giza (Wadi‘ 2009: 49–52):

- Giza, Franciscan Center, no. 16 (y. 1911), fol. 95v–104v (piece no. 7). The grammar at the end of a very particular corpus of grammars. A shorter (earlier?) version could lie under piece no. 4 (pp. 22r–29r) with the incipit: *Bab fi aqsam al-kalam al-qibti* (‘Chapter on the Parts of Coptic Speech’).[76]
- Giza, Franciscan Center, no. 17 (y. 1899), pp. 1–20 (piece no. 1). The grammar introduces the traditional corpus, followed, as usual, by the two vocabularies of Abu al-Barakat ibn Kabar and of al-Mu’taman ibn al-‘Assal. However, the *Qiladat al-tahrir* of Athanasius of Qus (Bohairic version) has slipped in there in the second position (pp. 21–66), and an unidentified, and as such very new, Greek–Bohairic–Arabic vocabulary concludes the miscellany (pp. 336–408). Interestingly enough, in the corresponding colophon the grammar is named *Muqaddimat al-Shaykh al-Samannudi* (‘The [Grammatical] Introduction of the Archon al-Samannudi’). Though it is presented in the heading as *Muqaddimat al-Sullam al-ma‘ruf bi-l-Samannudi*, the vocabulary as such does not appear at all.

As to the transmission of the Sahidic version of both philological works, there is now a comprehensive and critical appraisal of the whole material, including the many fragments and some Bohairic items, in Sidarus 2000b.

Notes

1 Khater and Khs-Burmester 1974: 321r; Samu’il and Dawud 1987: 165 (here with a textual lacuna). See also below the title of "Dean of the Bishops." On Pope Kyrillos and his time, apart from these two essential sources, see the historical sketch based on them, but to be read with caution, outlined by Nakhla 1951a. A critical and sociopolitical appraisal is given by Swanson 2010: 83–95 (ch. 6); see also Swanson 2012b. See further the monograph by Werthmuller 2010, based mainly on the correspondence archive of the patriarch (unique for the Middle Ages!). Otherwise, the information in the following reference works is deficient or outdated: Graf 1947: 360–69 (§116); Athanasiyus 2012: 422–36; Labib 1991e: 677a–677b. I am very grateful to Dr. Rachad Shoucri (Kingston, Ontario) for his linguistic review.

2 Graf 1947: 371, followed by Athanasiyus 2012: 422.

3 On the question of whether these two are the same person, see the portrait of the metropolitan in question at the beginning of MS 16 of Munich, discussed in the last section of this chapter.

4 See, for example, one colophon in MS Cairo, CopMus., Biblical 94, fol. 130v (see below, MS 2 in the section "Coptic–Arabic New Testament"), where the prototype used in the copying of the Pauline Epistles is said to be "in the handwriting *(bi-khatt)* of Anba Yu'annis, Bishop of Samannud, known as *(al-ma'ruf bi-)* al-Samannudi."

5 The same case applies to the well-known Bishop Yusab of Fuwwa, whose name before he became monk was Yusuf (Joseph); he maintained it as monk and bishop in that Coptic alternative form (Khater and Khs-Burmester 1974: 336v).

6 Incidentally, Muyser (1944: 154, *ad* p. 30, 1) states the same opinion, though it is not appropriate in the context in question. In any case, see the emblematic case of the celebrated bishop of Misr/Old Cairo Bulus al-Bushi, native of the village of Bush/Poushin in Middle Egypt. Note, by the way, the use of the same *nisba* by a Muslim *'alim* or *faqih* named 'Awad mentioned in the *History of the Patriarchs*: Khater and Khs-Burmester 1974: 320r; Samu'il and Dawud 1987: 163.

7 See the different versions and respective editions of the *History of the Patriarchs*, the essential of which is outlined by Swanson 2010: 6–8. Or see Müller 1991a: 1337a–1338b.

8 Timm 1987–92: 2254–62; Seeliger and Krumeich 2007: 13 (with the pertinent date indication on p. 7). The entry by R. Stewart in the *Coptic Encyclopedia* (Stewart 1991g: 2090a) is somewhat poor.

9 Munier 1943b: 39 #21, and 40 #6; Muyser 1944: 158–59. Mikhail 2014a: 63 refers inadvertently to another bishop of the same see with the name John, under Patriarch Michael/Kha'il (no. 46, r. 744–68); his actual name was Isaac.

10 Timm 1984–92: 1061–62. The Arabic sources show a great instability in the graphic rendering of the village's name, which corresponds today to Shubra Millis or Millas, a few kilometers southwest of Bana Abu Sir, district of Zifta. We will meet Bana, an old bishopric, again below.

11 See, too, for John V and Cosmas II, the different versions and respective editions of the History of the Patriarchs, the essential of which is outlined by Swanson 2010: 31–32, 35, 77–79. Or see Labib 1991f: 1340a–1341a and Labib 1991c: 636b–637b respectively. For the sequence numbers and the dates, we follow the ones adopted in the Coptic Encyclopedia: Atiya 1991e.

12 Timm 1984–92: 2259; Mikhail 2014a: 120 (with references to the sources). One must take into account the proximity of the military camp of Mahalla (al-Kubra).

13 Munier 1943b: 30–31; Muyser 1944: 154–55. Listing commented and put in context by Graf 1927.

14 See the *History of the Patriarchs* attributed to him (Samu'il and Dawud 1987: 179) near the end, where the text needs to be corrected according to what is said here.

15 Samu'il and Dawud 1987: 167–69. See also Nakhla 1951a: 29–32.

16 Graf 1947: 361–63 (§116.1–2); Athanasiyus 2012: 386–91. See also Khater and Khs-Burmester 1974: 327v–329r; Samu'il and Dawud 1987: 175–76; Nakhla 1951a: 103–105.

17 Samu'il and Dawud 1987: 179–81. See also Swanson 2010: 97–98; Samir 1985: 624–27.

18 Sidarus 2010: 317–18; see also 324–27; in the former shorter English version 2002: 145–46.

19 Heide 2014. See also Graf 1944: 388 (§104, [7 bis]) and Follet and Overwien 2016, where a section on the oriental versions is to be found (the volume is still in press; I owe the information to the kindness of the chief editor). For a contextualization within the reception of Greek wisdom by the Copts, see Sidarus 2013c: 351.

20 Heide 2014: *passim*. Text ed. on pp. 113–34 (§IV); German trans. on pp. 167–96 (§VII); linguistic analysis by Stefan Weninger on pp. 45–59 (§I.6).

21 In Heide's listing of the MSS, these copies are identified as P09 (sic) and P50. In the reading of the colophon of the first MS (Heide 2014: 11), *fama 'ana* should be corrected to *mimma* . . . , or repeat *'ana*. This results in the statement that the writing in question "reproduces the worthy work of translation from Coptic into Arabic by . . ." (*mimma 'ana bi-ikhrajihi min al-qibti ila al-'arabi* . . .). As to MS 275 (no. 2), note that the copyist is Ibn Quzman (Yusuf b. 'Atiyya *al-ma'ruf bi-* . . .), who lends his name to the recently discovered Coptic Arabic version of the *Alexander Romance*, which is sometimes found associated with the text under consideration, as in MS no. 3 (see the following note). As a matter of fact, Heide totally ignores the historical figure of Samannudi, making no mention of Graf or the *Coptic Encyclopedia*.

22 Wadi' 2006: 19–20. The information and the text were checked personally by me. On the second and last piece, which provides a Copto-Arabic version of the *Alexander Romance* in the line of Pseudo-Callisthenes, see Sidarus 2013a: 481.

23 According to the digital catalog available at the monastery. The text is followed by the lives of St. Antony and St. Paul of Thebes.

24 Heide 2014: 69–111 (§III), 139–66 (§VI). The relationships with the original Greek version are discussed on pp. 35–39 (§I.5). Before, on pp. 4–9 (§I.1.2), the author considers the relevance of the Arabic version together with the Ethiopian, which depends on it.

25 Perry 1964: 59–64, appendix 3. Information taken from Heide 2014: 3–4, 15.

26 Heide 2014: 14–17 (§I.3.2), with reproduction samples of the MSS on pp. 18–26.

27 Troupeau 1972: 35, 118, 272. Nothing of this is mentioned in Heide 2014 (Sigel P49, P50, P10; reference by means of two digits only). By identifying the Paris MSS, this author quotes older catalogs or inventories besides the most accurate and qualified catalog of Troupeau. Nonetheless, Troupeau, following Graf, overlooked Perry's edition, which is chiefly established on the basis of the BnF MSS.

28 The number 3 refers to the position in the original autonomous MS; it is the final item (17) of the whole collectanea. In the same line, the date 1606 given by Troupeau and Heide pertains to one of the three groups of texts or MSS bound together.

29 The text follows excerpts from the *Mukhtar al-hikam* by al-Mubashshir ibn Fatik (d. 1106?), about which see Sidarus 2013a: 484–85; Sidarus 2013c: 352.

30 Obviously the readings of the MS *SKND(Y)S* or *'SKNDRS* ('Alexander') apply to Secundus. In his identification of the MS, Heide (Sigel K) makes no reference to Simaika nor to the actual call number.

31 In Heide 2014: 16 the MS has no identification sigel, and it was not collated for the edition. Secundus text appears before a story on Alexander the Great; compare with the next MS and the Maadi MS (above, no. 3).

32 According to Heide Sigel K, this witness shows affinities with the Bodleian MS (below, no. 16), and both of these with the Geez version. On the former piece

no. 11, concerning a short account about Alexander the Great, see Sidarus 2013a: 484, with the *Annexe* on pp. 494–95.

33 Corresponding to no. 55 in Nicoll's catalog (1821: 58–59). See Heide Sigel O. Compare with what was said on the preceding MS in the previous footnote.

34 Del Río Sánchez 2008: 111–12. Corresponds to Sigel A in Heide's nomenclature. It is mentioned in Graf 1947: 495 as Sbath 1004, and as Sbath Fihris 2398 in the Addenda to Graf 1944 (see above), and was later inserted at the end of the reprint edition of this volume in 1966, p. 679.

35 Heide Sigel S. In Graf's listing it corresponds to Leningrad, Sammlung Gregor IV, no. 31.

36 Notice the existence in Coptic of a similar work by Patriarch John III the Merciful (see above), known as "The Questions of Theodore," on biblical issues (CPC 0180), edited and translated by Lantschoot (1957). See also Lantschoot 1958.

37 The slashes in the title are intended to indicate the *saj'* or rhymed composition.

38 The information is given by Wadi' 1997b: 467 (end of §44) without any allusion to item no. 3 in Graf's listing (p. 374), and blindly repeated in Athanasiyus's listing as an autonomous item no. 5 (2012: 446). Consequently, and according to a correct rendering of Graf's account (1947: no. 3), the three items nos. 2, 3, and 5 in that listing must be conflated. Obviously in item no. 3, the Arabic title given to the work under consideration reflects a back translation of Graf's German version and not the one stated in the manuscript.

39 But belonging to the episcopal see of Bana/Panaw as attested in the *passio*, either in Coptic or in Arabic. In Late Antiquity the see's name was Kynopolis Kato, to which also belongs al-Bandara, the homeland of St. Paphnutius, whom we will meet below. See Timm 1984–92: 318–24; and also Seeliger and Krumeich 2007: 10, 17–18.

40 The first toponym was not found in the reference works. Al-Bandara corresponds to Coptic Telpentourot and lies nowadays in the Samta District, not far away from Bana. On al-Qurashiya (this is the correct spelling; the catalog spelling is erroneous) in the same district, only some two kilometers south of Bana, see Timm 1984–92: 2171–72. Paphnutius's martyrdom is narrated in the next and last piece of the manuscript (fol. 116r–170v), as in other collections.

41 Zanetti 1986: no. 321: a commentary of the lectionary of Holy Week (y. 1614). The author says about these remains, which he dates to the fourteenth century: "fragment d'histoires monastiques (il semble s'agir de S. Jean de Šarmoulos)," referring to Graf 1944: 534, ll. 8 ff. It is difficult to see how the author connects his own evaluation of the content with what is said in Graf's laconic presentation of the text under consideration (according to the Paris MS, no. 5 above): "Martyrium und Wunder," nothing more.

42 CPC = Clavis Patrum Copticorum, in Tito Orlandi, *Corpus dei Manoscriti Copti Letterari*, http://www.cmlc.it/. BHO = Bibliotheca Hagiographica Orientalis (Brussels: Société Bollandiste). See now chapter 20 in the present volume, by Y.N. Youssef. His late dating of this Coptic text (fourteenth century) must be revisited according to what is said here.

43 Hebbelynck and Lantschoot 1937b: 413–16. Artistic study by Leroy 1974: 180–81 (no. 25); see also pp. 213, 231, and Pl. 99 (cf. fig. 1 here). We do not know why

Leroy omitted the description of the first painting, about which the catalog's authors give no clue.

44 Hebbelynck and Lantschoot 1937b: 416. It is edited and translated in Davis 1919: 320, but with an entirely different reading of the copyist's name (including the segment *bi-tarikh* . . .), which can be rejected according to the authoritative reading and appraisal of the catalog's authors. Interesting is the Arabic use of *wil(i) teki* (from Coptic–Greek *bubletheke*) and *qastali* (from Coptic–Greek *kastalis/on?*), later *qasr*, 'the fortified keep tower'. The first item is attested in Ibn Kabar's *Scala magna*, ed. Kircher 1643: 218.

45 Edition and translation by Hyvernat 1886b: 174–201.

46 Graf 1947: 414 (§127.8); Samir 1985: 624–31 (information gleaned from the *History of the Patriarchs* and manuscript colophons, with text edition and translation); MacCoull 1996; Bigoul 2007. See also Swanson 2010: 98–100; in connection with the copy of the Arabic *Pandectes* by Nikon of the Black Mountain (Antioch, eleventh century) that he mentions, see some details in Sidarus 2013b: 202n44 (with further literature).

47 Sidarus 1975: 23 with notes 82–83 and Doc. 9. See more below at the identification of the manuscripts.

48 Leroy 1974: 113–48 (nos. 16–17). See also some considerations with further bibliographical information in Sidarus 2002: 150–51; Sidarus 2010: 323–24.

49 See for example: Leroy 1974: 110–13 (no. 15), 148–57 (nos. 18–19), 178–80 (no. 24).

50 These are: al-As'ad Abu al-Faraj Hibatallah ibn al-'Assal, 'Alam al-Ri'asa Abu Ishaq Ibrahim ibn Katib Qaysar, and al-Wajih Yuhanna al-Qalyubi. See Graf 1947: 403–407 (§126), 387 (§122), and 375 (§120) in conjunction with Graf 1944: 162–63 (§35.3) and 179 (§39.2). See also the respective chapters in Athanasiyus's Arabic rendering (2012) of Graf's volume of 1947. On the Gospel translation of the first, see now the critical edition with a lengthy introduction by Moawad 2014a; see also Samir 1994. His Bohairic grammar is edited in a "diplomatic" way from one (old and good) MS by Wadi' 2005. On the scholar as such, see Wadi' 1997a: 89–96; some particulars and further information in Sidarus 2013b: 196–97 and *passim*. There is a recent updated notice on Ibn Katib Qaysar in Swanson 2012a.

51 Sidarus 2010: 318–19. In a shorter exposition of the general topic: Sidarus 2002: 146.

52 Langlois 1926: 28; Leroy 1974: 157–74 (MS no. 21) and plates 75–92. Among the bibliographical data provided by the authors, particular notice should be taken of Baumstark 1915, where the textual value is emphasized. See further MacCoull 1996: 393.

53 Macomber counts 221 ff. (probably according to the original folios or foliotation). Thus his references display two digits less than all the other authors. Artistic description and analysis by Leroy 1974: 174–77 (MS no. 22) and plates 93–95, 20.2 (where the MS number is to be corrected in 146). Further bibliography is provided there. Similarly, Hunt 1994: 404–405 (no. 2, with some inaccuracies) and 408–409 (figs. 2–3). Notice the reproductions nos. xxix–xxx in Simaika's catalog. As pointed out by Leroy, our MS was studied by many scholars and was displayed in many international expositions. Among the studies undertaken, the one by Cramer 1964 (together with other studies by her) must be underlined. See

more recently Abu al-Hamid 1981, where in ch. 1 the author studies this copy by Gabriel, together with other illuminated Coptic Arabic MSS, pointing out their founding achievement in the general framework of book art in the Ayyubid epoch. To that extent, Hunt's general appraisal (1994: 403)—"Many of the later manuscripts [from the fourteenth century] display a closer overlap with Islamic book production"—needs to be corrected and refined.

54 Crum 1905: no. 736 and 786. See further a full description by Horner 1898: ci ff. (MS H_2). The Coptic text was studied and edited by Horner and served as the main prototype for the critical edition of the text.

55 Both Simaika and Graf refer to the Pauline epistles only. Furthermore, Graf's description is very laconic and he has misinterpreted the actual dating.

56 Hunt 1994: 403. The publication of the final study by the author together with L.S.B. MacCoull, under the title *The Survey of the Illustrated Manuscripts in the Coptic Museum, Old Cairo*, has been announced for 2016. I am in debt to the kindness of Professor Hunt for this information and others she forwarded to me.

57 Samir 1985: 629–30; Leroy 1974: 177–78 (MS no. 23) + pl. 109.1; MacCoull 1996: 394. Notice the reproduction no. xxxiii in Simaika's catalog. After the Arabic colophon, there is a note on fol. 347r–346v (sic) concerning the divergences between the Coptic and Arabic translations of the Gospels, which could provide some clue about the real origin of both texts. For the Coptic and a general description of the MS, see the observations of Horner 1898: lxxxv–xciii. On the *arkhon* and his offspring, see Samir 1985: 628–32; Wadi' 1997a: 116–22; Sidarus 2013b: 190 (table 1) and 198.

58 The restitution of the last element in the onomastical chain is based on the graphical shape *(rasm)* together with what we know of the genealogy of the Banu al-'Asal, on which see Sidarus 2013b: 190–91, 195–96.

59 Zanetti's catalog (1986), where they have the same serial numbers.

60 Bigoul 2007. I was not able to check the paper and get more details on the manuscripts. My information comes from Swanson 2010: 199n4.

61 For further information on this point and the material that follows, see Sidarus 2000a; Sidarus 2001; Sidarus 2003. Actually these three essays are complementary.

62 The five grammars are those by al-Samannudi, Ibn Katib Qaysar, al-As'ad Abu al-Faraj ibn al-'Asal, al-Wajih al-Qalyubi, and al-Thiqa ibn al-Duhayri. There are also the grammatical works of Abu Shakir ibn al-Rahib and of Athanasius of Qus. On the generalization of the term *muqaddima* ('foreword, introduction') for a Coptic grammar, see Sidarus 2000a, §1.2; Sidarus 2001: 64. For the *Liber graduum* mentioned there, see now the critical presentation by Sidarus 2016.

63 See now the last report by Sidarus 2012.

64 See Sidarus 2000b: 290–91 (T19). This annexing in Bohairic may have originated from some corpora in which Ibn al-'Assal's grammar follows Samannudi's.

65 For further manuscripts, see below.

66 Lantschoot 1948: 4–63 (with Latin and Italian translation and occasional collation of MS 70 from the same library).

67 Sidarus 2000b: 277 (M6) together with 288 (T12) and 290 (T17). It was copied on behalf of a certain al-Shaykh al-As'ad. Contrary to what was suggested in

the references, the archon in question cannot be identified with Abu al-Faraj ibn al-'Assal, as the oldest copy of his translation of the Four Gospels, from the beginning of 1260, mentions him with the eulogy for the dead; Moawad 2014a: x; Wadi' 1997a: 96. On the other hand, there is a third archon with the same title, referred to in the *History of the Patriarchs* (Samu'il and Dawud 1987: 171–72) as al-As'ad Abu al-Karam, the grandson of the sister of Pope John VI, Kyrillos's predecessor (r. 1189–1216). See Nakhla 1951a: 94–95.

68 A new and full description of the MS by Khouzam 2002: xxv–xxxiv. Some critical considerations in Sidarus 2000b: 274–76 (M4).

69 Sidarus 1997: 298–302, 309–10. See also Sidarus 2000b: 273–74 (M1) in connection with T11 + T13 (p. 288) and T18 (p. 290).

70 Kircher 1643: 273–495. A recent presentation by Wadi' 1997a: 163–70. Completing information in Sidarus 2012: 96–97. A critical evaluation, with a discussion about the date of the composition and other aspects, can be found in Sidarus 2004: 6–12.

71 Sidarus 2016: 572 (§4), 577 (§5); see also the various tables.

72 Munier 1930: 1–43; Khouzam 2002: 8–93. In MS 44 (no. 4 above), the pertinent folios are 2r–23r.

73 In both listings the (old) 'Coptic' call numbers are no longer relevant. The so-called inventory serial number refers now to the Coptic collection.

74 Layton 1987: nos. 254–55 (oriental 8775 + 8789).

75 Sidarus 1975: 80–83, with corrections and additions in Sidarus 2004: 19. Consequently the *Scala ecclesiastica* appears in MS 16 on fol. 50r–84v precisely.

76 Actually, Samannudi's grammar often opens with those words. On the other hand, the *incipit* of this particular grammar (piece no. 7) corresponds to the one that frequently begins the corpus of 'The Five Grammars,' introducing the vocabularies referred to in the next item and elsewhere in this paper.

15 The Arabic Version of the Miracles of Apa Mina

Based on Two Unpublished Manuscripts in the Collection of the St. Shenouda the Archimandrite Coptic Society in Los Angeles

Hany N. Takla

Introduction

Egyptian texts concerning Apa Mina have came down to us in Sahidic and Arabic as hagiographic texts and in Bohairic mostly as liturgical texts.[1] From the Hamuli texts published by James Drescher (Drescher 1946), we see three distinct hagiographic/literary texts that survived complete or nearly complete in Sahidic: his martyrdom; his miracles, whose composition is attributed to Theophilus, Archbishop of Alexandria; and an encomium or eulogy by John, Archbishop of Alexandria. A liturgical text about him in Sahidic is found in the Hamuli Antiphonarium that was edited recently by Maria Cramer and Martin Krause (Cramer and Krause 2008: 110, 111). In Bohairic we find mostly liturgical texts in the form of doxologies and *psalis*, as well as Difnar entries published by De Lacy O'Leary (O'Leary 1926–30: 1:61–62; 3:18–19). In Arabic manuscripts, we have both the literary/hagiographic texts and the liturgical ones. This chapter will deal primarily with the Arabic text of the *Miracles of Apa Mina* as found in manuscript ML.MS.166 in the manuscript collection of St. Shenouda the Archimandrite Coptic Society in Los Angeles, and to a lesser extent with that of a digital copy of a manuscript brought to the Society in 2008 from Mar Mina Monastery in Maryut. It is catalogued as Ms.Mar.Mena.2 in the collection. The research on this text is still in its preliminary stages.

New Manuscripts

ML.MS.166

This manuscript was privately acquired in April 2014 from a Turkish dealer, from whom the St. Shenouda Society previously procured several manuscripts in its collection through eBay auctions. As usual, he did not offer any information about its history or provenance. The manuscript contains several works that may give some hints about the scribe and its provenance. It is a paper codex measuring 23.3 × 17.6 cm but has been remargined to fit into the current twentieth-century tight binding. Only 355 folios have survived, with at least one page of text missing in the beginning and an indeterminate number of folios at the end. The page numbering indicates that it may have been originally two separate manuscripts that were bound together, though the scribe is most likely the same person. Part 1 has 254 folios with text area 19.2 × 12.3 cm, with each column having fifteen lines. Part 2 has 101 folios with text area of 18–18.5 × 13 cm, with each column having between thirteen and fifteen lines. Part 1 is numbered originally in Arabic numerals on the recto of each folio with some exceptions. Part 2 does not have any physical numbers visible. There are no illuminations, but there are some margin texts by the original scribe to complete missing sentences. There are also later additions in modern blue ink, possibly by the last owner. It is written in black ink with the headings of each work written in red; sometimes subheadings are in red, though this is inconsistent. Watermarks that can be ascertained are either horizontal or vertical lines spaced 2.6 cm apart. There is no colophon at the end of each part except for indicating the conclusion of each of the works. The included works are mostly hagiographic and literary with no logical order. Its contents are as follows.

Part 1

f.1r–1v: missing
f.2r–22r: *Life* of Paul the monk, commemorated on 16 Ba'una
f.22v–39r: *Life* of St. Helena the Syrian (Mother of Emperor Constantine)
f.39v–40r: *Madiha* (hymn) for the fast of the Apostles
f.40v: blank
f.41r–141r: *Life* of St. Takla Haymanout
f.141v: *Vision of St. Pisentius* (title only)
f.142rv: blank
f.143r–163v: *Vision of St. Pisentius* (text)

f.164r–174r: Bayan Kamil Fadl Yawm al-Ahad wa Hiya al-Mas'ala al-Sadisa
f.174r–185v: Bayan Sabab Sawm al-Arba'a wa-l-Jum'a wa Hiya al-Mas'ala al-Sabi'a
f.186r–221v: *Vision of St. Gregory the Theologian*
f.222r–236r: *Vision of St. Shenouda the Archimandrite*
f.236v–254r: *Miracles of the Lord Jesus While He Was a Child* (including later miracles)
f.254v–255v: blank

Part 2

f.256r–307r: *Miamar* ('treatise' or 'discourse') of St. George by Theodosius of Jerusalem
f.307v–356v: *Miracles of Apa Mina*
f.357r–end: missing

Ms.Mar.Mena.2

This is a digitized private manuscript of unknown provenance that was repaired and photographed by Mar Mina Monastery in Maryut at an unspecified date. Folio dimensions are 22 × 16 cm per Fr. Polycarpos Avamena.[2] Text area is approximately 18.5 × 12.1 cm.[3] Arabic page numbers were added at a later date on each page, though not visible on every page, starting with the first page of text. Based on the digital copy, the manuscript has 215 folios, though the last page number on the verso of the last folio is 421. There is a colophon on folio 215v with a date of 1 Misra with a blank space where the Coptic year would be mentioned, though a Hijri year is written as 1180. This would correspond to AD 1760. No other codicological information was available. This manuscript is important because it includes a different version of the *Miracles of Apa Mina* from the one found in ML.MS.166.

Its contents are as follows.

f.1r: A modern Italian picture of the Lord Jesus in his youth
f.1v: A modern owner's (Kamel Shehata Ibrahim) inscription, dated 12 Tut AM 1627 (September 23 AD 1921)
f.2r–20v: *Miamar* of the *Martyrdom of Apa Mina* (15 Hatur)
f.21r–51v: *Miracles of Apa Mina* (seventeen miracles)
f.52r–56v: Homily of Ablawanus of Ephesus on Archangel Michael (12 Kiyahk)

f.57r–62r: Homily of Cyril of Jerusalem on the Twenty-four Priests (24 Hatur)
f.62v: Letter and heading illumination
f.63r–76r: *Life* of Abu Fana (25 Amshir)
f.76v: blank
f.77r–86v: *Martyrdom* of Salib the New Martyr (3 Kiyahk)
f.87r–99v: *Martyrdom* of Abnudi (3 Ba'una)
f.100r–113v: *Martyrdom* of Abaskhirun (7 Ba'una)
f.114r–119v: *Miamar* of Julius of Aqfahs on St. Abaskhirun (7 Kiyahk)
f.120r–124v: *Vision of Athanasius of Jerusalem*
f.125r: blank
f.125v–127r: *Madiha* (hymn) for Apa Mina
f.127v: blank
f.128r–139v: *Miracles of the Child Jesus*
f.140r–163r: *Miamar* of Timothy of Alexandria concerning Gabal al-Tayr
f.163v: blank
f.164r–170v: *On the Four Incorporeal Creatures* by John Chrysostom (8 Hatur)
f.171r–179v: *Miamar* of Jacob of Sarug on the Sacrifice of Abraham
f.180r–187r: On the Repose of Abraham the Patriarch
f.187v: blank
f.188r–193r: On the Repose of Isaac the Patriarch
f.193v: blank
f.194r–197r: On the Repose of Jacob the Patriarch
f.197v: blank
f.198r–215v: *Martyrdom* of St. James the Sawn-asunder (27 Hatur)
f.215v: Colophon dated AH 1180 (AD 1766/7)[4]

Analysis

Provenance of the manuscripts

ML.MS.166

According to the Turkish dealer from whom we purchased the manuscript, all his manuscripts came from Upper Egypt. The presence of the *Visions* of St. Pisentius and St. Shenouda along with the life of St. Takla Haymanout would be typical for an Upper Egyptian manuscript. Because the quality of the script is not the workmanship of a professional scribe, it is believed that the original owner was most likely its scribe. In the inside of the new binding there is an inscription in blue ink of the name "Talaat Ayad Attala Ebeid." The use of the quad name became common in the Nasser era in the 1950s and later. Thus, this would probably indicate that the binding is from that era. There is also another version of the name used inside the text in multiple places, which indicates that his family name is al-Birbawy. As many of the family names refer to the original village or town they came from, we can safely assume that this owner/scribe would have come from a place called Birba. This name is commonly used to refer to some ancient Egyptian temple that would have existed in the area. According to Mohammad Ramzi, there is a village with this name in the Girga Province in Upper Egypt, south of the modern-day Sohag/Akhmim area (Ramzi 1953–68: 2.4:108). He also lists its Coptic name as Tin, which is also listed in Stefan Timm's geographical dictionary (Timm 1984–92: 6:2682–85). It can also be assumed that the last owner may have been the inheritor of the manuscript rather than the original scribe, which would have been someone from an older generation, possibly a lay person living in that town in the mid-nineteenth century. As is the case for many of these manuscripts, the family members of the owner would have sold it to an agent of this Turkish dealer after the owner's passing. The contents of this codex probably came from multiple manuscripts in the region. The relationship of the Apa Mina text to St. Paul or St. Antony manuscripts will be discussed later in this chapter.

Ms.Mar.Mena. 2

Manuscripts that were brought to Mar Mina Monastery in Maryut for repair and photographing have come from various locations throughout Egypt. Fayoum is a very probable origin for this manuscript on the basis of the contents, the *Miracles of Mar Mina* having the same structure as the Sahidic one found in Archangel Michael Monastery at Phantoou, near the modern Fayoum village of al-Hamuli, now kept at the Pierpont Morgan Library in New York (Depuydt 1993: ciii–cxi).

Contents

Manuscripts

The text of the Sahidic Coptic version of the *Miracles of Mar Mina* has appeared in several scholarly publications by Walter Ewing Crum (Crum 1905: 156–57),[5] Henri Hyvernat (Hyvernat 1922b; 1922c), James Drescher

(Drescher 1946), Paul Devos (Devos 1960a), and most recently Seÿna Bacot (Bacot 2011). However, little scholarly work was done on the Arabic version of the *Miracles of Mar Mina* until 1993, when Felicitas Jaritz published in Germany a large volume on the Arabic texts related to Apa Mina. In it, she listed twenty-five manuscripts from Egyptian collections, but only sixteen included the miracles. The items in the list below are referenced by Jaritz designation.[6]

Cairo Coptic Museum: MSS F, M
Cairo Patriarchal Library: MSS A, R, Ṭ (3)
St. Antony Monastery: MSS Ṣ, Ẓ
St. Macarius Monastery: MSS Q, H
St. Paul Monastery: MSS Ğ, Ḫ
Suryan Monastery: MSS D, N, Ī
St. Catherine Monastery, Sinai: MSS Š, L

They range in date from the thirteenth century for the Sinai manuscripts to AD 1757–78 for manuscript Ṣ from St. Antony Monastery.

Attribution

Eight of the sixteen manuscripts do not have an author attribution for the collection (MSS Ḫ, Ī, A, Q, R, D, L, Ṭ). One of the early ones, which is similar to the Greek collection of these miracles, is attributed to Timothy of Alexandria (MS Š). The seemingly longer version is attributed to Mazdarius, archimandrite of the mount of Niaton,[7] which Jaritz mistakenly assumed to be Natrun (Jaritz 1993: 160 and n715). This attribution is found in five of the manuscripts (MSS M, Ğ, Ṣ, Ẓ, H), though the fourteenth-century MS M from the Coptic Museum did not agree in the contents and arrangements with the other four. Only the seventeenth-century MS F of the Coptic Museum indicates just a bishop of Alexandria as the author. ML.MS.166 does not have an attribution at the beginning of the text and the end is missing. Ms.Mar. Mena.2 mentions the name of Theophilus, Patriarch of Alexandria, as the author at the end of the text. However, there is a blank space in the beginning of the text where one would have expected to see such attribution.

Order of miracles

Jaritz lists all the miracle number variants among the sixteen manuscripts as well as the two Sahidic manuscripts published by Drescher from the Hamuli collection M590 and M585 (Jaritz 1993: 154–60). Using the data from her listing, the number and order of the miracles can be compared to the two unpublished manuscripts being discussed. First, the Ms.Mar.Mena.2 has the same exact order of the seventeen miracles as the Sahidic M590, which would allow us to reconstruct the large lacuna in Drescher's edition. Those two significantly differ from all the other manuscripts that Jaritz used, as well as from ML.MS.166. On the other hand, ML.MS.166, the primary manuscript in this discussion, is nearly identical to the order found in the two manuscripts from St. Paul Monastery and the two from St. Antony Monastery. Those four range in date from AD 1702 to 1758. There are minor differences between these four manuscripts based on Jaritz's listing, but it seems clear that ML.MS.166 had a parent text based either on one of these four or on a common one on which all five were based. Consequently, it can safely be assumed that it would have contained three more miracles in the missing part at its end, to agree with these other manuscripts.

Returning to our primary manuscript, we observe the following divisions in the text of the *Miracles of Apa Mina* as compared with Ms.Mar.Mena.2 (MM) and Jaritz 1993 (J).

f.307v–316v: Abbreviated *Life* of Apa Mina
f.316v–318r: First miracle: Man with the barren camel (MM1, J17)
f.318r–318v: Second miracle: Anastas the pig thief (MM5, J18)
f.318v–319v: Third miracle: Pagan man of Alexandria and his barren horse (MM6, J19)
f.319v–321v: Fourth miracle: Eight people from Alexandria and raising of the pigs (MM7, J20)
f.321v–325r: Fifth miracle: Jewish man of Alexandria and his Christian neighbor (MM8, J10)
f.325v–327v: Sixth miracle: Lame man and mute woman (MM9, J11)
f.327v–330v: Seventh miracle: Syrian man raised from the dead (MM2, J5)
f.330v–333v: Eighth miracle: Atrabius and the silver plates (MM3, J7)
f.333v–336r: Ninth miracle: Three men and their pigs (MM10, J12)
f.336r–338r: Tenth miracle: Rich man and donated wood (MM11–12, J13–14)
f.338r–339r: Eleventh miracle: Man and pig meat changing to stone (not in MM, J21–22)
f.339v–341r: Twelfth miracle: Widow and the soldier (MM13, J4)

f.341r–345v: Thirteenth miracle: Rich pagan man of Constantinople and the widow (MM14, J15)
f.346r–347r: Fourteenth miracle: Epileptic man of Alexandria (MM15, J24)
f.347r–351v: Fifteenth miracle: Sick Samaritan woman (MM16, J23)
f.351v–355v: Sixteenth miracle: Childless woman and the soldier (MM4, J9)
f.355v–[337r]: Seventeenth miracle: Philatika and the beautiful girl (not in MM, J2)

The probable missing miracles are as follows:
[Eighteenth miracle: Hebrew man and his demon-possessed son (not in MM, J3)]
[Nineteenth miracle: The thieves and the stolen wine compartment with the snake (not in MM, J8)]
[Twentieth miracle: Alexander the poor man and the borrowed gold (not in MM, J6)]

Themes and common elements

ML.MS.166 has many common elements, themes, or motifs among the miracles included in it. Some of these are as follows.

- The Church of the Saint in Maryut referred to as al-Bay'at[8]
- Reneging on vow to the Church and its bad consequences (1, 8, 11)
- Appearance of the saint:
  - In a vision (1, 6)
  - In person (2, 3, 8, 9, 11, 16)
  - In person anonymously (4, 12, 14, 15)
- Serving the Church as a result of the miracle (1, 12, 14, 15, 16)
- Healing (6, 12, 14, 15, 16)
- Raising from the dead (7, 9)
- Dying as a result of sin (2, 5, 13)
- Evil soldiers (10, 12, 15, 16)
- Good non-Christian and evil Christian (5, 15)
- Evil non-Christian (13)
- Animals:
  - Camels (1)

Horses, mostly ridden by St. Mina (3, 4, 5, 6, 7, 9, 10, 11, 12, 13, 15, 16)
Pigs (2, 4, 9, 10, 11, 14)
Sheep (13)

Summary of the miracles

The following is a brief description of the content of each miracle found in ML.MS.166.

Miracle 1

A camel herder had a barren camel. He prayed that if it gave birth, he would donate the young camel to the church of Apa Mina. The devil entered his heart and he reneged on his vow. He repeated the same request three times, and similarly ignored his vow all three times. Finally, Apa Mina appeared and took all three of the young camels, plus their mother, and placed them in the church. The camel herder was informed of what happened by a vision that night. He went to the church to investigate, and eventually gave all his money to the church and became their camel herder.

Miracle 2

A certain Anastas used to raid the pig herd of the church, and steal and eat them. One day when he did this, he cut the pig into big pieces and brought them to his house. When he decided to go again and steal some more, he found the pig's meat turned to stone. As he was going to steal at night, Apa Mina appeared to him and rebuked him for not recognizing the miracle of the pig meat turning to stone. As a punishment, Apa Mina turned him to half-man, half-stone. Eventually he was brought to the church and he died there.

Miracle 3

A rich man from Alexandria was a practicing pagan. He prayed to the saint that his very valuable yet barren horse would give birth, vowing three-quarters of its fruit to the church. The mare gave birth to a foal with three limbs. That night Apa Mina appeared to him, telling him that he gave him what he had asked for, and that his idol could give him the fourth limb. Consequently, he repented and converted to Christianity and donated all his money and efforts to the Church.

Miracle 4

Eight men from Alexandria pooled their resources and bought a pig to present it to the church steward with half (of the proceeds?) to be given to the Church and the other half to be spent on them. Before they boarded the ship going there, the devil killed the pig on shore, and they felt unworthy and decided to cancel their journey. Apa Mina appeared to them without their recognizing him, and he eventually brought the pig to life again and disappeared. They brought the pig to the church and donated all of it there, and stayed seven days telling the pilgrims about this miracle.

Miracle 5

A rich Jewish Alexandrian merchant used to deposit all his money with his Christian neighbor every time he traveled. After doing this for six years, the Christian conspired with his wife to keep the money because there was no witness. The Jewish man told him that if he would go to the church of Apa Mina and swear to them that he did not take anything from him, he would not ask for the money again. Eventually the saint sent a message through a third person to the wife to have her return the money. The Christian died as a result of his action and the Jewish man converted.

Miracle 6

This interesting story is about a lame man and a mute woman who came to the festival of the saint at the church. The saint appeared to him in a vision and told him to crawl and sleep with the woman in her bed. He refused to do this, until a third vision prompted him to comply. When he crawled there as he was asked and touched the woman, she was terrified. He jumped up and ran, and the mute woman began arguing with him. After the situation was explained to the angry crowd that gathered, they all recognized the saint's action.

Miracle 7

A prominent Syrian Orthodox merchant came to Alexandria for business and, upon hearing of the wonders of the saint, he decided to visit the church bearing gifts. On the way he spent the night with a marketplace merchant, who killed and dismembered him when he saw the gold he was taking to the church. When that merchant's attempt to dispose of the body was foiled by the appearance of the saint to him, he repented and brought back the dismembered body to the church, along with the gold and more of his own money to give to the church. The saint resurrected the body and all marveled.

Miracle 8

A wealthy believer called Atrabius commissioned two identical silver plates to be made, one with his name on it and another to be given to the church of Apa Mina. When the silversmith made one bigger than the other, Atrabius asked that his name be put on the bigger one. When he was traveling to church to offer the gift, his own plate fell from the hand of his servant, who jumped into the sea, fearing his master's wrath. Atrabius was very sad and prayed that the body of the servant would wash ashore. The servant was found alive with the plate in his hand. The servant then told him how the saint saved him, and Atrabius ended up offering both plates to the church.

Miracle 9

Three men each took one pig to offer to the church. When they went ashore a crocodile attacked and mauled one of the men and pulled him into the water. Eventually the saint came and rescued him, healed him, and brought him inside the church while the doors were closed. The saint then appeared to his other two friends and encouraged them to continue their journey, and they would find their friend whole. They went and found him, and the injured man and his companions told the person in charge what had happened.

Miracle 10

This miracle is actually two consecutive stories merged together. In the first, a man was donating wood to the church. As his servant was carrying the load of wood, he was stopped by a soldier who wanted to take money from him in lieu of confiscating the wood. The saint appeared and gave the servant the money to give, and then snatched the bad soldier by the hair and brought him to the church. There he suspended him in the air by his hair. That soldier repented and gave the money he took, plus some of his own. The second story reports that, as the soldier was leaving, he found another soldier on the road who had fallen off his horse because of the action of one of the pigs belonging to the church. That soldier did not listen to the people who warned him not to harm the pig because it was the property of the church, and he slew it in anger. The saint did a similar thing to him as to the first soldier, and he was found hanging by the hair in the church. When he was loosened and came around, he confessed his deed, repented, and offered to give another pig to the church in lieu of the one he killed.

Miracle 11

This story also combines two different miracles that happened to persons who met each other. In the first, a man decided to offer one of his nine pigs to the church. When the pig grew to be bigger than the other ones, he changed his mind and slew the pig, to offer only half of it to the church. In the morning, when he went to get some of the meat to feed his children, he found it turned to stone. As he took three dinars to give to the church instead, he met the second man on the road and told him the story. That other man apparently was offering a horse to the church. Upon hearing the story he got up immediately to fulfill his promise. He then offered one horse each year until the year of his death. On his last trip the saint appeared to him and praised his action. He then told him that after he took the gift to the church, he should go where the saint's body was, and whatever he found there would be his. There he found plenty of gold and went home content.

Miracle 12

A widow was traveling to the saint's church with her offerings. On the way she was met by a soldier, who took her offerings and beat her. When he sat down to look at what he had stolen, he tied his horse to his leg. Suddenly the horse jumped up and dragged him all the way to the church. There he confessed his sin and offered to give the church a quarter of his money. The saint then appeared and healed him. Meanwhile the widow, upon seeing what happened, decided to stay and serve the church the rest of her days.

Miracle 13

A rich non-Christian man in Constantinople, married to a Christian woman, coveted the one sole sheep that his poor widowed neighbor had. He made a clever plan to go with his wife to the church in Egypt to disprove the miracles he was told about. As they were leaving, he had one of his servants steal the widow's sheep and prepare it as food for the traveling pilgrims. Eventually the widow was told what had happened. She traveled to the saint's church and told his wife. She in turned asked him to swear on the body of the saint that he did not take the widow's sheep. Arrogantly, he did swear falsely, and all his body turned to stone except for his mouth, to tell his wrongdoing. Then he offered the widow four times what he stole from her. But the saint appeared and told him that he would die in this condition. His wife nursed him for a long time at the church until she was told he would die. So she went back and gave a generous offering of her wealth to the church. Every year thereafter, she would return to the church and give more generous alms.

Miracle 14

The relatives of a possessed non-Christian man from Alexandria took him to the church to be healed. On the way the saint appeared as a soldier and dragged him to the church, as his relatives were not able to control him. There he eventually was healed, and he stayed and served the church until he died.

Miracle 15

A very rich Samaritan woman from Alexandria had suffered from severe pains in her head for years, spending great sums of money on physicians to no avail. Christian women told her to go with them to the church to be healed. On the way she was deceived by a Christian man, who gave her shelter in his home and tried to rape her. When she refused, he tried to kill her with his sword. She prayed for the saint to save her, and he did so by paralyzing the man's hand. Eventually Apa Mina took her to the church, and she was healed and converted to Christianity.

Miracle 16

This again is two merged stories. The main one is about a rich woman named Sofia who was childless and wanted to give all her possessions to the church. As she gathered them and was on her way, she was met by an evil soldier who threatened her and tried to rape her. She called upon the name of the saint, and he snatched her from his grasp and put her on the soldier's horse, which was tied to his leg. The horse galloped to the church, with the woman riding on it and the soldier being dragged by it. There he confessed, repented, and was healed by the saint. The woman gave the church her offering. In the second episode she asked the priest to pray over the body of the saint for water for the pilgrims, and the Archangel Gabriel came and struck a rock and water flowed.

Miracle 17

A servant of the church, named Philatika, was accused of sleeping with the daughter of a rich man from Nikiou who stayed at his house while he was taking care of church affairs. His accuser was the servant, who actually slept with the daughter. When that servant dragged him to the mayor, a statue of the saint spoke and declared the innocence of his servant Philatika. The girl's father sent Philatika back to the church with offerings, and he punished the guilty servant until he confessed.

Conclusion

These two unpublished manuscripts, which were not available to Jaritz, represent two different versions of the Egyptian collection of the *Miracles of Mar Mina*. It can be safely concluded that ML.MS.166 represents a more expanded text that was extant in Upper Egypt. The development of the St. Antony and St. Paul monastic libraries has not been adequately studied yet. The question therefore still remains whether they all had a parent Upper Egyptian text, or whether ML.MS.166 is just a copy of the four manuscripts from those two monasteries. In any case, it allows us to conclude that ML.MS.166 is missing several sheets at the end of the preserved codex that would contain three more miracles. The close similarity of the text in Ms.Mar.Mena.2 to the Hamuli Sahidic manuscripts probably means that the origin of the latter manuscript is farther north, in Fayoum or even farther than that. In any case, more work is still needed to record and analyze the variants of these unpublished manuscripts against the others that Jaritz listed. In particular, more content analysis is needed to further clarify the relationship of these manuscripts to their presumed parent. The relationship of the brief history of the saint at the beginning of the text to the larger martyrdom or eulogy texts is another topic for research. Lastly, it is hoped that the introduction of these manuscripts will help future researchers in mapping the textual development of this important hagiographic text.

Notes

1 Detailed discussion of the Greek version of these miracles has not been included because it is considered to be of a different tradition than the one found in Coptic and Arabic manuscripts, to which the two unpublished manuscripts discussed here belong.

2 The manuscript was mistakenly assumed to be from Asyut due to its presence with other recently photographed manuscripts that were originally photographed from various places in Asyut by a member of the Society. Fr. Polycarpos Avamena corrected me after my presentation at the symposium and provided me with the dimensions in an email dated March 3, 2015.

3 Text area dimensions were approximated by taking a screen ratio of a single folio from the digitized copy of the manuscript.

4 The corresponding AD date was obtained from Chaîne 1925: 216.
5 Crum 1905, in his catalog entry no. 340 (p. 156), mistakenly lists the manuscript as Or. 5439(2). He later corrected it in the volume *Additions and Corrections* on p. 520 as Or 4919(4). Bacot 2011 n.8 lists the incorrect catalog entry.
6 For full description of these manuscripts, consult Jaritz 1993: 56–62.
7 Niaton is most probably an Arabized name of the Greek Enaton or Dayr al-Zujaj (Gascou 1991a).
8 All references in the miracles are to the Church of Apa Mina in Maryut, where the saint's body is located and where there is a priest present. There is no mention of a monastery per se there. It can thus be presumed that all the miracles occurred prior to the ninth-century destruction of the Apa Mina pilgrimage city (Drescher 1946: xxxii).

16 Life of Pope Cyril VI (Kyrillos VI)

Teddawos Ava Mina and
Youhanna Nessim Youssef

THE PERSONALITY OF Pope Cyril VI has always been admired by many western scholars, such as Theodore Hall Partrick (Partrick 1996: 163–85), Nelly Van Doorn-Harder (Guirguis and Van Doorn-Harder 2011: 127–55), Christine Chaillot (Chaillot 2005: 25–26, 48), Maurice Martin S.J., Christian Nipsen S.J., Fadel Sidarous S.J. (Martin, Nipsen, and Sidarous 1990: 245–57), Otto F.A. Meinardus (Meinardus 1999: 77–79), and John Watson (Watson 1996; Watson 2000: 46–64). In addition he was admired in the writings of such Egyptian Muslim scholars as Dina El-Khawaga (El-Khawaga 1991: 115–34) and Sanaa Hasan (Hasan 2002: 1–30).

This chapter will highlight some landmark events in the life of Pope Cyril VI.

Early Childhood and Youth

Pope Cyril VI was from a village called Tukh Dalaka or Tukh al-Nasara, which has the dependency of the Monastery of Baramus (Meinardus 1977: 264–65). Hence he came into contact with monks from his early childhood. According to a story reported by his brother, when Azer (his lay name) was only four years old, a monk from the Monastery of Baramus, Fr. Tadros, prophesied that the child would become a monk (Atta and Ava Mena 1998: 9).

After Azer spent his early childhood in Tukh Dalaka, his whole family moved to Alexandria. There, he finished his high-school education and started to work with Thomas Cook Shipping Company as a clerk. He then came in contact with the Coptic pope of his time, John XIX (Shoucri 1991c: 1351). Pope John later gave Azer his recommendation to enter the Monastery of Baramus, where he eventually became a monk under the name of Mina al-Baramusi.

The Monastic Life of Pope Cyril VI

On the morning of July 27, 1927, Azer went to the monastery, where he was admitted by the hegumen of the monastery, Fr. Shenouda al-Baramusi, as a novice. In addition to the daily tasks, he spent his time in learning the canons of monasticism, the lives of saints, and the homilies of St. Isaac the Syrian. He became a disciple to an elder learned monk, Fr. 'Abd al-Masih Salib al-Mas'udi (1848–1935) (Atiya 1991b: 7). He scribed several manuscripts of Isaac of Nineveh. He was consecrated a monk on February 25, 1928, and took the name of Mina al-Baramusi. On July 18, 1931, he was ordained priest by Demetrius, the metropolitan of Munufiya. He was later sent to the theological seminary of the monks in Helwan (Atta and Ava Mena 1998: 18–20).

Monastic Life near Cairo

Due to conflict in the monastery, Fr. Mina al-Baramusi was expelled and lived in an abandoned windmill on the outskirts of Cairo. He spent his time in prayer and praises. When his reputation reached the ears of Metropolitan Athanasius of Beni Suef, he summoned him and installed him as abbot of the Monastery of St. Samuel the confessor in Qalamun. This monastery had been reinhabited in 1896 by Fr. Isaac al-Baramusi, who left his monastery in Wadi al-Natrun and came to this monastery with ten monks. The monastery was very poor and not recognized by the Coptic Church as a canonical monastery (Meinardus 1992b: 151). Fr. Mina al-Baramusi put all his efforts into renovating the church of the dependency in al-Zurah and other buildings in the monastery. After his elevation as patriarch, he made a decision to recognize the monastery.

His Stay at the Church of St. Mina in Old Cairo

After leaving his cell in the windmill, Fr. Mina built a church named after his patron saint, Mina, in Old Cairo. This church attracted many disciples, among them Nazir Gayid (later Pope Shenouda III), Sa'd 'Aziz (later Bishop Samuel), 'Abd al-Masih Bishara (later Bishop Athanasius of Beni

Suef), and many others who followed his example and became monks and later leaders in the Coptic Church.

Mina al-Baramusi Is Ordained as Cyril VI

After the patriarchal throne had been vacant for more than three years, Fr. Mina al-Baramusi was elected as patriarch. On Sunday, May 10, 1959, he was consecrated as Pope Cyril VI. On this occasion he addressed the church with the following words: "If our mission is great and important, it also requires the union of all powers and efforts so that we may accomplish with joy our way to God" (Meinardus 1970: 138–41).

Pope Cyril VI was able to manage the church in difficult times. The renowned Egyptian journalist Mohamed Heikal wrote about him in 1983:

> The relationship between Gamal Abdel Nasser and Pope Cyril VI was excellent, recognized with their mutual admiration, and it was known that the Pope can meet Abdel Nasser, at any time. Pope Cyril was careful to avoid problems, and have [sic] benefited a lot from the good relationship with Nasser in solving many problems. (Heikel 1983: 157)

During his patriarchate, successful negotiations were carried out with the Roman Catholic pope, Paul VI, to obtain the return of the relics of St. Mark the Evangelist. On June 20, 1968, a delegation of bishops and notables from the Coptic and Ethiopian churches left Cairo for Rome to receive the relics. On June 25, Pope Cyril and President Gamal 'Abd al-Nasser inaugurated the new Cathedral of St. Mark in 'Abbasiya. On the following day he deposited the relics of St. Mark in the shrine under the main church (Meinardus 1999: 33–34).

Some of the Accomplishments of Pope Cyril VI

Ecumenical contacts

Pope Cyril received the Syriac patriarch Ignatius Ya'qub III in January 1959. Two years later, in May 1961, he accepted an invitation from the Syrian Orthodox patriarch to visit Damascus.

In Addis Ababa in 1965, the first conference of the non-Chalcedonian Churches took place, under the chairmanship of Pope Cyril VI. A follow-up conference of the non-Chalcedonian Churches was held in Cairo in January 1966 (Meinardus 1999: 126). The outcome of these meetings was the beginning of an opening with the Chalcedonian Churches, as the statement by the Oriental Orthodox Churches from Addis Ababa 1965 states clearly:

> Concerning the Christological controversy which caused the division, we hope that common studies in a spirit of mutual understanding can shed light on our understanding of each other's positions. So we have decided that we should institute formally a fresh study of the Christological doctrine in its historical setting to be undertaken by our scholars, taking into account the earlier studies on this subject as well as the informal consultations held in connection with the meetings of the World Council of Churches. Meanwhile, we express our agreement that our churches could seek closer relationship and cooperate with the Eastern Orthodox Churches in practical affairs. (Chaillot and Belopopsky 1998: 35)

Following this statement, a dialogue with the Chalcedonian Churches started unofficially.

Many prelates from Chalcedonian Churches visited him, among them the Ecumenical Patriarch (Athenagoras) of Constantinople in 1961, Archbishop Macarius of Cyprus in 1961, the Russian patriarch Alexis in 1961, the Bulgarian patriarch Kyrillos in 1962, and the Romanian patriarch Justinian in 1969.

As mentioned above, Pope Cyril VI was also in contact with the Roman Catholic pope Paul VI. In Austria, the Catholic group Pro Oriente started to make contacts with the Coptic Church. These contacts led to official meetings with Cyril's successor, Pope Shenouda III.

Hegumen Salib Suriel said on one occasion: "When I was in Rome in 1969 to attend a conference of Canon Law, I was pleased to visit Pope Paul VI and I told him: 'I offer you greetings from Pope Cyril VI personally.' He replied saying: 'The throne of your Church is headed now by a holy man and a man of prayer. Tell him to pray for me.'" When Father Suriel returned to Egypt, he commented: "Such words do not come from a normal Catholic at all; how much more does it mean when it is said by the top Catholic Shepherd! But the man sensed the radiation of the holiness of Pope Cyril VI to an extent that led him to recognize it."[1]

Theological teaching

Under the auspices of Pope Cyril VI, a theological college was built in the vicinity of the new St. Mark Cathedral. He encouraged students to continue their theological studies overseas. Several students were sent to the

United Kingdom, France, Germany, Greece, and other countries. Among the graduates were Dr. Wahib Gorgy, Dr. Maurice Tawadrus, Dr. George Habib Bebawi, and others.

Revival of monasticism

Many students who came in contact with Fr. Mina al-Baramusi took the monastic habit after their graduation and became monks. After his consecration as patriarch many of them were ordained as bishops, including the following:

- The late Metropolitan Basil of Jerusalem
- The late Metropolitan Athanasius of Beni Suef
- Bishop Shenouda, Bishop of Education, ordained on September 30, 1962, who later became Pope Shenouda III
- The late Bishop Samuel, Bishop of Public Services, who was assassinated along with President Sadat on October 6, 1981, by members of Islamic Jihad
- The late Metropolitan Domedius of Giza
- The late Bishop Gregorios, Bishop of Scientific Research and Graduate Studies, ordained on May 15, 1967, who was called "the Origen of the modern era"
- The late Bishop Andrew, Bishop of Damietta and the Monastery of St. Damiana
- The late Bishop Agapius, Bishop of Dayrut and Sanabu and Qusqam

In 1969, Pope Cyril VI appointed Fr. Matta al-Miskin ('Matthew the poor') as the spiritual father of the Monastery of St. Macarius in Wadi al-Natrun. Fr. Matta dedicated all his efforts to rebuild what was then a ruined monastery. Many university graduates joined this monastery.

The women's convents also flourished. Nuns adopted cenobitic monasticism practices in the convents of St. Mercurius and St. Dimiana (Van Doorn-Harder 1993; Stegeman 1969–70: 159–66).

The building of the Monastery of St. Mina

With the enthronement of Cyril VI in the patriarchal see of St. Mark, a new chapter of the history of the shrine of Mina was ushered in. On November 25, 1961, Cyril VI dedicated the first cells and the chapel of St. Samuel there, which constitute the first part of the new Monastery of St. Mina. In February 1962, some relics of St. Mina were translated from his church in

Fumm al-Khalig to the new monastery. The monastery is still flourishing and hundreds of monks now live there (Meinardus 1999: 154–55).

The apparition of the Holy Virgin Mary at Zaytun

This church was built in 1924 by Khalil Ibrahim Pasha for his family. It has attracted a large number of pilgrims, both Christian and Muslim, ever since the first apparition of the Holy Virgin Mary on April 2, 1968. For several weeks in 1968–69, thousands of pilgrims assembled every night in front of this church in anticipation of the apparition of the Holy Virgin in bright blue or orange light on the dome of the church (Meinardus 1999: 201).

The administration of the Coptic Church

On the domestic front, Cyril VI achieved far-reaching successes in reform. He was fully aware of the responsibility of the Church toward every individual, especially the needy and unemployed. He established the Bishopric of Social Services to help such people to help themselves through vocational and technical training. Thousands of families benefited from this organization by making use of their natural talents.

To settle the question of the administration of *waqfs* (land endowments of the Church), he was instrumental in the promulgation of Laws 1433 and 962 (1960 and 1966, respectively), whereby such endowments were brought under the sole authority of a well-organized administration (Shoucri 1991a).

Personal Characteristics of Pope Cyril VI

Pope Cyril VI was known for his love of prayer and the celebration of daily Eucharist and praises. Throughout his life he ate the same diet as when he was a monk, despite advancing age and increasing responsibility and work fatigue. His breakfast was one piece of bread with cumin powder, salt, or sesame. Only after incessant urging from his spiritual sons did he add to this portion two small tablespoons of beans.

He wore the simplest clothes. The inner clothing was rough ('bare-backed'), made of inferior thread called *aldmor*. He wore a leather belt called an *iskim* and over it a light black robe made of inexpensive cloth. He dressed in a robe *(za'but)* open in the front; over this he wore the traditional *farujiya*, or outer black robe. He wore a scarf over his head to conceal his hair, which he had vowed not to cut when he started his monastic life. His liturgical vestments during the liturgies, in sight of everybody, were plain and very simple. Many priests wore much more valuable clothing than his. Even on holidays and special occasions he wore the same, a testimony to his holiness. He refused to wear the ecclesiastical crown even on the opening day of the new cathedral at 'Abbasiya. He did not even wear the luxurious garments given to him by His Majesty Emperor Haile Selassie of Ethiopia for this occasion. He always repeated: "Christ has come fleeing to Egypt and he has no place to lay his head."

He slept very little. He would start his day with prayer at three o'clock in the morning and conduct meetings, receptions, and other responsibilities until late in the night. No matter how tired he was, when prayer time came His Holiness would wake up with amazing spirit and pleasure to perform his worship regimen.

The furniture of his cell was very simple: a copper bed with only one blanket in the summer and the winter. Several nights he slept in his chair. The Apostolic Nuncio admired the simplicity of his room when he visited him when he was ill, and asked his permission to furnish it for him. Pope Cyril VI simply thanked him, and said to him that he loved this simple place.

The Repose of Pope Cyril VI

On March 9, 1971, the papal office notified Egypt's president, Anwar al-Sadat, and other government officials, along with bishops, priests, and the churches' prelates around the world, that Pope Cyril had passed away to the victorious Church. The bells rang continuously until the prayers commenced. The official announcement which was released by the papal office read as follows:

> The Orthodox Church sadly announces that its first pastor, thrice-merciful and of blessed memory, Pope Cyril VI, Pope of Alexandria and the See of St. Mark, passed away to the heavenly glory at 10:30 yesterday morning.

The next day, Wednesday, March 10, at 7:15 p.m., President Sadat went to extend his condolences personally to the bishops in charge, the members of the Holy Synod, and all who were waiting to receive the pope's body. Other officials paying their respects were Dr. Kamal Ramzy Istino, Mr. Kamal Henry Abadir, and Eng. Ibrahim Naguib. President Sadat said, "I have always admired Pope Cyril VI, whom I love, and I hope that his successor will follow in his steps. I hope you will move forward in choosing his successor according to your rituals and in complete unity without divisions. I consider you family, and I wish there to be no divisions in my family."

Recognition of the Saintliness of Pope Cyril VI by the Holy Synod

Pope Cyril VI was famous for being a miracle worker, both before and after his death. Many people recounted many miracles, such as healing of incurable sicknesses and other matters. On November 23, 1972, his body was moved to the crypt under the main altar of the new basilica at St. Mina Monastery. This site has become one of the major pilgrimage centers in Lower Egypt, especially on 12 Ba'una (June 19) and 15 Hatur (November 24), the feast days of St. Mina. Extensive accommodations enable pilgrims to spend several days at the site. Two kiosks with a large assortment of devotional material serve the increasing number of visitors (Meinardus 2002a: 70). The anniversary of the repose of Pope Cyril VI, on March 9, always falls during Coptic Lent when the monastery is closed to pilgrims.

On Thursday, June 20, 2013, when the Holy Synod of the Coptic Orthodox Church met under the chairmanship of His Holiness Pope Tawadros II of Alexandria, the sainthood of Pope Cyril VI was recognized, forty-two years after his repose. Because of this decision, churches can now be built in his name, and his name is mentioned in the diptychs and the *memento sanctorum* in both the Holy Liturgy and the Holy Psalmody.

Pope Tawadros consecrated the first church named for Pope Cyril VI after recognition of his sainthood, at the Monastery of St. Mina in the Maryut Desert. Other churches and altars were built and consecrated in his name in various places in Egypt and in the Diaspora.

Conclusion

This short chapter sheds some light on a modern-day saint in the twentieth-century Coptic Church. He led the Church back from decades of spiritual decay and into a spiritual renewal. Under a mere dozen years of his leadership the Coptic Church was set again on the right path that gave rise to the renaissance witnessed over the past few decades. His name will forever be synonymous with St. Mina, miracles, and church reforms.

Notes

1 Personal communication from Fr. Raphael Ava Mina, former secretary to His Holiness Pope Cyril VI. The conversation is also mentioned briefly in el-Masri 1982: 445.

17 The Veneration of Anba Hadid and the Nile Delta in the Thirteenth Century

Asuka Tsuji

Introduction

This chapter will discuss the life of a little-known saint, Hadid, who resided in the Nile Delta in the thirteenth century, and some aspects of the Christian demography of the northwestern part of Lower Egypt during his life.

In the Islamic period, the social and religious landscape of Egypt—Christian under the rule of Byzantium—underwent great change. After the tax reform in the eighth century, Coptic churches and monasteries wielded less control over their lands and congregants. Arabization gradually advanced, and the Coptic language died out. However, the Islamization of Egypt, which proceeded slowly compared to other Middle Eastern areas, was never completed. The conditions of the Christian population during the Middle Ages remain obscure. We know that most Christians were farmers, but we have very little information about those who lived outside of Cairo before the Ottoman era.

Anba Hadid is commemorated in the Coptic *Synaxar* and the *Majma' al-Qiddisin* (3 Baramhat; Forget 1912: 2:5; *Kitab al-Sinaksar.* 1:15; *Kitab al-Ibsalmudiya*: 78).[1] He was born in Sinjar on Lake Burullus—not to be confused with Sinjar in northern Iraq—and spent most of his life as a priest in the village of Nutubis al-Rumman, located north of Fuwwa on the Rashidi branch of the Nile.[2] He died in 1286. He should not be confused with the saint also named Hadid who was martyred in 1387 (Nakhla 1952: 3:126–27).

It is argued here that the former Hadid died in 1286 rather than in 1386, as previous scholarship has held.[3] Hadid's disciple, Yuhanna al-Rabban, died in 1307 (Matta'us 2005: 24). A disciple cannot die eighty years before his master. Moreover, the *Life and Miracles of Anba Hadid* mentions the patriarchate of Yu'annis ibn Sa'id, the seventy-eighth patriarch (r. 1262–68, 1271–93) (*Life*: fol. 43a), placing Hadid's activities in the latter half of the thirteenth century.[4]

The *Life and Miracles of Anba Hadid* (hereafter, *Life*) exists as an unedited text in a few extant manuscripts.[5] The author is anonymous, but evidence in the narratives suggests that one or more of Hadid's disciples either related the saint's miracles to the author or directly composed the work. This *Life* seems to have been first mentioned in Salib al-Qiss Dimitri's article in *al-Kiraza* in the 1960s (Salib 1967: 30–33). This saint is best known from the pamphlet by Matta'us al-Suryani (Matta'us 2005).

Hadid's *Life*

According to the *Life*, Hadid's father was a fisherman, and his mother was told by an angel in a dream that she would bear a child whose name was to be Hadid and who would serve as head of the Lord's people *(ra's sha'b al-Rabb)*. Hadid grew up as a devout child; he engaged in fasting and prayers from the age of seven, while also helping his father fish (*Life*: fols. 4a–6a).

It is not clear how long Hadid worked as a fisherman. His charitable acts and devout way of life—he helped orphans and widows, and fasted—gradually brought him fame, and one day, Hadid chose to distance himself from Sinjar (*Life*: fols. 6a–6b). There are many obscurities in the descriptions of Hadid's early life in Sinjar, which gives the reader the impression that the author did not know much about Hadid's life before the saint came to Nutubis al-Rumman. According to the *Life*, Hadid first went to a church in Tabbana in the district of Burunbara in the northwest Delta.[6] However, that church was soon after destroyed. He then decided to travel to the Monastery of St. Macarius at Wadi al-Natrun. On his way, he saw a vision of the Virgin Mary in which he was told to go to the church bearing her name in the village of Nutubis al-Rumman and to spend the rest of his life there, serving his people (*Life*: fols. 7a–7b).

During his stay at Nutubis, people came to him from surrounding areas to seek his help with various matters, and eventually, the village *arkhon*s (notables or influential laymen) recommended to the bishop that he be ordained as a priest (*Life*: fols. 8a–8b). Hadid is credited with interceding on

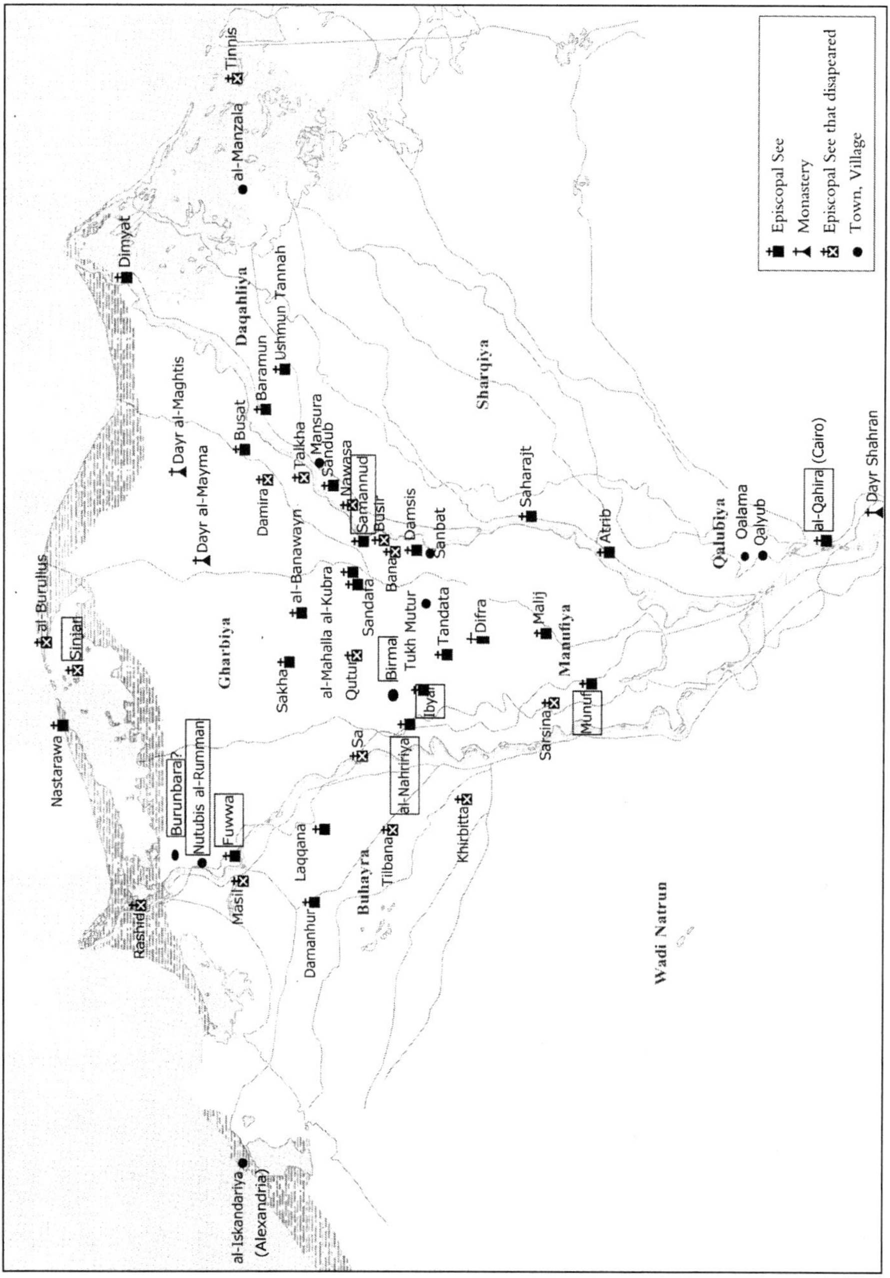

Fig. 17.1. Lower Egypt in the thirteenth century (Timm 1983).

the villagers' behalf with the patriarch, who was in Lower Egypt collecting taxes owed to Sultan Baybars (Miracle no. 31, *Life*: fols. 42b–44b). This episode places Hadid's residency sometime in the 1260s, when the Christians were made to pay a hefty tax, or ransom, by order of Sultan Baybars (r. 1260–77).[7] Hadid is also claimed to have translated a number of works (possibly liturgical) from Coptic into Arabic (*Life*: fol. 8a). Near the end of his life, the church at Nutubis al-Rumman was destroyed and Hadid was arrested, but then miraculously freed. He died after securing the local governor's *(wali)* promise that the church would be rebuilt (*Life*: fols. 44b–46b).

Description of the *Miracles*

The *Miracles of Anba Hadid* (hereafter, *Miracles*) consists of thirty-two or thirty-three miracle stories, mainly concerning various men from nearby towns and villages. The visitors seem to have been mostly commoners; high-ranking officials or clergy are rarely mentioned, nor are women.

The *Miracles* does mention Muslims. For example, in Miracle no. 22, a Muslim family from Munuf goes to Hadid in the hope of curing their child's disabilities. It is related that this family attempted to hide their child's disabilities from the people of Munuf, and moved to Fuwwa. Here, a neighbor advised the father to take his child to Anba Hadid and, as the father had also heard of the reputation of this saint from other people of Fuwwa, he decided to visit Hadid with his child (Miracle no. 22, *Life*: fols. 29b–30a). This episode goes hand in hand with an entry in the *Synaxar* stating, "Hadid cured believers and non-believers alike" (Forget 1912: 2:5). The men came to seek cures for themselves and their families, of which the *Synaxar* attributes many to Hadid. They also desired *baraka* (blessings), intercessions *(shafa'a)*, and advice, mostly about traveling on the Nile, which Nutubis al-Rumman faced and which was full of hazards in the Middle Ages.

A remarkable aspect of the *Miracles* is the mention of towns and villages from which the venerators of Hadid are claimed to have come. The author does not seem to be interested in recording the names or professions of the visitors, but he does take care to record their points of origin. Apart from Nutubis al-Rumman, where Hadid resided, those who visited him are said to have come from Sinjar, Hadid's native town (Miracles no. 3, 14, 28, and 29) and from towns and villages on the Rashidi branch of the Nile, such as Fuwwa (Miracle no. 22), Ibyar (Miracle no. 13), Birma, which is slightly inland (Miracles no. 13, 27), and Munuf (Miracle no. 22). The only town in the *Miracles* (apart from Cairo and Alexandria) that does not fit into this category is Samannud, an ancient and important Christian town in Gharbiya province (Miracle no. 20).

Many scholars question the authenticity and reliability of miracle stories in hagiographical literature. However, it seems that the author paints a realistic picture of Hadid's veneration. The people of Nutubis and Sinjar would have heard of Hadid, and those living on the Rashidi branch of the Nile, such as Fuwwa, Ibyar, and Munuf, would have had access to Nutubis al-Rumman by boat, the main means of transport in the Nile Delta.

Travels on the Nile

We learn from the *Miracles* that Christians (like all other Egyptians) were using the Nile in order to visit the saint, participate in festivals *(eid)*, and conduct business in Alexandria and Cairo. As traveling on the Nile was occasionally dangerous, people from Sinjar often came to receive Hadid's blessings *(baraka)* before traveling to Cairo on the river (Miracles no. 3, 28, and 29; *Life*: fols. 10b, 38b–40b).

In Miracle no. 3, the *arkhons* of Sinjar visit Hadid before traveling to Cairo to submit a petition, but are forced to wait in Nutubis for five days because their boat does not arrive (*Life*: fols. 10b–11b). Other men from Sinjar travel to Fustat by boat after seeing Hadid (Miracles no. 2 and 28; *Life*: fols. 10b–11b, 28a–28b). Some merchants on their way from Alexandria to Cairo stop at Nutubis to seek Hadid's blessing *(baraka)* (Miracles no. 21 and 27; *Life*: 28a–28b, 37a). Records from the Geniza documents indicate that it took five to six days to travel from Alexandria to Fustat on the Nile in the Middle Ages. Navigating ships on the Nile was by no means an easy task, as one risked shipwreck due to the shallow banks or storms as well as bandit raids (Goitein 1967: 1:295, 299).

The miracles attributed to Hadid are strongly connected to the Nile. Hadid cautioned merchants about the condition of the Nile and rescued them when they were shipwrecked (Miracle no. 21; *Life*: fols. 28a–28b). Few visitors are said to arrive by land and, in one story, Hadid urges a man to travel by land rather than on the Nile (Miracle no. 7; *Life*: fols. 14b–15a). However, the man ignores Hadid's caution and gets into a boat, only for it to capsize. This episode suggests that people preferred traveling by river to traveling by land, since even though traveling by river was hazardous, it was perhaps safer than traveling overland in those times. We know that Yusab, Bishop of Fuwwa, mentioned that he could not attend the synod of 1250 because of marauding Bedouins in this area (Yusab 2003: 279–80).

Christian Demography of Lower Egypt

M. Martin characterizes the late twelfth century as "the last glimpse of the Christians in Egypt" (Martin 1997: 191). However, lists of sees for the thirteenth to fourteenth centuries indicate a different situation, as they show that bishoprics were being restored or newly created (Munier 1943b: 30–41). The new bishoprics were mostly situated in the new, rising towns of Gharbiya province, the richest part of the Delta. Although not in Gharbiya, the places mentioned in the *Life and Miracles of Anba Hadid*—such as Fuwwa, Ibyar, Munuf, and Samannud—can be recognized as episcopal sees during the latter half of the thirteenth century, as H. Munier's study demonstrated (Munier 1943b: 30–41). That is, the names of bishops from these towns are present in the list of bishops who attended Church functions. The presence of a bishopric in the Middle Ages indicated a sizable Christian population (el-Leithy 2006: 86–87).

The only name mentioned in the *Miracles* that was not an episcopal see is Birma, in Gharbiya province. This village had existed since the Byzantine period and had three churches by the end of the twelfth century (Amélineau 1893: 101–102; Abu al-Makarim 1984a: 1:fol. 37a). The Church of Mar Girgis was also a famous pilgrimage site (Viaud 1979: 30). It seems reasonable, therefore, to presume that these towns and villages mentioned in the *Life and Miracles of Anba Hadid* had sizable Christian populations.

It is possible that Nutubis al-Rumman's accessibility was one of the factors that determined the geographical scope of Hadid's veneration in the Delta. It can also be presumed that the author of the *Miracles* was well acquainted with the geography of Lower Egypt and that the places he mentioned were towns and villages with sizable Christian populations during the thirteenth century.

Conclusion

Little information can be gathered about Hadid's early years, his presumably ascetic way of life, or his achievement of sainthood. The author of the *Life and Miracles of Anba Hadid* seems to have been more interested in recording Hadid's activities in Nutubis and the benefits that people derived from them—all of which made Hadid very much a 'local saint.' The *Life and Miracles of Anba Hadid* gives us a glimpse of the Christian way of life in the Nile Delta in the latter half of the thirteenth century, after the *Tarikh al-Kana'is* and before the persecutions of the fourteenth century destroyed many places of Christian veneration in the area (el-Leithy 2005: 200). The seemingly unremarkable character of Hadid's life and miracles suggests that there were other local saints like him during the Islamic period whose stories are not recorded in either the *Tarikh al-Batarika* or the *Synaxar.* It is to be hoped that such saints and their work will receive the attention they deserve in the near future, thus enhancing our understanding of the Coptic Church in the Middle Ages.

Notes

1 Hadid's name does not appear in R. Basset's edition.

2 The town of Sinjar dates back to the Byzantine period, and was an episcopal see from the eighth to the thirteenth century. It seems to have disappeared due to the rising waters of Lake Burullus in the sixteenth or seventeenth century (Meinardus 1977: 237–41); *Tarikh al-Kana'is* mentions that there were six churches in the village of Nutubis al-Rumman (Abu al-Makarim 1984a: 1:fol. 41a; Timm 1984–92: 1788–89; Halm 1982: 2: 67).

3 For past studies mentioning the Anba Hadid discussed here, see Abullif 1998: 2:152.

4 For more detailed discussion, see Tsuji (2016): 1155–56.

5 The known manuscripts are: Wadi al-Natrun, Dayr al-Suryan, MS *mayamir* 306 (eighteenth century), fols. 1a–46b (hereafter as *Life*); Dayr al-Suryan, MS *mayamir* 311 (AM 1267/AD 1551), fols. 28b–69b; Dayr Anba Antuni, MS *tarikh* 155 (n.d.), fols. 2–69; Wadi al-Natrun, Dayr Abu Maqar, MS Hag. 39 (fifteenth century?). I thank Abuna Bigoul for allowing me to consult the manuscripts at Dayr al-Suryan. The manuscript housed at Dayr Abu Maqar mentions the year of Hadid's death as AM 1002/AD 1286. See Zanetti 1986: 60.

6 I could not find any information on Tabbana. For the district of Burunbara, see Halm 1982: 2:465.

7 For this historical episode as related in the *Tarikh al-Batarika*, see Sawirus ibn al-Muqaffa' 1970: 3, pt. 3:134, 229–30.

18 Kellia and Monastic Epigraphy

Jacques van der Vliet

"Epigraphic Aggression"?

Graffiti covering the screens of a bus shelter or the walls of a subway station tend to give the average citizen a sense of insecurity, evoking violence and lawlessness. It was perhaps with this association in mind that the authors of the most recent Kellia volume qualified a dense group of over a hundred "disorderly" graffiti and *dipinti* that disfigure the walls of the sanctuary of one of the churches at Kom Qusur 'Isa (room 61) as a case of "epigraphic aggression," not befitting such a holy spot (Weidmann 2013: 311). These inscriptions represent only a small portion of the hundreds of Greek and Coptic graffiti and *dipinti* of varying length, contents, and interest that have been discovered by the French and Swiss missions at the various monastic settlements in and near Kellia since the 1960s.[1] The time has not yet come to attempt a synthesis of this rich material, which will only become possible when the comprehensive edition of the corpus, announced by Nathalie Bosson (Geneva), has appeared. In any case, as is well known, the interest of the corpus is great, from various points of view: linguistic, historical, and even theological. Yet the majority of the individual inscriptions are not at all that interesting and may seem mere acts of vandalism, as modern graffiti tend to be seen.

Instead of focusing on the more or less interesting contents of the inscriptions, the present chapter proposes a reading of the Kellia inscriptions as monastic epigraphy, that is, as witnesses to monastic life and practices. For this purpose, the chapter will first briefly sketch the characteristics of what could be called the 'monastic revolution' in epigraphy. Then three examples from the Kellia corpus of mural inscriptions will illustrate specific aspects of monastic epigraphy as it was part of the cultural practices of northern Egyptian monasticism. In the end some conclusions will be drawn that—needless to say—will not confirm the interpretation of the Kellia graffti as acts of vandalism.

The Revolution of Monastic Epigraphy[2]

The novel character of monastic epigraphy becomes rapidly apparent on comparison with the epigraphy of the Hellenistic and Latin traditions, perpetuated by the Christian empire. Traditional Greek epigraphy predominantly comprised public inscriptions, chiseled in stone, that had a commemorative function, either dedicatory or funerary in nature. The textual and visual strategies of such inscriptions were mainly aimed at conveying prestige, for instance the prestige of a rich patron in the case of dedicatory inscriptions, or the prestige of a family in the case of funerary monuments. They were meant to be seen and admired.

By contrast, the inscriptions of Kellia are in majority *dipinti*, painted on whitewashed walls, or even mere graffiti, crudely scratched into the relatively soft surface of a brick wall. And even the more carefully executed *dipinti* were not meant for showing off. Access to the rooms where they were found was limited and the inscriptions themselves are not particularly impressive by any standard. They rather bear a private character.

In order to understand these differences, two innovative aspects of monasticism need to be borne in mind. Firstly, monasticism gave rise to a new approach to habitat, that is, the living environment, as something spiritually significant. Where a monk lives is not irrelevant. That is why 'the cell' and 'the desert' are such important themes in Egyptian literature. The cell is part of a monk's life and its pedagogic role is highlighted by such authors as Paul of Tamma and Evagrius as well as by many of the *Sayings of the Desert Fathers*. One famous example from the latter may be quoted here:

> A brother visited Abba Moses in the Scetis, asking a word from him. The elder told him: "Go, sit down in your cell and your cell teaches you everything." (*Apophthegmata Patrum* alphab., Moses 6)

Instead of being a mere shelter, the living quarters of the monk inform and shape his way of life.

Secondly, monasticism inaugurated a novel way of contemplating written texts as a complement to the traditional oral/aural transmission of authority. As is well known, monasticism is generally considered to be the cradle of the practice of silent reading. In addition to the public reading of texts, which remained part of monastic communal practices, it favored a culture of private contemplation of texts, which is perhaps best exemplified by another *Saying of the Desert Fathers*:

> For those who can afford, acquiring Christian books is necessary. For the mere sight of the books makes us more averse to sin and encourages us to be more eager for righteousness. (*Apophthegmata Patrum* alphab., Epiphanius 8)

A monk should surround himself with texts that direct and inspire his way of life. What he reads, or even merely sees, is no less important than where he lives.

Monastic epigraphy brings these two strands, the assignment of spiritual significance to living quarters and the private contemplation of written texts, together. *All* epigraphy is witness to the interaction between space and text. Inscriptions are texts meant for a particular spatial setting; outside of this context they are practically meaningless. In *monastic* epigraphy, however, this setting is linked in a particularly intimate and private way to the spiritual life of the monk. Not only the space that he inhabits, his cell, but also the texts that adorn it are deemed spiritually significant.

The remainder of this chapter will briefly discuss three examples of the interaction of text and space in the typically monastic context of Kellia. The first is the famous text about the prayer to Jesus from room 12 at Qusur al-Ruba'iyat; the second is the case of "epigraphic aggression" in church 61 at Kom Qusur 'Isa, mentioned in the introduction to this chapter, and finally attention will be paid to the many funerary inscriptions on the Kellia walls.

Praying to Jesus

The Kellia text about the prayer to Jesus hardly needs introduction. It has been much discussed, in various contexts, ever since its first publication by Antoine Guillaumont and Rodolphe Kasser in 1969.[3] The text, in Bohairic

Coptic, is painted with considerable care on the plastered western face of a protruding part of the north wall in room 12 of the complex known as Qusur al-Ruba'iyat. The *dipinto* can—on circumstantial evidence—be dated to the seventh or eighth century. Formally it is an *apophthegma*, which is perhaps the most characteristic of all monastic genres and more often found on the walls of monastic sites in the Nile Valley.[4] As a primarily didactic tool, *apophthegmata* teach basic truths about monastic life in the form of a 'saying' of an 'elder,' a Desert Father. The present text is not known, however, from any of the printed collections of such sayings. It begins in this characteristic way:

> An elder said: "When the demons are attacking us, saying: 'When you cry out constantly: "Lord Jesus!," you are not praying to the Father nor to the Holy Spirit'—for we know that also such an attack is the work of the crafty one [i.e., the devil] . . ." (ll. 1–10).[5]

What follows is the refutation of this demonic insinuation. As the text argues, invoking Jesus is in fact praying to the Father and the Spirit as well and in no way violates the integrity of the Holy Trinity. An interesting parallel from the work of Shenoute shows that praying to Jesus was an object of monastic controversy already in the first half of the fifth century.[6] In this sense, the Kellia *dipinto* may be said to be about orthodoxy. Yet orthodoxy was certainly not its main concern. Its primarily didactic and practical purpose is apparent both from the text's literary form and from a study of its spatial context.[7]

The spatial context of the inscription is that of an oratory, a room for prayer. In fact, the reader of the inscription faced the east, in conformity with Christian praying practice. Gazing past the inscription, his gaze would inevitably meet a prayer niche, situated centrally in the eastern rear wall of the same room. This niche bore a painted representation of a bust of Christ imposed over the center of a decorated cross.[8] The painting, therefore, emphatically designates Christ as the focus of the monk's prayer and might be said to illustrate the inscription, if this were not an inadequate reading of the ensemble. In fact, as Elizabeth Bolman has aptly pointed out, the inscription, the figural representation, and their spatial setting together constituted a program that informed the praying practice of the monk or monks using the room (Bolman 2007: 417–18). Bolman here uses a term coined by Jaś Elsner, "ritual-centred visuality" (see Elsner 2000: 52–56). The whole visual layout of space, text, and painting is designed to guide and support the monk's prayer.

The inscription itself has a didactic character not only because of its textual form, but also by virtue of its specific spatial setting. The text is not primarily about orthodoxy nor even about Christology, but about monastic praying practice. It was meant to inspire the way of life of the monks who inhabited this particular building by teaching them how to pray and why.

Remaining Close to the Saints

An entirely different situation meets the eye in the southern basilica at Kom Qusur 'Isa (room 61).[9] Instead of one beautifully made inscription, the altar room of this church, the central sanctuary of the complex, shows a cloud of primitive and ugly *dipinti* (fourteen) and in particular graffiti (more than eighty) that have been dated to the middle and the second half of the seventh century.[10] Most of them are simply names, often badly written. Occasionally they take the form of brief prayers, such as this one in Bohairic Coptic:

> Remember this feeble person, Aba Georgi, that God may forgive him. Amen. (Weidmann 2013: 330, no. 74)

As we have seen, the editors of these rudimentary texts qualify this ensemble as a form of "epigraphic aggression" and consider their disorderly arrangement a violation of the sacred nature of the room (Weidmann 2013: 311). This chapter takes a diametrically opposite view and argues that this clustering of simple inscriptions precisely brings out the very sacred character of the place.

In the same volume where they publish the inscriptions, the excavators themselves provide the clue to the density of inscriptions at this particular spot. In the altar room of church 61, a secondary deposit has been found, containing the relics of a young man. These could be dated, by the C-14 method, to the third or fourth century. Wrapped in a piece of textile and contained within a small wooden pyxis, the relics had been let down in a pottery vessel under the altar floor. The entire deposit was then carefully covered by a marble tile. The excavators plausibly argue that these may be the relics of a martyr, perhaps even those of St. Menas (Mina), since the latter was probably depicted on a nearby wall painting (cf. Weidmann 2013: 427). Even though it is unlikely that the identity of the saint in question can ever be established with certainty, the find of his relics in the sanctuary of the church marks the place as a particularly sacred one, as a window on heaven.

With this in mind, the clustering of rudely inscribed names at this particular spot starts to make sense. These inscriptions are neither sacrilegious nor totally uninteresting. Instead, they bear witness to a vivid devotion focused on the relics of a saint. By leaving their names on this particular spot, monks and visitors wished to perpetuate their presence close to the relics of a saint who may have been a martyr from the great persecution, perhaps even St. Menas, and therefore near to God himself. Practical piety seems to be a better qualification than "epigraphic aggression."

The Quick and the Dead

A striking feature of the hermitages at Kellia (as well as the neighboring site of Pherme) is the high number of funerary inscriptions or epitaphs, painted on the walls of the residences of the living. As a group they are rather well known because some of them contain precise dates, names of patriarchs and emperors, or references to historical events.[11] An interesting example (in Bohairic Coptic) from the oratory of hermitage Qusur al-'Irayma 26 (ancient Pherme) runs thus:

> Our blessed father Simeon went to rest on the 28th of Paopi, in the fifth indiction year. The course [of his life] he completed, the faith he kept and now the crown of righteousness, which He [i.e., God] has promised to those who will love Him, is prepared for him [cf. 2 Tim. 4:7–8]. May the Lord Jesus Christ and the Holy Spirit grant his soul a place of rest together with all His saints. Amen. Pray for the feeble person who wrote this. Amen. Forgive me! Amen. (after N. Bosson in Bridel 2003: 375–76)

In this epitaph, the quote from 2 Timothy, recently discussed by Stephen J. Davis (2013, with the present text quoted at 360), is noteworthy. Otherwise, the text adheres to the standard format of funerary or commemorative texts, which usually feature names, dates (of decease), and brief prayer formulas only. Nor is the presence of funerary texts in a monastic context in itself remarkable. Remarkable in Kellia are rather the medium and, in particular, the spatial setting of the texts. Funerary inscriptions in Late Antiquity were typically stone inscriptions on tablets, so-called tombstones or funerary stelae. As a class of objects, they are frequently found also in monasteries—witness, for instance, the many funerary stelae from the neighborhood of the Monastery of Apa Jeremiah in Saqqara. In the Kellia region only one such stela has ever been found (published in Kasser, Favre, and Weidmann 1972: 82, fig. 33).

Tombstones, as the name suggests, are as a rule associated with tombs and thus situated in close proximity to the deceased themselves. Their natural habitat is the cemetery, a public space set apart from the world of the living and designated for the dead. The living would only come to the cemetery for the periodical commemoration of the dead, for which the inscribed tombstone provided—so to say—the scenario (with, again, a name, a date, and prayer formulas as its core elements). The commemoration of the dead by the living was a ritual process bound up with a liturgical cycle beginning with the date of departure of the deceased, usually culminating on the fortieth day after death and sometimes including one or more anniversaries. On such a day, the family or a larger social group would gather near the tomb or in a nearby chapel in order to pray for their deceased.[12]

In Kellia we find an entirely different situation. The Kellia funerary prayers were daily before the eyes of the inhabitants of a particular hermitage. The commemoration of the deceased no longer necessitates a physical move to a designated space beyond the domain of the living, nor is it necessarily bound to a liturgical cycle. The deceased themselves, moreover, are in most cases designated as "fathers" or "brothers," that is, as spiritual rather than natural family. Rather, the situation of the inscriptions shows that the place of the kin group, who usually paid for the tomb and its expensive tombstone, has here been taken by another, spiritual family, that of the living community that inhabits the hermitage in question. The inscriptions facilitate the commemoration of its spiritual ancestors on a daily and at the same time perpetual basis. Taking the argument one step further, one might say that in inscribing the walls of cells and oratories with funerary inscriptions, the community created its own pedigree and, beyond the cyclical commemoration of the deceased, wrote its own history.

Conclusions

The inscriptions of Kellia, as illustrated by these three examples, are key witnesses to the life of the monastic communities that inhabited the area. The famous *apophthegma* about prayer to Jesus in an oratory was part of a program that visually and textually directed the ritual practices of the monks. The clustering of crude graffiti in a particular part of a church bears witness to the desire of monks and visitors to remain in close contact with the relics of the saints. The funerary inscriptions in the cells and oratories of the living construct their spiritual pedigree outside of the conventional bounds of family and society. In each of these cases, it is the interaction of text, space, and ritual practices that give the inscriptions their meaning. As always in epigraphy, context is everything.

Notes

1 The most recent publications are, for the French mission, Ballet, Bosson, and Rassart-Debergh 2003, which lists 155 inscriptions (edited by N. Bosson at 209–326); for the Swiss, Weidmann 2013, with 154 (edited by N. Bosson, P. Cherix, and R. Kasser at 309–35; cf. Delattre, Dijkstra, and van der Vliet 2015: nos. 3–50), not counting *dipinti* on pottery. For the earlier bibliography, the reader is referred to these publications.

2 The following paragraphs present in a condensed form ideas discussed more extensively in van der Vliet (2017).

3 The present discussion of the inscription owes much to the fine essay by Bolman (2007).

4 Other examples are discussed in van der Vliet (2017).

5 For the text see Daumas and Guillaumont 1969: 1:99, with the corrections in Kasser 1996. See also Guillaumont 1979; Grillmeier and Hainthaler 1990: 191–92, with further references.

6 For the Shenoute text, best named after its incipit, *I am amazed*, see now Cristea 2011, in particular 205–15 and 274–79 (translation). Cf. Grillmeier and Hainthaler 1990: 188–92.

7 See Daumas and Guillaumont 1969: 1:47–49, pl. 6–7; 2:pl. XXXIX; other inscriptions in the same room: 1:100–101; cf. Guillaumont 1979: 168–73, 178–79.

8 Daumas and Guillaumont 1969: 2:pl. XXXIXb–c (photo and watercolor copy by B. Lenthéric); cf. Guillaumont 1979: 169–72; Bolman 2007: 415–17, with a line drawing at 417 and further references.

9 On this church, Weidmann 2013: 48–55; on the relics mentioned below: 427–31.

10 Ed. Bosson, Cherix, and Kasser, in Weidmann 2013: 324–35, nos. 30–128.

11 See, for example, R. Kasser, J. Partyka, and N. Bosson, in Bridel 1999: 12–17; Luisier 2007.

12 For further details see van der Vliet 2011.

19 Butrus al-Sadamanti al-Armani (Peter of Sadamant 'the Armenian')

Fr. Awad Wadi

BUTRUS AL-SADAMANTI WAS BORN (and/or lived) in Sadamant, near Ihnasiya (Coptic: Hnes), which is now in the province of Beni Suef. Its Greek name is Setment, and in Coptic Sotoment, or Soutoumit (Atiya 1991c: 431).[1] It seems that the place was never famous, and now it is a village (Timm 1991: 2222–25).[2] On the other hand, the Monastery of St. George in Sadamant has a great importance in the history of the liturgy. Ibn Kabar, in his *Misbah*, chapter 16, "On the Daily and Nightly Prayers," mentions that the monks in the Monastery of St. George in Sadamant have their own order of the distributions of the Psalms for these prayers (Ibn Kabar 2003: 394, 419–20, ¶¶177–85, 218–26; Villecourt 1924: 232–33; see Hanna 1996: 31–32). The same author mentions in chapter 18 that they have their own book for Holy Week (Ibn Kabar 2001: 264n77; Villecourt 1925: 280; see Hanna 1996: 32).

The very little information about Butrus al-Sadamanti comes from himself and from two medieval writers. Butrus, in his *Treatise on Belief (Maqala fi-l-i'tiqad)*, states that he wrote the treatise in AM 976, or AD 1260 (Vatican Arabe 126, fol 2r; FC M741, fol. 78r: 970; al-Sadamanti 1895: 2; Graf 1947: 353; al-Sadamanti 1972: 18; Samaan 1983: 30; Swanson 2008: 52; al-Maqari 2012: 349). A contemporary writer, al-Mu'taman ibn al-'Assal, mentions Butrus in the first chapter of his book *Majmu' usul al-din*.[3] According to Ibn al-'Assal, Butrus was a priest and he was called "al-Armani" (the Armenian). Some fifty years later we have the same statement from Ibn Kabar, who attributes only one work to him (Riedel 1902: 661 (text), 698 (trans.); Ibn Kabar 1971; see Vansleb 1677a: 336–37).

From the previous sources we can say that Butrus was born in the first quarter of the thirteenth century. He flourished in the second half of the thirteenth century; the only known date in his life is AD 1260, the possible date of one of his writings (see below). He was a monk-priest in one of the monasteries of Wadi al-Natrun or in the Monastery of St. George in Sadamant. He was considered a holy man. Cheikho (1924: 62, 236 ¶210) and Atiya (1991c) date him to the eleventh century, yet Atiya states that one of his writings is from AD 1260, when he wrote a work dedicated to his former colleague in the monastery, Yusab, Bishop of Akhmim (Samir 1991). Because of the title "al-Sadamanti," Graf believed that he lived in the Monastery of St. George in Sadamant (Graf 1947: 352; al-Maqari 2012: 342). At least one manuscript (FC M 741) attests that he was a monk in the desert of Scete (Shahit), that is, Wadi al-Natrun. Sadamant must be the place of his birth. The title "al-Armani" given to Butrus by the Vatican Arabic 126, fol. 2r, Ibn al-'Assal, and Ibn Kabar may mean that he was of Armenian origin,[4] even though he belonged to the Coptic Church. Butrus died after AD 1260.

The Works of Butrus

More works are attributed to Butrus than those he actually wrote, and some works are recorded under more than one title. His works can be divided into five categories: biblical, theological, moral or ethical, spiritual works, and edifying stories. His masterpiece is a commentary on the Passion of Christ preceded by an introduction on biblical hermeneutic, *al-Tashih fi alam al-Sayyid al-Masih* (The Correction [or Rectification] in the Sufferings of the Lord Christ), or *Tafsir alam al-Sayyid al-Masih* (Interpretation of the Sufferings of the Lord Christ). In the dogmatic field we have a treatise on Christian faith *(Maqala fi-l-i'tiqad [or al-'aqida])*. This has a small *urjuza* (poem). Several manuscripts wrongly attribute to Butrus a book consisting of five treatises, entitled *al-Burhan* (The Demonstration), but the book is by Butrus al-Jamil.

The following is a list of the abbreviations used:

BA = Bibliotheca Apostolica
BNF = Bibliothèque Nationale de France

BO = Bibliothèque Orientale
CM = Coptic Museum
CP = Coptic Patriarchate
DB = Dayr al-Baramus
FC = Franciscan Centre
G = Graf
GCB, SA = Greek Catholic Bishopric, Salim Association
MAM = Monastery of Anba Maqar
MSA = Monastery of St. Antony
MSP = Monastery of St. Paul
S = Simaika
SO = Selly Oak

Biblical work

This book has different titles:

- *Al-Tashih fi alam al-Sayyid al-Masih* (The Correction [or Rectification] in the Sufferings of the Lord Christ)
- *Tafsir alam al-Sayyid al-Masih* (Interpretation of the Sufferings of the Lord Christ)
- *Tashih al-i'tiqad fi alam al-Masih wa-bayan al-haqq fihi 'ala al-wajh al-sahih* (Rectification of the Belief in the Sufferings of Christ and the Statement of the Truth in It in the Right Way)

This is the only work included in Abu al-Barakat's list.

The work contains three introductions and a commentary on the Passion and Resurrection of Christ in the Gospels. The first introduction is on hermeneutics and contains seven sayings. The second introduction is on the economy *(tadbir)* in the life of Christ from his conception to his ascension. Sometimes we find the first or the second introduction in the manuscript without the rest of the book, with or without attribution to other authors; in particular, the second introduction was often attributed to al-Safi ibn al-'Assal. The third introduction contains two chapters and is the true introduction of the book. In his commentary on the Passion and Resurrection of Christ, the author follows the order of events as they appear in the Gospels. The authors mentioned are John Chrysostom, Gregory, Yahya ibn 'Adi, and 'Abdallah ibn al-Tayyib. Often the author does not specify his source. Even the work called *Hall shukuk*

(Resolution of the Doubts), which is found in some manuscripts as if it were an autonomous treatise, is actually part of this book, because the author, in his introduction, deals with the resolution of doubts. The book is translated into Ethiopic in manuscript Paris, Ethiopic 65.

The book apparently has no polemic or apologetic purpose, but the death of Christ is a topic frequently discussed in the Arab Christian as well as in Islamic writings. In the first introduction we find many expressions used by al-Safi ibn al-ʻAssal (see analysis in Samaan 1983: 90–197; Salah 2014).

Manuscripts

Cairo, CP, Theology 33 (S 215, G 604), 1r–17r (AD 1231): the first introduction
Cairo, CP, Theology 163 (S 476, G 360), 205 fol. (fourteenth century)
Paris, BNF, Arabic 90, fol. 1v–27v (fifteenth century?): the first introduction
Cairo, CP, Theology 162 (S 265, G 661), 81v–90v (AD 1589): the second introduction
Vatican, BA, Arabic 39, fol. 1v–32r (sixteenth/seventeenth century): the first introduction
Vatican, BA, Arabic 126, fol. 176v–3285v (AD 1687): the second and the third introduction
Cairo, Church of St. Sergius, Liturgy 33, fol. 1v–18v (AD 1623): the first introduction
Vatican, BA, Sbath 3, fol. 5v–234r (seventeenth century)
Cairo, Church of St. Mina, Theology 5, fol. 188r–192v (seventeenth century)
Sharfa (Lebanon), Monastery of the Deliverance, Syriac 9:5 (Karshuni), pp. 14–69 (seventeenth century?)
ʻAshqut (Lebanon), St. Peter and Paul School 55, fol. 1v–22r (1718): the first two introductions
Red Sea, MSP, Theology 45, 380 fol. (1738)
Red Sea, MSA, Theology 319, 223 fol. (1778/9)
Beirut, BO, 876 (Cheikho 459), 370 pp. (eighteenth century)
Beirut, BO, 876 (Cheikho 585), pp. 10–280 (eighteenth century)
Red Sea, MSA, Theology 103, 272 fol. (1792)
Red Sea, MSA, Theology 125, 268 fol. (1850)
Red Sea, MSA, Theology 102, 268 fol.

Aleppo, Heirs of Constantin Khudari, Sbath, al-Fihris, 75: the first two introductions
Red Sea, MSA, Theology 99, fol. 7–135
Cairo, FC, 741, fol. 132r–141v: part of the commentary

Editions and translations
al-Sadamanti 1871–72
al-Sadamanti 1926a, with titles, good division, and notes
Sbath 1929: 122–31, edition of the second introduction
al-Maqari and Manqaryus 1941: 5–23: the first introduction
al-Sadamanti 1972: 91–152, 1–54 (text), edition of the first introduction
Samaan 1983: 198–396: translation and edition of the second and third introduction and the prayer of Jesus in Gethsemane

Dogmatic works
***Maqala fi-l-i'tiqad* (Treatise on Belief) and *Maqala fi-l-'aqida* (Treatise on Dogma)**
The treatise, which looks like a short catechism, was composed on May 12, 1260. In the introduction, the author declares that the treatise is dedicated to his friend and former colleague in the monastery, Anba Yusab, Bishop of Akhmim. The treatise is divided into chapters (numbered in the FC M 741 as forty-nine chapters). Samaan also divides the treatise into numbers. The topics covered are the essence of God; creation and human sin; the Incarnation of Christ; the Trinity; the death, Resurrection, and Second Coming of Christ; and the end of the world. As we see, the author tries to follow the creed's sequence of subjects. The contents of the treatise are topics often disputed between Christianity and Islam, such as the Trinity, the Divinity of Christ, and his death on the cross. Speaking of final rewards, the author rejects the idea of the Islamic paradise, stating that it does not consist of eating, drinking, and sensual enjoyments (see analysis in Samaan 1983: 34–39).

Manuscripts
Cairo, CP, Liturgy 367 (S 747) (1493)
Aleppo, GCB, SA, Sbath 1027, pp. 1–31 (sixteenth century)
Vatican, BA, Arabic 126, fol. 2r–15r (1687)
Wadi al-Natrun, MAM, Hagiography 21, fol. 3v–28r
Red Sea, MSP, Theology 57 (1784)

Paris, BNF, Arabic 4786, fol. 45v–65r (1795/6)
Cairo, CP, Theology 203 (S 326, G 651), fol. 43r–56r (eighteenth century)
Cairo, CP, Theology 155 (S 529, G 350), fol. 74v–91v (1879)
Wadi al-Natrun, DB, Theology 4:67, fol. 190r–200v (1893)
Wadi al-Natrun, DB Theology 4:66, fol. 76r–87r (1891)
Birmingham, SO, Mingana 82 [20], 1r–11v (nineteenth century)
Cairo, CP, Theology 170 (S 318, G 365)
Cairo, FC, 741, fol. 78r–94r

Editions
al-Sadamanti 1895
al-Sadamanti 1926b

***Urjuza fi-l-i'tiqad* (*Urjuza* on Belief)**
The poem *(urjuza)* was written after the treatise, which dates to 1260. After a praise to the Trinity, it takes a quick look at the history of salvation, from the creation to the ministry of the Apostles, and it ends with moral exhortations to merit eternal life. The poet does not present any apologetic intent, but uses some Qur'anic terms, such as "al-Rahman" and other expressions (Samaan 1983: 40–43).

Manuscripts
Cairo, CP, Liturgy 367 (S 747) (1493)
Cairo, CP, Theology 110 (S 264, G 329), fol. 74v–91v (1562)
Cairo, CP, Theology 301 (S 291, G 541) (1661/2)
Vatican, BA, Arabic 126, fol. 241v–244v (1687)
Cairo, CP, Theology 303 (S 545, G 636), fol. 169v–171v (seventeenth century)
Cairo, CP, Theology 286 (S 366, G 338), fol. 155v–157v (1745)
Red Sea, MSP, Theology 57 (1784)
Cairo, CP, Theology 258 (S 452, G 388), fol. 155r–157v (eighteenth century)
Cairo, CP, Canon 30 (S 586) (1881)
Cairo, CP, Bible 169 (S 72, Graf 586) (1881)
Wadi al-Natrun, DB, Theology 4:67, fol. 164r–166r (1904)
Cairo, CP, Canon 25 (S 590) (1907)
Cairo, FC, 741, fol. 74r–77r

Editions
al-Sadamanti 1884: 16 pp. in the appendix
Jirjis 1927: appendix, 53–57
Anba Isudhurus: 55–60.

Ethical or moral writings

***Maqala fi-l-'amaliyyat* (Treatise on the Practical Life) and *Mukhtasar fi tahdhib al-nafs* (Compendium on the Education of the Soul)**

The Disciplining of the Soul in Practical Works (Mingana, p. 114)
This treatise follows the Treatise on Belief, and was also composed for Anba Yusab, Bishop of Akhmim; it must therefore date after AD 1260. In twelve chapters the author speaks about the virtues and perfection (see analysis in Samaan 1983: 50–60).

Manuscripts
Aleppo, GCB, SA, Sbath 1027, pp. 31–94 (sixteenth century)
Vatican, BA, Arabic 126, fol. 14v–41v (1687)
Wadi al-Natrun, MAM, Hagiography 21, fol. 29r–84v (1742)
Cairo, CP, Theology 155 (S 529, G 350), fol. 92r–127v (1879)
Birmingham, SO, Mingana 82 [20], 11v–34v (nineteenth century)
Cairo, FC, 741, fol. 95r–131r
Florence, Biblioteca Medicea-Palatina 417 (olim 70), 37v–117v

Editions
al-Sadamanti 1925–26[5]

***Ta'alim ruhaniyya wa-l-faz falsafiyya* (Spiritual Teachings and Philosophical Terms)**

The text deals with the same topics of the previous treatise, but with more biblical and canonical sources. The name of the author is mentioned only at the end, and only in Vatican Arabic 126; therefore the attribution must be accepted with some reservation.

Manuscripts
Aleppo, GCB, SA, Sbath 1027, pp. 94–182 (sixteenth century)
Vatican, BA, Arabic 126, fol. 42r–106r (1687)

Spiritual works

Al-Naja' fi-l-munaja'

Al-Khamsun tilba

In this book, the author imitates the Psalms. There is an introduction and fifty prayers. Samaan compares some prayers with their corresponding Psalms (Samaan 1983: 71–75).

Manuscripts

Cairo, CP, Liturgy 367 (S 747) (1493)
Red Sea, MSA, Liturgy 230, fol. 1–81 (1698)
Cairo, CP, Liturgy 212 (S 781, G 537), fol. 115v–209r (seventeenth century)
Vatican, BA, Sbath 288 (1712)
Red Sea, MSA, Theology 57 (1784)
Red Sea, MSA, Liturgy 200, fol. 151–214 (1715)
Red Sea, MSP, Ecclesiastical 258 (1780)
Red Sea, MSA, Liturgy 213, 86 fol. (1812)
Red Sea, MSA, Liturgy 214, 136 fol. (1812)
Red Sea, MSA, Liturgy 221 (1819)
Cairo, CP, Liturgy 211 (S 952) (1828)
Red Sea, MSA, Liturgy 200, fol. 1–146 (1831)
Red Sea, MSP, Ecclesiastical 306 (1869)
Red Sea, MSA, Liturgy 209, fol. 21–99 (1851)
Red Sea, MSP, Ecclesiastical 291 (1859)
Red Sea, MSP, Ecclesiastical 273 (1872)
Cairo, CP, Theology 155 (S 529, G 350), fol. 1r–74r (1879)
Cairo, CP, Liturgy 213 (S 794), fol. 115v–209r (seventeenth century)
Red Sea, MSA, Liturgy 685
Red Sea, MSA, Liturgy 192, 75 fol.
Red Sea, MSP, Ecclesiastical 252
Red Sea, MSP, Ecclesiastical 279
Cairo, FC, 741, fol. 3r–73v

Editions

al-Sadamanti 1890
al-Sadamanti 1976

Edifying stories

I put these three stories under the title of "Spiritual Works," rather than "Lives of Saints" or "Hagiography," because the contents of the three texts present a framework for the author to express his opinion on perfection in three types of life. The dialogues that the author uses in his moral teaching imitate the style of Kalila and Dimna. It does not seem that the persons of the stories are people known by the author or that they are saints, because they do not appear in any of the various Synaxaria (for more information see Schollmeier 1962; al-Sadamanti 1972: 33–34; Samaan 1983: 75–85).

The history of the rich man in Alexandria and his sons Isaia and Asia

Manuscripts

Vatican, BA, Arabic 126, fol. 106v–118r (1687)
Wadi al-Natrun, MAM, Hagiography 21, fol. 85r–110v (1742)
Cairo, CP, Theology 286 (S 366, G 338), fol. 140v–154v (eighteenth century)
Birmingham, SO, Mingana 82 [20], 34v–44r (nineteenth century)
Cairo, CP, Theology 155 (S 529, G 350), fol. 128r–143r
Cairo, CM, History 549 (S 120, G 706), fol. 18r–v

Editions

al-Sadamanti 2012a

The history of Isidurus of Alexandria and his family

Manuscripts

Aleppo, GCB, SA, Sbath 1027, pp. 182–245 (sixteenth century)
Vatican, BA, Arabic 126, fol. 129v–150v (1687)
Wadi al-Natrun, MAM, Hagiography 21, fol. 133r–176v (1742)
Red Sea, MSA, Theology 101 (1792)
Red Sea, MSP, Theology 99 (1858)
Birmingham, SO, Mingana 82 [20], fol. 44v–62v (nineteenth century)
Cairo, CP, Theology 155 (S 529, G 350), fol. 157v–184v

Editions

al-Sadamanti 2012c

The history of Babnuda al-Matardi

Manuscripts

Vatican, BA, Arabic 126, fol. 118v–129r (1687)
Wadi al-Natrun, MAM, Hagiography 21, fol. 110v–132v (1742)
Red Sea, MSA, Theology 101, fol. 86–103 (1792)
Cairo, CP, Theology 286 (S 366, G 338), fol. 127r–140r (eighteenth century)
Red Sea, MSP, Theology 99 (1858)
Cairo, CP, Theology 155 (S 529, G 350), fol. 143v–157r
Cairo, CM, History 549 (S 120, G 706), fol. 1r–9v
Red Sea, MSA, Theology 100, fol. 62–70
Red Sea, MSA, Theology 216
Wadi al-Natrun, MAM, Hagiography 23, fol. 106r–117v

Editions

al-Sadamanti 2012b

Doubtful and Spurious Works

Al-Ishraq (The Illumination): extracts (false attribution?)

From consulting the first manuscript, it seems that the text is from the book of Butrus al-Jamil (Wadi' 2012b). The work contains some philosophical and theological definitions, such as 'hypostasis,' 'essence,' 'attributes,' 'Incarnation,' and 'Resurrection'—basic terms for understanding theology and having a common basis for dialogue. Sbath speaks about chapters and not about definitions (Samaan 1983: 43–44).

Manuscripts

Cairo, CM, Theology 349 (S 74, G 704), fol. 111r–123r (eighteenth century) (without author's name)
Aleppo, GCB, SA, 1003, pp. 264–91 (eighteenth century)
Aleppo, GCB, SA, 1007, pp. 10–63 (nineteenth century)
Cairo, CP (G 396), fol. 55v–64v (nineteenth century)

Maqala tanfi al-Shakk wa-l-kufr 'an al-nasara al-muwahhidin li-Butrus al-Sadamant (Treatise Which Denies the Doubt and the Impiety from the Christians Who Believe in the Oneness of God)

In the only manuscript known so far this treatise is anonymous, so we must have reservations about its attribution to Butrus. In addition, we note that the same topics are included in the Treatise on Belief, but the terms are different. The aim of this treatise is clearly apologetic. It deals with the two most frequently discussed topics: the Trinity and the Divinity of Christ. A large part of the treatise is taken from Elijah, Bishop of Nisibis (§17–54), the great apologist (see analysis in Samaan 1983: 45–48).

Manuscripts

Vatican, BA, Arabic 120, fol. 239r–241r (1687)

Editions

Samir 1979

Kitab al-burhan (Book of the Demonstration)

The title and the contents of this book are attributed in other manuscripts to Butrus al-Jamil (Wadi' 2012b), who wrote shortly before Butrus al-Sadamanti. Rather than plagiarism, it is more likely a mistaken attribution by copyists (Graf 1947: 356). Likewise, the letter to Jamal al-Din al-Misri attributed in some manuscripts to Butrus al-Sadamanti is in reality the third treatise of the *Kitab al-burhan* of Butrus al-Jamil (see Samaan 1983: 49).

Manuscripts

Red Sea, MSA, Theology 282, 42 fol. (1743)
Cairo, CP, Theology 203 (S 326, G 651) (eighteenth century)
Aleppo, GCB, SA, 1021, pp. 1–72 (eighteenth century)
Red Sea, MSA, Theology 102, 310 fol. (1816)
Cairo, CP, Canon 26 (S 596, G 651) (eighteenth century)
Cairo, CP, Theology 170 (S 318, G 365)
Wadi al-Natrun, DB, Theology 4:67, fol. 201r–341v: the first three treatises
Cairo, FC, 741, fol. 142r–185r: the first three treatises

Notes

1 In Atiya 1991c it is written as "Sidmant."
2 There is no entry for Sadamant in the *Coptic Encyclopedia*.
3 Graf, 1912: 212–13; Ibn al-'Assal 1998. In note 4 the translator, Pirone, believes that the author alludes here to Butrus ibn al-Rahib.
4 Atiya rejects this interpretation.
5 I thank Rev. Father Misa'il al-Baramusi and Mr. Rafiq 'Adil who helped me obtain a scan from this rare article and for the correction of the date of the article, which was 1932, according to Graf 1947.

20 Julius of Aqfahs: The *Martyrdom* of John and Simon

Youhanna Nessim Youssef

Introduction

Julius of Aqfahs is commemorated in the Synaxarium on 22 Tut. The Synaxarium gives a brief biography.

> Julius was an officer whose sympathy was given to the martyrs whose sufferings he saw, and who did all in his power to assist them and was particularly careful in securing their relics after martyrdom. He is credited with being the means of preserving a great many of these relics. A special cycle of martyrdoms is formed of those at which Julius was present, or in some way showed his sympathy with the martyrs, or carried away their bodies, or composed the record of their sufferings: God had caused the heathen kings to overlook him so that he was not called upon to offer sacrifice but was left alone to allow him to write the martyrs' memorials. Toward the end of Diocletian's persecution, Julius, inflamed with a desire to follow the martyrs' examples, went to Arfaniyous (?) the governor of Samannud, and himself made public profession of Christianity. He was questioned and tortured, but refused to sacrifice to the seventy idols, and at his prayer the earth opened and swallowed the idols and 140 priests who served them. He was then sent to the governor of Atripe, who had him tortured and three times slain, his life being miraculously restored after the first

> two executions. On the third occasion the pagans killed Julius, his son Theodore, his brother Youqyas, his slaves, the governor of Samannud, and the governor of Atripe, both these latter having been converted in the course of the trial, and 1,500 other Christians.

Several *Martyrdoms* are attributed to Julius. They can be grouped in four categories.

1. The *Martyrdoms* of Middle Egypt (Shenoufe, Epima, Didymus, Heraclides, Chamoul, Panesnew)
2. The *Martyrdoms* of the east branch of the Nile in Lower Egypt (Ari, Anoub)
3. The *Martyrdom* of Paese and Thecla
4. Macarius, Macrobius(?), and Nahraw

This chapter will discuss one of these *Martyrdoms* that is attributed to him. John and Simon are two martyrs from Lower Egypt. The Coptic text of their *Martyrdom* survives in a single manuscript from the Vatican Library (Vatican, Copt. 60.3 ff. 62–85), published by Henri Hyvernat with a French translation (Hyvernat 1886–87: 174–201). The following is a summary of the text by De Lacy O'Leary.

> *John* and *Simon*, martyrs, 11 Abib (5 July). John was the son of the old age of Moses and Helena of Chenemoulos [Timm 1985: 1061–62], and Simon was his cousin. John's parents had prayed for a son and St. John Baptist had appeared in a dream and promised that they would have one. When the child was born they called him John and built a church in honour of St. John Baptist. One day the bishop came to their town and he and his clergy dined in Moses' house: after dinner various chapters of the Acts of the Apostles were discussed and the bishop ordered his clergy to recite psalms: the boy John, then aged twelve, stood by and corrected the clergy whenever they made a mistake. Next day the bishop took the boy and ordained him priest. John did not know how to read or to write, but quickly learned the three anaphoras, and every prayer by heart. A number of miracles are related of John. We are told that *Kontillianos* was "king" in those days. "The king had one daughter. When she was asleep a black serpent entered into her stomach and caused her great pain as she turned

> round. The girl uttered cries which caused the king great distress: in vain he tried to soothe her or relieve her pain. One of the officers of the palace told the king about John and the way he healed the sick, so he sent for him forthwith. But John was warned in a dream that the king would send for him, and in order to help the princess he was transported to Alexandria in a chariot of fire." Then Diocletian became Emperor and persecution commenced. At Alexandria John and Simon saw Armenius the Governor judging the Christians and offered themselves for martyrdom. After examination and torture in the usual manner they were beheaded. (O'Leary 1937a: 165–66)

Commentary

Narrative style

The *Martyrdom* of John and Simon has a unique style; it begins with the life of the saint even before his birth.[1] The texts commences with a call to the listeners: "Come and listen in order that I tell you the life of the men of God John and Simon. Listen, my beloved, and be amazed" (Hyvernat 1886–87: 174, l. 4). However, at the end of the text, we find that this biography was not just recited—it was in fact written: "He narrated all things . . . *I wrote them . . . I, myself, wrote them and I made Menas the notary to write them*" (Hyvernat 1886–87: 198, l. 16).

The birth of John

The text, following the rules of rhetoric, talks about the city and the family of the martyr and about his birth. It was on the feast of St. John the Baptist on 2 Ba'una that his father received the vision of "John son of Zacharia, the forerunner of the Christ." John the Baptist is commemorated in the Coptic calendar several times: 2 Tut is the commemoration of his martyrdom (Basset 1904: 5; O'Leary 1926: 2), and 2 Ba'una is the commemoration of the invention of the relics of John and Elisha.

> In his days Julian, the infidel, wished to [re]build the Temple of the Jews in Jerusalem, Vespasian, Emperor of Rome, and his son Titus having destroyed it, for Julian, by the wickedness of his works, wanted to make of no effect the word of the Lord, which He spoke in the Holy Gospel, Matthew 24:2. And Julian having thrice commanded the building of it, it was destroyed. And the Jews said, "In this place there are some bodies of Christian elders, and unless you cast them

out the Temple cannot be [re]built." And Julian commanded them to cast out the bodies from that place and to burn them with fire. . . . And when they cast the bodies out they found the bodies of Saint John the Baptist and Elisha the prophet, and they wanted to burn them with fire. And certain believers came and gave the soldiers much money, and they took away the bodies of the saints, after the soldiers had made them swear that they would [not] leave them in that city, so that the emperor might not hear of it, and destroy them . . . and those believing men brought the bodies of the saints, John the Baptist and Elisha the prophet, to the city of Alexandria, to Saint Abba Athanasius, and he rejoiced over them with a great joy; and he laid them by him, until he could build a church for them. And one day when Abba Athanasius was sitting in the garden of his fathers, his scribe Theophilus being with him, he said, "If God gives me good days, I will build in this place a church in the names of Saint John the Baptist and Elisha the prophet, and I will lay their bodies in it." And Saint Theophilus recorded the words, which Abba Athanasius spoke, and Abba Athanasius built a church; and he took many of his own priests, and all the Christian folk, and he went to the bodies of the saints, and carried them with great honour, and bore them to the church. And as they were passing along they came to a house wherein was an old woman who had suffered for forty days with the pains of labour, and she cried out in pain by day and by night until she was all but dead. And when she heard the singing of the priests, as they passed with the bodies of the saints, she looked from the window of her house, and asked [her servants], saying, "What is this?" And they said unto her, "The bodies of the saints, John the Baptist, and Elisha the prophet." And straightway she brought herself to believe, saying, "O John, thou saint of God, if thou wilt deliver me from this tribulation I [will become] a Christian." And before she had finished saying these words with her mouth, straightway she gave birth to a boy, and she called him "John"; and after this, she and all the men of her house were baptized with Christian baptism. And Abba Athanasius laid the bodies of the saints in the church, and great signs and miracles appeared through them. And Saint Abba Theophilus, and many of the saints, saw Saint John the Baptist and Elisha the prophet; and they went round in the church with the archbishop, and consecrated the church. (Basset 1924: 532 [1073]–534[1075])

The text of the Synaxarium is not the only witness narrating this episode. There is a homily attributed to Serapion mentioning the same story: "He (Athanasius) was served by Theophilus being his secretary" (Lantschoot 1931: 240). The same story was the source of the *History of the Patriarchs* in Coptic (Orlandi 1970b: 44–48) and in Arabic (Seybold 1904a: 75). There are homilies on the invention of the relics of John the Baptist attributed to John Chrysostom (Budge 1913: 128–45; Till 1958: 322–32; Winstedt 1906: 241–43) and to Demetrius of Antioch (Budge 1915: 103–104).

There is also a Greek text but with a different ending: "at Sebastia, a city in Egypt which depends on the same people, those cursed [Julian the Apostate and the Jews] opened the shrine of Saint John the Baptist and set it on fire and took the ashes" (Halkin 1985: 228 §5). The various legends concerning relics of John the Baptist contradict each other (Meinardus 1979: 26–63).

Dating of the *Martyrdom*

We can draw some conclusions from the following dates, which are known to be accurate:

- Julian the Apostate reigned from November 3, AD 361 to June 26, 363 (Grumel 1958: 355)
- Athanasius was patriarch from June 8, 328 to May 2, 373 (Grumel 1958: 442–43)
- Theophilus was patriarch from 384 to October 15, 412

According to the Synaxarium, Athanasius was contemporary to Julian the Apostate (which is true). And Theophilus was an indirect successor to Athanasius. We can accept the Synaxarium, which confirms the historical data. We may expect that the first feast of the invention of the relics took place in the first year of the patriarchate of Theophilus, AD 384. In our *Martyrdom*, we find that the feast of John the Baptist, 2 Ba'una, falls before the birth of the saint, and he will suffer martyrdom at the age of eighteen or more (Basset 1924: 644 [1186]) under the reign of Diocletian (AD 284–305). Hence, we can conclude that there is anachronism and a shifting of more than one century in the date of the martyr's death. Thus it is clear that the *Martyrdom* must have been written a long time after the events.

Geographical data

The author mentions that his father was a priest in Chenemoulos (Timm 1985: 1061–62). This village is also in the *Book of the Churches and Monasteries* as having a church of the Virgin and not a church of John the Baptist (Samuel 1992: 122).

It is important to mention that the other Acts of the Martyrs attributed to Julius of Aqfahs start only with the events leading up to the martyrdom, not before the martyr's birth as in this text.

John becomes a monk

After the episode of his birth we find that, at the age of twelve years, "His father wished to take for him a wife but the child told his father: 'If you take for me a wife, I will not dwell with her but I will go to Scetis in order to stay there'" (Hyvernat 1886–87: 178, l. 23–179, l. 5).

It was between the years 330 and 336 that Macarius the Egyptian founded the monastic life in Scetis, more than twenty years after the end of the Diocletian persecution (Chitty 1980: 44; Guillaumont 1991a: 1491–92; Evelyn-White 1933a: 17–42). If we follow our text, we find that John's discussion of marriage took place before the persecution, hence we have a discrepancy of several decades. Furthermore, teenagers were not accepted in Scetis, with a few exceptions, such as Zacharia son of Carion, who disfigured himself in order to avoid gossip (Chitty 1980: 141).

The *Martyrdom* continues its narration with the acts of the two saints and their virtues. According to the Arabic text of the *Martyrdom*, John was ordained at the age of eighteen. This age has a symbolic value, since its two digits are also the first two letters of the name of Jesus. After the ordination, the Coptic text mentions: "John did not know to write but God helped him until he learnt the three holy Anaphorae" (Hyvernat 1886–87: 180, l. 3). The account mentions that John had an excellent memory, and had learned by heart the book of Psalms, the Pauline Epistles, the Acts of the Apostles, and other scriptures.[2] It would not have been difficult for him to memorize three anaphorae. Thus it is difficult to understand why the writer would have said, "God helped him." It is important to mention that the limitation of the number of anaphorae to three is due to the patriarch Gabriel II ibn Turaik (r. 1131–45) in his twenty-sixth canon (Burmester 1935: 41). The manuscript containing the *Martyrdom* was copied in the year AM 971 (= AD 1254–55)—in other words, more than a century after the canons of Gabriel ibn Turaik. The number of anaphorae is therefore consistent with the dates that we are given.

Miracles in the *Martyrdom*

After the ordination, the text of the *Martyrdom* narrates a long series of miracles which shed some light about the life of the saint.

Healing of a soldier

The saint healed a one-eyed soldier. At this point, the text insists once more on the oral nature of its original transmission: "Listen also in order that I may tell you another marvel."

Healing of a princess

After this first healing, the scene changes, and we are transported to the royal palace in Antioch, with a legendary king called Kontillianos. In the palace, the daughter of the king swallows a dragon. The soldier who was healed before suggests that the king should consult St. John. The saint travels to the palace on a cloud and heals the daughter of the king.

King Kontillianos appears only once in the Coptic literature, in the *Martyrdom* of Theodore the Oriental, which is a translation of a lost Greek text (Youssef 1986–89: 107–10). It would be logical to assume that our text postdates the *Martyrdom* of Theodore, which is full of historic details such as the war on the Danube (Balestri and Hyvernat 1908: 39, l. 8). The travel on a cloud may be inspired from the book of Isaiah 19:2. In hagiographical texts we read that John the Dwarf went on a cloud to Babylon in order to search for the relics of the three young men (Amélineau 1894: 411–12). Likewise, St. Shenoute was carried on a cloud in order to return from Ephesus to his monastery.[3]

The theme of the sick daughter of the king is recurrent in hagiographical texts, such as Hilaria, daughter of Zeno (Drescher 1947: 124). In the *History of the Patriarchs*, Michael I (r. 744–68) also healed the daughter of the king:

> Yet the Lord Christ turned his [the king's] heart to love Abba Michael the patriarch, therefore he invited him to his palace and we accompanied him and he begged the patriarch to pray for him. And the governor's daughter, who was four years old, was possessed by an unclean spirit, and so her father requested the patriarch to pray for her. Then Abba Michael took oil and blessed it and anointed her with it and the devil went out of her immediately. (Evetts, 1909: 148 [402])

The saint's dwelling place

About the dwelling of this saint we read: "He built a small cell in his *topos*." The word *topos* is used twice in this *Martyrdom*. The father of the saint made a vow to build a *topos* in the name of the Baptist (Hyvernat 1886–87: 180, l. 13). The second occurrence is "Everyone who will make a gift to our *topos*" (Hyvernat 1886–87: 174, l. 12, l. 15).

The practice of the monk building his cell is very ancient, although not as old as the time of the persecutions. It was followed in Nitria and Scetis (Regnault 1990: 58). In the Middle Ages, the recluse who lived in the Monastery of St Mina in Ibyar received a visit from the sultan of Egypt, al-Malik al-Kamil (r. 1218–38) and anointed him with oil in order to heal him (Viaud 1975: 29, no. 11). Hence, we can deduce that the word *topos* should be understood as 'church,' which is the model of the medieval period.

It is surprising that we cannot find any allusion to manual work in the cell, but only prayers, which is an attitude similar to the Euchitia (heterodox monks) (Guillaumont 1980: 284–93). The Euchitia despised the practice of work other than prayer in cells. They believed that those who followed this practice spit the devil in the shape of a serpent going out of their mouth (Jarry 1968: 17). Could this idea have influenced the story of the princess with the snake in her stomach, in our text?

Death of the martyrs

Our text narrates that after nine months, the king died and Diocletian became a *cosmocrator.* After that, we find the episode of the war with the Persians, which is inspired by the martyrdom of Theodore the Oriental,[4] followed by the edict of persecution. The saint asks his disciple to go to Alexandria in order to suffer martyrdom in the name of Christ. In the other *Martyrdoms* attributed to Julius of Aqfahs, the saints go to suffer martyrdom after a heavenly vision. Simon, the disciple of John, sold his animals before going to Alexandria (Hyvernat 1886–87: 196, l. 16). We have here a monk who was allowed to keep his wealth, meaning that we are far from early monasticism. Beginning in the sixth and seventh centuries, the monks were allowed to keep their property, as is attested in many contracts (Wipszycka 1972: 161–62).

In Alexandria, John and Simon appear before the count Armenius. The interrogatory which follows is not different from the other epic *Martyrdoms*.

In this text, Julius of Aqfahs prepares a banquet for the two martyrs. This detail does not occur in any other *Martyrdom* attributed to Julius of Aqfahs. We find no information about the life of Julius, his family, or his titles. He is presented as a rich man but without any official power, which is unparalleled in any other text.

Julius took the bodies of Sts. John and Simon to their village, Chenemoulos, where a church was built and became a source of healing grace. The relics were later translated to different places (Youssef 2000: 339–50).

Conclusion

The *Martyrdom* of John and Simon does not follow the epic form of the other *Martyrdoms* attributed to Julius of Aqfahs, but follows the general themes of the panegyric.

It seems that this text began as an oral tradition, as it starts with the word "listen," and was written down later.

Our text provides several data about the life of a recluse in the Middle Ages. The cell was annexed to a church. The monk spent his time in recitation of the Scriptures, receiving visitors, and performing miracles, with no mention of manual labor. His economic status derived from the fact that he was the son of a rich priest in a village. He did not renounce his wealth.

We find two interesting liturgical notes: the feast of John the Baptist, which began in the fifth century, and the mention of the three anaphorae, which is from the twelfth century.

The author has access to the *Martyrdoms* of Theodore the Oriental, Hiliaria the daughter of Zeno, and others.

The typical themes of heavenly visions, horrible tortures, and the restoration of the body do not occur in our text.

From these indications, it is clear that the *Martyrdom* of John and Simon cannot be attributed to Julius of Aqfahs, and it is certain that it is based on a late redaction inspired by the lives of the recluses of the Middle Ages. This period was the Mamluk era, which was unfavorable for the Copts. An unknown author wanted to provide a model to his fellow Christians; he used a kind of 'copy–paste' system to create martyrs who corresponded to the circumstances of his own times.

Notes

1 Delehaye 1973: 143, which accurately explains the rules of panegyrics: preamble, the city, the family, the miracles, the life, his deeds, and the acts of the martyrs.

2 This is not surprising. In Egypt, children are able to learn the Qur'an by heart at the age of eight.

3 In the *Vitae* of Shenoute Coptic and Arabic; cf. Leipoldt 1906: 18§16; Amélineau 1888–95: 324–25.

4 Cf. Winstedt 1906.

21 The Bohairic *Acts of the Martyrs* as a Genre of Religious Discourse

Ewa D. Zakrzewska

The blood of the martyrs is the seed of the Church.
(after Tertullian, *Apologeticus*, chapter 50.13)

Introduction

The Egyptian *Acts of the Martyrs* have their background in the martyr cult of Late Antiquity. In their preserved form, however, most of them may date from after the Arab conquest of Egypt. The majority of preserved Bohairic manuscripts are from the tenth–eleventh centuries. It is in this period, when Coptic was about to fall into disuse as a language of communication, that Bohairic became the principal liturgical language of the Egyptian Orthodox Church and a considerable number of religious texts, originally written in Sahidic or Greek, had to be rewritten in Bohairic. The compilation of Bohairic Coptic religious texts, following their standardization for the use in liturgy ("synaxarial standardization," Orlandi 2013: 90), was one of the answers to the challenges facing Egyptian Christians in that period: religious Islamization on the one hand and linguistic Arabization on the other. Thanks to the far-sighted decisions of the Church authorities, Bohairic Coptic survived as a sacred language. Moreover, the cult of the martyrs became the cornerstone of Egyptian Christianity: the Coptic Orthodox Church was defined as the Church of the Martyrs (see Papaconstantinou 2006; Gemeinhardt and Leemans 2012).

Historians, literary critics, and theologians do not have a particularly favorable opinion about the *Acts of the Martyrs*, which they consider repetitive, historically unreliable, and lacking in theological profundity. And yet these narratives enjoyed, and still enjoy, great popularity among Egyptian Christians, and their importance for the Coptic Church is undeniable.[1] Clearly there are some other factors at work, underestimated by conventional scholarship. The aim of this contribution is therefore to look for such factors by asking how the *Acts of the Martyrs* functioned and what could have made them so influential despite their alleged shortcomings.

The present chapter is primarily based on the Bohairic *Acts of the Martyrs* edited by H. Hyvernat (1886b, abbr. *AM*) and elaborates on an earlier article (Zakrzewska 2011). In that article the narrative techniques applied by the writers of the *Acts of the Martyrs* were analyzed. This chapter will take a closer look at the social practices in which these texts functioned and interpret them as manifestations of religious discourse, where the term 'discourse' is used in a broad sense to refer to human linguistic behavior appropriate in given social circumstances regardless of the mode (oral or written). Consequently, social circumstances have to be included in the analysis (see De Fina and Georgakopoulou 2012). From this point of view, it is important to realize that the *Acts of the Martyrs*, which were intended to be read aloud during the liturgical commemoration of a martyr, were essentially persuasive texts: their main function was to influence the attitudes and behavior of their intended audience. The purpose of the analysis below is to reconstruct the strategies by which the realization of this persuasive aim was made possible.

Religious Discourse and Sacred Languages: Definitions and Social Functions

Sacred languages can be defined as languages or language varieties preferred for use in religious discourse, that is, in and around sacral practices, for example in liturgy, readings from sacred books (the Bible, the Qur'an), in sermons, prayers, edifying literature, religious songs, reports of mystical experiences and divination, and magical spells. Languages or language varieties used for these purposes often differ from the ones used by the same population in secular functional domains. Examples abound: the use of Latin in the Roman Catholic Church, of Bohairic Coptic in the Coptic Orthodox Church, of Qur'an Arabic by Arabic-speaking or non-Arabic-speaking Muslims, and so on.

In spite of this conspicuous divergence from the language of daily communication, and perhaps even thanks to this divergence, sacred languages function as very strong markers of identity for the members of the communities in which they are used, especially if membership in these communities (and consequently the use of an appropriate sacred language) is a matter of one's conscious choice, as it is in times of religious conflicts. In this way the use of sacred languages is instrumental for constructing social communities. Coptic is here a case in point: since the adoption of Coptic as the liturgical language of the Coptic Orthodox Church, it has been maintained for centuries until the present day, despite the population's language shift to Arabic.

Unfortunately, the issue of the social functions of Christian sacred languages is clearly underrepresented in sociolinguistic studies. This analysis will therefore examine the most conspicuous properties of religious discourse in which these languages are typically used, and will be illustrated with examples from the Bohairic *Acts of the Martyrs*.

Religious Discourse and Jakobson's Model of a Communicative Situation

The starting point of the discussion in the present chapter is the classic model of a communicative situation by Jakobson (1960: 353) with which the abovementioned article (Zakrzewska 2011) concludes:

	Context [Time] [Place]	
Addressee	**Message**	**Addresser** [Writer], [Speaker], etc.
	Contact channel [Aural] [Visual] etc. **Code** [Language use]	

In religious discourse all these parameters of a communicative situation are different from 'profane' discourse. They will be discussed in the remainder of this chapter in the following order: addressee; message; addresser; context; contact channel; code.

Addressee

The addressee—that is, the entity to whom religious discourse acts are directed—is primarily the Supernatural: most notably God but also spirits, either angelic or demonic. The addressee can be conceptualized in a variety of ways but always as an entity capable of receiving a message and acting appropriately, in other words, characterized by consciousness, will, and agency. Religious discourse is thus, first and foremost, communication with the Supernatural, and this is the single most important feature which distinguishes diverse genres of religious discourse from profane ones.

Members of a religious community can be intended as co-addressees of religious discourse acts. This was apparently the case of the *Acts of the Martyrs*, which becomes evident from *The Martyrdom of John of Phanijoit*, a very late Bohairic text (dated to the early thirteenth century) which contains a description of such an event.

> According to the custom of the southerners, the Christian believers, out of the greatness of their love for the ancient martyr . . . , Saint George the Meletonian, to whom they dedicated the seven Sundays of the fifty festive days,[2] *would read his Martyrdom* every Sunday with responsorial hymns and *psalis*[3] suited to his honor. (Zaborowski 2005: 72–75; translation modified, emphasis added)

A martyr's commemoration is described as a part of a liturgical celebration, that is, a church service meant to worship God in public, to offer him thanks, and to invoke his mercy through the intercession of the martyr. In such a service God is intended as the primary addressee of several varied discourse acts. Moreover, this liturgical ceremony is depicted as a distinct communicative situation, differentiated by specific features from other such situations. Some of these specific elements are explicitly mentioned in the text, for instance the reading aloud of the saint's *Martyrdom* and the singing of the various hymns. The reading of the *Martyrdom* is 'embedded' in the liturgy, and the audience—"multitudes" of believers (Zaborowski 2005: 75)—thus become co-addressees.

The message and its performance

The central segment of the Jakobsonian model of a communicative situation is the message. The most characteristic feature of the message within religious discourse is the fact that it is not intended as a statement about something but as verbal means to change something in reality. In the foregoing sections the term 'persuasive' has been used several times, as persuasive discourse acts are meant to affect the addressee's behavior or attitude. Prototypical persuasive acts include the following (Archer 2010: 382):

- directives (requests and orders)
- commissives (promises)
- expressives and acknowledgments (praises, curses, thanks, apologies)

As has been shown above, a persuasive variety of religious discourse, such as the reading of a *Martyrdom*, but also for example a sermon, should prototypically be 'embedded' in the liturgical service. The discourse acts which characterize the liturgy proper, and which obviously belong to the domain of religious discourse as well, should be characterized as performative.

Performative discourse acts, also called speech acts (see Austin 1962 and Searle 1969) or speech actions, are not intended as statements about something either, but as social actions in order to "effect changes in the state of affairs" (Keane 2004: 433). As they have no referential meaning they cannot be evaluated in terms of true or false, but as *felicitous* or *infelicitous* in a given situation: they have to be used in appropriate circumstances by persons 'legitimatized' to do so and according to specific rules, otherwise they will be void. Typical and generally known examples of performative acts are legal acts. For example, by using an appropriate formula ("I hereby do thee wed," Keane 2004: 433) in appropriate circumstances the candidate spouses become actually married. In the domain of religious discourse, performative acts form the backbone of the Divine Liturgy and the sacraments. The persuasive acts which are embedded in the liturgy, as sermons or readings of the saints' *Lives* or *Martyrdoms*, gain their authority and persuasive force precisely by virtue of their embedding in this performative context. Persuasive *texts* may be used also outside the performative context by the members of the community or, for example, by scholars, but this is a secondary, impoverished use, in which the persuasive function can actually become lost.

The term 'performative' is etymologically related to the terms 'to perform' and 'performance.' Performative acts are intimately connected to rituals, among others religious rituals. The rituals are performed, that is, dramatically enacted.

Religious rituals have the following goals:

- "to regulate the relations between the society and the supernatural (transcendental function),
- "to underline social values and create social identities and solidarity (normative/ideological function),

- "to construct, maintain and modify the society itself by confirming and reinforcing of shared traditions (social/cultural function)" (Bax 2010: 498, 505, and references)

In other words, participation in a publicly performed religious ritual is not only spiritually beneficial for an individual but also leads to a confirmation of one's membership in the community and eventually formation of group identity. Participation in liturgical commemorations obviously requires specific behavior on the part of both the performer and the audience, behavior that had to be learned either by formal training or by socialization processes and training through participation.

For such situations in their entirety, Foley's concept of the performance arena seems to be very useful. As Foley (1995: 47–49, 61–66) observes, the term 'performance arena' can be understood literally when referring to an actual performance situation, but it can also refer to a whole spectrum of rhetorical devices indicating indirectly such a situation. Zakrzewska (2011: 516) argues for broadening of the scope of this concept even further in order to apply it also to the cultural environment which shapes the expectations of the participants, the expectations that are to be met during a specific performance event. According to this interpretation, the performance arena is a tacit, culturally determined contract between the members of a given community which specifies how the work in question is to be presented, perceived, and understood. In other words, it is the performance arena where the behavioral and attitudinal facets of religious discourse show. For an analytical approach like the one here advocated, which considers narratives as social practices, the performance arena is as essential a component of a literary work as is the text itself.

An example will help to clarify this concept. We can imagine that the text of a *Martyrdom* could be read aloud by a priest or deacon to the pilgrims in the martyr's church during his religious commemoration and, on another occasion, read aloud by a professor to his or her students in a classroom for analytical purposes. In each of these cases, the participants' expectations and behavior would be different. Theoretically, we could even imagine that the same individual could participate in both gatherings and would in each case react and behave differently. The goal of the present chapter is to reconstruct, as far as possible, the original medieval performance arena of the *Acts of the Martyrs* via the analytical approach of a modern student of religious discourse.

Addresser

The addresser is the entity who produces the message. In profane discourse this is mostly a speaker or a writer of a given text. In the case of religious discourse the situation is not so straightforward, however, as there are several 'speaking agents' and several 'voices,' a phenomenon which has been labeled *heteroglossia* (Keane 2004: 440–43, after Bakhtin 1981 and Goffman 1981).

According to Keane (2004: 440), the following speaking agents should be distinguished:

- "the *principal* who bears the responsibility for what is said,
- "the *author* who formulates the words,[4]
- "the *animator* who utters them."

The clearest examples to illustrate these distinctions are the four Gospels, which we consider as the 'word of God' (= *the principal's word*), but also as texts written by four human *authors* and read aloud during religious services by *authorized animators* whom I call *performers*. These roles are also relevant in other genres of religious discourse, for example, if a distinction has to be made between prophetic speech and direct revelation, divination and glossolalia (speaking in tongues), with "a deity and a human using the same body but speaking in different voices, marked by contrasting prosodic and paralinguistic features, and sometimes distinct linguistic codes" (Keane 2004: 442).

The distinction between these three types of speaking agents concerns their respective responsibility not only for the content of what is said but also for the authority which is bestowed on this message. The lesser the status and authority of the principal, the more pronounced becomes the role of the author. Thus, as the *Acts of the Martyrs* were neither a part of the Bible nor belonged to the performative parts of the liturgy proper, their authors had some liberty to write what they considered appropriate. As Dijkstra and Van der Vliet (2015: 387) observe in the context of the Coptic *Lives of Saints*: "Their manuscript transmission, therefore, does not represent an effort at reproducing as faithfully as possible an '*Urtext*,' but rather an on-going process of updating the text. This is not an arbitrary process, guided by—for instance—esthetical criteria, but a deliberate effort at enhancing the effectiveness of the text as an edifying (or better, persuasive) text."

In the case of the *Acts of the Martyrs*, the distinction of principal vs. author can be creatively blurred and used as an authentication strategy: the text is claimed to have been written by an authoritative eyewitness (i.e., the principal and author are the same person):

> It is me, Julius of Khvehs, who wrote this memorial of Saint Father Macarius of Antioch and was sailing together with Arianus for (recording) these affairs in this way. My Lord Jesus Christ knows that I neither withheld nor added anything (*AM*, 69).

The role of the writer of liturgical manuscripts requires some commentary. Is there a difference between the copyist, who has no responsibility for the content of the text, and the author? The above observation by Dijkstra and Van der Vliet suggests that this difference can be blurred. However, one should also bear in mind that even in the case when a scribe merely copied a liturgical manuscript, he was nevertheless enhancing the authority of the message, especially in a cultural environment in which participation in literacy practices was accessible to a 'happy few' only. To quote Dijkstra and Van der Vliet (2015: 387) again, "a manuscript represented a value of its own that was both of a symbolic and an economic nature. It was copied on order for a well-to-do sponsor who donated it to a church or monastery, where it was lavishly bound and carefully kept, to be shown on solemn occasions only." Moreover, both the conscientious production of a liturgical manuscript and its commission were also performative actions which, when accompanied by appropriate prayers, could earn the scribe and the commissioner remission of their sins (see *AM*, 77). Liturgical books as material objects, rather than being simply 'data carriers,' had thus their own role to play in a religious ceremony and issued their own 'hidden voice' to underline the authority of the message.[5] This was also one of the reasons why such books were kept in the monasteries even when they went out of use, only to be found and purchased in later times by modern scholars as collections which Orlandi (2013: 91) calls *bibliological units*. The Bohairic *Acts of the Martyrs* discussed in this chapter form exactly such a bibliological unit.

In the case of the performative parts of the liturgy proper, a very important factor is "transformation of intentionality and agency" on the part of the performer, as "the efficacy of the action being performed by a rite depends on being accepted as something that can be repeated and that cannot be derived solely from the speaker's intentions" (Keane 2004: 443). Thus, the fact that the performer's own agency is downplayed ensures the correct communication with the Supernatural and therefore the fulfillment of the rite.

The *Acts of the Martyrs* belonged to the persuasive parts of the liturgy directed to the congregation as their co-addressee, and the performer could certainly stress the emotional appeal of the story by a skillful use of prosodic means. It is an open question whether the performer could also engage the audience by adding various modifiers such as vocatives or short comments for making the message more convincing (see Zakrzewska 2011: 511), but in any case he could 'guide' the audience through the text in the course of the ongoing oral performance: "Listen further and I will tell you another great miracle which happened through the saint" (*AM*, 183).

Similarly, the renderings of the characters' speeches, especially of those delivered by the martyr saint, were introduced by elaborate constructions called quotative indexes, "aural punctuation marks" as Foley (1999: 221) puts it, for example: "And Apater answered him . . . saying this" (*AM*, 97). Such direct speech reports were probably read on a different tone by the performer (Zakrzewska 2011: 509 and references), which increased their dramatic and moral appeal. According to Grig (2004: 42), "speech in the martyr acts could be a powerful tool for exposition, for confirmation and definition of the faith."

The performer in religious discourse is typically a member of the community, who is authorized to act on behalf of the community or some specific members of it, regardless of their physical presence or absence on the spot. However, if present, the members of the community are typically expected to actively co-perform, verbally or nonverbally, according to the format of a specific celebration, for example by singing, kneeling, or praying silently (see "Contact Channel" below). This aspect distinguishes the participants in a religious celebration from, for example, the audience in the theater, who merely watch and applaud the performers.

Context: time and place

As has been stated above, the *Acts of the Martyrs* must have been written in order to be read aloud to the pilgrims visiting the shrine of the martyr on the occasion of his festival. The preserved manuscripts, which had been compiled for liturgical purposes, contain several annotations to that effect, such as the date of the festival and instructions for the performer: *ōš* 'read' and *ša* 'up to [here]' (Hebbelynck and Van Lantschoot 1937a: 419).[6] Also *The Martyrdom of John of Phanijoit* mentions the place of the commemoration (the church dedicated to the martyr in a village called Ponmonros, near Cairo; Zaborowski 2005: 75) and its scheduled time: every Sunday of the time between Easter and Pentecost.

Time in religious discourse is conceived of as not linear but cyclic: a ritual performance takes place according to a certain schema every day, every week (for example, "every Sunday"), every year, and so on, without an end point, thus in theory eternally. This can be called heterochrony (Keunen 2011: 45, 123n11), as it contrasts significantly with most genres of profane discourse, in which a linear conception of time is observed: the events described are dated to a specific point on the time axis or to a specific segment of this axis.

As for the second important contextual parameter, place, it differs from daily, ordinary situations no less dramatically than the parameter of time. Religious celebrations typically take place in dedicated spaces in which the rules of the 'ordinary' world do not apply, as for example a temple, church, churchyard, or, as in our case, the shrine of a martyr. Such spaces have been called heterotopic (Foucault 1986; Keunen 2011: 44–46). The celebrations which took place at the shrine of the martyr were attended by "multitudes" of pilgrims. To complete the picture we should add the emotional arousal accompanying the pilgrimage: the excitement of traveling to the saint's shrine and temporary suspension of the day-to-day routine in favor of the extraordinary; exuberant feasts with wine, meat, and bread; crowds in festive mood where one could rub shoulders with all kinds of otherwise inaccessible dignitaries (for Christian pilgrimage see Turner and Turner 1978 and the discussion in Derks 2009: 25–41; for Egypt, see Papaconstantinou 2001: 317–25). Next to these worldly attractions, spiritual benefits were no less important: by joining the martyr's commemoration, the believers could earn a plenary indulgence of their sins and return home spiritually reborn (Papaconstantinou 2001: 323).

These special values of the parameters of time and space provide the very raison d'être for the *Acts of the Martyrs*, which were intended to justify the veneration of a specific martyr in a specific place in which his relics were allegedly kept (= space) on a specific day, the anniversary of his death, typically the final temporal boundary of the martyr's story (= time). In this way, performing the *Acts of the Martyrs* contributed to the ideological sacralization of the landscape and Christianization of the calendar (Van der Vliet

2006: 48–55; 2013: 226–30). Moreover, as Van der Vliet argues, the combination of these three parameters—veneration of the martyr, place, and time—is actually the only really historical information which can be found in the *Acts*. By providing an explanation for existing worship, the *Acts of the Martyrs* write "performative history," as Van der Vliet (2006: 54) puts it.[7]

Contact channel: multimodal interaction

The contact channel is the 'path' by which the message, issued by the addresser, reaches the addressee. For example, a spoken message is typically perceived aurally, while a written or signed one is perceived visually. In religious discourse, the message can be delivered in a variety of ways, including nonverbally. The following list will illustrate this variation.

- Variations in the aural channel: melodic recitation, music, chant
- Visual channel: images, viewed as performative by virtue of being depicted in an appropriate place and in an appropriate form ("ritual-centered visuality," Elsner 2000: 55, 60–63); liturgical vestments (compare with judges or lawyers), gestures and movements, for instance crossing oneself, kneeling, changing position around the altar (the human body as a medium of communication; see Müller et al. 2013-14); light and darkness
- Tactile channel: touching the martyr's grave or an icon
- Olfactory channel: incense
- Gustatory channel: Holy Communion, a special kind of white bread (called *artos katharos* or *katharion*; Papaconstantinou 2001: 319)
- Mental channel: inner speech and/or silent meditation

In the preceding sections it has been argued that the addressees in religious discourse are the Supernatural with the members of the community as co-addressees, while the message is delivered by the performer with the members as co-performers. These multiple roles of the interactants are matched by the *multimodal* character of the interaction, which engages all one's senses as well as one's body, thoughts, emotions, and imagination. Moreover, the interaction with the Supernatural has its material and social sides: the prescribed use of liturgical vestments and objects, including books, holy water and oil, candles, and so forth on the material side, and the participants' sense of performing, thus belonging together, on the social one. This makes religious discourse, seen as a social practice, an all-encompassing experience.

Code

As has been demonstrated, all the parameters of a communicative situation differentiate religious discourse acts from profane ones:

- the message: not referential but performative and/or persuasive
- the participants: a 'heteroglossic' performer vis-à-vis the Supernatural, with the members of the community as both co-performers and co-addressees
- context: heterochrony and heterotopia
- contact channel: multimodal interaction

All these differences justify the use of a divergent linguistic code in religious discourse: a dedicated variety of the standard language (classic diglossia) or another, genetically unrelated language (extended diglossia; see, e.g., Myers-Scotton 2006: 76–89; Coulmas 2013: 53–57; for Coptic see Zakrzewska [2017]). What classic and extended diglossia have in common is that the varieties in question are used for texts of respectively high and low status. The high-status variety in a diglossic society is typically used in writing and not learned as a mother tongue in infancy but acquired in the course of formal education. This has two consequences. First, high-status varieties, although based on a natural language, do not develop in a natural way but are more or less constructed by authorized agents. Second, in a society in which educational opportunities are restricted and literacy practices are nevertheless highly valued, mastering of the high-status variety represents considerable symbolic capital (see Bourdieu 1991).

Generally speaking, religious texts enjoy high status, but linguistic varieties used in persuasive acts are typically less removed from standard than the ones used in performative acts. In present-day Egypt, for example, in the Coptic Orthodox Church the liturgy proper may be performed in Coptic (with some Greek), while sermons are delivered in Arabic. When diverse varieties of Coptic were spoken in Egypt, the liturgical language was Hellenistic Greek (not vernacular Greek). We know, however, that Sahidic Coptic was used, next to Greek, for sermons in Pachomian monasteries and interpreters were available for those visitors who could not understand it (Goehring 1986: 200). It was only when Coptic was no longer used as a living language of written communication that it became a liturgical language and acquired in this way the highest status in the eyes of its users. This must have been a deliberate decision of the Church authorities, as it was not Sahidic but Bohairic, the dialect of Lower Egypt, as used in the monastic complex of Wadi al-Natrun, that was chosen for the use in liturgy, while the earliest, unsystematic attempts to translate liturgical texts were translations into Sahidic.

Linguistic varieties used in religious discourse have some properties which differentiate them from high-status varieties used in other circumstances and which point to their constructed character, that is, to deliberate control of linguistic resources. One of these properties is a preference for chant or melodic recitation (see "Contact Channel," above) in which religious texts have to be delivered in public. This can be interpreted as a means to control the prosody and intonation in order to stress the singularity of a religious performance. Another conspicuous property is the use of lists of names which occur outside 'normal' clausal patterns. Examples are litanies and lists in magical texts (see Gordon 1999). This can be seen as controlling the syntax.

Probably the most striking property of religious language use, which can be interpreted as controlling both the grammar and the lexicon, is, however, a marked preference for formulaic expressions and constructions, that is, more or less fixed combinations of words or phrases which function as a single lexical unit. Contrary to popular opinion, formulas are not clichés that one has to reproduce slavishly, but play an essential role in a variety of social practices in which they have to be expertly applied. Consequently, as Foley (2002: 18) puts it, formulas are "bigger words"; they have not only referential but also social meaning.

The referential meaning of formulas (explicated, for example, in *The Oxford Dictionary of Idiomatic English*) makes them similar to words. Their social meaning evokes the shared social and cultural background of the interactants and thus confirms one's social identity. The appropriate use of formulary expressions in a given context allows the participants mutual recognition as members of the same social milieu who share the same conventions of verbal behavior. As argued by Edwards and Sienkewicz (1990: 199), in oral cultures a formula is "a symbol of the shared knowledge and experience" which gives the speakers "the assurance both of the wisdom of what they are saying and of social approval of their contribution." Moreover, formulas are essential in performative functions (ensuring ritual efficacy) and discursive ones (marking off certain text segments). To quote Foley again: "We don't merely *repeat* [formulaic expressions] but rather use such phrases because the social situation warrants it, and only when the situation warrants it" (Foley 2002: 137–38; emphasis in original).

From a grammatical point of view, formulas should be considered as "partly lexicalized frames" with "slots for variable material" (Wray 2008: 12, 16). In the context of the Bohairic *Acts of the Martyrs* this can be illustrated by the different variants of the frequently occurring formula: "the imperishable crown which Christ has prepared for those who will struggle for the sake of His holy name" (*AM*, 119).

The formula and its constituent segments evoke Holy Scripture (see, e.g., 1 Peter 5:4), with its authority and wealth of intertextual associations. In the *Acts of the Martyrs*, the only invariable segment of this formula is the noun ⲙ-ⲡⲓⲭⲗⲟⲙ 'wreath/crown' used as the direct object: $ⲙ_{ACC}$-$ⲡⲓ_{SDEF}$-ⲭⲗⲟⲙ. The most frequent verb in the formula is ϭⲓ 'receive' with which the noun or pronoun referring to the martyr appears as the subject ('the martyr receives the crown'); less frequent are the verbs ⲣⲭⲁⲣⲓⲍⲉⲥⲑⲉ 'give' and ⲥⲟⲃϯ 'prepare' with Christ as the subject and the martyr as the indirect object ('Christ gives/prepares the crown for the martyr'). The richest variation pertains to the attributes of the noun 'crown,' which in their turn can be expanded by adverbs. These attributes and adverbs are likewise also formulaic. Schematically this can be represented as follows:

ATTRIBUTE	ADVERB
• ⲛⲁⲧⲧⲁⲕⲟ 'imperishable' • ⲛⲁⲧⲗⲱⲙ 'unfading' • ⲛⲧⲉ ⲡⲱⲟⲩ 'of glory' • ⲛⲧⲉ ⲛⲓⲙⲁⲣⲧⲩⲣⲟⲥ 'of the martyrs' • ⲛⲧⲉ ϯⲙⲉⲧⲙⲁⲣⲧⲩⲣⲟⲥ 'of martyrdom'	• ϣⲁ ⲉⲛⲉϩ 'till eternity' • ϧⲉⲛ ϯⲙⲉⲧⲟⲩⲣⲟ ⲛⲛⲓⲫⲏⲟⲩⲓ 'in the kingdom of heavens' • ϧⲉⲛ ⲛⲛⲓⲫⲏⲟⲩⲓ 'in the heavens' • ϧⲉⲛ ⲡⲓⲁⲏⲣ 'in the sky' • ϧⲉⲛ ⲟⲩϩⲓⲣⲏⲛⲏ 'in peace'

The writer can choose one segment from each column and is able to construct diverse variants of the formula with one of the three abovementioned verbs: 3 verbs × 5 attributes × 5 adverbs makes 75 possible variants! In this way the writer can 'kill two birds with one stone': ensure textual variation and at the same time evoke early Christian agonistic imagery in which martyrdom is depicted as a struggle *(agon)* which the martyr completes not as a pitiful victim but as the crowned winner.

Conclusions

The introduction to this chapter asked how it is that the *Acts of the Martyrs* have such a powerful appeal to their audiences. The analysis describes two factors which must have had a particular importance for the functioning of these narratives: the liturgical context in which they were performed and their linguistic form.

As for the linguistic aspects, as is argued elsewhere (Zakrzewska 2015; 2017), Coptic, as it has come down to us in several written varieties, was throughout its history a deliberately constructed prestige idiom used to express group identity: first by the members of ascetic and monastic communities and later also by those members of the laity who wanted to align themselves with the local monasteries. In the diglossic linguistic situation of Egypt, Coptic was thus a suitable high-status variety for use in religious discourse, especially after the rise of Arabic as a dominant *spoken* language. Coptic continued then to express group membership and therefore group solidarity of the members of the Egyptian Church. This special combination of high status and solidarity has helped Coptic to survive into modern times.

As for the performativity of religious discourse, it has been demonstrated that all its communicative parameters differ systematically from their counterparts in profane discourse. For the clarity of the discussion, each of these parameters—addressee, message, addresser, context, and contact channel—was analyzed separately. The specificity of religious discourse is, however, that all these factors operate together and engage the participants' whole personality: body, mind, emotions, imagination, and sense of social identity.

The individual response to the performance of the *Acts of the Martyrs* was thus intensified by a sense of group solidarity and by sharing the ritual experience. It is beyond the scope of the present chapter to analyze the impact of the collective experience of the sacred thus produced, but it goes without saying that this impact could have been profound. In fact, the liturgy is considered a crucial factor for preserving Christianity in Egypt.

Interestingly, *The Martyrdom of John of Phanijoit* confirms our expectations of the beneficial effects of the Divine Liturgy:

> Now when the blessed John noticed the multitudes flocking there, he arose and went there with them so that he might complete the festival of Saint George with the troop of the Christians. And when the clerics had completed the evening prayer and the nocturnal *psalmodia*, thus in the early morning, and while they were singing to Saint

> George with odes and prayers, then he, the believer in the Lord, Saint John, came to his senses [and declared:] "By the power of my Lord Jesus Christ I myself too shall die by the sword and shed my blood too for His holy name." (Zaborowski 2005: 74–77, translation modified; for the nocturnal *psalmodia* and odes, see Kuhn 2011: 64–68)

In this way, a collective religious experience becomes personalized and leads to the repentance of a sinner who eventually becomes a saint. Obviously, this is the most desirable effect to which a writer of a persuasive text can aspire.

Notes

1 See Armanios 2011: ix for the author's personal account; see also Leemans 2005.
2 That is, of the time between Easter and Pentecost.
3 Kuhn (2011: 69–70) defines *psali* as a genre of hymns sung in honor of Christ and the saints. During a saint's anniversary a *psali* is sung devoted specifically to this saint. *Psali*s must thus not be confused with psalms.
4 For the sake of simplicity, the distinction between the author of a narrative and the narrator has been disregarded. For this distinction, see, for example, Zakrzewska 2011: 500–501, 504–505, 511–12.
5 See, for example, Latour (2005) for 'agency' and 'performativity' of material objects, considered not as passively reflecting social relations but as actually shaping them.
6 Significantly, the Coptic word for 'read,' *ōš* (Egyptian and Demotic *ʿš*), is polysemic and can also mean 'cry,' 'announce,' 'sound' (Crum 1939a: 533–34), just like Arabic *qara'* (Vycichl 1983: 251; see Zakrzewska 2011: 506).
7 For 'performing' the *Acts of the Martyrs*, see also Grig 2004: 4–5, 34–53.

22 Remnants of a Byzantine Church at Athribis

Tomasz Górecki

Excavations at the site of Kom Sidi Yusuf at Tell Atrib (now Benha; Greek: Athribis; Arabic: Tell Atrib) were initiated by Prof. Pahor Labib of the Coptic Committee, who invited the Polish Center of Archaeology in Cairo to conduct excavations on the site. The Coptic party suggested an investigation of this *kom*,[1] which, according to local tradition, covered ruins of a church. Given the fact that Athribis was a large urban center and the seat of a bishopric probably until the sixteenth century (Seeliger and Krumeich 2007: 60–62),[2] there must have been many churches located there. Nonetheless, only one particular church, namely the Holy Virgin Mary Church, is known from written sources, which give an idealized description of it (Amélineau 1893: 67–68). After the *kom* yielded many good-quality architectural fragments in 1969 and 1979–84, it became clear that they must have originated from an important sacral building. Despite the scarcity of evidence, both archaeological and written, the structure was labeled as dedicated to the Holy Virgin.[3]

Almost all finds (fragments of architectural details, stuccos, mosaics, bronze chandeliers which doubtlessly belonged to a church) were found in one particular spot—a rubble dump, uncovered after a few seasons of exploration of the *kom*.[4] This concentration of finds in that place suggested they were remnants of a single building, thrown away over a brief period of time. Apart from artifacts, the rubble dump also yielded a large amount of scorched lime mortar, mixed with ashes, from a burned-down structure.

Without doubt, this ash deposit was not a byproduct of some craft activity,[5] as it was heavily mingled with fragments of marble architectural details, stuccos, and other elements of the interior decoration, including mosaics, floor tiles, and remnants of liturgical furnishing, such as the chancel barrier, ciborium(?), ambo(?), and altar mensae.

The objects from the rubble dump seem to have been thrown away indiscriminately, indicating that those who carried them to the *kom* considered this material not reusable. This suggests that the rubble containing church elements was relocated shortly after the structure was destroyed (by fire?), but it is impossible to say whether it was done for the purpose of clearing the site before rebuilding, or whether there was no such intent whatsoever. Nonetheless, the stratigraphy of Kom Sidi Yusuf disproved an initial hypothesis that the rubble was discarded there in modern times by the fellahin leveling the foot of the *kom*, in order to widen the neighboring cultivated area.

It is puzzling why all of the architectural details were preserved only very fragmentarily. Was it because the destruction of the church was caused by a serious—possibly accidental—fire,[6] which resulted in the collapse of the structure? Or was it intentionally destroyed by man, for instance, after the conquest of Egypt by the Persians or, slightly later, by the Arabs?[7] The historical sources and, even more so, the archaeological ones, are inconclusive on this matter.

The most important groups of finds are as follows.

Marble Architectural Details

Column pedestals

The unearthed archaeological material lacked any remnants of 'typical' bases, though there were sparse examples of square pedestal fragments.[8] Due to their poor state of preservation, it was impossible to determine their size, but some estimation could be given based on the diameters of preserved small fragments of columns.

Columns

It was possible to distinguish several groups of columns based on size, as determined by their diameter. It seems logical that groups of columns with similar diameters were placed in various parts of the structure, depending on the function. Therefore, starting with the smallest diameters, the fragments may have formed the columns of a chancel barrier (templon), ambo, ciborium, galleries, and columns between the naves. Although it is difficult to fully determine the function of a column by its size, it nonetheless seems plausible that columns with diameters of 16–21 cm belonged to the chancel barrier or, perhaps, the ambo; those measuring 24–28 cm (fig. 22.1a–c) in diameter may have been parts of the ciborium; columns with diameters of 34–37 cm (fig. 22.1d) possibly upheld the dome of the ciborium, or flanked the entrance (Holy Door) into the sanctuary;[9] the largest examples, 52–56 cm in diameter, supported the roof.

On many fragments of the columns there were visible traces of gilding (Ruszczyc 1997: 34),[10] which was particularly well preserved on their ends—the tori and the furrows above them (fig. 22.1). Most interestingly, on several tori a kind of checkered pattern was identified, although the corners of the rectangles were not adjacent (fig. 22.1c–d). A spectroscopic analysis revealed that genuine gold was used for the gilding.

The thin layer of gold had been scraped off the marbles for remelting. Traces of such activity were apparent on one gilded column fragment (fig. 22.1a). Columns measuring 24–28 and 34–37 cm in diameter, with preserved gilding and the above-described decoration, may have been placed in some special spot, for instance, flanking the entrance into the sanctuary or supporting the dome of the ciborium.

Column capitals

All unearthed capitals were late Corinthian ones. Most of the fragments bore traces of gilding. Any reconstruction of the full form of a capital seems impossible due to the fragmentariness of finds in this group (Ruszczyc 1997: fig. 8).[11]

Pilaster capitals

Over a dozen fragments of gilded marble slabs were found, 1.8–2.3 cm thick, featuring floral decoration executed in bas-relief (Ruszczyc 1986: fig. 9). Pilaster capitals with similar composition were excavated by Carl Maria Kaufmann at Abu Mina (Kaufmann 1910a: pl. 65.8–9). Examples from both Abu Mina and Athribis feature a pair of simplified flower buds, leaning toward or away from one another.

Ciborium(?) pedestals

The measurements of several octagonal pedestals[12] indicate they were supporting columns larger than barrier colonnettes. It is possible that they belonged to the ciborium or stood, for instance, at the end of the solea, in the entrance leading to the sanctuary.[13]

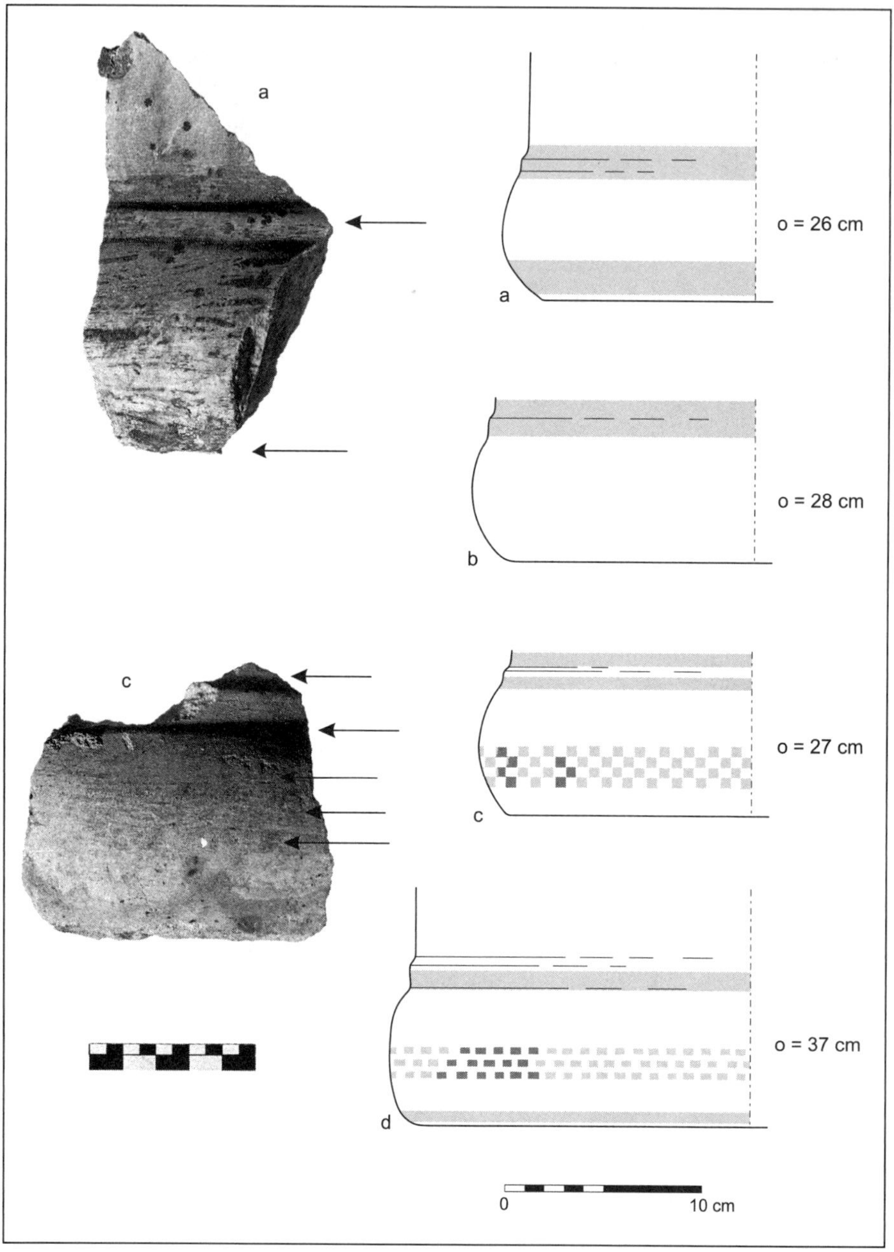

Fig. 22.1. Athribis: fragments of columns with traces of gilding (photograph: Zbigniew Doliński; drawing: Tomasz Górecki; digitizing: Marta Momot).

Fig. 22.2. Athribis: two elements of the chancel barrier structure: (a) an octagonal post with a groove; (b) a slab fragment with cross in circle bas-relief (photograph: Zbigniew Doliński).

Barrier posts (figs. 22.2a, 22.3)

The posts were octagonal in section, but round in their topmost part. These ends also served as bases for barrier colonnettes supporting an architrave.[14] On almost the entire height of the posts' sides there were carved vertical grooves, 3–4 cm wide, used for fastening barrier slabs in upright position. The upper surface of the posts/colonnettes' round base featured holes measuring 5–6 cm in diameter, and 9–10 cm deep, in which dowels were placed for fastening posts and colonnettes together.

Barrier colonnettes

The site yielded fragments of small columns, 16–21 cm in diameter, executed mainly in light or, sometimes, colored marble, though other stones were also used, for instance, porphyry and serpentinite. The colonnettes, some of which were decorated with spiral fluting, most probably belonged to the upper part of the chancel barrier and supported an architrave. In order to fully conceal the sanctuary from the aisle, textile curtains could be hung in the intercolumniations.[15]

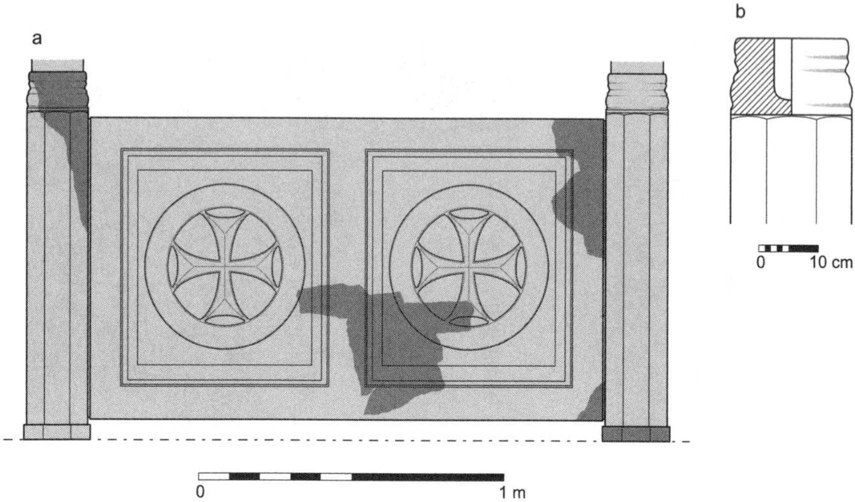

Fig. 22.3. Athribis: (a) Reconstruction of a chancel barrier segment—darker shade marks original fragments; (b) upper part of the post (drawing: Tomasz Górecki; digitizing: Marta Momot).

Fig. 22.4. Athribis: ambo(?) post (photograph: Zbigniew Doliński).

Barrier slabs (figs. 22.2b, 22.3a)

All unearthed slab fragments testify to the fact that only their exterior face was decorated. The decoration was a simple bas-relief, with the surface divided into two square fields, each with a Greek cross in a circle (symbolically, a cross in a wreath). Slab reconstruction (fig. 22.3a) determined its length as 170–175 cm (Ruszczyc 1997: fig. 5; reprinted in Seeliger and Krumeich 2007: fig. 7).[16] Slabs varied in thickness, ranging from 3.9 to 6.9 cm. The width of the slabs' tongues, which were fitted into the grooves of the posts, was 2.8–3.5 cm.

A rectangular post (fig. 22.4) of an ambo(?)

Probably a quadrilateral post, ending in a dome-shaped element; it might be one of the posts flanking the entrance to the ambo. A groove was carved only in one of its sides, possibly for fastening a barrier slab along the stairs to the platform. The post could also be a remnant of the church's previous furnishing phase. The practice of reusing architectural elements was common in Egypt, even if the effect was not formally or aesthetically consistent.[17]

Stuccos (figs. 22.5a–b)

Decorative stucco elements imitated the floral decoration of marble capitals (fig. 22.5c). Due to its fragility, stucco could only be used for pilaster capitals, similar in size to column capitals. The best-preserved examples were large fragments of an acanthus, as well as one fragment of an abacus, and one of a base. The stucco's white-gray color toned well with marble.

Fig. 22.5. Athribis: architectural decoration fragments: (a–b) stucco acanthus; (c) fragment of marble capital with acanthus ornament (photograph: Zbigniew Doliński).

Floor and Wall(?) Tiles

The small stone tiles were mostly examples of floor decoration made in the *opus sectile* technique. They also displayed a range of colors and thicknesses. The thickest examples measured 2.4 cm, while the slimmest ones were only 0.8 cm thick, though most tiles were 1.3–1.8 cm thick. It is possible that some of the tiles decorated the church's walls, as sometimes they had visible holes in their sides, 0.5–0.7 cm in diameter. Inside the holes, traces of iron were found, indicating the use of metal dowels for fastening tiles together. However, apart from the assertion that the tiles served as floor or wall decoration, not much can be said about this group.

Wall Decoration

Small and sparse fragments of painted plaster attested only to the presence of this type of decoration in some part of the church. Somewhere within the building, probably in the apse, there was also a mosaic wall decoration (Ruszczyc 1986: fig. 10), more likely a figural than a geometric one.[18] It was composed of tesserae—quadrilaterals with side length of 0.5–1.2 cm—present in nine colors, and made of marble, glass, or mother-of-pearl plates. Some of the mother-of-pearl plates were arranged in rows, pressed into wet plaster at an angle of 30–40 degrees in relation to the wall surface. As a result, they reflected light differently from other tesserae. Lamplight or daylight entering through windows was reflected as if by a mirror, not only by the mother-of-pearl plates, but also by the gilded columns, providing additional illumination in the church.

Fragments of Mensae

A rectangular mensa (fig. 22.6a)

A single, rather small (3.4 cm thick), but quite characteristic fragment of a rectangular mensa was found at the site. Generally, rectangular mensae were quite large and typically functioned as the central element of the main altar (Piccirillo and Alliata 1998: nos. 55–57; Tkaczow 2008: 92–93, nos. 1207, 1214),[19] but apart from indicating that the liturgical equipment of the church included such mensae, this particular find yields no further information.

A sigma-shaped(?) mensa (fig. 22.6b)

One mensa fragment featured a characteristic, protruding edge, most typical of sigma-shaped mensae. The fragment measured 5.6 cm in height, and approximately 80 cm in diameter (parallels in Dyggve and Egger 1939: pl. 8,

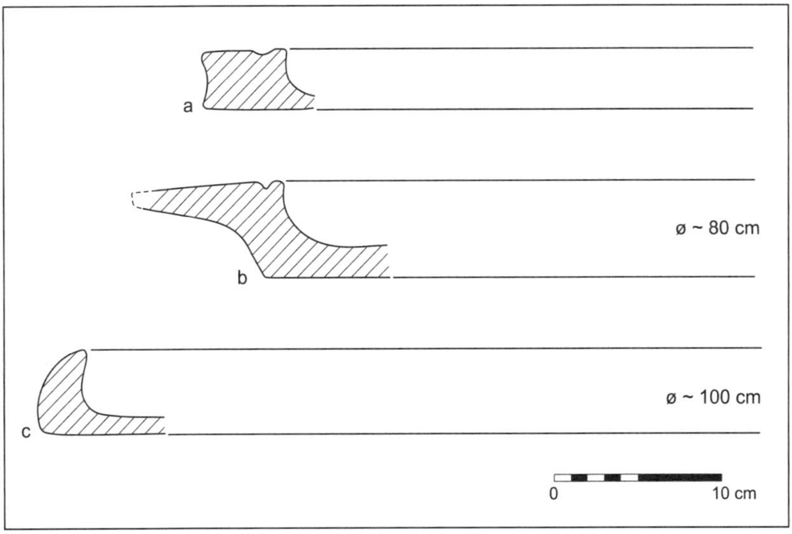

Fig. 22.6. Athribis: fragments of altar mensae, sectional views (drawing: Tomasz Górecki; digitizing: Marta Momot).

mensa H/12; Evelyn-White 1933b: 215–16, fig. 17, pl. LXXVI; Nussbaum 1961; Nussbaum 1965: 111–15; Piccirillo and Alliata 1998: nos. 64–65; Rücker 1920; Tkaczow 2008: no. 1227; Weitzmann 1979: cat. no. 576).

A mensa with inverted rim (fig. 22.6c)

Mensae characterized by such molding were exclusively rounded, with diameters reaching 120 cm (Piccirillo and Alliata 1998: nos. 75–78; Tkaczow 2008: no. 1222). The unearthed fragment measured 4.9 cm in height, and approximately 100 cm in diameter.

Lighting in the Church

A notable and abundant group of finds comprised remnants of bronze chandeliers fitted with glass receptacles for oil, which served as a fuel source for illuminating the church interior.

Chandeliers *(coronae)* with foldable lamp holders

Among the fragments of hanging bronze lamps, it was possible to discern two ring chandeliers.[20] They had protruding glass oil lamp holders attached by hinges, making them foldable.

Flat chandeliers *(diskoi)* with openings for lamps

Fragments of at least four chandeliers of this type were found at the site. They were characterized by a flat hoop or disc with six to twelve openings for glass lamps (Ruszczyc 1997: fig. 10; Górecki 2015: fig. 9.2). If not hollow, the middle of the chandelier featured either an openwork Greek cross, or a simplified chi-rho, in the center of which there was another opening for a lamp. The hoop and the ornament were cast as one piece.

A hand-held candlestick

This small, portable bronze candlestick was either deliberately executed in such a form, or was adapted from a broken lampstand (Górecki 2014).

Attempt at Reconstruction of the Church Interior

Based on fragments of marble furnishing, stuccos, mosaics, and lighting elements, it is possible to present a plausible, albeit general and limited, reconstruction of the interior, as well as to theorize about the size of the church.

The structure was supported by columns with pedestals rectangular in top view. The columns were either partly or entirely gilded, as were their Corinthian capitals. It is difficult to say which part of the church was decorated by plastered brick pilasters with stucco bases and capitals. While such decoration was surely aesthetically harmonious with the dominant marble embellishments, it probably adorned some less important part of the church, supplementing the marble elements, imitating or even straightforwardly copying their style. Some part of the church was embellished with pilasters ending in gilded marble capitals, decorated with floral bas-relief, which were stylistically consistent with the character of the full-size capitals. Logic suggests that gilded marble elements decorated the sanctuary, while more modest marble and stucco embellishments adorned other parts of the church. Moreover, probably all plastered walls were covered in paintings, but it is next to impossible to infer their character based on the fragmentary remnants of unearthed plaster. There were also preserved patches of plaster with embedded tesserae, indicating the presence of mosaic compositions. Judging by the tesserae's quality and arrangement, as well as by their rich color palette, the mosaics in the church were of excellent handiwork. This mastery is further exemplified by rows of rectangular mother-of-pearl plates, deliberately pressed into plaster at a certain angle to make them reflect the natural and artificial light.

The sanctuary was separated from the aisle with a barrier of monolithic marble slabs, approximately 90 cm high, inserted between octagonal posts. The slabs featured a bas-relief depicting a pair of Greek crosses. Above the row of slabs, there was an architrave supported on small colonnettes (approximately 20 cm in diameter), possibly of different colors.[21] The entire barrier was quite high, with the colonnette-supported architrave suggesting a possibility of concealing the liturgy with curtains.

Assuming that a slab, approximately 175 cm long, formed the barrier running perpendicularly to the axis of the aisle, it is possible to estimate the width of the aisle. Counting four posts and two slabs flanking the Holy Door, the aisle was at least 7 meters, or perhaps even 11–12 meters, wide, if there were two slabs on each side of the entrance.

Unearthed fragments of mensae indicate the presence of at least three altars. The large rectangular mensa must have belonged to the main altar, where the Eucharistic liturgy was served. The two remaining mensae could have been located, though it is unknown if simultaneously, in a chamber *(pastophorium)* adjoining the apse from the north, where offerings were made and the Eucharistic bread and wine were prepared. It is also possible that only the round mensa was in the *pastophorium*, while the sigma-shaped one was placed in a different chamber, or—given its form—in a semicircular wall niche.

A few dozen bronze chandelier fragments were found, amounting to at least six examples. Without doubt, these represent but a small portion of the original lighting equipment. Therefore, the kind of lamps used may be determined, but not their number.

Given the relatively sparse archaeological material, only a broad dating of the church may be given. Although the structure could have been erected as early as the end of the fifth century, most architectural details seem to be of the Justinian period. Based on these modest data, it can be stated that these are remnants of a church, the interior of which was shaped sometime in the mid-sixth century. It probably had the structure and the plan of a basilica, similar to the two largest churches at Abu Mina. Also like those two churches, the one at Athribis probably had a timber roof truss, which would account for the inflammability of the church regardless of whether the fire was accidental or intentional.

Given the fact that some of the architectural details may have been reused from earlier structures, the dating of the church is complicated, and, perforce, quite broad. Moreover, it cannot be excluded that the interior, especially the small architecture of the sanctuary, underwent modifications while already in use. Therefore, it stands to reason that the architectural elements were not necessarily all of the same period.

Pinpointing the date of the fire constitutes the most challenging aspect of the church's history. According to a local oral legend, the building was burned down during persecutions (1004–14) under the caliph al-Hakim. However, Barbara Ruszczyc argues that the event happened much earlier, in the beginning of the eighth century (see note 7). What may confirm this claim is the dating of a small pottery deposit found inside a brick-walled storage pit, dug into the layer superimposing the debris from the church (Ruszczyc 1997: fig. 4 (layer 8); reprinted in Seeliger and Krumeich 2007: fig. 8). This deposit can be dated to the mid-eighth to the ninth century, though the layer into which it was dug was quite thick, and its natural accumulation could have lasted relatively long, up to a hundred years. Therefore, it is possible that the church was destroyed earlier than in the first half of the eighth century. Perhaps, as in the case of the Martyr Church at Abu Mina, the destruction occurred during the Persian conquest. Other, purely theoretical, dates of the fire worth mentioning are the Arab conquest of Egypt or the period during and after one of the joint Coptic–Muslim agrarian revolts in the Nile Delta in 725 or 831.

To conclude, the destruction (conflagration) of the Justinian-era church at Athribis could have taken place between 619 and 850, but its cause remains obscure. It is also unknown if the church was ever rebuilt. Likewise, it is impossible to identify to whom it was dedicated, whether it functioned as a diocesan church, or whether it was some other notable church in Athribis.

Notes

1 A *kom* is an artificial mound, usually formed upon ruins of ancient structures. Works at Kom Sidi Yusuf were conducted in 1969, and then yearly 1979–84. The Coptic party was represented by Prof. Pahor Labib, while the works were directed by Barbara Ruszczyc (Ruszczyc 1975; 1986; 1990; 1997).

2 As late as the fourteenth century, there was a diocesan church dedicated to the Virgin Mary, rebuilt after destruction in the second half of the ninth century; see Timm 1984a: 261–62. Conversely, Maqrizi mentions a ruined Holy Mary convent at Atrib, situated on the bank of the Nile, and inhabited by three monks (Wüstenfeld 1845: 108).

3 According to Ruszczyc (1997) the church was dedicated to the Virgin Mary. The author assumed that there was only one large, richly decorated church at Athribis and was therefore convinced that the remnants she discovered must have been parts of the structure mentioned in the written sources. Meanwhile, the

only certain fact is that remnants of a Byzantine church with a richly decorated interior were unearthed, but the dedicatee remains unknown.

4 It was unearthed in trench D, a test trench approximately fifty meters long and three to four meters deep. For plan and section of trench D, see Ruszczyc 1997: figs. 3–4; Seeliger and Krumeich 2007: figs. 6, 8 (reprints). For the plan of the site, including Kom Sidi Yusuf, see: Myśliwiec 2000: figs. 1–3; Ruszczyc 1986: figs. 1, 3. For other plans of Athribis, see Dąbrowski 1962: pls. I–II. For the Roman history of Athribis, see Dietze 2004: 612–22.

5 For instance, a common practice in Athribis/Tell Atrib was burning marble for lime, as an abundance of remnants of marble architectural details were found in the ruins of the Roman city. For a discussion of lime kilns on the site, see Ruszczyc 1986: 337–38; 1997: 29–31.

6 The ease and the intensity of the spread of fire may have been caused by the fact that the roof truss was most probably made of wood, like in the Martyr Church at Abu Mina; see Grossmann 1989: 90–91, 93, plans 7–8 (truss reconstruction). Grossmann's uniquely comprehensive study will be referenced throughout the present chapter, as it provides excellent comparative material for the finds from Athribis.

7 Perhaps the fire occurred at the same time as the destruction at Abu Mina; see Grossmann 1989: 15–16n15, 183–84 (destruction by the Persians in 619). Another possibility is that the church was destroyed during one of the many agrarian revolts, more specifically in 725 or 831, which took place mainly in the Nile Delta. These were joint Coptic–Muslim rebellions against the authorities; see Mikhail 2014a: 75, 119, 120, 125. Alternatively, it may have happened under Caliph 'Umar II in the beginning of the eighth century; see Ruszczyc 1997: 43–44.

8 Similar pedestals can be found in Severin and Severin 1987: fig. 15; Grossmann 1989: fig. 9; Kaufmann 1910a: pl. 69.4.

9 On the Byzantine ambo, solea, and sanctuary, see Xydis 1947. The validity of the terminology describing various parts of Byzantine sanctuaries is discussed in Walter 1995: 95–106.

10 Traces of gilding were also found on capitals of columns and pilasters, but not on the barrier slabs or posts. The practice of gilding of architectural details is also attested in literary sources and archaeological evidence from Abu Mina; see Grossmann 1989: 16; Kaufmann 1910a: 100. Literary sources (on Hagia Sophia) can be found in Mango 1972: 72, 76, 93–94, 98–101.

11 For parallels, see Severin and Severin 1987: figs. 32, 39.

12 They are smaller than quadrilateral column pedestals, but larger than barrier posts.

13 The present author wishes to express his deep gratitude to Peter Grossmann for the opportunity to personally conduct measurements of the chancel barrier remnants (including posts and the spacing between them, equaling the length of the slabs) in the Great Basilica during his stay in Abu Mina (see also note 16). In the Great Basilica, the octagonal posts in both corners where the solea ends and the sanctuary begins (see also note 9) are larger than others, measuring a little over 40 cm in diameter. For similar, though significantly larger (approx. 65 cm in diameter), octagonal pedestals, see Grossmann 1989: 100, 102, figs. 20–21, pl. 57b. At Abu Mina, there were four sizes of octagonal pedestals (Severin and Severin 1987: 28). See also Kaufmann 1910a: fig. 64, pl. 20 (pedestal size undetermined).

14 Mango (1972: 93) quotes Paulus Silentiarius's description of the interior of Hagia Sophia, rebuilt in 558–62, with the following account of the chancel barrier's posts/pedestals: "The mason has beautifully carved the eight sides of each pedestal, while the steel carving-tool has bound its round neck [with a collar] so that the column should rest securely upon the circular [top of] the pedestal that is affixed underneath."

15 For a discussion on the function of sanctuary curtains, see Mathews 1971: 169–71.

16 Parallels can be found in Grossmann (1989: 64, fig. 12, pls. 2–3), including an unfinished chancel barrier slab, 190 × 95 cm, later reworked into a mensa, subsequently reused as an altar substructure in the Martyr Church. The slab featured two rectangular panels for (unrealized) decoration. In the Great Basilica, each slab composing two rows of the solea barrier was 171–175 cm long, while the ones constituting the sanctuary's western border were approximately 215 cm long. Slabs forming the northern and southern rows of the sanctuary barrier were less consistent in length; most of them measured about 145 cm, but two slabs abutting the western barrier were approximately 200 cm. Ulbert (1969) lists dimensions of around a hundred fully preserved slabs, often exceeding 200 cm in length. The longest one (no. 168), found at Thessaloniki, was 280 cm long. As the publication features no photographs, it gives little ground for dating particular depictions. According to Ulbert (1969: 22–33), slabs with symbolic representations (various forms of crosses, also in wreaths or circles) could be dated to the mid-fifth to mid-sixth centuries.

17 For well-documented instances of the practice of reusing architectural material, see Grossmann 1989: 258–65, pl. 43; Severin and Severin 1987: figs. 12, 13, 18, 19.

18 Byzantine wall mosaics in Egypt are known mainly from Abu Mina; see Grossmann 1989: 144, 225–27, 680–81; Kaufmann 1910a: fig. 16.

19 See also Dyggve and Egger 1939: fig. 53, pl. 8 (rectangular mensa H/5 measuring 164 × 82 × 4.8 cm; other such mensae on plate 8: H/4, H/6, H/8, H/10).

20 One of them resembles an example from Falck and Lichtwark (1996: cat. no. 226). Another one is identical with an example from Piccirillo (1994: figs. 1, 4); see also Górecki 2015: fig. 9.1.

21 Not every barrier featured a colonnette-supported architrave. On various forms of the chancel barrier, see Mathews 1971: 168.

23 Architecture in Kellia

Gisèle Hadji-Minaglou

FROM THE MIDDLE of the fourth to the ninth centuries, Lower Egypt was home to three large ascetic communities: Nitria, Kellia, and Scetis, which were established along an axis approximately parallel to the eastern Nile branch.[1] Although the classical sources of Egyptian monasticism, the *Historia monachorum in Aegypto*, the *Historia Lausiaca*, the *Collationes* by Cassian, and the *Apophthegmata Patrum*, contain a great deal of information concerning the position of each settlement in relation to one of the other sites, their actual geographical location has not been easy to determine.

The situation of Nitria and Scetis was definitively established by H.G. Evelyn-White (Evelyn-White 1932: 17–42), and that of Kellia was finally identified by A. Guillaumont (Guillaumont 1964). Nitria, the nearest to Alexandria, was situated on the site of the modern village of al-Barnugi, about fifteen kilometers south of Damanhur, and Scetis, now Wadi al-Natrun, is situated approximately sixty kilometers to the south of Nitria. Kellia was halfway between these two monastic centers (Guillaumont 1964: 44–48). When Guillaumont visited the site in March 1964, it was still there, lying under the sand of the desert, but part of it had already been destroyed by agricultural expansion in the area (Guillaumont 1965: 220). Faced with the threat of devastation of the remains, the Institut français d'archéologie orientale and the University of Geneva undertook rescue excavations one year later.[2] This was the beginning of the archaeological exploration of Kellia, which was interrupted from

1969 to 1975 because of hostilities involving Egypt. Work resumed in 1976 and went on until 1990, when archaeological work was finally discontinued.

Topography and Archaeological Exploration

At the height of its development, Kellia extended over an area of twenty-seven square kilometers and consisted of five settlements stretching approximately twenty kilometers along the Nubariya Canal: these are, from west to east, Qasr Waheida, Qusur al-Ruba'iyat, Qusur al-Izayla, Qusur al-'Abid, and Qusur 'Isa. Two smaller communities were settled fifteen kilometers to the southeast of Qusur al-'Abid at Qusur al-'Irayma and Qusur al-Higayla.[3]

Qusur al-Ruba'iyat is the largest of these settlements, with a central core surrounded by smaller settlements, one of which is Qasr Waheida. The topographical maps of the area made by the French and Swiss missions show the distribution of the *koms*, the small hills which shelter archaeological remains: 616 were listed in 1972.[4] Eleven of these *koms*, dating from the sixth–seventh centuries to the eighth century, have been excavated by the French mission in Qusur al-Ruba'iyat: *kom* 219 (Daumas and Guillaumont 1969), *koms* 1, 2, 3, 4, and 6 (Daumas 1967), *koms* 88 and 16 (Coquin 1984–85), *kom* 167 (Andreu et al. 1981), *kom* 171 (Coquin 1982), and *kom* 195 (Henein and Wuttmann 2000). Another one, *kom* 34, has been unearthed in Qasr Waheida (Daumas 1968: 395–402; Daumas 1969; Andreu, Castel, and Coquin 1980: 350–68 and pl. XCIX–CII). *Kom* 34 sheltered one of only two ecclesiastic centers found in the Kellia region.

Qusur al-Izayla was situated a little less than two kilometers from Qusur al-Ruba'iyat and numbered up to 250 *koms* (Kasser 1967: 14, fig. 4); only 133 of them were preserved in 1981. The first buildings appeared toward the middle of the sixth century, but the main occupation of the settlement dates to the seventh century. The site was abandoned toward the middle of the eighth century (Weidmann 1986b: 257–58). The plans of 164 monastic buildings (referred to as *ri* in the main publication, MSAC 1983) of Qusur al-Izayla and its immediate environment have been drawn, thus allowing, better than elsewhere, a study of the evolution of the architecture of Kellia (MSAC 1983: 399–421; Weidmann 1986a).

Qusur al-'Abid is the smallest settlement of all, with a hundred *koms* located on a surface area of 0.25 square kilometers. One of them, endangered by the rapid encroachment of modern cultivation, was excavated and published at the very beginning of the archaeological exploration of Kellia (Kasser 1967: 41–53).

Qusur 'Isa, of which Qusur al-'Abid might have been a suburb, was quite a large settlement, covering a surface area of four square kilometers and including about six hundred *koms*. Only a dozen of them remained in 1965 (Kasser 1967: 20), and one, named Qusur 'Isa I by the excavators, was completely unearthed in the southwestern part of the settlement (Kasser 1967: 25–40). The remains found in Qusur 'Isa I ranged from the second half of the fourth century to the first half of the eighth century, from simple cells to a large complex including two churches and community buildings (Bridel 1988a: 44–48; Thirard 2012: 23–24).

Qusur al-Higayla and Qusur al-'Irayma amounted all together to about 120 hermitages (Kasser 1969; MSAC 1989); the plans of most of them were established by the Swiss mission thanks to a surface survey, but only a dozen were excavated (Kasser 2003). The settlement of Qusur al-Higayla appears to have developed in the second quarter of the fifth century around the cell, or the cells, of hermits whose bones became venerated relics. The first constructions at Qusur al-'Irayma were set down in the middle of the sixth century. Both settlements were abandoned at the end of the seventh century (Kasser 2003: 16).

The railway line linking Alexandria to Kom Hamada, initiated in 1977, crossed the site of Kellia from southeast to northwest (Bridel 1990: 22; Thirard 2012: 116, fig. 17), destroying about thirty hermitages in the very heart of Qusur al-Ruba'iyat. Before the start of the earthmoving works, the Egyptian Antiquities Service undertook the excavation of twenty-five of these hermitages. The excavations were continued by the Swiss mission, which also published the results (Kasser 1994: 195–274).

Architecture

The hermitages

Little is known of the first cells of the Kellia settlement. The only ones which have been unearthed belong to the two communal complexes of Qusur 'Isa I and QR 34: they date to the second half of the fourth century or the first half of the fifth century and consist of small half-buried rooms. The cells of Qusur 'Isa I, which were the best preserved, were covered with vaults, which rested directly on the ground and were hardly visible from the outside (Weidmann 2013: 28–30, 121–22; see in particular 122, fig. 26). Some other isolated cells, probably dating to the same period as the cells of Qusur 'Isa I, have been located in the desert outside the main settlements (Weidmann 2013: unnumbered plate entitled "Plan d'ensemble interprétatif").

At their maximum development, in the sixth and seventh centuries, the settlements of Kellia were covered with hermitages established at a certain distance from each other. These autonomous units were demarcated by enclosures whose size varied, depending on the number of occupants. Nevertheless, the repetitive nature of the plans allows us to record the main elements of their composition, independently of their size or wealth. To describe this pattern we will use as an example the plan of QR 195 (figs. 23.1–23.3), excavated in the Qusur al-Ruba'iyat settlement by the French mission (Henein and Wuttmann 2000).[5] This hermitage was built in the first quarter or the first half of the seventh century and abandoned at the end of the eighth or possibly the beginning of the ninth century.

The enclosures were rectangular in shape with a general southeast–northwest orientation and the habitations were predominantly established in their western corner. The entrance of the hermitage was usually in the south, thus protected from the prevailing winds. In some cases, however, it opened in the eastern wall of the enclosure, in particular when the surface of a hermitage had been enlarged. A well, dug in the southeastern part of the courtyard, provided the inhabitants with the water for their daily needs as well as for the watering of the garden. Latrines were installed against the southern wall and the sewage was drained out of the enclosure toward the south.

The entrance to the habitation was on the eastern side and opened onto a rectangular hall with a south–north orientation. This hall was sometimes divided into two parts by an arch. It led westward, directly or through a corridor, to a large room situated in the northwestern corner of the construction; this room possessed a niche cut into the eastern wall. The position, the size, the ornamentation, the painted cross, and the inscriptions associated with this niche indicate that this room was the oratory of the hermitage.[6] The oratory was often connected to a smaller room, situated to the east of it and accessible only from it. To the south the oratory gave access to another room equipped with a small storeroom.

South of the entrance hall was a pantry or a workshop leading to a kitchen as well as to another room with a storeroom. Except for the oratory and the kitchen, nothing in the layout of the rooms leads to a definite interpretation of their function. They could be living rooms, bedrooms, or workshops. In QR 195, the oratory, room 4, and the rooms around it, 3, 5, and 6, were interpreted as the elder's apartment, and the three spaces 7, 8, and 9 formed the disciple's apartment.

Over time, with the growth of the community, this pattern of the primary hermitage evolved by the addition of new constructions along the perimeter wall of the enclosure. This wall was often doubled by a second one, in order to support the pressure exerted by the vaults of the new buildings. The first additions were new habitations, including an oratory and a room with its storeroom, and sometimes a kitchen. In QR 195, the modifications were progressive. The first constructions to be added were in the southwestern corner of the courtyard; their similarity with rooms 6 and 7 in the primary habitation led the excavators to recognize them as new living quarters. Then two new apartments were installed, one in the southwest corner of the enclosure, the other one along its northern wall.

The enlargement of the community might also lead to the extension of the area of the hermitage, either by extending the area of the enclosure itself or by constructing an additional courtyard. In the case of QR 195, a third of the area of the primary enclosure was increased toward the north and the east: to this end, the northern apartment was knocked down, together with the eastern wall.

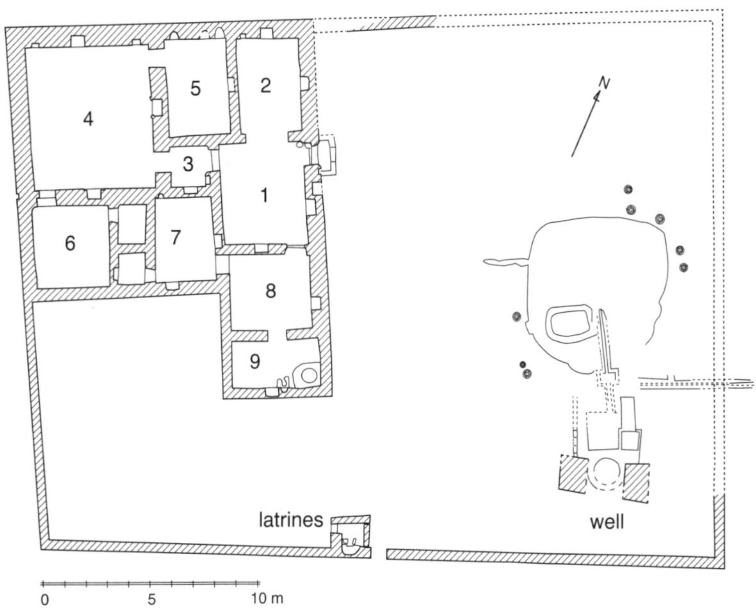

Fig. 23.1. QR 195. Plan of the primary hermitage (after Henein and Wuttmann 2000: plan 1).

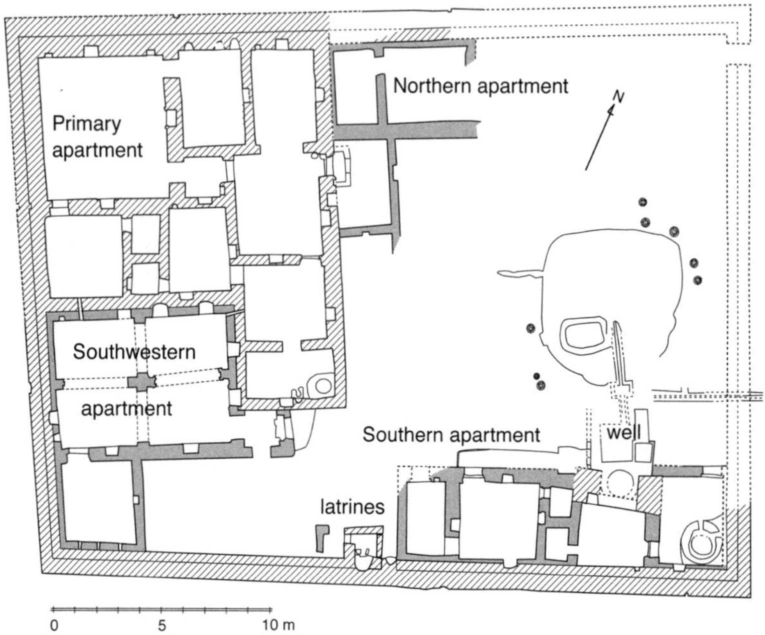

Fig. 23.2. QR 195. Plan of the hermitage after the addition of new constructions (after Henein and Wuttmann 2000: plan 2′).

An additional apartment was installed in the northwestern corner of the newly created space: it consisted of a double-bayed vestibule (1), an oratory (2), and two rooms; this plan differs from the primary habitation by the lack of storerooms and kitchen. As a matter of fact, the kitchen was installed outside the habitation, next to the entrance (3). Adjacent to this kitchen—and belonging to the same building—was a two-bayed hall.

Although not systematic, the presence of a two-bayed hall is fairly common in the Kellia settlements, especially from the second half of the seventh century. Its pattern, similar to that of the entrance hall of the monks' apartments, suggests that it was a space for the reception of visitors. It might also have been used as a refectory as well as a dormitory or even as a prayer area. Some of these reception halls are divided into three bays (Bridel 1986: 146–51).

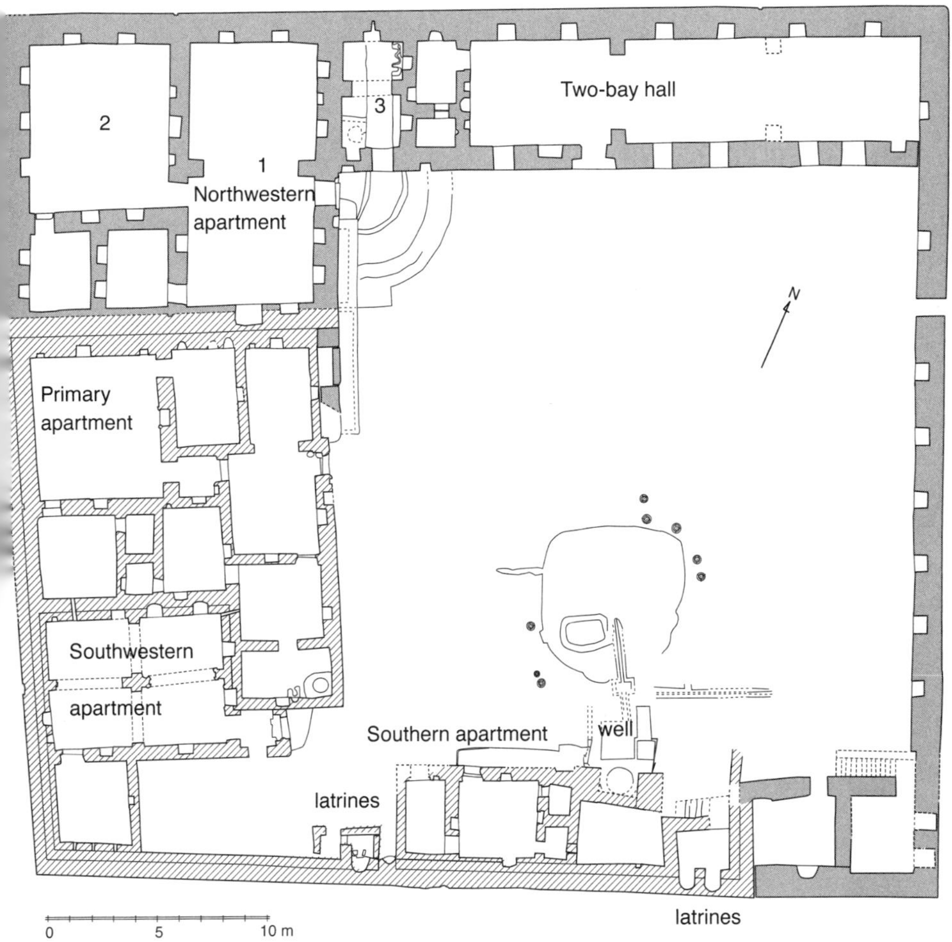

Fig. 23.3. QR 195. Plan of the hermitage after the extension of the enclosure (after Henein and Wuttmann 2000: plan 9).

The churches and the community complexes

As discussed above, in each hermitage there were prayer areas, private areas like the oratory, which was the main room in every monk's apartment, or prayer areas shared with the visitors, like the two-bayed hall. The larger hermitages also had a church. Eight of these churches have been detected in Qusur al-Izayla and four have been unearthed: QIz 14 (MSAC 1983:

fasc. 1, 122–25 and fasc. 2, 27, pl. XIV), QIz 16 (MSAC 1983: fasc. 1, 128–31 and fasc. 2, 31, pl. XVI), QIz 19–20 (MSAC 1983: fasc. 1, 136–41, in particular 139–40, and fasc. 2, 37, pl. XIX), and QIz 45 (MSAC 1983: fasc. 1, 193–96, in particular 195, and fasc. 2, 83–85, pl. XLIII–XLV). They all date to the seventh century and had been added at some separate time after the construction of the main hermitage. Their plans all have in common a two-bay naos, but the treatment of the sanctuary differs from one building to another.

According to the excavators, the church of QIz 19–20 was built before AD 630 in the southern part of a courtyard installed to the east of the primary enclosure. The naos was covered with domes and the sanctuary was divided into three rooms separated by an arch. The entrance of the church was in the northern wall of the naos. Another building of QIz 19–20 has been interpreted as a church. It was situated inside the primary enclosure, against its northern wall, and it consisted of a room divided by an arch; in the eastern part was a shrine, a bench for the celebrant, and a niche for the lamp (Descœudres 1990: 51, fig. 37–38, and 52, fig. 40). The other three churches belong to the second half of the seventh century.

The church of QIz 14 was added outside the main enclosure of the hermitage, to the south of it. The two-bayed naos led to the sanctuary, which consisted of a single room of the same breadth as the naos. The entrance to the church was on the north. The church of QIz 16 was established in the northeast corner of the enclosure, where it replaced an earlier habitation. As was the case for QIz 14, the sanctuary was made from one room as large as the naos, but it had an annex to the south, connected to a staircase that jutted out from the façade of the building. The church of QIz 45 was established outside of the enclosure, in the southeastern corner. The sanctuary was divided in three by two arches.

Not all the churches attached to the hermitages had a simple two-bayed naos. In Qusur ʻIsa, hermitage 366, which was occupied between 625 and the end of the eighth century (Haeny and Leibundgut 1999: 39), the church was a basilica with three naves and a three-part sanctuary. It was installed outside the enclosure, along the northern wall. The southern part of the sanctuary led to a building consisting of three rooms with a baptistery (Haeny and Leibundgut 1999: 8, fig. 1, and 15, fig. 2).

The emergence, around the middle of the seventh century, of churches integrated into the hermitages has been explained by the decay, during the same period, of the community complexes where the monks gathered on

Saturdays and Sundays for their meal in common and for the celebration of the Mass and the Eucharist. According to the ancient sources, the Kellia region had only one church in the fourth century and the first half of the fifth century. After the Council of Chalcedon (451), the texts mention two churches. As a matter of fact, two community centers with churches were found in Kellia, at Qusur 'Isa (Qusur 'Isa I) and at Qasr Waheida (QR 34). The first occupation in these two complexes dates to the second half of the fourth century, but the first church, at Qusur 'Isa I, was not built before the end of the fourth or the beginning of the fifth century, and the first church of QR 34 was installed in the third quarter of the fifth century.[7] The community center of Qusur 'Isa I was transformed into a cemetery in the middle of the seventh century and was definitively deserted at the beginning of the eight century. The chronology of QR 34 is not very different although the date of its final abandonment has not been determined with certainty.

At the end of the fifth century the community center of Qusur 'Isa I developed around a half-buried hermitage (Weidmann 2013: 122, fig. 26), to which was added another cell and the first church (Weidmann 2013: 124, fig. 27). The cells were probably in a courtyard with a well and the church was outside the enclosure. This church is the most ancient monastic church ever discovered by archaeological investigation in Egypt. The first community installations appear in the first quarter of the fifth century. They consisted of a new enclosure which included the church, a meeting room, and a new apartment (Weidmann 2013: 126, fig. 28). Soon after this event, the enclosure was enlarged toward the north and new rooms were added in that direction (Weidmann 2013: 127, fig. 29).

The most spectacular changes happened in the second half of the fifth century, when the enclosure was extended toward the east and the south, with an entrance gateway to the east. The reason for this change was the building of a new church, a basilica with a three-aisled naos and a three-part sanctuary, while the structure of the first church remained unchanged. The northern side room of the basilica contained a baptistery. The primary cells were backfilled and new dwellings were added to the courtyard: one of them was planned with special attention and might have been intended for distinguished visitors. To the east of the first church was an underground room, which has been interpreted as a *memoria* (Weidmann 2013: 129, fig. 30). For about a century, the modifications did not significantly change the organization of the center. The enclosure was enlarged once again, a new well was added, and the habitations were modified, but the most important change was the construction of a tower. The appearance of this refuge tower might have been due to the climate of insecurity which prevailed in the area during the fifth century (Weidmann 2013: 132, fig. 31).

Between the last quarter of the sixth century and the beginning of the seventh century a new and even more important change was made: the first church was destroyed and a new one was built on its location. Like the second church, it was a basilica with a three-aisled naos and a three-part sanctuary. The other changes during the same period involved the apartments and the courtyards (Weidmann 2013: 134, fig. 32).

During the first quarter of the seventh century, the complex underwent a final major transformation: the western residential area was destroyed and replaced by a new large complex consisting of an L-shaped portico connected to a large hall, probably intended for visitors, who became very numerous during the first half of the seventh century when the population of the Kellia region was at its peak. New apartments were also created, together with workshops and a new bakery (Weidmann 2013: 136, fig. 33). The construction program definitively stopped in the second quarter of the seventh century and the complex was gradually abandoned. A cemetery developed then in the northern and eastern part of the *kom*, perhaps initially in relation to the churches (Weidmann 2013: 138, fig. 34).

The organization of QR 34 was similar to that of Qusur ʻIsa I and its development followed the same pattern. Likewise, the community center developed around the first monastic cells (Weidmann 2013: 114, fig. 22) and, in the middle of the sixth century, the first enclosure included a church, a complex of dwelling rooms with a large communal reception hall, a well, and several other small constructions (Weidmann 2013: 115, fig. 23).[8] Later on, during the second half of the sixth century, the enclosure was extended toward the east, a new church was added, larger than the first one, and close to it a tower was built; a very large meeting room replaced the previous reception hall. A construction which the excavators believed to have had a liturgical function and which was interpreted as a *memoria* was also installed (Weidmann 2013: 117, fig. 24).

In the first half of the seventh century, a second tower was built in a new extension toward the east of the enclosure (Weidmann 2013: 118, fig. 25). After the abandonment of the complex, a cemetery developed in the area: by that time the buildings had been completely ruined and covered with windblown sand.

Although little has been excavated of the Kellia settlements, compared to the number of complexes the site contained before its destruction, the results of the French and, even more, the Swiss excavations are impressive in every aspect, particularly in regard to the architecture, painting, pottery, and epigraphy. This chapter has dealt only with some of the architectural aspects and has concentrated on the function and the spatial organization of the hermitages. Both aspects reflect the actual way of life of the monks of Kellia, who lived isolated in their hermitage during the week and met with their community on the weekend.

The plan of the hermitages illustrates the solitary life of the monks, protected inside the enclosure walls, where they were self-sufficient thanks to the well and the vegetable garden. In their apartments, the dominating feature of the oratory clearly reflects their life of prayer, while on the other hand, the entrance hall, together with the two-bayed hall, also shows the importance placed on hospitality. Inside the enclosure of the community centers—one was established at the western end of the site (Qasr Waheida) and the other at its eastern end (Qusur 'Isa I)—the buildings were all for community use, except for the few dwelling places, which were intended for special visitors and for the monks in charge of the housekeeping. Both centers were abandoned in the middle of the seventh century; this abandonment coincided with the increase of the monastic population and the emergence of churches in the hermitages.

To complete this brief overview of the architectural environment of the monks of Kellia, the reader is referred to the chapters concerning the architectural elements in the main publications: Henein and Wuttmann 2000: 73–241; MSAC 1983: 71–93; and Descœudres 1988: 87–89. The papers focusing on a specific subject are also helpful, such as Coquin 1988, which draws a parallel between texts and archaeology, and Bridel 1986, which analyzes the ways people moved around inside the hermitages in order to bring to light the hierarchy between private and public spaces.

Notes

1 I am grateful to Vivienne G. Callender, who has kindly reviewed my English.

2 The following year the two institutions decided to work separately (see Kasser 1967: 4).

3 See the map published in Bridel 1990: 22 and repeated in Thirard 2012: 116, fig. 17. The sites are named according to the *Survey of Egypt, Atlas of the Normal 1:100,000 Scale Topographical Series of Egypt*, sheet 88/54, Giza 1929 (see Kasser 1967: 18–19; Kasser 2003: 151, pl. 1).

4 The French and the Swiss worked independently. The plan established by the French has been published in Daumas and Guillaumont 1969: fasc. 2, pl. I. The plan established by the Swiss has been published in Kasser 1972, where the *koms* represented on the French map are listed in numerical order on pp. 147–49, with their coordinates on the Swiss map.

5 The main documentation for the plan of the primary habitation comes from the survey and the excavations in the Qusur al-Izayla settlement, where the plan of 164 hermitages was drawn (MSAC 1983: 399–421). The observations made at Qusur al-Izayla also apply to the other *qusur*.

6 For a typology and a description of the oratories of the Kellia hermitages, see Bridel 1986.

7 The most recent publication concerning Qusur 'Isa I is Weidmann 2013. QR 34 was only partially published by the excavators (Daumas 1968; Daumas 1969; Andreu, Castel, and Coquin 1980), but a comparative study of the two complexes by D. Weidmann and G. Nogara (Weidmann 2013: 112–19) analyzes clearly the architectural and functional organization of QR 34. Although the identification of Qusur 'Isa I with the headquarters of the sole church of Kellia before the Council of Chalcedon and that of QR 34 with the second church, built after the Council of Chalcedon, is evident because of their dating, nothing in their architectural features helps to determine which one was pro-Chalcedonian and which one anti-Chalcedonian. G. Descœudres has suggested that QR 34 was the actual headquarters of the pro-Chalcedonian community (Kasser 1999: 490–92), but this hypothesis is not generally accepted (Weidmann 2013: 117, 137–38).

8 The first constructions appeared in the third quarter of the fifth century, that is to say, half a century after the Qusur 'Isa I structure (see note 7).

24 Kellia: Its Decoration in Painting and Stucco

Karel C. Innemée

Introduction

According to a tradition found in the *Apophthegmata Patrum*, Kellia was founded by Ammoun of Nitria, at the instigation of St. Antony, when he noticed that the settlement of Nitria was getting too crowded.[1] According to the text the distance between Nitria and Kellia was only about nineteen kilometers, which suggests that even then the new settlement was close to the Delta and its villages and cultivation. The exact location of Kellia was established by A. Guillaumont in 1964, and in the two decades that followed, French and Swiss archaeologists surveyed the area and excavated parts of it. Since then most of the sites have been sacrificed to agriculture.

The sites cover an area of approximately twenty-seven square kilometers, and within this vast area a number of clusters can be distinguished, of which the most important ones are (from west to east): Qusur al-Ruba'iyat (abbreviated as QR), Qusur al-Izayla (QIz), and Qusur 'Isa (QI).

Although Kellia was founded for those who were seeking a higher degree of seclusion, life here must have been of only moderately ascetic character. Only a small number of cells for a solitary inhabitant were discovered, sometimes half underground. This type seems to belong to the very early period, and soon afterward a model of hermitage for more than one inhabitant became the standard. These walled compounds, offering accommodation to small groups of anchorites, were not only at a relatively close distance to 'the world,' but also close to each other.

Each compound had units of one or more rooms for its inhabitants and common facilities such as a kitchen, storage rooms, and a latrine. Whereas the oldest type of *manshubiya*[2] was probably no more than a half-underground, simple dwelling, the later types show in their vast majority variations on the theme of the courtyard house, a kind of residential building that has been found in Egypt since the Middle Kingdom or earlier.[3] Although several variants occur, the majority of the *manshubiya*s were based on a more or less common plan, consisting of a courtyard with living quarters and facilities built in a U- or L-shape within the perimeter wall. Apart from this type of dwelling, a number of remains of what must have been towers, often incorporated in a *manshubiya*, have been found. In Scetis, towers must have existed from an early date, but these probably served the purpose of a retreat in times of siege and a safe storage place for valuable objects (Grossmann 2002: 301–306). The towers in Kellia, on the other hand, were probably meant for permanent habitation (Descœudres 1998: 75). Similar tower houses must have occurred in the Nile Delta in Late Antiquity (Lehmann 2013), and although our knowledge of Egyptian domestic architecture is far from complete, it seems likely that, apart from a number of buildings that developed over the centuries into specific community centers with churches, the architecture of Kellia was directly inspired by secular architecture of the Nile Delta. A group of hermits living under the guidance of a spiritual father must have had different architectural requirements from those of an average (extended) family in the Delta, but a common element with secular house architecture is the division into common, semi-private, and private space, a tripartite division that is clearly recognizable in the architecture of Kellia.

In numerous buildings, decorations of some sort have been found, ranging from simple graffito-like drawings in red ocher to elaborate painted stucco imitations of columns.[4] Most of these decorations were found in the oratories, the private or communal rooms for prayer. The number of churches in Kellia was limited and the walls have rarely survived up to a level of more than two meters. From the remains of these buildings no traces of monumental painted decoration with figurative representations have survived that are comparable to those in churches elsewhere, as for instance in Scetis.[5]

Many of the paintings are of a decorative character and do not show any religious characteristics. Red ocher was often used for painting floors and a dado decoration that reached to approximately one meter high on the walls of certain rooms. Geometrical, floral, and animal motifs were used, while crosses are the most frequent elements with an obvious Christian meaning. Representations of human figures are rare,[6] and here we see an important difference with contemporary paintings from monastic contexts such as in Scetis, Bawit, and Saqqara. The paintings found in Kellia date back to the last, and most prosperous, phase of the settlements, roughly speaking the sixth to the eighth centuries. This is also the period to which the paintings in Bawit and Saqqara are dated and the time of the earliest known paintings from Scetis. The differences are conspicuous: the prayer niches in Saqqara and Bawit show a variety of *Majestas Domini* representations and paintings of the Virgin, angels, and apostles in various configurations. In Kellia the oratories and, within these, the prayer niches in the eastern wall were the focal points of painted decoration, but instead of representations of Christ and the Virgin, the main theme here was the cross, appearing in countless varieties. The other motifs used in the painted decoration are floral patterns, birds of various kinds (peacocks, partridges, doves), horses, camels, giraffes, and other animals. In addition to these there are geometrical patterns in endless varieties. Apart from the two-dimensional decorations, there were numerous embellishments of the architecture in stucco: frames around niches, semi-columns, some flanking niches, and others attached to the supports of diaphragm arches.

One of the questions that suggests itself is how these decorations should be interpreted as part of a wider context. If the architecture in which they have been applied was influenced by domestic architecture, can it be assumed that the painted and stucco decorations have also been inspired by what was usual in the interior decoration of Christian houses in the Delta in the sixth to eighth centuries? Were these decorations the product of the anchorites themselves or of professional artisans? And if they are compared to the earliest decorations that we know from Scetis, can similarities be seen?

Craftsmanship

There is a considerable variety in the quality of the mural paintings. Some are no more than graffiti and could be the product of the inhabitants, while other decorations, in fact the majority, seem to be the work of trained or professional painters. It seems that, so far, no results of chemical analyses of pigments and binders are available, which makes it difficult to compare the paintings of Kellia to other material in their technical aspects. In addition to this, a total lack of preserved painted decorations in contemporary houses in the Delta makes it impossible to draw any direct parallels, but considering the nearness of the Delta and similarities in domestic architecture, it may be plausible that there was a resemblance between the decoration of monastic and village and town houses.

By contrast, the last phase of painting in Kellia is contemporary with the earliest datable paintings that are known from Scetis and here a number of parallels are evident. Some of these parallels are of such a kind that it seems likely that the same painters and artisans were active in both regions. So far only a few *manshubiya*s have been excavated in Scetis, but from this limited material some interesting parallels are known.[7]

During a survey around the St. Macarius monastery in 2012, a mud-brick building was found that has a painted decoration in red ocher on the lower walls (fig. 24.1). At the upper edge of this red surface a frieze of triangles with a pomegranate has been painted, a pattern found in several varieties in Qusur al-Izayla (fig. 24.2).[8] This pattern was also found in the remains of a monk's cell in Dayr al-Baramus, a context that was datable to the sixth–seventh centuries (fig. 24.3).

Fig. 24.1. Upper edge of a dado decoration, building 25, Dayr Abu Maqar (Karel C. Innemée).

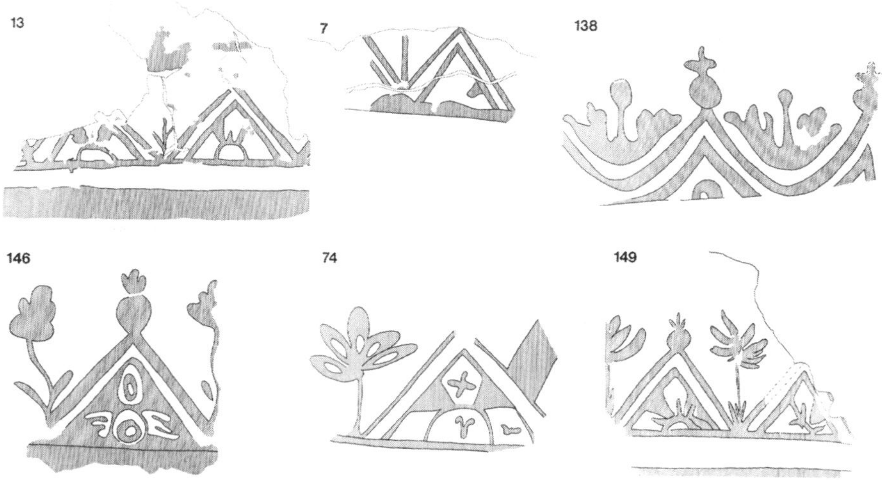

Fig. 24.2. Various decorations, Qusur Izayla (after Kasser 1983).

Fig. 24.3. Decorative painting from Dayr al-Baramus (Karel C. Innemée).

Fig. 24.4. Dado with marble imitation from the southern nave in the Church of the Virgin, Dayr al-Suryan (Karel C. Innemée).

51

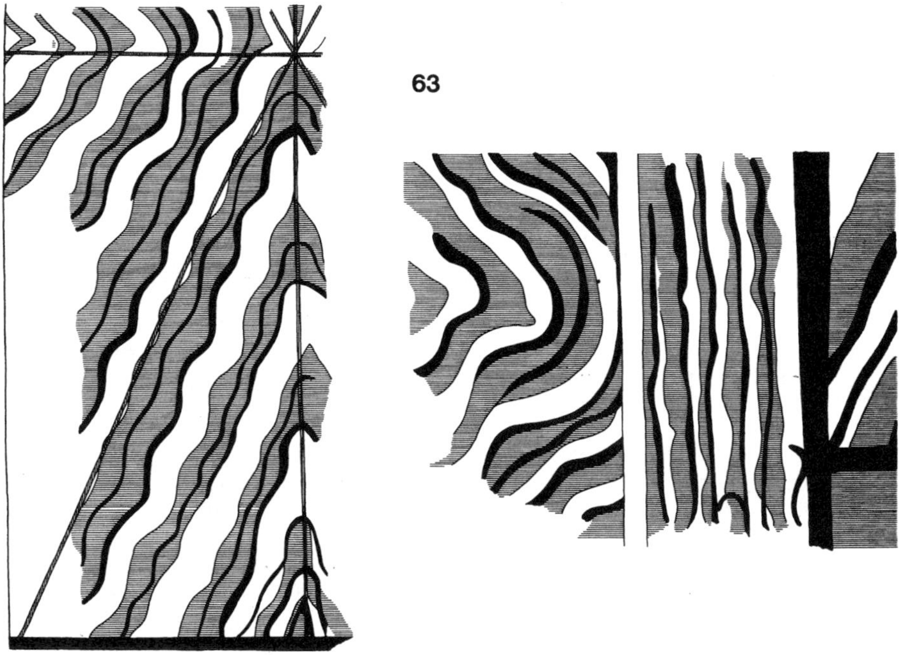

Fig. 24.5. Fragment of dado from Qusur Izayla (after Kasser 1983).

The first paintings, belonging to the second phase of decoration of the Church of the Virgin in Dayr al-Suryan, probably date back to the late seventh or early eighth century and show a number of decorative elements that have close parallels in Kellia. In many places these paintings were covered by later decoration, but the southern wall of the *khurus* still carries important remains of crosses, peacocks, and a decorative border at the edge of the arch. The decorative border around a niche in QR 195 has an almost identical floral pattern (Rassart-Debergh 2003: photo 52).[9] The motif of the cross, encircled by a floral wreath on the south wall of the *khurus*, has various close parallels in Kellia.[10] All around the church a dado decoration was painted that consists of an imitation of marble paneling. Each panel consists of four 'slabs' of marble with a pattern of diagonal veins (fig. 24.4). A fragment of a similar dado was found in the church of QIz 45 (Kasser 1983: pl. CLXVIII) (fig. 24.5).

Wall niches, framed by decorative columns or other stucco decorations, were found in numerous cells, and similar niches, some with a religious function, must have been common in houses. In Karanis such a decorated niche, probably serving as a house altar, was found in house C119E (Frankfurter 2012: fig. 20.2).

Apart from a similarity in the painted decoration, there is also a remarkable resemblance between certain details in Kellia and Scetis in the use of stucco decoration. The use of marble elements was quite limited and most architectural elements such as columns, half-columns, and capitals were made as imitations in stucco. A real marble column would consist of a base, a shaft, and a capital as three superimposed elements. In the process of putting up the column, wooden wedges would be placed between the base and the shaft, so that the shaft could be put perfectly perpendicular. Some stucco workers in Kellia went so far as to imitate these wooden wedges in plaster as well. Examples of this kind of imitation were found in QR 219, salle XVI (Daumas and Guillaumont 1969: Pl. XXXVIII), QR 227, rooms 46–48 (Kasser 1994: Pl. 2.4), and the church building in QIs 366 (Haeny and Leibundgut 1999: pl. 15.3). In the *khurus* of the church of the Virgin in Dayr al-Suryan, semi-columns have been made in stucco that show exactly the same detail (fig. 24.6). This part of the decoration of the church dates back to the time of its construction, the middle of the seventh century, and is therefore probably almost contemporary with the buildings in Kellia mentioned before.

Although the painted and stucco decoration evokes the impression of an environment with a certain degree of luxury, one could also argue that all these decorations are in fact relatively cheap imitations of the real luxury that must have been enjoyed elsewhere. As the columns and some of the paintings imitate marble, so there are other paintings that are meant to evoke the impression of textile furnishings. This phenomenon is not unique to Kellia. In several churches in Egypt and the Mediterranean, painted imitations of wall hangings are known.[11]

Between two stucco columns in QR 219 there was a painted decoration consisting of a diagonal pattern of lozenges and triangles (fig. 24.7).

A wall hanging dated to the fourth century, now in the Textile Museum in Washington, DC, shows the same motif: two columns with a geometrical pattern of squares and triangles in between (Rutschowskaya 1990: 65). A mid-fifth-century tapestry in the Musées Royaux d'Art et d'Histoire in Brussels shows a comparable composition: two columns with a geometrical

Fig. 24.6. Base of a stucco column, khurus of the Church of the Virgin, Dayr al-Suryan (Karel C. Innemée).

Fig. 24.7. Stucco columns and geometric painting in QR 219 (after Daumas and Guillaumont 1969).

pattern of diagonal lines in between (Rutschowskaya 1990: 47). A variation of the same pattern can be found on the northern wall of the *haykal* of the Three Youths in Dayr Abu Maqar (fig. 24.8).

The cross, flanked by birds or other animals, a subject frequently occurring in Kellia, was also used in textiles of various kinds, such as a tapestry ornament of a veil (altar cloth?), now in the Museu Textil in Tarrasa (Cabrera 2009: fig. 12a), and a curtain or veil in the Metropolitan Museum of Art in New York.[12]

It is not only wall hangings that may have served as a source of inspiration for the paintings; rugs were also imitated. In the large, three-bayed hall of QR 227 (rooms 46–48) there are remains of three pedestals or bases that probably supported marble table tops. That, at least, is the impression one gains from the patterns painted in red on the floor around the bases, imitating rugs of a size and shape that correspond to marble table tops (Kasser 1994: 63, 525, fig. 22, Pl. 30.7, 30.8).[13] One is round, the other two

Fig. 24.8. Geometrical pattern in the *haykal* of the Three Youths, Dayr Abu Maqar (Karel C. Innemée).

sigma-shaped, and their presence is an indication that this room was used as a refectory. It also shows that probably in private houses, apart from the luxury of marble dining tables, rugs or carpets could be used in the *triclinia* and other rooms. The fact that in Kellia one had to be satisfied with a painted imitation is therefore rather a matter of abstinence than of luxury.

A number of decorative panels painted on walls may also have been an imitation of the more expensive *opus sectile* work (Rassart-Debergh 1986: 185). Real *opus sectile* is extremely rare in Kellia,[14] and here as well the painted imitation can be seen as a sign of sobriety.

Painted imitations of precious materials such as marble, porphyry, and other kinds of stone and imitations in stucco of marble columns must have been used in middle-class houses in Roman Egypt. Although such houses have rarely survived, especially in the Nile Valley and the Delta, an indirect proof of their existence can be found in the necropolis of Tuna al-Gabal, where tombs were constructed that were meant to be emulations of residential architecture (Lembke 2014: 87, pl. 6, 7).

In conclusion we can say that, with a number of adaptations, architecture in Kellia and its interior decoration were probably inspired by town and village houses in the Nile Valley. The similarities to decorations in churches and other buildings in Scetis could be taken as an indication that artisans, active in the Delta, were commissioned to do decoration work not only in Kellia, but also in the farther-off monastic settlements of Scetis.

Iconography

At first sight the architecture in Kellia and its decoration seem to have been created with a strong influence of the secular arts and crafts. Decorative motifs such as birds, other animals, and geometrical patterns form the majority, while depictions of human beings are rare. One of the elements in the iconography of its paintings that is the most conspicuous mark of its Christian character is the frequent use of the cross. This in itself is not necessarily a characteristic of monastic or ecclesiastic architecture; crosses carved in lintels of doors can be found in traditional houses inhabited by Copts all over Egypt. Crosses occur in a wide variety and a distinction can be made, not only in the skill with which they have been painted, but also in the iconography, depending on the details and the place where they have been painted. Rassart-Debergh mentions three varieties in the crosses as they appear in Kellia: prophylactic *(prophylactique)*, decorative, and liturgical (Rassart-Debergh 1986: 186; Rassart-Debergh 2003: 349–51). Indeed, these aspects can be recognized, but more can be said about this categorization. In the first place, the decorative character of crosses cannot be seen as an independent characteristic. As a symbol it has a meaning that can be combined with a decorative design, but primarily this meaning comes first. The protective or apotropaic function of the cross as a sign is widespread, in jewelry as well as in architectural and other decoration; the numerous crosses that can be found on walls of houses and hermitages all over Egypt no doubt had this as their primary function. In particular, crosses near entrances can be interpreted in this way. They often combine this function with a decorative aspect. The term 'liturgical' for crosses in prayer niches may not be the most appropriate. The prayer niches must have had a function in personal devotion, and celebration of the liturgy must have taken place in churches. Indeed, we see that in the niches of oratories in Saqqara and Bawit themes are represented that are reminiscent of apse compositions: Christ and/or the Virgin enthroned, sometimes flanked by angels. This does not imply that such niches were used for liturgical celebrations; for personal prayers, an image that can be characterized as 'epiphanic' or 'theophanic' can play an essential role as a focal point of devotion. The crosses in the niches of Kellia can also be called theophanic, in the sense that they remind the beholder of the appearance of Christ. The best example of this is the cross in QR 219, room XII (Daumas and Guillaumont 1969: Pl. XXXIX, C), which shows a great similarity to the cross in the apse of San Apollinare in Classe. In both cases we see a representation of a golden cross, decorated with gems *(crux gemmata)*, with a medallion bearing a bust of Christ in the center. Erich Dinkler has shown convincingly that this cross has a double theophanic meaning: flanked by Moses and Elijah it stands for Christ in his divine appearance, while in conjunction with the paradise-like garden below it refers to the Second Coming of Christ, announced by the appearance of the "sign of the Son of Man" in the sky, as described in Matthew 24:30 (Dinkler 1964: 22–100).

A conspicuous difference between this cross in QR 219 and the one in Ravenna is the chains hanging between the arms, from which little bells or round ornaments are hanging. The same kind of decoration can be seen in other crosses in Kellia. Most of these crosses seem to stand on firm ground and are sometimes flanked by birds or other animals (Rassart-Debergh 1986: figs. 6, 7; Kasser 1983: Pl. CLXXXIII–CLXXXV). This kind of representation could refer to monumental crosses of metal, erected in churches or public places. The most famous example of this was the cross on the site of the Crucifixion, erected by Theodosius II (Theophanes, *Chronographia* 86, 26–29, De Boor 1883), but in a general sense we can say that these three-dimensional crosses and their painted representations are both expressions of the cross as a *tropaion*, a sign of victory, more specifically the victory of Christ over death.[15] Death, in Christian tradition, is the result of the original sin committed by Adam and Eve, and was overcome and reversed by the sacrifice of Christ; for this reason the cross became the sign of victory and the *lignum vitae*.[16] The crosses in Kellia often appear against a backdrop of, or surrounded by, flowers and plants; together with the flanking animals, this appears to be meant as a representation of the regained paradise, expected after the Second Coming of Christ. The cross as a central theme in early Christian apses was not widespread, but apart from the abovementioned apse of San Apollinare in Classe, there were at least two other apse mosaics where the cross as a *tropaion* or *crux gemmata* is represented in an eschatological setting. The apses (now lost) of the churches of Fundi and Nola in Italy (both around AD 400) had a cross as a central element, in Nola appearing in the sky, in Fundi on a throne, as the announcement of the *parousia* (Ihm 1960: 80–81). Closely connected to the theophanic/eschatological background of the cross in an apse or prayer niche is the cross, flanked by peacocks or other birds, associated with a funerary context. This motif is represented on a number of sarcophagi from Ravenna (fifth–sixth centuries) (Bovini 1954: 35–44), sometimes on a short side, sometimes as the main theme on the front. The cross as the announcer of the Last Judgment here apparently expresses the hope of the deceased for a life in paradise. This theme occurs in Bawit, probably to underscore the symbolism of the monk's dwelling as a tomb (Clédat 1904–1906: pl. XXIX; Innemée 2015: 247), and in Kellia a similar thought may have been the background behind certain crosses.

Summarizing, we can distinguish three aspects in the crosses from Kellia. First is the apotropaic meaning and function, an aspect that is widespread in the Christian world and not specifically monastic. Second, the frequent appearance of the cross in prayer niches has a clear iconographic connection with apse decorations; this theophanic aspect can be found in the prayer niches in Saqqara and Bawit as well, although the most popular themes in those two locales are Christ and the Virgin. A third and related aspect is the cross as a funerary theme. In this respect as well, there may be a thematic correspondence with Bawit, where references to funerary iconography are frequent.

Apart from crosses there is another subject that occurs frequently in the mural decoration of Kellia: the sailing ship.[17] Marguerite Rassart-Debergh, in an article where she discusses the iconography of boat graffiti in Kellia and a number of other sites in Egypt, suggests that, apart from the possibility that it concerns simply sketches from everyday life, a number of religious meanings could be attached to these representations. The passage to the hereafter, the boat as an image of the soul or of the Church, are among the possible meanings that she mentions (Rassart-Debergh 1992: 57, 72–73). In the case of Kellia, however, no solid evidence permits us to go beyond speculation.

All these representations of ships have a graffito-like character and therefore seem to be the work of the inhabitants, unless visitors made them. Not only in Kellia, but as far south as Faras, graffiti of ships have been found in a monastic context. The so-called anchorite's grotto there has several ships on its wall (Griffith 1927: pl. LXII.2, LXIII.1, LXIV.2, LXVI.2). A clue to an interpretation is lacking so far, or at least no thorough studies have been undertaken concerning this theme in its modest execution. The remarkable fact is, however, that graffiti of ships in a religious context occur not only in the Nile Valley, but in a number of places in the world. More or less systematic inventories have been made in England and Scandinavia, where hundreds of ships were scratched on the walls of churches.[18] The dates for these graffiti seem to range from the late medieval era to the seventeenth century. The reason for scratching such images on church walls is still obscure. They occur not only in churches near the coast, but also farther inland. Graffiti of ships in a religious context are apparently not limited to Christian culture: they have been found on the walls of the Bronze Age Temple 1 in Kition (Cyprus) (Wachsmann 1998: 147–48) and on the temple of Musawwarat al-Sufra in Sudan.[19] On the temple walls in Tarxien (Malta), graffiti of ships have been made, possibly starting in the second millennium BC (Muscat 2000). It appears that an interpretation of the ship's graffiti in Kellia will require a study that covers more than just Christian Egypt.

Kellia lies at the border of the Delta, an area that can be seen, in more than one respect, as an area of transition between the secular world and the monastic landscape of the Western Desert. The moderate degree of seclusion and asceticism in Kellia seems to be reflected in its material culture, which was probably created under the influence of nearby towns and villages. The limited time that was granted to archaeologists to excavate means that only a small percentage of its heritage of decorative arts was documented, and the attention paid to it in publications seems to be too limited, even if we consider that it does not concern painting and stucco of monumental quality. The artistic heritage of Kellia deserves more attention.

Notes

1. *Apophthegmata Patrum*, Antony 34; Ward 1975a: 8.
2. Arabic term to indicate a hermitage for one or more inhabitants (from the Coptic word *mansjoope*, which means 'dwelling place').
3. For a detailed analysis of the plan of the Egyptian mud-brick house, see Correas Amador 2013. The courtyard house and tripartite living units are discussed on pp. 37–40.
4. Apart from the descriptions of such paintings in the respective excavation reports, a general and overall analysis of paintings in Kellia has not been published yet. An elaborate description of paintings from QR 195 was published in Rassart-Debergh 2003. A number of articles on painting in Kellia in general have been published by Marguerite Rassart-Debergh: Rassart-Debergh 1986; Rassart-Debergh 1991.
5. Absence of proof is no proof of absence in this case. Churches with elaborate decoration may have existed, but in most cases they have been preserved up to a relatively low level, so that figurative paintings higher up on the walls have survived barely or not at all, as for instance in QI 1 (Weidmann 2013). In QI 1 one fragment of a face was found (Haeny and Leibundgut 1999: pl. 23.1).
6. There are some exceptions, such as three military saints in QI 14, a bust of Christ in a medallion in QR 306 (Rassart-Debergh 1989, fig. 45, 52), and a cross with a bust of Christ in QR 219 (Daumas and Guillaumont 1969, pl. XXXIX).
7. Unpublished surveys by the author around Dayr al-Baramus and Dayr al-Suryan have shown the presence of several hundred monastic structures, many of which are or were in areas that are privately owned, and many of these must have disappeared since the surveys were taken.
8. Kasser 1983: 2, Pl. CLXXV, CLXXVI.
9. As was previously stated, so far no analyses of pigments and binders of paintings from Kellia are available. The paintings in Dayr al-Suryan are done in a combination of tempera and encaustic.
10. For instance, in several hermitages in QI; Kasser 1983: Pl. CLXXXI–CLXXXV.
11. Well-known examples are the niches in the *haykal* of the church of the Red Monastery and the lower zones of walls in Santa Maria Antiqua in Rome.
12. http://www.metmuseum.org/art/collection/search/444287
13. Such marble tops of various shapes and sizes were used frequently in monasteries and churches in Egypt. Some of them were (re-)used as altar tables, others as dining tables in refectories, as is still the case in Byzantine monasteries, such as Vatopedi on Mount Athos: http://athosweblog.com/2009/05/03/783-refectory-vatopedi/
14. The best example of such a rare *opus sectile* panel is the one from the church of QI 1 (Weidmann 2013: Pl. 65).

15 For a general introduction to the iconography of the cross, see Dinkler 1990.

16 In the decoration of the church, rock-cut dwellings, and other buildings in Dayr al-Dik near Antinoopolis there is a great variety of crosses that are comparable to those in Kellia (Martin 1971: 27–33, 49). One of these crosses has the clear shape of a tree, apparently referring to the Tree of Life in paradise. The absence of human representations is another similarity to the decoration in Kellia.

17 Some of the many examples of this kind can be found in Rassart-Debergh 1986: figs. 3–5.

18 http://www.pasthorizonspr.com/index.php/archives/12/2013/signs-sailors-ship-graffiti-medieval-churches; http://www.vikingeskibsmuseet.dk/en/professions/education/method/picture-sources/ship-graffiti/; http://winchelsea.net/community/was/graffiti.htm; Kastholm 2011.

19 http://musawwaratgraffiti.mpiwg-berlin.mpg.de/graffitidb/browse/catalog/result_graffiti.pt?-display=image&-size=10&-op_motif_key=in&motif_key=075+078+076+077

25 Highlights from the Polish Excavations at Marea/ Philoxenite 2000–14

Krzysztof Babraj and Daria Tarara

The site of Marea/Philoxenite is located forty-five kilometers southwest of Alexandria, on the southern shore of Lake Maryut. The city was a major port, active during the Roman and Byzantine periods, and perhaps even earlier, during the Ptolemaic era. There is uncertainty as to the ancient, original name of the city and complex at Marea, and this is one of the fundamental tasks of the mission. Given the variety and volume of ruins agglomerated in Late Antiquity, another goal is to determine the role and importance of the Byzantine complex as a religious center. The basilica at Marea is the second largest in Egypt, yet, astonishingly, contemporary document sources are silent on its very existence.

During fifteen seasons of excavations, the Polish Archaeological Mission has revealed two independent architectural complexes: a bath complex supported by a *saqya* and a funerary chapel, and a Christian basilica. Both complexes were active from the beginning of the sixth to the beginning of the eighth century (Szymańska and Babraj 2008).

History of the Site

On the southwestern shore of Lake Maryut the remains of the port facilities can be found, the most impressive of which are at Marea (fig. 25.1).

Mahmoud Bey al-Falaki (1872), the court astronomer for the viceregent of Egypt, Ismail Pasha, first identified the ruins as ancient Marea (Μαρεία).[1]

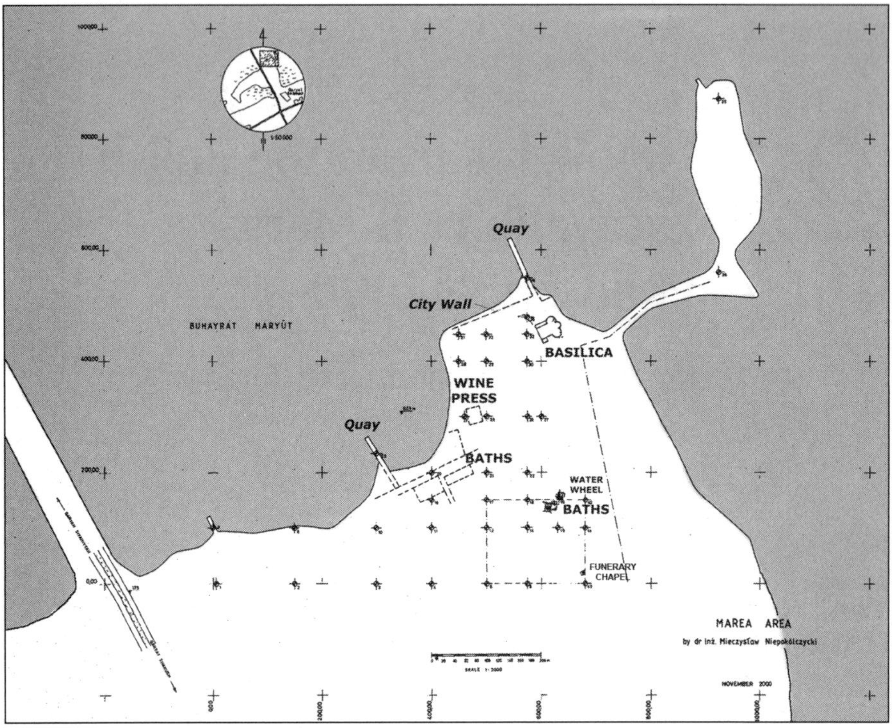

Fig. 25.1. Plan of the site of Marea (Daria Tarara).

However, this remains uncertain, with no evidence on site as to the identification. The ruins of a big city beside Lake Maryut (ancient Mareotis), forty-five kilometers from Alexandria, near the village of Hawwariya, has long aroused the interest of researchers. One of the first maps of the coast which indicated key architectural remains was prepared by A. de Cosson.[2]

This magnificent port city had four massive piers, adapted for mooring of vessels, and docks to protect against wind and waves. Much of its pre-Christian history can be reconstructed from ancient sources. According to Herodotus, during the reign of Psamtik I in the Twenty-sixth Dynasty, Marea was strategically located with a military garrison defending the border with Libya (Herodotus 1976). Another source reported that General Amasis defeated the army of Pharaoh Apries at Marea and became ruler of the country in 570 BC (Diodorus 1989). During the period of Persian rule, the city was the capital of an independent Libyan–Egyptian kingdom that stretched from the Canopic branch of the Nile to Cyrenaica. Its ruler, named Inaros II, took up arms against the Persians, which cost him his life in 454 BC, after the fall of Memphis (Thucydides 1928).

Even after the founding of Alexandria, Marea did not lose importance as a commercial port, and Mareotis remained the most important agricultural region in northwestern Egypt. During Ptolemaic and Roman times, the lake was an important transport route for goods coming from inland to Alexandria, and from there to other cities in the Greco-Roman world.[3] At the time, the Mareotis region was extremely fertile, famous for the cultivation of grapevines, olive orchards, and papyrus. Indeed, ancient writers praise the wine sent to Rome from this region as of very high quality.[4] The many presses discovered in the area confirm intensive wine production (Rodziewicz 1998a). The remains of almost thirty kilns for production of amphorae, dating from the beginning of the Hellenistic period to Late Antiquity, have been discovered on the southern shore of the lake, including the exceptionally large example uncovered by the Polish mission under the basilica, and numerous remains of glass workshops (Empereur and Picon 1998; el-Ashmawi 1998). These complete a picture of the region as a significant center of craft.

Silting of the channels in the eighth and ninth centuries and the lack of supply of fresh water from the Nile caused the partial drying of the lake. In 1801 the lake filled with sea water because of the opening of the locks by the English, who wanted to cut off the fresh-water supply of Napoleon's camp in the region. Currently, the lake surface is approximately ninety square kilometers, and its average depth is 1.50 meters (Blue and Ramses 2005).

Conversion of Mareotis to Christianity

In AD 260, Patriarch Dionysius of Alexandria, as he went into exile in Libya, noted that there were no Christians in Mareotis (Eusebius 1932; Timm 1988). Later, it was documented that converts to Christianity were sent to the Mareotis region as an act of persecution and repression. In 538, in accordance with the edict of Justinian, the region previously forming part of the Roman province of Aegyptus Prima was ceded to Libya (Justinian 1877a). It was only after the conquest of Egypt by the Arabs in 641 that it returned to Egypt. The few references to Mareotis in Coptic texts show that by the end of the Byzantine domination of the region, it was no longer a significant center of activity.[5] The total collapse of the city may have been caused by the aforementioned lack of fresh water, as well as political and social factors. In the late fifth and early sixth centuries, there is evidence of unrest in the region, with neighboring Abu Mina hosting a garrison of 1,200 troops, stationed to protect the sanctuary and pilgrims. At the beginning of the eighth century, during the reign of the Abbasids, and probably after the collapse of the city in Mareotis, a new wave of Arab nomads began to take increasing control of the local church institutions. The area was no longer safe for Christians, and especially not as a stopover for pilgrims. By contrast, wine from Mareotis was still famous in the seventh century, according to a story about abstinent monks, quoted by John Moschos (Moschos and Baynes 1947).

Identification

Doubts as to the identification of the ruins as ancient Marea have surfaced, based mainly on findings from pottery dating from the sixth to the beginning of the eighth century and the distinctive Byzantine character of the architecture.[6] Mieczyslaw Rodziewicz advanced the argument that the ruins visible on the surface belonged to a city founded as a staging point for pilgrims traveling to the Monastery of St. Mina in Abu Mina, twenty kilometers away (Rodziewicz 1983).[7] His text mentions numerous facilities for travelers, such as hotels, markets, porticos, and even a kind of luggage storage facility. The purported founder of this resort was the prefect of Emperor Anastasius (r. 491–518), named Philoxenos, from which the city received its name, Philoxenite. Ewa Wipszycka identifies this dignitary as Consul Philoxenos Soterichos, who was in office in 525 (Wipszycka 2002; Wipszycka 2012; Grossmann 2003).

However, the size of the port installations and the large size of the basilica, as well as fragments of pottery from the early Roman period, suggest that a large urban center existed there before the Byzantine buildings were constructed. This is also indicated by the size and high quality of the municipal wastewater treatment for the city. There is a possibility that Consul Philoxenos built a city close to the existing port installations, which for some reason ceased to function as a town center before the channels silted up and restricted the supply of fresh water from the lake.

There is little doubt that the pilgrimage to the Shrine of the Holy Martyr passed through this area, not least because of its proximity to the lake. This can be supported by evidence that a late Roman *villa rustica*, discovered in the village of Hawwariya, was converted to a dormitory in the mid-sixth century, with a small church inside (Rodziewicz 1988: 271–73, fig. 2). A large urban center with extensive port facilities would certainly have been an obvious place to stop for tired, often sick travelers.

Bath Complex

The bath complex (fig. 25.2)[8] includes a stand-alone bath and a system to supply water from a well, supported by a *saqya*, as well as ancillary shops. The rectangular bath, of 170 square meters, was enclosed within 642 square meters of courtyards and was built of kiln-fired bricks with foundation.

The complex consists of east and west courtyards with porticos. To the north at the outer wall were a latrine and shops. The bath complex was divided into two unequal parts: the larger southern part was designed for men and the smaller northern part for women.[9] Each part was heated by a separate furnace, which provided heat to four hypocausts (under-floor heating systems). Access to the men's part was from the west side; visitors were conducted from the courtyard directly into the apodyterium, which consisted of the tepidarium and two caldaria. The women's part had poorer facilities; access was from the large courtyard located on the east side, and it had only three rooms: apodyterium and two caldaria.

There were a total of fourteen small bathing pools: eight inside, and six open-air. The pools had diverse shapes: semicircular, rectangular, or round, according to the different phases of construction.

The bath rooms probably had vaulted ceilings. The extrapolated height of the rooms was 3.50 meters, based on the ratio of the preserved parts of the building. The shops probably had flat roofing.[10]

The underground part of the building included a basement for storage, two furnaces for heating caldaria and one for heating the water, and four under-floor spaces as part of the hypocausts: two under the men's part and two under the women's part.

The bath complex provides evidence of a luxury establishment, which consisted of marble floor coverings, columns with Corinthian capitals, and several layers of polychrome wall with a multicolored floral frieze. Even the floors, and sometimes the walls of the basins and water tanks, were lined with marble slabs. The bath complex was connected to an extensive network of solid municipal channels, indicating the probable presence of other such establishments within the city.

The lack of a clear stratigraphy does not allow for precise determination of the chronology of the bath complex, and also hinders clear separation of the successive phases of its reconstruction and maintenance. Ceramic finds on site help establish a chronological framework for the functioning of the baths in the period between the first half of the sixth century and the first thirty years of the eighth century, that is, before the advent of the Arab

Fig. 25.2. Baths, seen from the west (Tomasz Kalarus).

Early Lead Glazed wares (Majcherek 2008; Fagan 1999). Finds of Arab coins minted after monetary reform in AD 686, and in circulation until approximately 750, confirm the operation of the baths after the Persian invasion and after the Arab conquest (Malarczyk 2008). The most intensive use of the baths appears to have been during the first half of the seventh century, as evidenced by both ceramic finds and the dominance of coins from the reign of Khosrau (Chosroes) II (Lichocka 2008).

From the clear signs of collapsed buildings, one cannot exclude the initial assumption that an earthquake was the cause of destruction. A second hypothesis, that the destruction occurred during the invasion by the Persian king Khosrau II Parviz in 619, is not justified, due to numerous coins from the time of this ruler and from later periods found during excavations in the bath.[11]

Saqya

At a distance of five meters north of the baths, a water well supported by a *saqya* was discovered.[12] The well had a depth of five meters, with a rectangular plan (1 m × 3.40 m). It was built of stone blocks with stone support beams inside, placed horizontally, one above the other. The well was filled from a fresh-water source that was discovered near the northwest corner, derived from an underground aquifer. In the northern wall of the well was a rectangular inlet channel, which led to a cistern with a vaulted brick ceiling. At a distance of 3.80 meters from the inlet to the channel was a shaft presumably used to provide access in order to clean the whole structure. Small footholds were cut into the side walls, again to allow access. At the bottom of the well and tanks, a large volume of ceramic fragments were found, dating from the sixth and seventh centuries, among which were a large number of fragments of the vessels (*gawadis*) used in the *saqya*.[13] The well was located in a stone circle with an outer diameter of eight meters. Still visible on some of the stone blocks is the sign of the cross painted in red. The entire structure is supported by stone buttresses, four on the west side and two on the east side. Adjacent to the south of the *saqya* there is a reservoir measuring 10 × 5.5 meters, which stored water from the well; the bottom of this reservoir retains its kiln-fired bricks and waterproof mortar.

The area between the well and the stone circle was filled with regularly arranged layers of alternating clay and gravel stone. This was a suitable base for walking a tethered animal operating the *saqya*. Because *saqya*s remain in use today in the villages of Egypt, reconstruction of the ancient form of the *saqya* was not difficult.[14]

The wealth of sources from the Byzantine period proves that the *saqya* was very widespread in Egypt (Bonneau 1993).[15] This device was used both in rural households, for watering fields and gardens, and in urban areas.[16]

The only ancient pictorial representation of a *saqya* is located on a piece of wall painting from the necropolis of Minat al-Basal (Wardian). The device, which in this case is depicted as watering a garden, also draws water from a well.[17]

The Marea baths used a very simple hydraulic system based on the principle of the siphon. This hydraulic system may be one of the very few found in Egypt, and is the only example in the published literature.

All indications are that, within the larger conurbation at Marea, this was not the only *saqya*. During our research, we came across a surface area west of the bath where the remains of a similar structure exist (fig. 25.3).

Funerary Chapel

The funerary chapel is located at a distance of 110 meters southeast of the bath complex. Its dimensions are 9 × 7.70 meters, and it is built with stone blocks. It includes a small apse facing east, in accordance with early Christian custom.[18] The interior of the chapel is divided into three parts. Within

1. bath - part for women
2. bath - part for men
3. courtyard on east side
4. courtyard on west side
5. latrine

6. shops
7 saqya
8. reservoir
9. well

Fig. 25.3. Reconstruction of baths (Daria Tarara).

the chapel are three graves of standard size—2.5 × 1.75 meters with a depth of 2 meters. Contained in each grave were the interred bodies of several individuals. Since the skeletons were probably disturbed, it is difficult to document their original position. It seems, however, that they were placed with their heads in a westerly direction. Burial objects were limited to simple brown rings and some loose glass beads (one amethyst), as well as several coins. Judging from the brown color of the soil surrounding the bones, some of the bodies were wrapped in cloth.[19]

The chapel was built in the sixth century, as suggested by coins found in graves, as well as the Gaza-type amphora that lay directly under the floor of the apse. The building was in use probably up to the beginning of the eighth century, similar to the bath complex.

Basilica (Szymańska and Babraj 2006)

The ruins of the basilica, located on high ground near the eastern pier, were discovered by W. Müller-Wiener in 1967, one of the first researchers of the pilgrimage center of Abu Mina (Müller-Wiener 1967). In 1986 his successor, Peter Grossmann, sketched a plan of the basilica (Grossmann 1993; Grossmann 2002). Despite its large size, it is not mentioned in any contemporary ancient source. It is one of only four churches with transepts known in Christian Egypt. The others are Abu Mina, Hermopolis Magna, and possibly Dikhaylah, where the unfinished excavations do not allow for certainty in the plan of the church (fig. 25.4).

It is possible that the basilica was modeled on Alexandrian churches from the same period. The Polish mission has uncovered the full extent of the building with dimensions of 49 × 47 meters, divided into three naves: a large central nave and two side naves, separated by columns (Szymańska and Babraj 2005a, 2005c, 2005d; Babraj and Szymańska 2004). In front of the entrance was a covered portico. This separated the basilica from a number of small buildings, most likely shops to serve pilgrims.

An interesting feature of the transept is the semicircular shape. No other example of this design has been found in Egypt (fig. 25.5).

Four large pillars were located in the transept, at the corners of the altar.

The external walls of the basilica were approximately one meter thick, and possibly too weak for the structure. Examples of buttresses are visible, supporting the external wall of the transept. These buttresses were repaired and added to over many years. This may be evidence of a heavy roof or dome, which the original construction could not support.

Two baptisteries were discovered, one near the altar and the other on the south wall of the basilica.[20] This second baptistery was part of the original layout of the basilica. The baptistery near the altar is probably from a previous sanctuary on the site.

The area around the altar was dedicated exclusively to the clergy and was surrounded by decorated marble partition screens supported by pillars, about one meter high.

There is ample evidence that the basilica was very richly decorated. This is evidenced by marble columns of different sizes and Corinthian capitals, the marble coming from Prokonez, Turkey, imported through Alexandria. In addition, there are stucco pilasters crowned by capitals which may have been painted. The floors were arranged in the *opus sectile* technique with multicolored marble tiles found in large numbers in different places. The relatively large altar area was separated from the rest of the church during various stages of its reconstruction by marble barriers called cancelli, consisting of marble support pillars and decorated slabs.

The apse was also richly decorated. A number of fragments of mosaic were found, made of multicolored glass cubes, some of which were still in the mortar. A few of them were layered with gold foil.

In the apse, two crypts were discovered, containing the remains of more than one hundred people of both sexes, including children, newborns, and even unborn children.[21] It is possible that they were the victims of an assault by the Persian army of Khosrau II in 619 that destroyed Alexandria and plundered the countryside.

Kiln for Firing Amphora

Under the apse of the church, at a depth of 1.80 meters, the unexpected discovery was made of a blast furnace, or kiln, for firing amphorae, but which was used by the builders of the basilica as the foundation for part of the liturgical tabernacle. The kiln is eight meters in diameter, with a half-meter-thick grill, the second largest Roman ceramic kiln in Egypt. Only a height of 0.9 meter remains of sections of the outer wall of mud brick. Still sitting on the grill were examples of whole, and fragments of, amphorae dating from the second and third centuries.[22]

The large amount of pottery, mainly amphorae, found on site in Mareotis argues for the existence here of a large amphorae production center in the early Roman period.

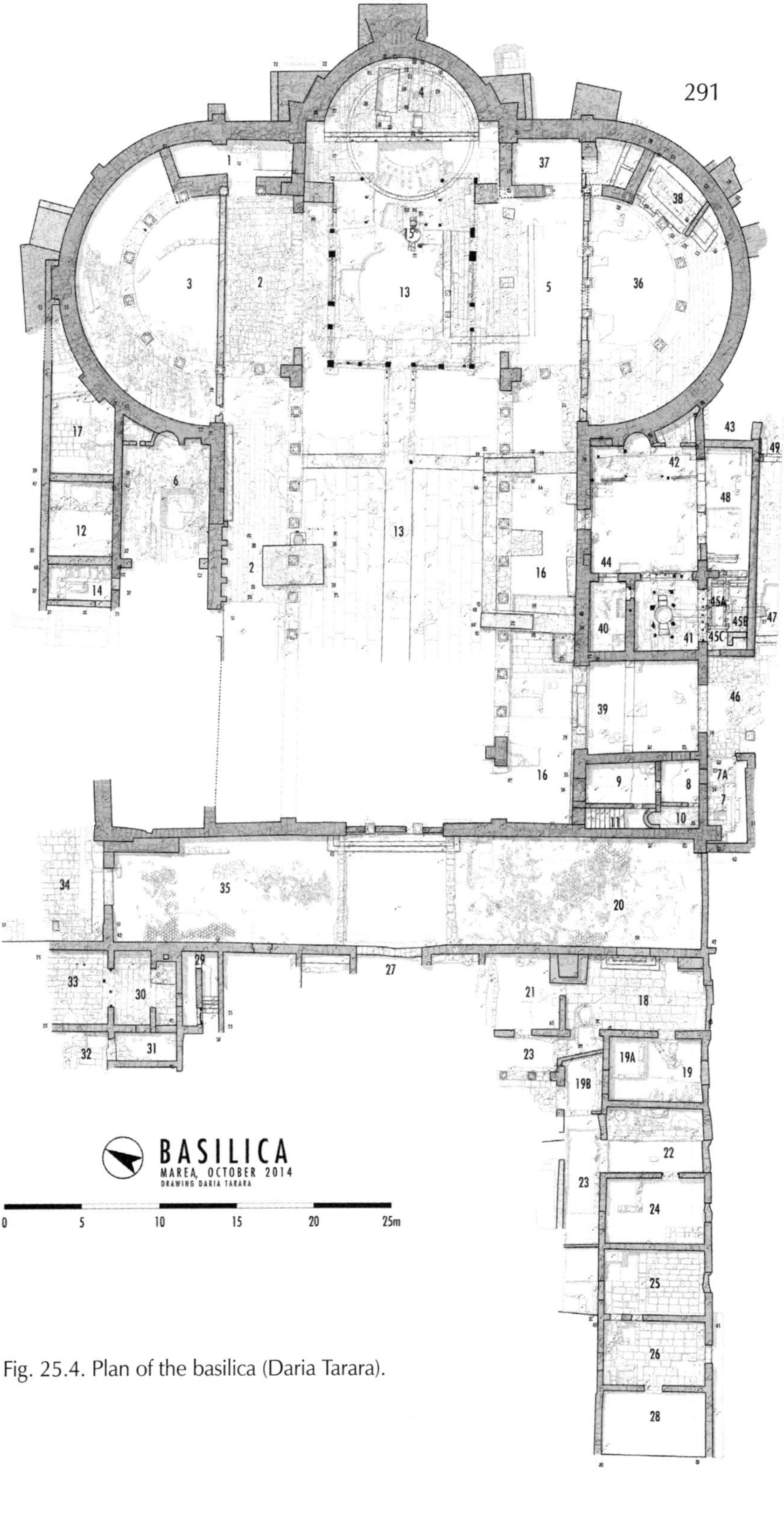

Fig. 25.4. Plan of the basilica (Daria Tarara).

Fig. 25.5. Top: basilica, view of the south transept (Tomasz Skrzypiec); bottom: basilica, view of the apse (Jacek Kucy).

Other debris and items were found in the kiln, including pillars, brickwork, and screens (cancelli). They probably fell into the kiln from the apse during the collapse of the main structure.

Ostraca

In the area beyond the apse of the basilica, port facilities and a building called the "villa" were found. Also in this area were a large volume of ostraca—pieces of broken pottery used for writing on. Over 164 pieces of ostraca with readable text were discovered, with an additional 120 examples where the text could not be read (fig. 25.6).

Most of the text was very mundane information (lists of salaries, material costs, etc.). For example, on one set of fragments, the relative pay given to each type of artist/worker on the site was deciphered.

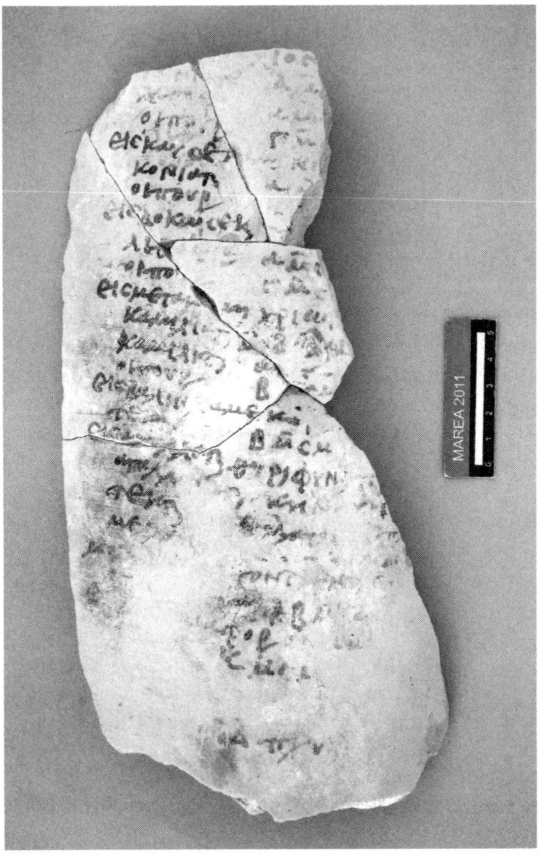

Fig. 25.6. Infrared photograph of an ostracon (Joanna Babraj).

Conclusions

Over its fifteen years of continuous excavation of the site at Marea, the Polish Archaeological Mission has made many unique and interesting discoveries, which place Marea at the center of a major pilgrimage route to Abu Mina. However, the city also had great importance prior to the Christian era, with strong evidence of significant Roman activities on an industrial scale reflected in both the investment in port facilities and the discovery of sophisticated water and bathing systems and a large kiln. There remains some uncertainty as to the exact identification of the city; however, the circumstantial evidence is compelling that this may well be the location of the ancient city of Marea.

We would like to dedicate this chapter to the memory of Professor Hanna Szymańska, leader of the mission to Marea from 2000 to 2010.

Notes

1 For further discussion of the location and history of Marea, see Kees 1930; Calderini 1980; Gomaà 1980; Babraj and Szymańska 2005; Babraj and Szymańska 2010.

2 De Cosson 1935: 131. According to this author, a strategic route from Africa to Alexandria passed close to Marea. This route was taken by both Julius Caesar and 'Amr ibn al-'As of Fustat, and in more modern times by Napoleon.

3 Strabo (1997: 83) reports that the port of Marea imported far more goods by sea than Alexandria. To the south of Alexandria was a port, now sunken, called Portus Mareoticus, which catered for the lake ships. From there, a canal flowing through Alexandria connected to the Mediterranean. For details of the channels connecting Mareotis with the Canopic branch of the Nile, see Rodziewicz 1983; Rodziewicz 1988; Empereur 1998.

4 Virgil 1999; Strabo 1997: 105; Horace 2004; Athenaeus 1927. Even today one of the best crops of Egyptian wine grapes is located at the southern edge of the Mareotis region.

5 For further discussion of the medieval history of Mareotis (seventh to early sixteenth centuries), see Décobert 2002: 127–67.

6 Fraser (1972: 146) first drew attention to a possible error in identifying the position.

7 Rodziewicz relied on Coptic Encomium St. Mina from the patriarch Johannes IV (r. 775–89), quoted by Drescher (1946: 147–48), who described Philoxenite. In a recently published article Rodziewicz argues that this thesis lacks the support of defensive equipment and garrisons in the Late Period, traces of which should have been found. In addition, the city was built, according to him, as a result of a single, coherent architectural concept (Rodziewicz 2003: 27–47).

8 A detailed description of the bath complex has been published in Szymańska and Babraj 2008.

9 Vitruvius 1956: 5, 10, 1 i VI, 4, 1. Such a device is found in Pompeii (baths at the forum) and Herculaneum (baths of the forum); see Yegül 1992: 65, figs. 65 and 66. Such a division of the bathing areas occurred in Egypt during the Ptolemaic period; cf el-Khashab 1949: 51. This is supported by papyrology research; cf. Meyer 1992.

10 The reconstruction was based on a preserved vault in the Hunting Baths at Leptis Magna; cf. Yegül 1992: 243, fig. 290.

11 The Persian army destroyed the area around Abu Mina in 619; see Grossmann and Kościuk 1991: 65.

12 A detailed description of the *saqya* is included in Szymańska and Babraj 2008: 85–99.

13 The word *gadus* has its origin from the Greek κάδος, which means 'the vessel used in a *saqya*.' On the Arabic word *saqya*, cf. Littmann 1967.

14 Modern *saqya* design does not differ from the ancient design; see Ménassa and Laferrière 1974. For further reading on the subject of the ancient *saqya*, see Stórk 1984; Oleson 2000: 267–72. A drawing showing a *saqya* as a typical Egyptian device is given in *Description de l'Egypte* (1832: II, pl. 5). After the commissioning of the Aswan dam, this type of device ceased to be constructed.

15 In a story from Sulpicius Severus (*Dialogorum libri II*, I 13, PL 20, pp. 183–222), from the early fifth century, there is a description of this unit (called *machina rotalis*) irrigating gardens at the desert monastery.

16 A wealth of data regarding the use of the *saqya* in Arsinoë in Fayoum from AD 113 is provided on the recently released papyrus P. Lond. 1117. In the text are descriptions of the various water systems including *saqya* (βοηλάται μηχαναί), information about the costs of their implementation, and the persons responsible for their maintenance (Habermann 2000).

17 The date of this fresco is still a topic of debate. It has been placed in both the second century BC and the third century AD. For a discussion of the chronology of this fresco, see Venit 2002: 96–118 and a review in Babraj and Gorzelany 2002.

18 The chapel was initially described in Szymańska and Babraj 2008.

19 According to the anthropologists Kaczmarek and el-Merghany, the burial remains contained twelve subjects aged one through eighteen, males between forty and fifty years of age, and women between thirty and forty (Szymańska and Babraj 2005b: 125).

20 Baptisteries of this type can be found in the Great Basilica of Abu Mina (Khatchatrian 1962: 8, 60; Grossmann 2004a).

21 Anthropological studies of human remains of the crypts were made by Maria Kaczmarek and Samia el-Merghany (Szymańska and Babraj 2006: 111).

22 Chronology of ceramics was determined by G. Majcherek.

26 Conservation of Mural Paintings in the Coptic Museum

Michael Jones

In 2004–2006, the American Research Center in Egypt (ARCE) undertook a project to protect and conserve the seven painted niches from the Monastery of Apa Jeremiah at Saqqara, the two painted niches from the Monastery of Apa Apollo at Bawit, and the mural painting of Adam and Eve from Tebtunis, now in the Coptic Museum, Cairo.[1] The project was a response to the urgent need to safeguard these paintings during building renovations and redesigning of the display galleries.[2] The selection criteria rested on the particular vulnerability of the niches and their art historical importance as perceived 'masterpieces' of Coptic art; the iconographic significance of the niches, all of which show Christ and the Virgin Mary often in the company of apostles and saints, that had served as devotional icons in their original settings; and the unique quality of the Tebtunis painting. Building renovations were already well advanced by the time ARCE became involved. The team of Italian wall painting conservators, already well known for their work at St. Antony's and St. Paul's monasteries, carried out emergency stabilization and protective measures to safeguard the niches and the Tebtunis mural, and removed them from the galleries for storage until the renovations were complete.[3]

The recent conservation history began very soon after the paintings were discovered when they were detached from their archaeological contexts and taken to Cairo. This approach is seldom followed today since detachment can cause irreversible damage and introduces risks that inevitably lead to cycles of well-intentioned but poorly implemented retreatment.[4] Although the Bawit and Saqqara niches exhibit all these damaging effects, removal to the museum undeniably guaranteed their survival, as also with the Tebtunis mural, since the paintings that were left in situ perished as the supporting masonry decayed.[5]

The Bawit niches, now CM7118 and CM8012, were excavated in 1913.[6] They went first to the Egyptian Museum, where CM7118 was accessioned in the same year under the number JE44232, and CM8012 under tr12.12.20.2 some seven years later.[7] CM8012 is a modern composition created by inserting a niche painting found in one room into the outer frame and arch of another niche found nearby.[8] The excavator noted important conservation details. The niche that would be used for the outer frame and arch had already been moved anciently to the position where it was found and adjusted to fit into its new space where the wall had been modified to receive it. When excavated, the two pilasters from either side had already disappeared without trace.[9] The niche that would form the interior of CM8012 was found with sand, which the excavator eventually removed, adhering very firmly to the painted surface.[10] The conservators noted that the surface was particularly abraded, with widespread micro paint losses and adhesion flaws in the encaustic green (copper-verdigris) pigments. It is not known whether the two niches were joined together on site or assembled at the Egyptian Museum.[11]

The Saqqara niches were excavated between 1906 and 1910.[12] The Egyptian Museum accession registers provide scant information, although all seven niches undoubtedly went to the museum with the other detached wall paintings from Quibell's excavations. Only two registered niches are identifiable by references to Quibell's published photographs. Tr18.1.21.4 is an "armoire renfermant des fragments de décoration murale (peinture au plâtre): une niche avec la Vierge . . ." identifiable as CM8013; tr18.1.21.7 is an "armoire" also containing fragments of mural decoration including "niche (Vierge allaitant l'enfant)" identifiable as CM7987.[13] In 1939 the Bawit and Saqqara niches were transferred to the recently constructed new wing of the Coptic Museum and installed in the galleries, where they remained until 2004.[14] The Tebtunis mural, CM3962, found in March–April 1933,[15] was not registered in the Egyptian Museum and undoubtedly went straight to the Coptic Museum.[16]

In keeping with Egyptian tradition, all the paintings are painted on plaster *a secco*. The Saqqara niches were constructed of mud brick lined with a white lime plaster *arricio*, often quite coarse and uneven, containing siliceous alluvial sand and some occasional plant fibers. The *intonaco* varies in application from not present (CM7984 and 7995) to a fine white lime wash, thin and discontinuous (CM7978), to three layers of thin washes (CM7987). The *intonaco* of CM7989 was intentionally rendered gray by adding lampblack to the mixture. Excavation photographs show that where the supporting masonry was preserved, the interior plaster surfaces of the walls had not always survived well.[17] However, the removal processes and various undocumented interventions subsequently caused considerable damage, the most serious losses attributable to methods used for removal and transfer to Cairo and possibly prolonged storage as indicated by the Egyptian Museum register. The second move to the Coptic Museum would have placed further stress on the already fragile niches.

Abundant traces of amber and brown varnish with impressions of a coarse fabric resembling the weave of hessian were noted on the painted surfaces of all the Saqqara niches, indicating the method of securing the painted surfaces with cloth and varnish adhesive during removal from the site and transfer to Cairo. These materials were unevenly applied, leaving parts of the niches, particularly uneven edges, exposed to damage. Later, they were clumsily removed, in some cases taking the original paint layer with them. During the actual detachment from the walls, counter-molds and containment structures were imprecisely and only selectively used. The backs of the niches were strengthened by applying several layers of hessian soaked in liquid plaster of Paris varying in thickness between 2.0 and 5.0 centimeters. Poor adhesion between the original plaster and this supporting material created cavities that in turn introduced further areas of risk. With each application of plaster-soaked cloth, a thicker and more viscous layer of plaster was spread and leveled with a spatula, into which wooden wedges and iron bars were inserted. This means of supporting the backs of the niches ultimately proved inadequate, leading to a slow process of structural collapse while the niches remained in storage and after they went on display. Fissures caused movement in the plaster layers with resulting losses of alignment in the levels of plaster and painted images. More than one attempt had been made in the past to reposition unaligned fragments that had probably detached during the moves.[18]

The two niches from Bawit were painted on mud with only a thin white lime wash applied for the paintings, rendering them considerably more delicate than the Saqqara niches. A section through a sample from the original backing of CM8012 indicated a continuous mass of silty clay mixed with siliceous sand and moderate amounts of vegetable fiber and no trace of gypsum. Two layers were distinguished, but only from the different ratio of clay to vegetable fibers, with the outer 3.0–3.5 mm of the sample having a higher amount of clay. There is no visible (×10 magnification) interruption between the two layers, suggesting they were applied in quick succession. The Bawit niches were removed and transported in a much more systematic way than were the Saqqara pieces, indicating greater conservator confidence, and they seem to have been treated with much greater care. Only skilled technicians able to manipulate the fragile structure and painted plaster without causing further damage could have achieved the combined Bawit niche CM8012.[19]

On arrival at the Coptic Museum, the niches were mounted against the gallery walls in individual cases built of red brick set in cement, fixed to the walls with iron bars and brackets and closed at the front with glass. Each display replicated the curve of the niche in the form of an apse extending to the floor. Inside these cases, the paintings were mounted in wood and plaster frames tailor-made to fit each piece. The painting of Adam and Eve from Tebtunis (CM3962), with one broad flat surface, was removed from the wall of the church and placed in a wooden rectangular frame with reinforcing vertical, horizontal, and corner braces. A wire mesh with 1.0-centimeter squares was fixed on the back within this framework using plasterboard and copious amounts of plaster of Paris applied very irregularly, causing it to overlap the edges of the frame. The painting was mounted on the museum wall in this support structure using iron brackets attached to bars set into the masonry. The structural integrity of this piece was maintained remarkably well by the backing applied in 1933, although extensive horizontal cracks had developed in the original plaster, with resulting losses in the paint layer.

Most previous conservation treatments to the Saqqara and Bawit niches had focused on removing and replacing previously applied mortars that often overlapped on the original paint. It is not known whether these interventions began in the Egyptian Museum or later in the Coptic Museum. These undocumented operations also involved perfunctory cleaning and extensive interventions better described as 'restoration' that sometimes included actual repainting and varnishing of the images. Modern industrially produced paints were detected in two samples from CM7989 (fig. 26.1). Pale blue paint containing synthetic pigment (cerulean blue) and a

Fig. 26.1. Detail of niche painting of Christ enthroned from Saqqara (CM7989) showing the extent of modern restoration infilling and cracks in the plaster and paint layers before conservation. ARCE 05-501-08 (Tim Loveless).

green layer containing a synthetic ultramarine and a yellow pigment overlay an original yellow-orange pigment of red and yellow iron pigments (hematite and jarosite) dispersed in an organic binder.[20] More recent interventions were characterized by less restoring and cleaning, in keeping with recent trends in conservation, and were limited to replacing old fillings. Nevertheless, thick layers of acrylic resin had been applied instead of the older varnishes and paints.[21] The previous treatments caused discoloring and abrasions to the surfaces, as they were usually applied without removing accretions such as dust, wax, and smoke residues from the paint layers or from previous applications (fig. 26.2). Atmospheric particulates were also present since the display cases were not sealed. Analysis showed that lack of cleaning had preserved ancient wax and smoke residue from candles on the painted surface of Saqqara niche CM7987.[22]

The first phases of direct intervention in 2004 were emergency treatments in preparation for removal from the gallery walls and for packing and storage.[23] While still in position, each painting was checked for micro and macro cracks, the state of adhesion of the paint layers, and the state of the supporting plaster. This was followed by cleaning the surfaces with soft brushes to remove dust and with solvents to remove the layers of varnish and acrylic resin applied in previous treatments. Consolidation of the plaster layers was made by injection with an acrylic emulsion (Primal AC 33) diluted 1:1 in distilled water. Flaking or detached paint layers were fixed using Paraloid B72 in a 5 percent solution of acetone applied by brushing or by a gentle low-pressure spray where surfaces were too fragile for direct contact. Cracks and different levels where surfaces had separated were filled using gypsum and calcium carbonate in a ratio of 1:3 to provide surface continuity and adhesion for all seven niches from Saqqara (fig. 26.2). In the case of the two niches from Bawit and the Tebtunis mural, a mortar composed of eight parts yellow powdered limestone, four parts lime, one part gypsum, and a small amount of natural umber to provide a suitable color was used. This mixture is softer than the gypsum and calcium carbonate mixture employed on the Saqqara niches and more appropriate for the mud mortar of the original backings of the Bawit and Tebtunis paintings.

Following consolidation of painted surfaces and plaster layers, facing materials were applied to protect the paint layers. In the case of the Saqqara niches, four different materials were used. First, polyamide paper cut into 10.0 × 25.0-centimeter strips was applied directly onto the paint layer of each niche in successive overlapping stages from the bottom upward to

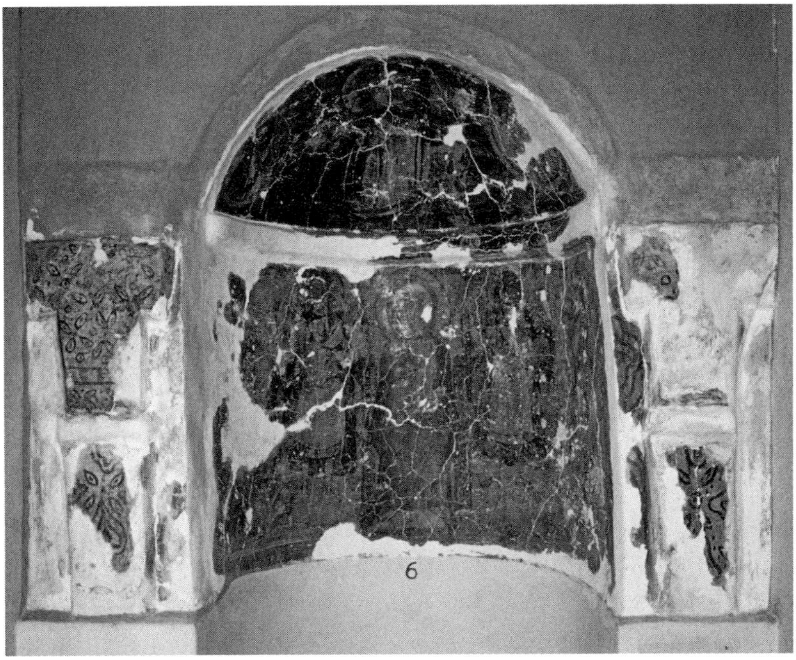

Fig. 26.2. Niche painting from Saqqara (CM8013) with seated Virgin Mary and Christ child flanked by archangels and two figures, possibly Enoch and Jeremiah, with Christ in the vaulting of the niche, showing modern infilling in plaster losses replaced with new gypsum and calcium carbonate, and the dark discoloration from previous applications of varnish before conservation. ARCE 04-56-14 (Lutfi Hassan).

prevent adhesive dripping down onto the uncovered paint layers. Each piece of paper was coated with acrylic resin in a 15 percent solution with acetone. A second facing made of gauze strips 10.0–20.0 centimeters wide was applied over the polyamide paper in successive layers. Each gauze piece was coated in acrylic resin (Paraloid B72) in a 15 percent acetone solution. Next, a layer of cotton gauze with a finer tissue structure and cut in pieces larger than in the second layer was applied in a 15 percent solution of Paraloid B72 in acetone. The cotton gauze had been first washed to reduce the starch content and dried while stretched out to prevent distortion at the edges. Aluminum foil cut into 10.0 × 10.0-centimeter squares was then applied using a 10 percent solution of Paraloid B72 in acetone. The foil was put on from top to bottom to resist any tendency toward pushing

Fig. 26.3. Niche CM7984 from Saqqara in the process of applying protective covering of aluminum foil over layers of paper and gauze prior to removal from the gallery wall (Lutfi Hassan).

and distortion from the polyurethane foam that would be used in the final operation (fig. 26.3). The Bawit niches received only paper and aluminum foil facings to avoid adding extra weight to the fragile surfaces. The Tebtunis painting, with its uniformly flat surface and stronger adhesion of paint and plaster, also required only paper and aluminum foil. Finally, individually made and precisely fitting protective wooden supports were constructed for each piece. An interior panel of thin plywood shaped to fit each niche supported the interior space, separated from the aluminum foil by foam rubber. A wooden framework was constructed over the front of each niche to avert any physical contact.

The niches and the Tebtunis mural were now ready for removal from the galleries. The niches were cut from the walls, together with the modern brick and cement masonry surrounds, and slid onto stainless steel sheets mounted on mobile trolleys. A wooden framework was constructed at the back of each niche and joined to the similar framework already fitted on the front to create a portable wooden carrying cage. Liquid foam that expanded and dried in an almost weightless mass was injected into the framework to buffer the niches during transportation and storage. Each piece was then placed in an individual wooden crate labeled with its museum registration number, a photograph, the project intervention number, and its former location in the museum galleries (fig. 26.4). The painting of Adam and Eve from Tebtunis was detached from the wall within its display frame. A wooden cage was constructed around it and the panel was then transferred to a wooden case without the need for a double wooden framework and foam buffering.

The paintings remained in storage until July 2005, when the conservation project began.[24] The niches and the Tebtunis mural were still inside their protective frames and coverings, and so could be handled easily without risk. The first task was to stabilize the early twentieth-century supports that had been applied when the niches were first removed from their archaeological

Fig. 26.4. Niches CM7978 and CM7984 from Saqqara, removed from the gallery walls and prepared for storage inside wooden frames with internal protective covering and foam padding. ARCE 05-36-04 (R.K. Vincent).

locations. The niches were placed face downward with the base perpendicular to the work surface. Each Saqqara niche was given a new base. A thin layer of cotton gauze was spread across the open lower cavity and coated with acrylic resin in emulsion. After it had dried, a 2.0-millimeter-thick fiberglass sheet, profiled to fit the exact shape of the niche, was glued on using epoxy resin loaded with micronized silica gel. The niches were then placed upright on a sheet of aerolam (a rigid fiberglass panel with a lightweight honeycomb pattern center) that rested on a stainless steel frame at the base of each niche (fig. 26.5). The new bases were connected to the structure of the niches with aluminum L-shaped brackets anchored to the base and to the plaster backing with stainless steel screws. Epoxy resin with micronized silica gel was used to fill the gaps between the brackets and the plaster support, a treatment with good reversibility. The upper surface was coated with a gypsum-based mortar compatible with the surrounding structure. This arrangement addressed two issues: it provided a good support for the niches and simultaneously rectified a misunderstanding in the way the niches had been displayed previously in the museum. In their original monastic contexts, the Saqqara niches were situated in alcoves above a shelf made of either limestone slabs or mud bricks, but in the museum they had been placed at the top of semi-cylindrical apses that extended to the floor, making no reference to the original architecture. The new bases replicated the original aspect in a way that gave permanent stability to each piece. The Bawit niches were treated in a similar way by inserting a horizontal panel supported on a steel frame to act as workbenches. However, the Bawit niches had originally extended to the ground, so these temporary bases were removed on completion of conservation.

Once the niches were secured either permanently or temporarily to their new bases, the process of removing all the protective coverings could begin. First the wooden framework was dismantled, followed by sawing away the polyurethane foam filling. Scalpels were used to detach the foam where it touched the aluminum foil facing, which was also removed mechanically, with small infiltrations of acetone to loosen it where necessary. The layers of paper and gauze facings were removed by absorbing the resin used as adhesive with cotton swabs soaked in acetone.

Treatment of the plaster layers required mechanical removal of old fillings using scalpels. In some cases removal revealed original details that had been obscured by earlier plaster repairs: part of a finger of Christ's blessing hand on CM7989; part of the face of the angel on the viewer's right in the small cupola with Christ in a mandorla on CM7118; part of the face of the Christ

Fig. 26.5. Niche painting from Saqqara (CM7978) of Christ in a mandorla above and the Virgin Mary and Christ child below flanked by two archangels, showing the new aerolam base fitted, old infillings replaced, and a cleaning test on the outer face of the right frame. ARCE 05-501-01 (Tim Loveless).

child on CM7995 and CM7987. During cleaning of the Tebtunis painting of Adam and Eve a *battitura di filo* line in red paint that served as the original draftsman's guideline was discovered (fig. 26.6). New plaster fillings compatible with the original plasters were made to fill cavities around the edges of the niches to reintegrate the plaster panels made when they were installed in the museum. Original detached or cracked plasters were re-adhered using infiltrations of liquid mortar. Where greater adhesion was necessary, small connections were made with acrylic resin in emulsion (Acryl 33 at 30 percent solution in distilled water). In some cases it was necessary to load the solution with a small percentage of micronized calcium carbonate. Adhesion of paint layers was achieved using infiltrations of acrylic resin in emulsions (primal AC33 at 15 percent in distilled water). Where the paint layer had lifted, pressure was applied with a plastic spatula interposed with a sheet of silicone paper or polyethylene. Acrylic resin (Paraloid B72 in 2 percent solution in nitro-thinner) was brushed on to consolidate cohesion faults.

Varnishes and resins applied to the painted surfaces in the past were removed by alternating applications of acetone, nitro-thinner, and in some cases, nitro-thinner with dimethylformamide added in a ratio of 4:1. Waxy deposits on the painted surfaces were removed using chlorinated solvents (trichloroethylene and methyl chloroform) heated in a bain-marie to a

Fig. 26.6. Detail of the painting of Adam and Eve from Tebtunis (CM3962) after conservation. The arrows indicate the *battitura di fori* line. ARCE 05-503-31 (Tim Loveless).

temperature of 45 degrees centigrade. These solvents were used only to remove waxy deposits on surfaces other than encaustic paint layers that had been prepared using a wax binding medium. Old painting reintegration using modern oil paints was removed with a polar solution (70 grams of ammonium carbonate per liter of distilled water) applied with cotton swabs. Carbonaceous deposits, oily residues, and light salt efflorescence were removed with a solution of 10 drops of ammonia per 200 centiliters of distilled water. Heavier salt efflorescence was reduced with fiberglass nibs and removed mechanically with scalpels. The final phases of treatment involved 'aesthetic presentation,' an application of watercolor washes in various tones to areas where repairs to loss and damage would otherwise interfere with an appreciation of the original painting. Paraloid B72 in a 1.5 percent solution in nitro-thinner was applied with brushes as a final protection on all ten pieces.[25]

The treatments summarized in this chapter saved the paintings from risks during the museum renovations, and the conservation project prepared the paintings in a robust way for display in the new museum galleries. Mounting work, cleaning, and stabilizing of the paint and plaster layers and the ancient and modern support materials should ensure the long-term preservation of these important wall paintings. Placement of the conserved paintings in the renovated galleries was carried out by others according to designs approved by the SCA.[26]

Notes

1 For help in writing this chapter I would like to thank D.J. Ian Begg for information on Gilberto Bagnani's Tebtunis archives, Jere Bacharach for help with bibliographic research, and Yasmin el-Shazli and Eman Mohammed Amin for access to the Egyptian Museum Cairo catalog database. Special thanks are due to Abuna Maximous al-Antony for his constant support for ARCE's work with Coptic cultural heritage. Dr. Zahi Hawass, then secretary general of the Supreme Council of Antiquities (SCA), and Dr. Gawdat Gabra initiated the project (Gabra, van Loon, Reif, and Swelim 2013: 10–11). Philip Habib, director of the Coptic Museum, Victor Girguis, and Ahmed Shu'aib facilitated the work.

2 In March 2004, Dr. Hawass officially requested assistance from ARCE. The project was funded by the United States Agency for International Development.

3 Vincent 2010. Unpublished interim and final reports are held in the ARCE Archives in Cairo. Final reports are: Hassan 2004; Badamo 2005, 2006; De Cesaris and Sucato 2006a, 2006b, 2006c; Poggi 2006.

4 Brajer 1999: 65. On current practice, ICOMOS 2003: Article 6.

5 On a recent case study of a wall painting emergency detachment at the threatened site of Qasr Ibrim: Singleton, Miller, and Rose 2006: 15–23.

6 CM7118: Maspero and Drioton 1931: vii and pls. XXI–XXIV (the text reproduces Maspero 1913: 289–92, 295–96); Bénazeth 1988: 59–60. For CM8012 see note 8 below. Schlumberger 1919: 243–48 summarizes Jean Maspero's 1913 finds. On recent excavations, Bénazeth 2008: 11–22 and Bénazeth 2010: 17–24; Rutschowskaya 2010: 50 for wall paintings and proposed sixth- to seventh-century dating.

7 CM refers to Coptic Museum inventory numbers. JE and tr refer to Egyptian Museum Cairo Journal d'Entrée and temporary register numbers respectively. In the catalog, temporary register numbers are arranged left to right around a cross recording when the object was registered, beginning upper left with the day and month and below with the year and registration number. Tr12.12.20.2 indicates 12 December 1920, second object registered, implying that this niche remained unregistered for seven years despite its inclusion in Maspero 1915: 249 no. 1120 and 248, fig. 89. On niche CM7118/JE 44232 see Bénazeth 1997: 45n2, 64.

8 CM8012 inner part: Maspero and Drioton 1931: x–xi, 10–11, 32, pls. XXXI–XXXIV. CM8012 outer frame and arch: Maspero and Drioton 1931: viii–ix, 1–2, 15, pl. IIIB and C during excavation and pls. V–VII. Pl. VIII shows the damaged niche painting originally in the outer frame that was replaced when the two elements were combined.

9 Maspero and Drioton 1931: xi, 32.

10 Maspero and Drioton 1931: 10.

11 Maspero 1915: 248, fig. 89 shows the niche painting that would become the interior of CM8012 with the original architectural surround as found. This image is not from the same negative as Maspero and Drioton 1931: pl. XXXI and may have been taken in Cairo before the two pieces became one, or it may be an unpublished site photograph taken while the niche was still in situ.

12 CM8014: Quibell 1908: 63–64 and pls. X–XLIII. CM7989: Quibell 1909: 99 and pls. VIII and frontispiece. CM7978: Quibell 1912: 23 cell 1723, 135, and pl. XXV upper. CM7984: Quibell 1912: 28 cell 1795, 135, and pl. XXV lower. CM7987: Quibell 1912: 23 cell 1725, 134, and pls. XXII and XXIII upper. CM7995: Quibell 1912: 23 cell 1719, and pl. XXIII. CM8013: Quibell 1912: 22 cell 1727, 134–35, and pl. XXIV. Quibell 1912: pl. XXII shows CM7987 partly detached on site. Important studies on the entire repertoire of paintings from the Monastery of Apa Jeremiah are Rassart-Debergh 1981a; Rassart-Debergh 1981b; Rassart-Debergh and Debergh 1981; van Moorsel and Huijbers 1981.

13 Both were still in storage when registered on January 18, 1921, just over a month after the Bawit niche tr.12.12.20.2 (see note 7).

14 Bénazeth 1997: 45; Habib 1967: 14, 24. The gallery locations of all the paintings except three Saqqara niches (CM7984, 7989, and 7995) are given at Habib 1967: 33 no. 30 (CM7118 Bawit); 37 nos. 58 (CM7182 Saqqara) and 59 (CM7987 Saqqara); 40 nos. 83 (CM3962 Tebtunis), 85 (CM8012 Bawit), and 88 (CM8014 Saqqara); 41 no. 88 (CM8014).

15 Bagnani 1933: 126–29 and fig. 18; Dhormé 1934: 77. The mural was discovered by the Italian Expedition to Tebtunis, led by Gilberto Bagnani, in a church richly decorated with well-preserved wall paintings: Galazzi and Hadji-Minaglou 1989: 186–87. Part of another wall painting found in situ in the same church was removed to the Coptic Museum (CM3963): Bagnani 1933: fig. 15. Both murals are illustrated in color at

Atalla 1989: 23. I am grateful to D.J. Ian Begg for drawing my attention to CM3963. Watercolors of others are in the Bagnani archives at Trent University, Canada: Furness and Fitzgibbon 2011: 3. Grossmann 2005: 203 suggests the church dates "more or less in the seventh century" and that it may not have been used for very long owing to the lack of a *khurus*, while Gayraud 1992: 39 proposes "l'église ayant été datée de l'époque fatimide." Bagnani records several rebuilding phases and successive paint layers: Begg 2008. On dating the mural, Elizabeth Bolman states (personal communication, July 15, 2015), "based on style, it could be anywhere from the 7th to the 10th centuries." Ceramic evidence suggests the end of occupation at Tebtunis "aux alentours de la fin du XIe ou au début du XIIe siècle" (Roussert and Marchand 1999: 216). Keenan 2003: 129–39 reviews archaeological and papyrological evidence for this period, particularly 132–34 for this church. See also Walters 1989: 205–206.

16 Simaika 1937: 45 and pl. CIII with its inventory number 3962 and location in "salle 25." In 1939 the painting was moved to Room 9 of the New Wing; Habib 1967: 14, 40 no. 83, and 169, fig. 27.

17 Quibell 1912: pls. XX–XXI.

18 Van Moorsel and Huijbers 1981: 129–68 and pl. A (CM7984); pl. D (CM7987); pls. I–III (CM8014); pls. VII–IX (CM7989); pls. XIV–XVII (CM7995); pls. XVIII–XIX (CM7978); pls. XX–XXII (CM7987); pls. XXIII–XXVa (CM8013); pls. XXVIa, d–XXVII (CM7984) provide good descriptions and photographs of the Saqqara niches before cleaning and conservation; no trace of the suggested moss or algae was found on CM7987; 156n1. For color images of Saqqara niches before conservation see Atalla 1989: 16–17 (CM7984); 19 (CM7987); 21 upper (CM7989); 21 lower (CM7978 wrongly numbered 7987); 151 upper (CM7995).

19 For color images of Bawit niches before conservation see Atalla 1989: front cover, 9–11 (CM7118); 25 upper (CM8012).

20 Hematite is the mineral form of iron oxide; jarosite is a basic hydrous sulfate of potassium and iron.

21 No traces were found of the often-used but unstable consolidant cellulose nitrate: Selwitz 1988; Shashoua, Bradley, and Daniels 1992. On the darkening effect of cellulose nitrate on mural paintings: Weatherhead 2001: 56; Weatherhead 2007: 142, 167–68, 167n53.

22 Poggi 2006: sample 3.

23 Emergency stabilization, removal, packing, and storage were carried out by Lotfi Khaled Hassan, Alberto Sucato, Emiliano Ricchi, Giorgio Capriotti, and Abuna Maximous al-Antony during July and August 2004.

24 Conservators were Luigi De Cesaris, Chiara Di Marco, Diego Pistone, Emiliano Ricchi, Alberto Sucato, and Gianlucca Tancioni.

25 Although no comprehensive publication with post-treatment color photographs has appeared, select examples can be found in recent related literature: Gabra 2014: cover image (CM7989); van Loon 2014: 199, fig. 16.3 (CM7989) and 200, fig. 16.4; René 2014: 277, fig. 20.3 (CM7118); Gabra and Eaton-Krauss 2005: 75, 48 (CM7984) and 76, 49 (CM7989).

26 The two niches from Bawit are displayed in Room 8 on the ground floor of the museum and the seven niches from Saqqara are in Room 6 on the ground floor. The painting of Adam and Eve from Tebtunis is displayed in Room 11 on the first floor.

Abbreviations

AB	*Analecta Bollandiana*
ARCE	American Research Center in Egypt
ASAE	*Annales du Service des Antiquités de l'Égypte*
BASP	*Bulletin of the American Society of Papyrologists*
BIFAO	*Bulletin de l'Institut Français d'Archéologie Orientale*
BSAA	*Bulletin de la Société d'Archéologie d'Alexandrie*
BSAC	*Bulletin de la Société d'Archéologie Copte*
CE	*The Coptic Encyclopedia*
CPC	Clavis Patrum Copticorum
CPG	Clavis Patrum Graecorum
CSCO	Corpus Scriptorum Christianorum Orientalium
EK	Ekklesias kellion
FIFAO	Fouilles de l'Institut Français d'Archéologie Orientale
IFAO	Institut Français d'Archéologie Orientale
JARCE	*Journal of the American Research Center in Egypt*
JCS	*Journal of Coptic Studies*
JEA	*Journal of Egyptian Archaeology*
JECS	*Journal of Early Christian Studies*
JTS	*Journal of Theological Studies*

MDAIK	*Mitteilungen des Deutschen Archäologischen Instituts Kairo*
MSAC	Mission suisse d'archéologie copte de l'Université de Genève
OCA	Orientalia Christiana Analecta
OCP	*Orientalia Christiana Periodica*
OLA	Orientalia Louvaniensia Analecta
PO	Patrologia Orientalis
PSBA	*Proceedings of the Society of Biblical Archaeology*
SAC	Société d'Archéologie Copte
SKCO	Sprachen und Kulturen des christlichen Orients
SOCC	Studia Orientalia Christiana Collectanea
SOCM	Studia Orientalia Christiana Monographiae
STAC	Studien und Texte zu Antike und Christentum
TAVO	Tübinger Atlas des vorderen Orients
ZÄSA	*Zeitschrift für Ägyptische Sprache und Altertumskunde*
ZPE	*Zeitschrift für Papyrologie und Epigraphik*

Bibliography

'Abd al-Malek, M.B. 2005. "Carl Maria Kaufmann (AD 1872–1952)." *Rakhoti* 2:26–28.

———. 2009. *Al-Kitab al-tidhkari bimunasabit murur sab'at 'ashr qarnan 'ala istishhad al-shahid al-misri Mar Mina al-'Agaibi*. 1st ed. Alexandria: Gam'iyat Mar Mina al-'Agaibi li-l-Dirasat al-Qibtiya.

Abu al-Hamid, M. 1981. "The Miniature Paintings of the Ayyubid Manuscripts." MA thesis, University of Cairo.

Abu al-Makarim. 1895. *The Churches and Monasteries of Egypt and Some Neighbouring Countries*, attributed to Abu Salih the Armenian. Edited by T.A. Evetts and A.J. Butler. Oxford: Clarendon Press.

———. 1984a. *Tarikh Abu al-Makarim: al-Kana'is wa-l-adyira fi-l-qarn al-thani 'ashar*. Vol. 1. Edited by S. al-Suryani. Wadi al-Natrun: Dayr al-Suryan.

———. 1984b. *Tarikh al-kana'is wa-l-adyira*. Edited by S. al-Suryani. 4 vols. Cairo: Samu'il al-Suryani.

Abullif, W. 1998. "Hadid." In *Bibliotheca sanctorum orientalium. Enciclopedia dei santi: le Chiese orientali*, edited by J.N. Cañellas and S. Virgulin, vol. 2, 152. Rome: Città Nuova.

———. 1998–99. "Ruways." In *Bibliotheca sanctorum orientalium. Enciclopedia dei santi: Le chiese orientali*, edited by J.N. Cañellas and S. Virgulin, vol. 2, 889–92. Rome: Città Nuova.

Abu Salih al-Armani. 1895. *The Churches and Monasteries of Egypt*. Edited by B.T.A. Evetts and A. Butler. Oxford: Clarendon Press.

Adalian, R. 2010. *Historical Dictionary of Armenia*. Historical Dictionaries of Europe No. 77. Lanham, MD: Scarecrow Press.

Afifi, M. 1992. *al-Aqbat fi-l-'ahd al-'uthmani*. Tarikh al-Misriyin Series. Cairo: Egyptian General Organization for Books.

Agapios (Hieromonachus), ed. 1957. *The Rudder (Pedalion): Of the Metaphorical Ship of the One Holy Catholic and Apostolic Church of the Orthodox Christians, or All the Sacred and Divine Canons.* Translated by D. Cummings. Chicago: Orthodox Christian Educational Society.

Alboyadjian, A. 1941, 1955, 1961. *History of Armenian Migrations.* 3 vols. Cairo: Sahag-Mesrop Press. (in Armenian).

Amélineau, É. 1873. *La Géographie de l'Égypte à l'époque copte.* Paris: Imprimerie Nationale.

———. 1888. "Histoire des deux filles de l'empereur Zenon." *PSBA* 10, no. 18: 181–206.

———. 1888–95. "Vie arabe de Schenoudi." In *Monuments pour servir à l'histoire de l'Égypte chrétienne aux IVe–Ve siècle.* Mémoires publiés par les membres de la Mission archéologique française au Caire 4. Cairo: IFAO.

———. 1889. *Fragments coptes pour servir à l'histoire de la Conquête de l'Égypte par les Arabes.* Paris: Imprimerie nationale.

———. 1890. *Les actes des martyrs de l'église copte.* Étude critique. Paris: Ernest Leroux.

———. 1893. *La géographie de l'Égypte à l'époque copte.* Paris: Imprimerie Nationale.

———. 1894. *Histoire des monastères de la Basse-Égypte.* Annales du Musée Guimet 25. Paris: Leroux.

Andraous, E. 2012a. "al-Qiddis anba Barsum al-'Aryan." In *Encyclopedia of History of Copts of Egypt.* http://www.coptichistory.org/new_page_589.htm

———. 2012b. "Dayr al-anba Barsum al-'Aryan: al-Ma'sara, Halwan." *Encyclopedia of History of Copts of Egypt.* http://www.coptichistory.org/new_page_6770.htm

Andreu, G., G. Castel, and R.-G. Coquin. 1980. "Sixième campagne de fouilles aux Kellia (1979–1980): Rapport préliminaire." *BIFAO* 80:347–68.

Andreu, G., R.-G. Coquin, P. Ballet, G. Castel, P. Deleuze, and P.-H. Laferrière. 1981. "Septième campagne de fouilles aux Kellia (avril 1981): Rapport préliminaire." *BIFAO* 81:159–88.

Archer, D. 2010. "Speech Acts." In *Historical Pragmatics,* edited by A.H. Jucker and I. Taavitsainen, 379–417. Berlin and New York: De Gruyter Mouton.

Armala, E. 1925. *The Syrians in Egypt.* Beirut.

Armanios, F.Y. 2003. "Coptic Christians in Ottoman Egypt: Religious Worldview and Communal Beliefs." PhD diss., Ohio State University.

———. 2011. *Coptic Christianity in Ottoman Egypt.* Oxford: Oxford University Press.

el-Ashmawi, F. 1998. "Pottery Kiln and Wine-Factory at Burg el Arab." In *Commerce et artisanat dans l'Alexandrie hellénistique et romaine: Actes du colloque d'Athènes 11–12 décembre 1988,* edited by J.-Y. Empereur, 55–64. Bulletin de Correspondance Hellénique, suppl. 33. Athens: École française d'Athènes.

Atalla, N.S. 1989. *Coptic Art: Wall Paintings.* Vol. 1. Cairo: Lehnert & Landrock.

———. 1998. *Coptic Icons.* Part 2. Cairo: Lenhert & Landrock.

Athanasius. *Defense of His Flight* 24. In Szymusiak 1987: 234–36.

Athanasiyus al-Maqari. 2012. *Fihris kitabat aba' kanisat al-Iskandariya: al-kitabat al-'arabiya.* Vol. 1, *Masadir tuqus al-kanisa.* Wadi al-Natrun: Monastery of St. Macarius.

Athenaeus. 1927. *The Deipnosophists.* Translated by C.B. Gulick. Loeb Classical Library 204. Cambridge, MA: Harvard University Press.

Atiya, A.S., ed. 1959. *History of the Patriarchs of the Egyptian Church Known as the History of the Holy Church.* Vol. 2, part 3, *Christodulos–Michael, AD 1046–1102.* Cairo: SAC.

———. 1991a. *The Coptic Encyclopedia.* 8 vols. New York: Macmillan (= *CE*). http://ccdl.libraries. claremont.edu/col/cce

———. 1991b. "'Abd al-Masih Salih al-Masu'di." *CE* 1:7.

———. 1991c. "Butrus al-Sidmanti." *CE* 2:431–32.

———. 1991d. "Higher Institute of Coptic Studies." *CE* 4:1230.

———. 1991e. "Patriarchs, Dates and Succession of." *CE* 5:1913b–1920a.

Atta, H., and Aba Mina Roufaeel. 1981. *Mudhkirati 'an hayat al-Baba Kyrilus al-Sadis baba al-Iskandariya wa Batriark al-Karaza al-Murqsiya.* Cairo: Dar Nubar.

———. 1998. *Mudhakirati 'an hayat al-Baba Kyrilus al-Sadis.* Cairo: Dar Nubar.

Attyia, M. 2011. *The Coptic Orthodox Church and the Ecumenical Movement.* Cairo: Bishopric of Youth Affairs.

Austin, J.L. 1962. *How to Do Things with Words.* Oxford: Oxford University Press.

Awad, Girgis Filuthawus. 1948. *Mimar al-shahida Dimyana.* Cairo: Matba'at al-Shams al-Haditha.

Ayres, L. 2010. "The Holy Spirit as the 'Undiminished Giver': Didymus the Blind's *De Spiritu Sancto* and the Development of Nicene Pneumatology." In *The Holy Spirit in the Fathers of the Church: The Proceedings of the Seventh International Patristic Conference*, edited by V. Twomey and J. Rutherford, 57–72. Dublin: Four Courts Press.

Babraj, K., and D. Gorzelany. 2002. "Monumental Tombs of Ancient Alexandria: The Theater of the Dead." *Archeologia* 53:166–69.

Babraj, K., and H. Szymańska. 2004. "Die vierte Grabungssaison in Marea, Ägypten: Grabkapelle und Basilike." *Kemet* 13, no. 3: 61–64.

———. 2005. "Fünfte Grabungssaison in Marea, Ägypten: Basilika." *Kemet* 14, no. 3: 63–67.

———. 2010. "Marea or Philoxenite: Polish Excavations in the Mareotic Region 2000–2007." In *Lake Mareotis: Reconstructing the Past: Proceedings of the International Conference on the Archaeology of the Mareotic Region Held at Alexandria University, Egypt, 5–6 April 2008*, edited by L. Blue and E. Khalil, 75–85. BAR International Series 2113. Oxford: Archaeopress.

Bacot, Seÿna. 2011. "Quatre miracles de saint Ménas dans un manuscrit copte de l'IFAO (Inv. 315–322)." *BIFAO* 111:35–73.

Badamo, H. 2005. "The Coptic Museum: Conservation of Wall Paintings in the Coptic Museum." Unpublished art history research report submitted to ARCE, July 2005.

———. 2006. "Conservation of Wall Paintings in the Coptic Museum." Unpublished art history research report submitted to ARCE, July 2006.

Bagnall, R.S., and D.W. Rathbone, eds. 2008. *Egypt from Alexander to the Copts: An Archaeological and Historical Guide.* Cairo: American University in Cairo Press.

Bagnani, G. 1933. "Gli Scavi di Tebtunis." *Bolletino d'Arte del Ministero dell'Educazione Nazionale* 27:119–34 and figs. 1–22.

Bakhtin, M.M. 1981. *The Dialogic Imagination: Four Essays*. Austin: University of Texas Press.

Balestri, G., and H. Hyvernat. 1908. *Acta Martyrum*. CSCO 3. Paris: Typographeo republicae.

Ballet, P., N. Bosson, and M. Rassart-Debergh. 2003. *Kellia II: L'ermitage copte QR 195*. Vol. 2, *La céramique, les inscriptions, les décors*. FIFAO 49. Cairo: IFAO.

Bammel, C.P. 1996. "Problems of the 'Historia Monachorum.'" *JTS* 47:92–104.

Bartelink, G.J.M. 1987. "Les rapports entre le monachisme égyptien et l'épiscopat d'Alexandrie." In ΑΛΕΞΑΝΔΡΙΝΑ*: Hellénisme, judaïsme et christianisme à Alexandrie: Mélanges offerts au P. Claude Mondésert*. 365–79. Paris: Éditions du Cerf.

———. 1994. *Vie d'Antoine*. Paris: Éditions du Cerf.

Bartelink, G.J.M., Christine Mohrmann, and Marino Barchiesi. 1974. *La storia Lausiaca*. Milan: Mondadori (Fondazione Lorenzo Valla).

Basset, R., ed. 1904. *Le Synaxaire Arabe Jacobite (rédaction Copte)*. Vol. 1, *Les mois de Tout et Babeh*. PO 1, fasc. 3. Paris: Firmin-Didot.

———. 1906. *Le Synaxaire Arabe Jacobite. Rédaction copte*. Vol. 2, *Les mois de Hatour et de Kihak*. PO 3. Turnhout: Brepols.

———. 1909. *Le Synaxaire Arabe Jacobite (mois de Hatour et de Kiahk)*. PO 3. Paris: Rue Jacob.

———. 1922a. *Le Synaxaire Arabe Jacobite*. Vol. 4, *Les mois de Baramahat, Baramouda et Bachons*. PO 26. Paris: Rue Jacob.

———. 1922b. *Le Synaxaire Arabe Jacobite*. Vol. 5, *Les mois de Baounah, Abib, Mésoré et jours complémentaires*. PO 17, fasc. 3. Turnhout: Brepols.

———. 1924. *Le Synaxaire Arabe Jacobite (rédaction Copte)*. Vol. 5, *Les mois de Baounah, Abib, Mesoré et les jours complémentaires*. PO 17, fasc. 3, no. 84. Paris: Firmin-Didot.

———. 1971a. *Le Synaxaire Arabe Jacobite (rédaction Copte)*. PO, vol. 3, fasc. 3, no. 13. Turnhout: Brepols.

———. 1971b. *Le Synaxaire Arabe Jacobite (rédaction Copte)*. PO, vol. 11, fasc. 5. Turnhout: Brepols.

———. 1989. *Synaxaire arabe jacobite (rédaction copte)*. 5 vols. Mardesous, Belgium: Brepols.

Baumstark, A. 1915. "Ein illustriertes koptisches Evangelienbuch von Jahre 1250." *Oriens Christianus*, new series 4:341–44.

Bax, M. 2010. "Rituals." In *Historical Pragmatics*, edited by A.H. Jucker and I. Taavitsainen, 483–519. Berlin and New York: De Gruyter Mouton.

Begg, D.I. 2008. "Excavating Churches at Tebtunis." Paper presented at the First Annual Coptic Studies Symposium, Toronto. Unpublished.

Behrens-Abouseif, D. 1985. *Azbakiyya and Its Environs: From Azbak to Isma'il: 1476–1879*. Cairo: IFAO.

———. 1986. "Locations of Non-Muslim Quarters in Medieval Cairo." *Annales islamologiques* 22:117–32.

Bell, H.I., and E.W. Crum. 1925. "A Greek-Coptic Glossary." *Aegyptus* 6:177–226.

Bénazeth, D. 1988. "Histoire des fouilles de Baouît." In *Études Coptes IV: Quatrième Journée d'études, Strasbourg 26–27 mai 1988*, 51–62. Paris and Louvain: Peeters.

———. 1997. "Un monastère dispersé: Les antiquités de Baouît conservées dans les musées d'Égypte." *BIFAO* 97:43–66.

———. 2008. "Nouvelle campagne de fouilles à Baouît." In *Études Coptes X: Douzième journée d'études (Lyon, 19–21 mai 2005)*, edited by A. Boud'hors and C. Louis, 11–22. Paris: De Boccard.

———. 2010. "Nouvelle campagne de fouilles à Baouît (2005, 2006)." In *Études Coptes XI: Treizième journée d'études (Marseille, 7–9 juin 2007)*, edited by A. Boud'hors and C. Louis, 17–24. Paris: De Boccard.

Bennett. B.J. 2001. "Didymus the Blind's Knowledge of Manichaeism." In *The Light and the Darkness: Studies in Manichaeism and Its World, Nag Hammadi and Manichaean Studies*, edited by P. Mirecki and J. BeDuhn, 38–67. Leiden: Brill.

Bianchi, R.S. 2003. "Book Review: *Taposiris Magna, Port of Isis* by Gyozo Vörös." *JARCE* 40:190–91.

Bigoul al-Suryani. 2007. "New Elements in the History of the Pope Gabriel III the 77th." In *Actes du Huitième Congrès International d'Études Coptes (Paris, 2004)*, edited by A. Boud'hors et al., vol. 1, 15–23. OLA 164. Louvain: Peeters.

Binns, J. 2002. *An Introduction to the Christian Orthodox Churches*. Cambridge, UK: Cambridge University Press.

Blue, L., and S. Ramses. 2005. "Lake Mareotis Research Project: Preliminary Report from Pilot Survey August 2004." *Newsletter of the Archaeological Society of Alexandria* 15:5–16.

Bolman, E.S., ed. 2002. *Monastic Visions: Wall Paintings in the Monastery of St. Antony at the Red Sea*. New Haven and London: Yale University Press.

Bolman, E.S. 2007. "Depicting the Kingdom of Heaven: Paintings and Monastic Practice in Early Byzantine Egypt." In *Egypt in the Byzantine World, 300–700*, edited by R.S. Bagnall, 408–33. Cambridge and New York: Cambridge University Press.

Bonneau, D. 1993. *Le régime administratif de l'eau du Nil dans l'Égypte grecque, romaine et byzantine*. Leiden, New York, and Cologne: Brill.

Bonnet, F. 1986. "Les possibilités de datation de la période d'abandon des ermitages kelliotes." In *Le site monastique copte des Kellia: Sources historiques et explorations archéologiques. Actes du colloque de Genève, 13–15 août 1984*, edited by Ph. Bridel. Geneva: MSAC.

Boon, A. 1932. *Pachomiana Latina: Règle et Épitres de S. Pachôme, Épitre de S. Théodore et "Liber" de S. Orsiesius. Textes latins de S. Jérome*. Louvain: Bureaux de la Revue.

Boud'hors, A., and R.W. Boutros. 2001. *L'homélie sur l'église du Rocher attribuée à Timothée Aelure, texte copte et arabe*. PO 49, fasc. 1, no. 217. Rome: Pontifico Istituto orientale.

Bourdieu, P. 1991. *Language and Symbolic Power*. Cambridge: Polity Press.

Bouriant, M.U. 1892. *Fragments coptes relatifs au Concile d'Éphèse (431)*. Mémoires publiés par les membres de la mission archéologique française au Caire 8. Paris: Leroux.

Bovini, G. 1954. *Sarcofagi Paleocristiani di Ravenna*. Rome: Pontificio Istituto di Archeologia Cristiana.

Brajer, I. 1999. "Aspects of Reversibility in Transferring Paintings." In *Reversibility: Does It Exist?*, edited by A. Oddy and S. Carol, 63–71. Occasional Paper 135. London: British Museum.

Brakke, D. 1995. *Athanasius and the Politics of Asceticism*. Oxford: Clarendon Press.

———. 2006. "Research and Publications in Egyptian Monasticism, 2000–2004." In *Huitième congrès international d'études coptes (Paris 2004): 1. Bilans et perspectives 2000–2004*, edited by A. Boud'hors and D. Vaillancourt, 111–26. Cahiers de la Bibliothèque Copte 15. Paris: De Boccard.

———. 2008. "From Temple to Cell, from Gods to Demons: Pagan Temples in the Monastic Topography of Fourth-century Egypt." In *From Temple to Church: Destruction and Renewal of Local Cultic Topography in Late Antiquity*, edited by J. Hahn, S. Emmel, and U. Gotter, 91–112. Religions in the Graeco-Roman World 163. Leiden: Brill.

———. 2009. *Evagrius of Pontus: Talking Back: A Monastic Handbook for Combating Demons*. Cistercian Studies Series 229. Collegeville, MN: Liturgical Press.

Breccia, E. 1907. "D'un édifice d'époque chrétienne à el-Dekhela et de l'emplacement du Ennaton." *BSAA* 9:3–12.

———. 1914. "Duo nuovi epitaffi di monaci alessandrini." *BSAA* 15.

———. 1919. "Ancora un epitaffio di monaco alessandrino." *BSAA* 17.

Bridel, Ph. 1986. "La dialectique de l'isolement et de l'ouverture dans les monastères kelliotes: espaces réservés–espaces d'accueil." *Le site monastique copte des Kellia: Sources historiques et exploration archéologique, Actes du colloque de Genève, 13–15 août 1984*, edited by Ph. Bridel, 145–61. Geneva: MSAC.

———. 1988a. "Les bâtiments de la vie communautaire." *Dossiers, histoire et archéologie* 133:44–59.

———. 1988b. "L'installation dans le désert." *Dossiers, histoire et archéologie* 133:16–19.

———. 1990. "Le site des Kellia et son exploration par la mission suisse." In *Les Kellia, ermitages coptes en Basse-Égypte. Musée d'art et d'histoire de Genève, 12 octobre 1989–7 janvier 1990*, edited by Y. Mottier and N. Bosson, 21–32. Geneva: Éditions du Tricorne.

———, ed. 1999. *Explorations aux Qouçoûr el-Izeila lors des campagnes 1981, 1982, 1984, 1985, 1986, 1989 et 1990*. EK 8184, vol. 3. Louvain: Peeters.

———. 2003. *Explorations aux Qouçoûr Hégeila et 'Éreima lors des campagnes 1987, 1988 et 1989*. EK 8184, vol. 4. Louvain: Peeters.

Budge, E.A.W. n.d. *Synaxarium: The Book of the Saints of the Ethiopian Orthodox Tewahedo Church*. Garland, TX: Ethiopian Orthodox Tewahedo Debre Meheret St. Michael Church.

———. 1909. *Texts Relating to Saint Mena of Egypt and Canons of Nicaea in a Nubian Dialect*. London: British Museum Press.

———. 1913. *Coptic Apocrypha in the Dialect of Upper Egypt*. London: British Museum.

———. 1915. *Miscellaneous Coptic Texts in the Dialect of Upper Egypt*. London: British Museum.

———. 1920. *An Ancient Egyptian Hieroglyphic Dictionary*, vol. 2, 1030. London: John Murray.

Bulgakov, S.N. 1997. *The Holy Grail and the Eucharist*. Hudson, NY: Lindisfarne Books.

Burmester, O.H.E. 1935. "Canons of Gabriel ibn Turaik the 70th Patriarch of Alexandria." *OCP* 1:5–45.

———. 1938. "On the Date and Authorship of the Arabic Synaxarium of the Coptic Church." *JTS* 39:249–53.

Butcher, E.L. 1897. *The Story of the Church in Egypt*. London: Smith, Edder, & Co.

Butler, A.J. 1884. *The Ancient Coptic Churches of Egypt*. Vol. 1. Oxford: Clarendon Press.

———. 1978. *The Arab Conquest of Egypt and the Last Thirty Years of the Roman Dominion*. 2nd ed. New York: Oxford University Press.

Butler, C. 1898–1904. *The Lausiac History of Palladius I–II*. Texts and Studies V–VI. Cambridge: Cambridge University Press.

Cabrera, A. 2009. "Late Roman and Byzantine Textiles from Egypt: Some Examples of Furnishing Textiles from Spanish Public Collections." In *Clothing the House: Furnishing Textiles of the 1st Millennium AD from Egypt and Neighbouring Countries*, edited by A. de Moor and C. Fluck, 89–99. Antwerp: Lannoo.

Cabrol, F., and H. Leclerq. 1925–53. *Dictionnaire d'archéologie chrétienne et de liturgie*. Vol. 1, no. 2; vol. 15, no. 2. Paris: Librairie Letouzey et Ané.

Calderini, A. 1980. *Dizionario dei nomi geografici e topografici dell'Egitto Greco-Romano*. Vol. 3, fasc. 3. Milan: Cisalpino Goliartica.

Casanova, P. 1901. "Les noms coptes du Caire et localités voisines." *BIFAO* 1:139–224.

Chaillot, C. 2005. *The Coptic Orthodox Church: A Brief Introduction to Its Life and Spirituality*. Paris: Inter-Orthodox Dialogue.

———. 2011. *Vie et spiritualité des Églises orthodoxes orientales des traditions syriaque, arménienne, copte et éthiopienne*. Patrimoine Orthodoxe. Paris: Cerf.

Chaillot, C., and A. Belopopsky. 1998. *Towards Unity: The Theological Dialogue between the Orthodox Church and the Oriental Orthodox Churches*. Paris: Inter-Orthodox Dialogue.

Chaîne, M. 1925. *La chronologie des temps chrétiens de l'Égypte et de l'Éthiopie*. Paris: Geuthner.

Chakmakjian, H. 1965. *Armenian Christology and Evangelization of Islam*. Leiden: E.J. Brill.

Cheikho, L. 1924. *Catalogue des manuscrits des auteurs arabes chrétiens*. Beirut: Dar al-Machreq.

Chitty, D.J. 1977. *The Desert a City: An Introduction to the Study of Egyptian and Palestinian Monasticism under the Christian Empire*. Crestwood, NY: St. Vladimir's Seminary Press.

———. 1980. *Et le désert devint une cité*. Spiritualité Orientale 31. Solesmes: Abbaye de Bellefontaine.

Clark, E.A. 1992. *The Origenist Controversy: The Cultural Construction of an Early Christian Debate*. Princeton: Princeton University Press.

Clédat, J. 1904–1906. *Le monastère et la nécropole de Baouît.* Mémoires publiés par les membres de l'Institut Français d'Archéologie Orientale du Caire 12. Cairo: IFAO.

Colin, G. 2004. *Le livre éthiopien des miracles de Marie.* Collection Patrimoines, Christianisme. Paris: Cerf.

Coquin, R.-G. 1982. "Huitième campagne de fouilles aux Kellia (avril 1982): Rapport préliminaire." *BIFAO* 82:363–77.

———. 1984–85. "Neuvième campagne de fouilles aux Kellia (avril 1983): Rapport préliminaire." *ASAE* 70:107–24, pl. 1–5.

———. 1988. "L'évolution de la vie monastique." *Dossiers, histoire et archéologie* 133:60–65.

———. 1991a. "Dayr." *CE* 3:695.

———. 1991b. "Dayr al-Maghtis." *CE* 3:818–19.

———. 1991c. "Dayr Sitt Dimyanah: History." *CE* 3:870–72.

———. 1991d. "Deir al-Maymah." *CE* 3:837–38.

———. 1991e. "Menas." *CE* 5:1588–89.

———. 1991f. "Menas, Saint." *CE* 5:1589.

———. 1991g. "Patriarchal Residences." *CE* 6:1913.

———. 1991h. "Victor of Tabennese." *CE* 7:2308.

———. 1993. "Langue et littérature arabes chrétiennes." In *Christianismes orientaux*, edited by M. Albert, 35–106. Paris: Éditions du Cerf.

Coquin, R.-G., and M. Martin. 1991a. "Dayr al-Khandaq." *CE* 3:814.

———. 1991b. "Dayr Anba Bishoi." *CE* 3:736–37.

———. 1991c. "Deir al-Askar." *CE* 3:783–84.

———. 1991d. "Naquizah." *CE* 6:1174b–1175a.

Coquin, R.-G., M. Martin, and P. Grossman. 1991. "Dayr al-Qusayr (Turah)." *CE* 3:853b–855a.

Corboud, P. 1986. "L'oratoire et les niches-oratoires: les lieux de la prière." *Le site monastique copte des Kellia: Sources historiques et exploration archéologique, Actes du colloque de Genève, 13–15 août 1984*, edited by Ph. Bridel, 85–92. Geneva: MSAC.

Correas Amador, M. 2013. "Ethnoarchaeology of Egyptian Mudbrick Houses: Towards a Holistic Understanding of Ancient Egyptian Domestic Architecture." PhD diss., Durham University. http://etheses.dur.ac.uk/6916/

Coulmas, F. 2013. *Writing and Society: An Introduction.* Cambridge: Cambridge University Press.

CPC. Orlandi, T., et al. n.d. *Clavis Patrum Copticorum.* http://www.cmcl.it/~cmcl/chiam_clavis.html.

CPG. Geerard, M. 1974–2003. *Clavis Patrum Graecorum.* Turnhout: Brepols.

Cramer, M. 1964. *Koptische Buchmalerei: Illuminationen in Manuskripten des christlich-koptischen Ägyptens von 4. bis 19. Jahrhundert.* Recklinghausen: Bongers.

Cramer, M., and M. Krause, eds. 2008. *Das koptische Antiphonar (M 575 und P 11967).* Münster: Aschendorff Verlag.

Cristea, H.-J. 2011. *Schenute von Atripe: Contra Origenistas.* STAC 60. Tübingen: Mohr Siebeck.

Cross, F.L. 1997. *The Oxford Dictionary of the Christian Church*. 3rd ed. Oxford: Oxford University Press.

Crum, W.E. 1899–1900. "Christian Egypt." *Archeological Report*: 46–51.

———. 1905. *Catalogue of the Coptic Manuscripts in the British Museum*. London: British Museum.

———. 1915. *Der Papyruscodex saec. VI–VII der Phillippsbibliothek in Cheltenham*. Strassburg: Trübner.

———. 1939a. *A Coptic Dictionary*. Oxford: Clarendon Press.

———. 1939b. "Coptic Documents in Greek Script." *Proceedings of the British Academy* 25:249–71.

Dąbrowski, L. 1962. "La topographie d'Athribis à l'époque romaine." *ASAE* 57:19–31.

Dadoyan, S. 1997. *The Fatimid Armenians: Cultural and Political Interaction in the Near East*. Leiden: E.J. Brill.

———. 2013. *The Armenians in the Medieval Islamic World: Paradigm of Interaction, Seventh to Fourteenth Century*. Vol. 2. New Brunswick, NJ: Transaction Publishers.

Daly, R.J., trans. 1992. *Treatise on the Passover and Dialogue of Origen with Heraclides and His Fellow Bishops on the Father, the Son, and the Soul*. Ancient Christian Writers 54. Mahwah, NJ: Paulist Press.

Daowd, N.K. 2003. *Tarikh kanisat al-Malak Mikha'il al-Bahari, Hada'iq al-Qubba, al-Qahira*. Cairo: Kanisat al-Malak Mikha'il al-Bahari.

Daumas, F. 1965. "Rapport sur les travaux scientifiques de l'I.F.A.O. durant l'année 1964–1965." *Comptes-rendus des séances de l'Académie des Inscriptions et Belles-Lettres* 109, no. 2: 383–90.

———. 1967. "La 4e campagne au Désert des Cellules." *Comptes-rendus des séances de l'Académie des Inscriptions et Belles-Lettres* 111, no. 3: 438–52.

———. 1968. "Fouilles et travaux de l'Institut français d'archéologie orientale durant l'année 1967–1968." *Comptes-rendus des séances de l'Académie des Inscriptions et Belles-Lettres* 112, no. 3: 395–408.

———. 1969. "Rapport sur l'activité de l'Institut français d'archéologie orientale du Caire au cours des années 1968–1969." *Comptes-rendus des séances de l'Académie des Inscriptions et Belles-Lettres* 113, no. 3: 496–507.

Daumas, F., and A. Guillaumont. 1969. *Kellia I, Kom 219: fouilles effectuées en 1964 et 1965*. FIFAO 28, 1–2. Cairo: IFAO.

Davis, M.H., ed. and trans. 1919. *The Life of Abba John Kahmé*. PO 14.2, no. 68. Reprint, Paris: Turnhout, 2009.

Davis, S. 1998. "Pilgrimage and the Cult of Saint Thecla in Late Antique Egypt." In *Pilgrimage and Holy Space in Late Antique Egypt*, edited by D. Frankfurter, 303–39. Leiden and Boston: Brill.

———. 2001. *The Cult of Saint Thecla*. Oxford: Oxford University Press.

———. 2004. *The Early Coptic Papacy: The Egyptian Church and Its Leadership in Late Antiquity*. The Popes of Egypt 1. Cairo: American University in Cairo Press.

———. 2008. *Coptic Christology in Practice: Incarnation and Divine Participation in Late Antique and Medieval Egypt*. Oxford and New York: Oxford University Press.

———. 2013. "Completing the Race and Receiving the Crown: 2 Timothy 4:7–8 in Early Christian Monastic Epitaphs at Kellia and Pherme." In *Asceticism and Exegesis in Early Christianity: The Reception of New Testament Texts in Ancient Ascetic Discourses*, edited by H.-U. Weidemann, 334–73. Novum Testamentum et orbis antiquus/Studien zur Umwelt des Neuen Testaments 101. Göttingen: Vandenhoeck & Ruprecht.

De Boor, C., ed. 1883. *Theophanis Chronographia*. Vol. 1. Leipzig: n.p.

De Cesaris, L., and A. Sucato. 2006a. "Final Report: Coptic Museum—Old Cairo Conservation of the Wall Paintings." Report prepared for the Egyptian Antiquities Project, ARCE, July 2006. Unpublished.

———. 2006b. "Appendix to the Final Report: Coptic Museum—Old Cairo Conservation of the Wall Paintings." Report prepared for the Egyptian Antiquities Project, ARCE, July 2006. Unpublished.

———. 2006c. "Maps of Damage and Maps of Interventions (Graphic Documentation)." August 2006. ARCE Archive.

Dechow, J.F. 1988. *Dogma and Mysticism in Early Christianity: Epiphanius of Cyprus and the Legacy of Origen*. North American Patristic Society Patristic Monograph Series 13. Macon, GA: Mercer University Press.

Décobert, Ch. 2002. "Maréotide médiévale: des Bédouins et des chrétiens." In *Alexandrie médiévale 2*, edited by Ch. Décobert, 127–67. Études Alexandrines 8. Cairo: IFAO.

De Cosson, A. 1935. *Mareotis: Being a Short Account of the History and Ancient Monuments of the North-Western Desert of Egypt and of Lake Mareotis*. London: Country Life.

———. 1937. "The Desert City of El Muna." *Bulletin de la Société royale d'archéologie d'Alexandrie* 31:247–53.

De Fina, A., and A. Georgakopoulou. 2012. *Analyzing Narrative: Discourse and Sociolinguistic Perspectives*. Cambridge, UK: Cambridge University Press.

Deghadou. 2015. Quarterly magazine of the Armenian General Benevolent Union Cairo. No. 75 (April). (in Armenian).

de Lagarde, P. 1886. *Catenae in evangelia Aegyptiacae quae supersunt*. Göttingen: Arnoldi Hoyer. Reprint, Osnabrück: Otto Zeller, 1971.

Delattre, A., J. Dijkstra, and J. van der Vliet. 2015. "Christian Inscriptions from Egypt and Nubia 2 (2014)." *BASP* 52:297–314.

DelCogliano, M., A. Radde-Gallwitz, and L. Ayres, trans. 2011. *Works on the Spirit: Athanasius the Great and Didymus the Blind*. Popular Patristics Series 43. Yonkers, NY: St. Vladimir's Seminary Press.

Delehaye, H. 1910. "L'invention des reliques de Saint Ménas à Constantinople." *AB* 29:117–56.

———. 1922. "Les martyrs d'Égypte." *AB* 40:5–154.

———. 1925. "Les recueils antiques des miracles des saints." *AB* 43:5–85.

———. 1973. *Les passions des martyrs et les genres littéraires*. Subsidia Hagiographica 17. Brussels: Société des Bollandistes.

Del Río Sánchez, Fr. 2008. *Catalogue des manuscrits de la Fondation Georges et Mathilde Salem (Alep, Syrie)*. SKCO 16. Wiesbaden: Harrassowitz.

Depuydt, L. 1990. "In Sinuthium graecum." *Orientalia* 59:67–71.

———. 1993. *Catalogue of the Coptic Manuscripts in the Pierpont Morgan Library*. 2 vols. Louvain: Peeters.

Derks, S.W. 2009. *Power and Pilgrimage: Dealing with Class, Gender and Inequality at a Bolivian Marian Shrine*. Nijmegen: LIT.

Descœudres, G. 1988. "L'architecture des Kellia." *Le Monde Copte* 14/15:75–96.

———. 1990. "L'architecture des ermitages et des sanctuaires." *Les Kellia, ermitages coptes en Basse-Égypte: Musée d'art et d'histoire de Genève, 12 octobre 1989–7 janvier 1990*, edited by Y. Mottier and N. Bosson, 33–55. Geneva: Éditions du Tricorne.

———. 1998. "Wohntürme in Klöstern und Ermitagen Ägyptens." In *ΘΕΜΕΛΙΑ: Spätantike und koptologische Studien Peter Grossmann zum 65. Geburtstag*, 69–80. Wiesbaden: Reichert Verlag.

Description de l'Égypte. 1822–29. Paris: C.L.F. Panckoucke.

Detlef, C., and D.G.G. Müller. 1991. "Zacharias, Saint." *CE* 7:2368–69.

Devos, P. 1960a. "Le juif et le chrétien: Un miracle de Saint Ménas." *AB* 78:275–308.

———. 1960b. "Un récit des miracles de S. Ménas en copte et en éthiopien." *AB* 78:154–60.

———. 1969. "Fragments coptes de l'*Historia Monachorum in Aegypto*: S. Jean de Lyco et la Tentatrice." *AB* 87:417–41.

Dhormé, É. 1934. "Les Fouilles." *Chronique d'Égypte* 9:65–84.

Dietze, G. 2004. "Römische Stadtstrukturen in Nordafrika und Ägypten: Eine vergleichende Studie an Hand des Materials aus Thugga/Dougga (Tunesien) und Narmuthis/Medinet Madi (Fayum, Ägypten) und Berücksichtigung der Ägyptischen Metropoleis." PhD diss., Katholieke Universiteit Leuven.

Difnar: Kul Ayyâm al-Sana. 1985. Beni Suef: Bishopric of Beni Suef.

Dijkstra, J., and J. van der Vliet. 2015. "The Earliest Manuscript of the Coptic *Life of Aaron* (British Library, Or. 7558 [89] [93] [150])." *Vigiliae Christianae* 69:368–92.

Dinkler, E. 1964. *Das Apsismosaik von S. Apollinare in Classe*. Cologne and Opladen: Westdeutscher Verlag.

———. 1990. "Kreuz." In *Lexikon der christlichen Ikonographie*, edited by E. Kirschbaum, vol. 2, col. 562–90. Rome, Freiburg, and Vienna: Herder Verlag.

Diodorus Siculus. 1989. *Diodorus Siculus I*. Translated by C.H. Oldfather. Loeb Classical Library 279. Cambridge, MA: Harvard University Press.

D'Orléans, P.Ch. 2002. *al-Qiddisin al-misriyin*. Vol. 2, *Mikha'il Maksi Iskandar and Maryam Gamil Sulaiman*. Cairo: Maktabat al-Mahaba.

Doutreleau, L. 1955. "Que savons-nous aujourd'hui des papyrus de Toura?" *Recherches de science religieuse* 43:161–93.

Doutreleau, L., and L. Koenen. 1967. "Nouvel inventaire des papyrus de Toura." *Recherches de science religieuse* 55:547–64.

Drescher, J. 1941. "St. Menas' Camels Once More." *BSAC* 7:19–32.

———. 1942. "More about St. Menas." *ASAE* 41:53–70.

———, ed. 1946. *Apa Mena: A Selection of Coptic Texts Relating to St. Menas*. Cairo: SAC.

———, ed. and trans. 1947. *Three Coptic Legends: Hilaria, Archellites, the Seven Sleepers*. Supplément des ASAE 4. Cairo: IFAO.

Dulaurier, É. 1949. "Grammaire copte-arabe de Samannoudi." In *Catalogue Général des Manuscrits des Bibliothèques Publiques des Départements*, 1:718–39. Paris.

Dutilh, E.D.T. 1904. "St. Menas of Alexandria." *BSAA* 5–6, no. 1, fasc. 1: 38–52, 56–68, 69–73.

Dyggve, E., and R. Egger, eds. 1939. *Der altchristliche Friedhof Marusinac*. Forschungen in Salona 3. Vienna: Rudolf M. Rohrer.

Ebied, R.Y. 1981. *Peter of Callinicum: Anti-Tritheist Dossier.* Louvain: Peeters.

Edwards, V., and Th.J. Sienkewicz. 1990. *Oral Cultures Past and Present: Rappin' and Homer*. Oxford: Blackwell.

Ehrman, B.D. 1986. *Didymus the Blind and the Text of the Gospels*. Atlanta, GA: Society of Biblical Literature.

Elsner, J. 2000. "Between Mimesis and Divine Power: Visuality in the Greco-Roman World." In *Visuality before and beyond the Renaissance: Seeing as Others Saw*, edited by R.S. Nelson, 45–69. Cambridge: Cambridge University Press (reprinted in J. Elsner, *Roman Eyes: Visuality and Subjectivity in Art and Text*, 1–26. Princeton and Oxford: Princeton University Press, 2007).

Emmel, S. 2002. "From the Other Side of the Nile: Shenute and Panopolis." In *Perspectives on Panopolis: An Egyptian Town from Alexander the Great to the Arab Conquest. Acts from an International Symposium Held in Leiden on 16, 17 and 18 December 1998 (P. L. Bat. 31)*, edited by A. Egberts, B.P. Muhs, and J. van der Vliet, 95–113. Leiden: Brill.

———. 2004. *Shenoute's Literary Corpus*. 2 vols. CSCO 599–600, Subsidia 111–12. Louvain: Peeters.

———. 2005. "The Library of the Monastery of the Archangel Michael at Phantoou (al-Hamuli)." In *Christianity and Monasticism in the Fayoum Oasis*, edited by G. Gabra, 63–70. Cairo: American University in Cairo Press.

Empereur, J.-Y., ed. 1998. *Commerce et artisanat dans l'Alexandrie hellénistique et romaine: Actes du colloque d'Athènes 11–12 décembre 1988*. Bulletin de Correspondance Hellénique, suppl. 33. Athens: École française d'Athènes.

Empereur, J.-Y., and M. Picon. 1998. "Les ateliers d'amphores du lac Mariout." In *Commerce et artisanat dans l'Alexandrie hellénistique et romaine: Actes du colloque d'Athènes 11–12 décembre 1988*, edited by J.-Y. Empereur, 75–91. Bulletin de Correspondance Hellénique, suppl. 33. Athens: École française d'Athènes.

Eusebius. 1932. *Ecclesiastical History*. Translated by J.E.L. Oulton. Loeb Classical Library 265. Cambridge, MA: Harvard University Press.

Evelyn-White, H.G. 1932. *The Monasteries of the Wâdi 'n Natrûn*. Part 2, *The History of the Monasteries of Nitria and of Scetis*. Metropolitan Museum of Art Egyptian Expedition 7. New York: Metropolitan Museum of Art.

———. 1933a. *The Monasteries of the Wâdi 'n Natrûn*. Egyptian Expedition, vol. 2. New York: The Metropolitan Museum of Art.

———. 1933b. *The Monasteries of the Wâdi 'n Natrûn*. Part 3, *The Architecture and Archaeology*. New York: Metropolitan Museum of Art. Reprint, Arno Press, 1973.

Evelyn-White, H.G., W. Hauser, and A.M. Lythgoe. 1932. *The Monasteries of the Wâdi 'N Natrûn*. Part 2, *The History of the Monasteries of Nitria and of Scetis*. New York: Metropolitan Museum of Art.

Evetts, B., trans. 1907a. *History of the Patriarchs of the Coptic Church of Alexandria*. Vol. 2, *Peter I to Benjamin I (661)*. PO 1.4. Paris: Firmin-Didot.

———, trans. 1907b. *History of the Patriarchs of the Coptic Church of Alexandria*. Vol. 1/2. PO 2. Paris: Firmin-Didot.

———, trans. 1909. *History of the Patriarchs of the Coptic Church of Alexandria*. Vol. 3, *Agathon to Michael I*. PO 5, fasc. 1, no. 21. Paris: Firmin-Didot.

Fagan, G.G. 1999. *Bathing in Public in the Roman World*. Ann Arbor: University of Michigan Press.

al-Falaki, Mahmoud Bey. 1872. *Mémoire sur l'antique Alexandrie, ses faubourgs et environs découverts par les fouilles, sondages, nivellement et autres recherches*. Copenhagen.

Falck, M. von, and F. Lichtwark, eds. 1996. *Ägypten, Schätze aus dem Wüstensand: Kunst und Kultur der Christen am Nil. Katalog zur Ausstellung herausgegeben vom Gustav-Lübcke-Museum der Stadt Hamm und dem Museum für Spätantike und Byzantinische Kunst, Staatliche Museen zu Berlin—Preussischer Kulturbesitz*. Wiesbaden: Dr. Ludwig Reichert Verlag.

Falls, J.C.E. 1913. *Three Years in the Libyan Desert: Travels, Discoveries and Excavations of the Menas Expedition (Kaufmann Expedition)*. Translated by E. Lee. London: T. Fisher Unwin.

Fanning, S. 2001. *Mystics of the Christian Tradition*. London: Routledge.

Favre, S. 1988. "L'architecture des ermitages." *Dossiers, histoire et archéologie* 133:20–29.

Fedalto, G. 1984. "Liste vescovili del Patriarcato di Alessandria." *Studia Patavina–Rivista di Scienze religiose* 31:249–323.

———. 1990. *Rufino di Concordia (345 c.–410/411) tra oriente e occidente*. Rome: Città nuova.

Fedotov, G., ed. 1969. *Treasury of Russian Spirituality*. Gloucester: Peter Smith.

Ferré, A. 1991a. "Abu al-'Ala Fahd ibn Ibrahim." *CE* 1:17.

———. 1991b. "Fatimids and the Copts." *CE* 4:1097.

Festugière, A.-J. 1961. *Historia monachorum in Aegypto*. Subsidia Hagiographica 34. Brussels: Société des Bollandistes.

———. 1964. *Les moines d'Orient*. Vol. 4, part 1. Paris: Éditions du Cerf.

Foley, J.M. 1995. *The Singer of Tales in Performance*. Bloomington: Indiana University Press.

———. 1999. *Homer's Traditional Art*. University Park: Pennsylvania State University Press.

———. 2002. *How to Read an Oral Poem*. Urbana: University of Illinois Press.

Follet, S., and O. Overwien. 2016. "Secundus le Taciturne." In *Dictionnaire des philosophes antiques*, edited by R. Goulet, vol. 6, 166–70 (no. S 36). Paris: CNRS Éditions.

Forget, J., ed. 1912. *Synaxarium Alexandrinum*. 2 vols. CSCO Scriptores Arabici series 3, vols. 18–19. Beirut: Typographeo Catholico.

———. 1963. *Synaxarium Alexandrinum*. CSCO Scriptores Arabici 3, 4, 5, vols. 47–49. Louvain: Peeters.

Forster, E.M. 1990. *Alexandrie: Une histoire et un guide*. Translated from English by C. Blanc. Paris: Quai Voltaire.

Foucault, M. 1986. "Of Other Spaces." Translation by J. Miskowiec of "Des espaces autres." *Diacritics* 16:22–27.

Les fouilles de l'expédition de Francfort au Karm Abu Mina (1re période: novembre 1905–juin 1906). 1906. Alexandria: Société de publications égyptiennes.

Fournet, J.-L., and J. Gascou. 2002. "Moines pachômiens et batellerie." Alexandrie Médiévale 2. *Études alexandrines* 8:23–45.

Frankfurter, D. 2012. "Religious Practice and Piety." In *The Oxford Handbook of Roman Egypt*, edited by C. Griggs, 319–36. Oxford: Oxford University Press.

Fraser, P.M. 1972. *Ptolemaic Alexandria I*. Oxford: Clarendon Press.

Frend, W.H.C. 1972. *The Rise of the Monophysite Movement*. Cambridge, UK: Cambridge University Press.

———. 1991. "Timothy Salofaciolus." *CE* 7:2268–69.

Furness, A.M., and G. Fitzgibbon. 2011. "Description and Finding Aid: Gilbert and Stewart Bagnani Fonds CA OTAG SC036." E.P. Taylor Research Library and Archives: Art Gallery of Ontario, Canada.

Gabra, G. 1999. *Cairo: The Coptic Museum and Old Cairo Churches*. Cairo: Egyptian International Publishing Company–Longman. (Reprint of 1993 original.)

———, ed. 2001. *Be Thou There: The Holy Family's Journey in Egypt*. Cairo: American University in Cairo Press.

Gabra, G. 2002. *Coptic Monasteries: Egypt's Monastic Art and Architecture*. Cairo: American University in Cairo Press.

———. 2003. "The Revolts of the Bashmuric Copts in the Eighth and Ninth Centuries." In *Die koptische Kirche in den ersten drei islamischen Jahrhunderten*, edited by W. Beltz, 111–19. Hallesche Beiträge zur Orientwissenschaft 36. Halle (Saale): Institut für Orientalistik, Martin-Luther-Universität.

———. 2008. *Historical Dictionary of the Coptic Church*. Cairo: American University in Cairo Press.

———, ed. 2014. *Coptic Civilization: Two Thousand Years of Christianity in Egypt*. Cairo: American University in Cairo Press.

Gabra, G., and M. Eaton-Krauss. 2005. *Treasures of Coptic Art in the Coptic Museum and Churches of Old Cairo*. Cairo: American University in Cairo Press.

Gabra, G., G. van Loon, S. Reif, and T. Swelim. 2013. *The History and Religions of Old Cairo: Its Fortress, Churches, Synagogue, and Mosque*. Edited by C. Ludwig and M. Jackson. Cairo: American University in Cairo Press.

Gabra, G., G. van Loon, and S. Sonbol. 2012. *The Churches of Egypt: From the Journey of the Holy Family to the Present Day*. Los Angeles and Cairo: Ludwig Publishing/American University in Cairo Press. (Reprint of 2007 original.)

Galazzi, C., and G. Hadji-Minaglou. 1989. "Fouilles anciennes et nouvelles sur le site de Tebtynis." *BIFAO* 89:179–202, pls. XXV–XXVII.

Galtier, E. 1905. "Contributions à l'étude de la littérature arabe–copte. 3. Les Actes de Victor fils de Romanos." *BIFAO* 4:127–40.

Garitte, G. 1949. *S. Antonii vitae versio Sahidica*. CSCO 117–18, Scriptores Coptici 13–14. Louvain: Peeters.

Gascou, Jean. 1976. "*P. Fouad* 87: Les monastères Pachômiens et l'état byzantin." *BIFAO* 76:157–84.

———. 1991a. "Enaton." *CE* 3:954–58.

———. 1991b. "Metanoia, Monastery of the." *CE* 5:1608–11.

Gayraud, R.-P. 1992. "Tebtynis: Quelques notes sur le site islamique." In *Itinéraires d'Égypte: Mélanges offerts au père Maurice Martin*, edited by C. Décobert, 31–44. Cairo: IFAO.

Gemeinhardt, P., and J. Leemans. 2012. "Christian Martyrdom in Late Antiquity: Some Introductory Perspectives." In *Christian Martyrdom in Late Antiquity (300–450 AD): History and Discourse, Tradition and Religious Identity*, edited by P. Gemeinhardt and J. Leemans, 1–11. Berlin: De Gruyter.

El Gendi, S.S. 2007. "al-Qita' al-athariya allati tahmil tasawir al-qiddis Mar Mina al-' Aja'ibi." *Annals of the Faculty of Arts/Ain Shams University* 32, no. 2: 499–546.

Georgii, F.A. 1794. *Di miraculis S. Coluthi*. Rome: Antonius Fulgonius.

Giamberardini, G. 1972. "Orientamenti teologici della Chiesa copta." *Antonianum* 47:213–94.

Girardet, K. 1970. "Philologos und philologein." *Kleronomia* 2:323–33.

Goehring, J.E. 1986. *The Letter of Ammon and Pachomian Monasticism*. Patristische Texte und Studien 27. Berlin: Walter de Gruyter.

———. 2006. "Remembering Abraham of Farshut: History, Hagiography, and the Fate of the Pachomian Tradition." *JECS* 14:1–26.

———. 2011. "The Ship of the Pachomian Federation: Metaphor and Meaning in a Late Account of Pachomian Monasticism." In *Christianity in Egypt: Literary Production and Intellectual Trends. Studies in Honor of Tito Orlandi*, edited by P. Buzi and A. Camplan, 289–303. Rome: Institutum Patristicum Augustinianum.

———. 2012. *Politics, Monasticism, and Miracles in Sixth-Century Upper Egypt*. STAC 69. Tübingen: Mohr Siebeck.

Goffman, E. 1981. "Footing." In *Forms of Talk*, 124–57. Philadelphia: University of Pennsylvania Press.

Goitein, S.D. 1967. *A Mediterranean Society: The Jewish Communities of the Arab World as Portrayed in the Documents of the Cairo Geniza*. Vol. 1, *Economic Foundations*. Berkeley: University of California Press.

Golitzin, A. 2003. "The Vision of God and the Form of Glory: More Reflections on the Anthropomorphite Controversy of AD 399." In *Abba: The Tradition of Orthodoxy in the West: Festschrift for Bishop Kallistos (Ware) of Diokleia*, edited by J. Behr, A. Louth, and C. Dimitri, 273–97. Crestwood, NY: St. Vladimir's Seminary Press.

Gomaà, F. 1980. "Kom el-Idris (Marea)." In *Lexikon der Ägyptologie*, edited by W. Helck and E. Otto, vol. 3, 647. Wiesbaden: Harrassowitz.

Gordon, R. 1999. "'What's in a List?' Listing in Greek and Graeco-Roman Malign Magical Texts." In *The World of Ancient Magic: Papers from the First International Samson Eitrem Seminar at the Norwegian Institute at Athens, 4–8 May*

1997, edited by D.R. Jordan, H. Montgomery, and E. Thomassen, 239–77. Bergen: Norwegian Institute at Athens [= Papers from the Norwegian Institute at Athens 4].

Górecki, T. 2014. "Ręczne (przenośne) candelabrum z bizantyńskiego kościoła w Athribis w Egipcie."/"Hand (Portable) Candelabrum from a Byzantine Church in Athribis in Egypt." *Rocznik Muzeum Narodowego w Warszawie*, Nowa Seria/*Journal of the National Museum in Warsaw*, new series 3, no. 39: 135–46.

———. 2015. "Appendix B: Lighting of the Churches' Interior." In *The Alexandrian Church: People and Institutions*, edited by E. Wipszycka, 343–48. Journal of Juristic Papyrology, Supplement 25. Warsaw: Faculty of Law and Administration of University of Warsaw.

Graf, G. 1912. "Das Schriftstellerverzeichnis des Abu Ishaq Ibn al-'Assal." *Oriens Christianus*, new series 2:205–206, 212–13.

———. 1927. "Die Rangordnung der Bischöfe Ägyptens nach einem protokollarischen Bericht des Patriarchen Kyrillos Ibn Laqlaq (hg./übers.)." *Oriens Christianus* 24:299–337.

———. 1933. "Exegetische Schriften zum Neuen Testament in arabischer Sprache bis zum 14. Jahrhundert." *Biblische Zeitschrift* 21:22–40, 161–69.

———. 1934. *Catalogue des manuscrits arabes chrétiens conservés au Caire*. Studi e Testi 63. Vatican City: Biblioteca Apostolica Vaticana.

———. 1944. *Geschichte der christlichen arabischen Literatur*. Studi e Testi 118, vol. 1. Reprint 1966. Vatican City: Biblioteca Apostolica Vaticana.

———. 1944–53. *Geschichte der christlichen arabischen Literatur*. 5 vols. Vatican City: Biblioteca Apostolica Vaticana.

———. 1947. *Geschichte der christlichen arabischen Literatur*. Studi e Testi 133, vol. 2. Reprint 1966. Vatican City: Biblioteca Apostolica Vaticana.

Gregorios, Bishop. 1991. "Anba Ruways." *CE* 1:128.

Griffith, F.L. 1927. "Oxford Excavations in Nubia." *Liverpool Annals of Archaeology and Anthropology* 14:57–115.

Griffith, S. 1997. "From Aramaic to Arabic: The Language of the Monasteries of Palestine in the Byzantine and Early Islamic Period." *Dumbarton Oaks Papers* 51:11–31.

Grig, L. 2004. *Making Martyrs in Late Antiquity*. London: Duckworth.

Griggs, C.W. 1991. "Carpocrates." *CE* 2:461.

Grillmeier, A., and Th. Hainthaler. 1990. *Jesus der Christus im Glauben der Kirche*. Vol. 2, *Die Kirche von Alexandrien mit Nubien und Äthiopien nach 451*. Freiburg, Basel, and Vienna: Herder.

Grossmann, P. 1982. "Abu Mina: Zehnter Vorläufiger Bericht: Kompagnen 1981 und 1982." *MDAIK* 38:131–54.

———. 1986. *Abu Mina: A Guide to the Ancient Pilgrimage*. Cairo: Fotiadis and Co. Press.

———. 1989. *Abu Mina I: Die Gruftkirche und die Gruft*. Mainz am Rhein: Verlag Philipp von Zabern.

———. 1991a. "Dayr al-'Izam." *CE* 3:810.

———. 1991b. "Dayr Sitt Dimyanah: Architecture." *CE* 3:872.

———. 1993. "Die Querschiffbasilika von Hauwariya und die übrigen Bauten dieses Typus in Ägypten als Repräsentanten der verlorenen frühchristlichen Architektur Alexandreias." In *In Memoriam Daoud. BSAA* 45:107–21.

———. 2002. *Christliche Architektur in Ägypten*. Leiden: Brill.

———. 2003. "Nochmals zu Marea und Philoxenite." *BSAC* 42:13–29.

———. 2004a. *Abu Mina II: Das Baptysterium*. Mainz: Zabern-Verlag.

———. 2004b. "Report on the Excavations at Abu Mina in Spring 2003." *BSAC* 43:33–43, pls. VII–X.

———. 2005. "The Early Christian Churches of Tebtunis Discovered by the Italian Mission in 1930–1933." In *Christianity and Monasticism in the Fayoum Oasis*, edited by G. Gabra, 197–208. Cairo: American University in Cairo Press.

Grossmann, P., and H. Jaritz. 1982. "Abu Mina: Neunter Vorläufiger Bericht: Kompagnen 1977, 1978 und 1979." *MDAIK* 36:203–27.

Grossmann, P., and J. Kościuk. 1991. "Report on the Excavations at Abu Mina in Autumn 1989." *BSAC* 30:65–75.

Grumel, V. 1958. *Traité d'Études Byzantines*. Vol. 1, *La Chronologie*. Paris: PUF.

Guéraud, O., and P. Nautin, eds. 1979. *Origène sur la Pâque*. Paris: Éditions Beauchesne.

Guillaumont, A. 1964. "Le site des 'Cellia' (Basse Égypte)." *Revue Archéologique* 2 (July–December): 43–50.

———. 1965. "Premières fouilles au site des Kellia (Basse-Égypte)." *Comptes-rendus des séances de l'Académie des Inscriptions et Belles-Lettres* 109, no. 1: 218–25.

———. 1979. "Une inscription copte sur la 'Prière de Jésus.'" In *Aux origines du monachisme chrétien*, 167–83. Bégrolles-en-Mauges: Abbaye de Bellefontaine.

———. 1980. "Le problème de la prière continuelle dans le monachisme ancien." *L'expérience de la prière dans les grandes religions: Actes du colloque de Louvain-la-Neuve et Liège (22–23 novembre 1978)*, edited by H. Limet and J. Ries, 284–93. Homo Religiosus 5. Louvain: Université Catholique Louvain-la-Neuve.

———. 1991a. "Macarius the Egyptian, Saint." *CE* 5:1491–92.

———. 1991b. "Nitria." *CE* 6:1795b–1796b.

———. 2004. *Un philosophe au désert: Evagre le Pontique*. Paris: Vrin.

Guirguis, M., and N. van Doorn-Harder. 2011. *The Emergence of the Modern Coptic Papacy: The Egyptian Church and Its Leadership from the Ottoman Period to the Present*. Cairo: American University in Cairo Press.

Guy, J.-Cl. 1974. "Jean de Lycopolis." In *Dictionnaire de spiritualité ascétique et mystique*, vol. 8, 619–20. Paris: Beauchesne.

Gwynn, D.M. 2011. "Athanasius in Oriental Historical Tradition." In *Unclassical Traditions*. Vol. 2, *Perspectives from East and West in Late Antiquity*, edited by C. Kelly, R. Flower, and M.S. Williams, 43–58. Cambridge: Cambridge Philological Society.

———. 2012. *Athanasius of Alexandria: Bishop, Theologian, Ascetic, Father*. Oxford: Oxford University Press.

———. 2013. "Athanasius of Alexandria in Greek and Coptic Historical Tradition." *JCS* 15:43–54.

Habermann, W. 2000. *Zur Wasserversorgung einer Metropole in kaiserzeitlichen Ägypten. Neuedition von P.Lond III 117. Text—Übersetzung—Kommentar.* Munich: Beck.

Habib, D. 1996. *Iyris Habib al-Masri, mu'arrikhat qissat al-kanisa al-qibtiya.* Cairo: Dora al-Masry.

Habib, I. n.d. *Qissat al-kanisa al-qibtiya.* Vol. 7. Cairo: Mahabba Bookshop.

Habib, R. 1967. *The Coptic Museum: A General Guide.* Cairo: Ministry of Culture.

Hacikyan, A., G. Basmajian, and E. Franchuk. 2005. "An Overview from the Eighteenth to the Beginning of the Twentieth Century." In *The Heritage of Armenian Literature from the Eighteenth Century to Modern Times*, vol. 3, 34–35. Detroit: Wayne State University Press.

Haeny, G., and A. Leibundgut. 1999. *Kellia: Kôm Qouçoûr Isa 366 und seine Kirchenanlagen.* Recherches suisses d'archéologie copte 5. Louvain: Peeters.

Hafiz, F. 1986. *History of the Armenian People from Origin to Nowadays.* Cairo: AGBU.

Hakim, A., and Y. Mansour. 1969. *'Ashar sanawat majida fi tarikh al-kanisa.* Cairo: n.p.

Halkin, F. 1932. *Sancti Pachomii Vitae Graecae.* Subsidia hagiographica 19. Brussels: Société des Bollandistes.

———. 1985. "La passion de saint Marc d'Aréthuse BHG 2248." *AB* 103:217–29.

Halm, H. 1982. *Ägypten nach den mamlukischen Lehensregistern.* Vol. 2, *Das Delta.* Wiesbaden: Dr. Ludwig Reichert.

Hanna, B.J. 1996. *Tarikh dayr Mar Jirjis bi Sadamant al-Jabal bayn al-madi wa-l-hadir.* Cairo: Lajnat al-Tahrir wa-l-Nashr.

Hansen, G.C. 1995. *Sokrates Kirchengeschichte.* Griechischen Christlichen Schriftsteller, n.s. 1. Berlin: Akademie.

Hasan, S. 2002. *The Struggle for Coptic Equality: Christian versus Muslim Egypt.* Oxford: Oxford University Press.

Hassan, L.K. 2004. "Emergency Stabilization and Transport of Wall Paintings in the Coptic Museum." Report prepared for the Egyptian Antiquities Project, ARCE, December 2004. Unpublished.

Hawkes-Teeples, S., ed. 2011. *The Liturgical Commentaries: St. Symeon of Thessalonika.* Toronto: Pontifical Institute of Mediaeval Studies.

Hayreneik Association. 1980. "The Armenian Colony of Egypt during the Reign of Muhamed Ali (1805–1848)." *Armenian Review* 33:118–30.

Hebbelynck, A., and A. van Lantschoot. 1937a. *Codices Coptici Vaticani, Barberiniani, Borgiani, Rossiani.* Bibliothecae Apostolicae Vaticanae codices manu scripti rec. iussu Pii 9. Rome: Biblioteca Apostolica Vaticana.

———. 1937b. *Codices Coptici Vaticani, Barberiniani, Borgiani, Rossiani.* Vol. 1, *Codices Coptici Vaticani.* Vatican City: Biblioteca Apostolica Vaticana.

Heide, M. 2014. *Secundus Taciturnus: Die arabischen, äthiopischen und syrischen Textzeugen einer didaktischen Novelle aus der römischen Kaiserzeit.* Äthiopische Forschungen 81. Wiesbaden: Harrassowitz Verlag.

Heikel, M. 1983. *Autumn of Fury.* London: Andre Deutsch.

Helmbold, A.K. 1967. *The Nag Hammadi Gnostic Texts and the Bible*. Baker Studies in Biblical Archaeology 5. Grand Rapids, MI: Baker Book House.

Henein, N.H., and M. Wuttmann. 2000. *Kellia II: L'ermitage copte QR 195. Archéologie et architecture* 1–2. FIFAO 41. Cairo: IFAO.

Hengstenberg, W. 1922. "Pachomiana mit einem Anhang über die Liturgie von Alexandrien." In *Beiträge zur Geschichte des christlichen Altertums und der byzantinischen Literatur: Festgabe Albert Ehrhard*, edited by A.M. Koeniger, 238–52. Bonn: Kurt Schroeder Verlag.

Herodotus. 1976. *Herodotus Book II*. Edited by A.B. Lloyd. Études préliminaires aux religions orientales dans l'Empire romain 43. Leiden: Brill.

Hooff, G. van. 1884. "Acta Sancti Menæ: Martyris Aegyptii." *AB* 3:258–70.

Horace. 2004. *Odes and Epodes*. Translated by N. Rudd. Loeb Classical Library 33. Cambridge, MA: Harvard University Press.

Horner, G.W., ed. and trans. 1898–1905. *The Coptic Version of the New Testament in the Northern Dialect*. 4 vols. Oxford: Clarendon Press.

Huller, S. 2009. "The Rediscovery of the Original Episcopal Throne of the Alexandrian See of St. Mark." *JCS* 11:71–114.

Hulsman, C. 2001. "Tracing the Route of the Holy Family Today." In *Be Thou There: The Holy Family's Journey in Egypt*, edited by G. Gabra, 31–131. Cairo: American University in Cairo Press.

Hunt, L.-A. 1985. "Christian–Muslim Relations in Painting in Egypt of the Twelfth to Mid-thirteenth Centuries: Sources of Wallpainting at Deir es-Suriani and the Illustration of the New Testament Manuscript MS Paris, Copte-Arabe 1/Cairo, Bibl. 94." *Cahiers Archéologiques* 33:111–55. Reprinted in Hunt 1998–2000: 205–81.

———. 1994. "Introducing the Catalogue in Progress of the Illustrated Manuscripts of the Coptic Museum [in Old Cairo]." *Parole de l'Orient* 19:401–13.

———. 1998–2000. *Byzantium, Eastern Christendom and Islam: Art at the Crossroads of the Medieval Mediterranean*. 2 vols. London: Pindar Press.

Hyvernat, H., ed. and trans. 1886a. *Les actes des martyrs de l'Égypte tirés des manuscrits coptes de la Bibliothèque Vaticane et du Musée Borgia*. Texte copte et traduction française 1. Paris: Ernest Leroux.

———. 1886b. *Les actes des martyrs de l'Égypte*. Vol. 1. Paris: Ernest Leroux. Reprint 1977, Hildesheim and New York: Olms.

———. 1886–87. *Les Actes des Martyrs de l'Égypte tirés des manuscrits Copte de la Bibliothèque Vaticane et du Musée Borgia*. Texte copte et traduction française. Paris: E. Leroux.

———. 1909. "Coptic Literature." In *Catholic Encyclopedia* 5:362. New York: Robert Appleton Company.

———. 1922a. *Bybliothecae Pierpont Morgan codices coptici photographice expressi*. 56 vols. Rome: Biblioteca Apostolica Vaticana.

———. 1922b. *Bibliothecae Pierpont Morgan codices coptici photographice expressi*. Vol. 21, *Passio s. Menae militis. Miracula per s. Menam patrata narrante Theophilo archiespicopo Alexandrino. Iohannis archiepiscopi Alexandrini ermo in laudem s. Menae*. Rome: Biblioteca Apostolica Vaticana.

———. 1922c. *Bibliothecae Pierpont Morgan codices coptici photographice expressi.* Vol. 38, *Passio s. Leontii Arabis et Publii. Severi Antiochensi sermo in laudem s. Leontii Arabic. Miracula per s. Menam a Deo Patrata.* Rome: Biblioteca Apostolica Vaticana.

———. 1977. *Les Actes des martyrs de l'Égypte tirés des manuscrits coptes de la Bibliothèque Vaticane et du Musée Borgia*, reprint Hildesheim: Georg Olms Verlag. (Original edition, Paris: Leroux, 1886).

Ibn 'Abd al-Zaher, Abu al-Fadl 'Abdallah. 1996. *al-Ruda al-bahiya al-zahira fi khitat al-mu'aziya, al-Qahira.* Edited by A.F. al-Sayed. Cairo: Dar al-'Arabiya li-l-Kitab.

Ibn al-'Assal, al-Mu'taman. 1998. *Majmu' usul al-din wa-masmu' mahsul al-yaqin* (Summa dei principi della religione). Vol. 1, 43. Edited by A. Wadi. SOCM 6. Ed. A. Wadi. Cairo: Franciscan Center of Oriental Studies. 1/13; 43. Translated into Italian as *Summa dei principi della religione* by B. Pirone, vol. 1, 60. SOCM, 1998.

Ibn Duqmaq. 1893. *al-Intisar li-wasita 'aqd al-amsar.* Vol. 4. Cairo: Imprimerie nationale.

Ibn Kabar, Shams al-Ri'asa Abu al-Barakat. 1971. *Misbah al-zulma fi iydah al-khidma.* Cairo: Maktabat al-Karuz.

———. 2001. "Il digiuno e la settimana santa." In *Misbah al-zulma*, edited by A. Wadi, 233–322. SOCC 34. Cairo: Franciscan Centre of Oriental Studies.

———. 2002–2003. "Le preghiere del giorno e della notte." In *Misbah al-zulma*, edited by A. Wadi, 365–456. SOCC 35–36. Cairo: Franciscan Centre of Oriental Studies.

Ibn Taghri Birdi, Gamal al-Din Abi al-Mahassen Youssef al-Atabki. 1992. *al-Nujum al-zahira fi muluk Misr wa-l-Qahira.* Edited by M.H. Shams al-Din. Vol. 4. Lebanon: Dar al-Kutub al-'Ilmiya.

ICOMOS (International Council on Monuments and Sites). 2003. *Principles for the Preservation and Conservation/Restoration of Wall Paintings.* http://www.icomos.org/en/179-articles-en-francais/ressources/charters-and-standards/166-icomos-principles-for-the-preservation-and-conservationrestoration-of-wall-paintings

Ihm, C. 1960. *Die Programme der christlichen Apsismalerei vom vierten Jahrhundert bis zur Mitte des achten Jahrhunderts.* Wiesbaden: Franz Steiner Verlag.

Imam, M.R. 2014. "al-Mukhayam al-armani bi Bor Sa'id 15 September 1915–24 November 1919." *AREK* 49 (September):11–15.

Immerzeel, M. 2012–13. "The Renovation of the Churches of Cairo in the Fatimid and Early Ayyubid Periods According to Abu al-Makarim's *Churches and Monasteries of Egypt.*" In *Eastern Christian Art in Its Late Antique and Islamic Contexts*, vol. 9, 41–42. Louvain: Peeters.

Innemée, K.C. 2015. "Funerary Aspects in the Paintings from the Apollo Monastery at Bawit." In *Christianity and Monasticism in Middle Egypt*, edited by G. Gabra and H.N. Takla, 241–53. Cairo: American University in Cairo Press.

Innemée, K.C., and L. Van Rompay. 2002. "Deir al-Surian (Egypt)." *Hugoye: Journal of Syriac Studies* 5, no. 2: 245–63.

Innemée, K.C., and D. Zielińska. Forthcoming. "The King and the Cross: The Iconography of a Painting in the Throne-hall of Dongola." In *Festschrift for W. Godlewski.*

Isidorus, Bishop. 2002a. *al-Kharida al-nafisa fi tarikh al-kanisa.* Cairo: Maktabat al-Mahabba.

———. 2002b. *al-Kharida al-nafisa.* Part 2. Cairo: al-Mahabba Bookshop.

Iskandar, M.M. 2005. *Tarikh al-masihiya wa-athariha fi-l-khams mudun al-gharbiya.* Vol. 2. 2nd ed. Cairo: Matba'it Dar al-'Allam al-'Arabi.

Iskarus, T. 1910. *Nawabigh al-aqbat wa mashahirihim fi-l-qarn al-tasi' 'ashr.* Vol. 1. Cairo: Matba'at al-Tawfiq.

Isudhurus, Anba. n.d. *Mu'jizat al-anba' abram usquf al-Fayyum.* Cairo: Matba'at al-Shams.

Jacques, J. 1968. "Réflexions sur la portée théologique d'une fresque d'Umm-el-Barakat (Tebtunis)." *BIFAO* 66:139–42, pl. XV.

Jakobson, R. 1960. "Linguistics and Poetics." In *Style in Language*, edited by T.A. Sebeok, 350–77. Cambridge, MA: MIT Press.

Jaritz, F. 1993. *Die arabischen Quellen zum Heiligen Menas.* Heidelberg: Heidelberger Orientverlag.

Jarry, J. 1968. *Hérésies et faction dans l'empire byzantine du IV au VII siècle.* Recherches d'Archéologie, de Philologie et d'Histoire 14. Cairo: IFAO.

Jirjis, M., ed. 1927. *Kitab al-qawanin alladhi jama'ahu al-shaykh al-safi al-'alim Ibn al-'Assal min kutub al-qawanin wa-allafahu fi sanat 955 li-l-shuhada' al-athar.* Cairo: Matba'at al-Shams.

Joannou, P.-P. 1963. *Les Canons des pères grecs.* Vol. 2 of *Fonti: Discipline generale antique (IVe–IXe s.).* Rome: Grottaferrata.

Johnson, D.W. 1980. *A Panegyric on Macarius Bishop of Tkôw Attributed to Dioscorus of Alexandria.* CSCO 415–16. Louvain: Secrétariat du CSCO.

Johnson, L.J. 2009. *Worship in the Early Church: An Anthology of Historical Sources.* Collegeville, MN: Liturgical Press.

Jullien, M. 1891. *L'Égypte: Souvenirs bibliques et chrétiens.* Lille: Desclée de Brouwer.

Justinian. 1877a. Edict, *Corpus Iuris Civilis. Codex Justinianus, II.* Edited by Krüger.

———. 1877b. *Novellae.* Edited by R. Scholl and G. Kroll. Dublin and Zürich, 1972.

Kalvesmaki, J., ed. 2014. "Life of Evagrius Ponticus." *Guide to Evagrius Ponticus.* http://evagriusponticus.net/life.htm

Kasser, R., ed. 1967. *Kellia 1965: Topographie générale, mensurations et fouilles aux Qouçoûr 'Isâ et aux Qouçoûr el-'Abîd, mensurations aux Qouçoûr el-'Izeila.* Recherches suisses d'archéologie copte 1. Geneva: Librairie de l'Université.

Kasser, R. 1969. "Exploration dans le désert Occidental: Qouçour Hégeila et Qouçour Ereima." *Kêmi* 19:103–10.

———, ed. 1972. *Kellia: Topographie.* Recherches suisses d'archéologie copte 2. Geneva: Librairie de l'Université.

Kasser, R. 1975. "L'idiome de Bachmour." *BIFAO* 75:401–27.

———. 1983. *Survey archéologique des Kellia (Basse-Égypte): Rapport de la campagne 1981.* Louvain: Peeters.

———. 1991. "Bashmuric." *CE* 8:47–48.

———, ed. 1994. *Explorations aux Qouçoûr er-Roubâ'îyât: Rapport des campagnes 1982 et 1983.* Louvain: Peeters.

Kasser, R. 1996. "La 'Prière de Jésus' kelliote réexaminée en quelques points." *OCP* 62:407–10.

———, ed. 1999. *Explorations aux Qouçour el-Izeila lors des campagnes 1981, 1982, 1984, 1985, 1986, 1989 et 1990.* Mission suisse d'archéologie copte de l'Université de Genève EK 8184 III. Louvain: Peeters.

———. 2003. *Explorations aux Qouçoûr Hégeila et 'Éreima lors des campagnes 1987, 1988 et 1989.* Mission suisse d'archéologie copte de l'Université de Genève EK 8184 IV. Louvain: Peeters.

Kasser, R., S. Favre, and D. Weidmann. 1972. *Kellia: topographie.* Recherches suisses d'archéologie copte 2. Geneva: Georg.

Kastholm, O.T. 2011. "Six Ships Graffiti from Himmelev Church." *Maritime Archaeology Newsletter from Denmark* 26:28–31.

Katos, D.S. 2011. *Palladius of Helenopolis: The Origenist Advocate.* Oxford: Oxford University Press.

Kaufmann, C.M. 1908. *La découverte des sanctuaires de saint Ménas.* Translated from German by A. Hartmann. Alexandria: Société des publications égyptiennes.

———. 1910a. *Die Menasstadt und das Nationalheiligtum der altchristlichen Ägypten in der westalexandrinischen Wüste: Ausgrabungen der Frankfurter Expedition am Karm Abu Mina 1905–1907.* Leipzig: Verlag von Karl W. Hiersemann.

———. 1910b. *Zur Ikonographie der Menas-ampullen; mit besonderer Berücksichtigung der Funde in der Menastadt nebst einem einführenden Kapitel über die neuentdeckten Nubischen und Ethiopischen Menastexte.* Cairo: F. Diemer, Finck & Baylaender, Succ.

———. 1920. "Ikon mit der Darstellung eines Menaswunders aus der Koptischen Kirche der Mari Mina in Kairo." In *Ehrengabe deutscher Wissenschaft (Festschrift für Hans Georg zu Sachsen)*, edited by F. Fessler. Freiburg im Breisgau: Herder.

Keane, W. 2004. "Language and Religion." In *A Companion to Linguistic Anthropology*, edited by A. Duranti, 431–48. Malden, MA: Blackwell.

Keenan, J.G. 2003. "Deserted Villages: From the Ancient to the Medieval Fayyum." *BASP* 40:119–39.

Kees, H. 1930. "Marea, Mareotis." In *Real Encyklopädie der classischen Altertumswissenschaft*, edited by A. de Cosson, vol. 14, no. 2, 1676–78. London.

Kelly, C. 2004. *Ruling the Later Roman Empire.* Cambridge, MA: Harvard University Press.

Keunen, B. 2011. *Time and Imagination: Chronotopes in Western Narrative Culture.* Evanston, IL: Northwestern University Press.

Khalil, S. 1991. "Victor Stratelates." *CE* 7:2305–2308.

el-Khashab, Abd el-Mohsen. 1949. *Ptolemaic and Roman Baths of Kom el Ahmar.* Annales du Service des Antiquités de l'Égypte, suppl. 10. Cairo: IFAO.

Khatchatrian, A. 1962. *Les baptistères paléochrétiens.* Paris: Klincksieck, École pratique des Hautes Études.

Khater, A. 1961–62. "La translation des reliques de Saint Ménas à son église du Caire." *BSAC* 16:161–81.

Khater, A., and O.H.E. Khs-Burmester, eds. and trans. 1974. *History of the Patriarchs of the Egyptian Church.* Vol. 4, parts 1–2. Textes et Documents 14–15. Cairo: SAC.

El-Khawaga, D. 1991. "Le renouveau copte actuel: raisons d'émergence et mode de fonctionnement." In *Modernisation et nouvelles formes de mobilisation sociale: Égypte–Brésil (1970–1989)*, edited by I. Farag, 115–34. Cairo: Centre d'Études et de Documentation Économique et Juridique (CEDEJ).

Khouzam, A.F., ed. 2002. *La langue égyptienne au moyen âge: Le manuscrit copte 44 de Paris de la Bibliothèque Nationale de France*, vol. 1. Paris: L'Harmattan.

King, A. 2007. *Rites of Eastern Christendom*. Piscataway, NJ: Gorgias Press.

Kircher, A., ed. and trans. 1643. *Lingua aegyptiaca restitua*. Roma: apud Ludovicum Grignanum.

Kiss, Z. 1989. *Les ampoules de Saint Ménas*. Warsaw: PWN–Éditions scientifiques de Pologne.

Kitab al-ibsalmudiya al-muqaddasa al-sanawiya: Hasab tartib aba' al-kanisa al-qibtiya al-urthudhuksiya. n.d. Cairo: n.p.

Kitab al-sinaksar al-jami' li-akhbar al-anbiya' wa-l-rusul wa-l-shuhada' wa-l-qiddisin al-mustam'al fi kana'is al-kiraza al-marqusiya fi-ayyam wa ahad al-sana al-tutiya. 1972. 2 vols. 3rd ed. Cairo: Maktabat al-Mahabba.

Kosack, W. 1971. *Historisches Kartenwerk Ägyptens*. Bonn: Rudolf Habelt.

Kraatz, W. 1904. *Koptische Akten zum Ephesinischen Konzil vom Jahre 431*. Leipzig: Hinrichs.

Krause, M. 1990. "Karm Abu Mena." In *Reallexikon zur byzantinischen Kunst*, edited by K. Wessel, vol. 3, cols. 1116–58. Stuttgart: Anton Hiersemann.

———. 1991a. "Menas the Miracle Maker, Saint." *CE* 5:1589–90.

———. 1991b. "Papyrus Discoveries." *CE* 6:1898a–1900b.

Kuhn, M. 2011. *Koptische liturgische Melodien: die Relation zwischen Text und Musik in der koptischen Psalmodia*. Louvain: Peeters.

al-Laali' al-saniya fi-l-mayamir wa-l-'aja'ib al-maryamiya. 1936. Edited by N. Sarkis. 1st ed. Cairo.

Labib, S. 1991a. "Badr al-Jamali." *CE* 2:324–26.

———. 1991b. "Christodoulus." *CE* 2:545.

———. 1991c. "Cosmas II." *CE* 2:636b–637b.

———. 1991d. "Cyril II." *CE* 3:675–77.

———. 1991e. "Cyril III." *CE* 3:677a–677b.

———. 1991f. "John V." *CE* 4:1340a–1341a.

———. 1991g. "Mina I." *CE* 5:1631–32.

———. 1991h. "Mina II." *CE* 5:1632–33.

Langlois, M. 1926. *La Bibliothèque de l'Institut Catholique de Paris*. Vol. 3, *Séries spéciales*. Paris: Institut Catholique.

Lantschoot, A. van. 1931. "Fragment copte d'un panégyrique de saint Jean Baptiste." *Le Muséon* 44:235–54.

———. 1934. "Allocution de Timothée d'Alexandrie prononcée à l'occasion de la dédicace de l'église de Pachôme à Pboou." *Museon* 47:13–56.

———. 1946. "Fragments coptes d'une homélie de Jean de Parallos contre les livres hérétiques." *Miscellanea Giovanni Mercati* 1, offprint with own pagination. Studi e Testi 121, 1–31, 296–326. Vatican City: Biblioteca Apostolica Vaticana.

———. 1947. "Un texte palimpseste de Vat. copte 65." *Le Muséon* 60:261–68.

———, ed. and trans. 1948. *Un précurseur d'Athanase Kircher: Thomas Obicini et la scala Vat. copte 71*. Bibliothèque du Muséon 22. Louvain: Institut Orientaliste.

———. 1957. *Les "Questions de Théodore": Texte sahidique, recensions arabes et éthiopienne*. Studi e Testi 192. Vatican City: Biblioteca Apostolica Vaticana.

Lantschoot, A. van. 1958. "Les Questions-Réponses du ms. Vat. arabe 155." *Le Muséon* 71:279–98.

Latour, B. 2005. *Reassembling the Social: An Introduction to Actor-Network Theory*. Oxford: Oxford University Press.

Layton, B. 1987. *Catalogue of Coptic Literary Manuscripts in the British Library Acquired since the Year 1906*. London: British Library.

———. 2014. *The Canons of the Fathers: Monastic Rules of Shenoute*. Oxford: Oxford University Press.

Layton, R.A. 2004. *Didymus the Blind and His Circle in Late-Antique Alexandria: Virtue and Narrative in Biblical Scholarship*. Urbana: University of Illinois Press.

Leclerq, H. 1920. "Dekhela." In *Dictionnaire d'archéologie chrétienne et de liturgie*, edited by F. Cabrol and H. Leclerq, vol. 5, part 1, col. 508–14. Paris: Librarie Letouzey et Ane.

Leemans, J. 2005. "Introduction." In *More than a Memory: The Discourse of Martyrdom and the Construction of Christian Identity in the History of Christianity*, edited by J. Leemans, xi–xvi. Louvain: Peeters.

Lefebvre, G. 1907. *Recueil des inscriptions grecques-chrétiennes d'Égypte*. Cairo: Imprimerie de l'IFAO.

Lefort, L.Th. 1925. *S. Pachomii vita bohairice scripta*. CSCO 89. Paris: E typographeo reipublicae; reprint Louvain: Secrétariat du CSCO, 1965.

———. 1939. "Les premiers monastères pachômiens: Exploration topographique." *Muséon* 52:379–407.

———. 1942. *Les Vies coptes de Saint Pachôme et de ses premiers successeurs*. Bibliothèque du Muséon 16. Louvain: Institut Orientaliste.

Lehmann, M. 2013. "Skylines, Bridges and Mud in the Delta and Elsewhere: A Comparison of Egyptian and Yemeni Tower Houses." In *Delta Survey Workshop 22–23 March 2013, British Council, Cairo*. http://ees.ac.uk/rersearch/Delta_Workshop.html

Leipoldt, I. 1906. *Sinuthii Archimandritae vite et opera omnia*. CSCO, Scriptores Coptici 2, 18§16. Paris: Typographeo Reipublicae.

el-Leithy, T. 2005. "Coptic Culture and Conversion in Medieval Cairo: 1293–1524 A.D." PhD diss., Princeton University.

———. 2006. "Sufis, Copts, and the Politics of Piety: Moral Regulation in Fourteenth-century Upper Egypt." In *Le développement du soufisme en Égypte à l'époque mamelouke*, edited by R. McGregor and A. Sabra, 75–119. Cairo: IFAO.

Lembke, K. 2014. "City of the Dead: The Necropolis of Tuna el-Gebel during the Roman Period." In *Egypt in the First Millennium AD: Perspectives from New Fieldwork*, edited by E. O'Connell. Louvain: Peeters.

Leroy, J. 1974. *Les manuscrits coptes et copto-arabes illustrés*. Paris: Paul Geuthner.

———. 1982. *Les peintures des couvents du Ouadi Natroun*. Cairo: Imprimerie de l'IFAO.

Leroy, L. 1908. "Les couvents des chrétiens, traduction de l'arabe d'al-Makrisi." *Revue de l'Orient Chrétien* 13:33–46, 192–204.

Lichocka, B. 2008. "The Early Byzantine Coins." In *Byzantine Marea: Excavations in 2000–2003 and 2006, Marea*, edited by H. Szymańska and K. Babraj, vol. 1, 145–52, figs. 50–53. Biblioteka Muzeum Archeologicznego w Krakowie 4. Krakow: Muzeum Archeologiczne w Krakowie.

Life and Miracles of Anba Hadid. Wadi al-Natrun, Dayr al-Suryan, MS *mayamir* 306 (eighteenth century), fols. 1a–46b.

Littmann, E. 1967. "Die Sâqiya." *ZÄSA* 76:45–54.

López, A.G. 2013. *Shenoute of Atripe and the Uses of Poverty: Rural Patronage, Religious Conflict, and Monasticism in Late Antique Egypt.* Transformation of the Classical Heritage 50. Berkeley: University of California Press.

Lucchesi, E. 1981. "Chénouté a-t-il écrit en grec?" In *Mélanges Antoine Guillaumont: Contributions à l'étude des christianismes orientaux*, edited by R.-G. Coquin, 201–10. Geneva: P. Cramer.

———. 2003. "L'homélie de nativitate de Damien d'Alexandrie: un témoin copte du Monastère Blanc." *Aegyptus* 83:1–2, 229–32.

Luisier, Ph. 2007. "Les années de l'indiction dans les inscriptions des Kellia." *ZPE* 159:217–22.

Lyster, W. 1999. *Monastery of St. Paul.* Cairo: Palm Press.

MacCoull, L.S.B. 1996. "A Note on the Career of Gabriel III, Scribe and Patriarch of Alexandria." *Arabica* 43:357–60.

Macfarlane, R.T. 2014. "Re-Collection of Tourah Codex V, Didymos, and Its Codicology." http://papyrology.blogspot.com/2014/11/elsewhere-at-sbl.html

Macomber, W.F. 1995. *Final Inventory of the Microfilmed MSS of the Coptic Museum, Old Cairo, Egypt.* 4 vols. Provo, UT: Brigham Young University. https://archive.org/details/MacomberCopticMuseum.I.BYURollsA120

———. 1997. *Inventory of the Microfilmed Manuscripts of the Coptic Orthodox Patriarchate, al-Azbakiyah, Cairo.* 2 vols. Provo, UT: Brigham Young University. https://archive.org/details/MacomberCopticOrthodoxPatriarchate.IBYUMicrofilms

Mahe, J.P. 1980. "Les Arméniens et l'Égypte." *Le Monde Copte* 9:23–27.

Mai, A. 1831. *Scriptorum veterum nova collectio.* Vol. 4. Rome: Bibliotheca Vaticanae Praefecto.

Majcherek, G. 2008. "The Pottery Assemblage from the Baths and Saqiyah." In *Byzantine Marea: Excavations in 2000–2003 and 2006, Marea*, edited by H. Szymańska and K. Babraj, vol. 1, 105–27. Biblioteka Muzeum Archeologicznego w Krakowie 4. Krakow: Muzeum Archeologiczne w Krakowie.

Malarczyk, D. 2008. "Ummayad Coins." In *Byzantine Marea: Excavations in 2000–2003 and 2006, Marea*, edited by H. Szymańska and K. Babraj, vol. 1, 153–54, figs. 53–54. Biblioteka Muzeum Archeologicznego w Krakowie 4. Krakow: Muzeum Archeologiczne w Krakowie.

Malaspina, E. 1992. "John Talaias." In *Encyclopedia of the Early Church*, edited by A. Di Berardino, translated by A. Walford. 2 vols. Vol. 1, 447. New York: Oxford University Press.

Malaty, T.Y. 1993. *Introduction to the Coptic Church*. Alexandria: St. George's Coptic Orthodox Church.

———. 1996. *The Dictionary of the Church Fathers and Its Saints*. Cairo: Anba Reweis Printing House.

Mango, C., ed. 1972. *The Art of the Byzantine Empire 312–1453: Sources and Documents*. Englewood Cliffs, NJ: Prentice-Hall.

Mansi, Y. 1983. *The History of the Coptic Church*. Cairo: al-Mahaba Bookshop.

Manteuffel, J. 1939. *Tell Edfou. Fouilles franco-polonaise 1939: Les papyrus et les ostraca grecs* (= P. Edfou Greek 8 [140153 MN/ 1549 UW]). Cairo.

al-Maqari, A. 2012. *Fihris kitabat aba' kanisat al-Iskandariya, al-kitabat al-'arabiya*. Vol. 1. Cairo: Matba'at Nubar.

al-Maqari, F., and Y. Manqaryus, eds. 1941. *Tuhfat al-amjad fi tafsir fusul al-ahad wa-l-a'yad*. Cairo: Matba'at al-Qiddis Makaryus.

al-Maqrizi, Taqi al-Din Ahmad. 1835. *Kitab al-mawa'iz wa-l-i'tibar bi dhikr al-khitat wa-l-athar*. Vols. 1 and 2. Bulaq ed. Cairo: Dar al-Fikr al-'Arabi.

———. 1853. *al-Mawa'iz wa-l-i'tibar fi dhikr al-khitat wa-l-athar*. Vol. 2. Cairo: Édition Bulaq.

———. 1996. *Itti'az al-hunafa bi akhbar al-a'ima al-fatimiyyin al-khulafa'*. Edited by M.H.M. Ahmed. Vol. 3. Cairo: al-Majlis al-'Ala li-l-Shu'un al-Islamiya.

———. 1998a. *al-Khutat al-maqriziya*. Part 3. Cairo: Madbuly Bookshop.

———. 1998b. *Tarikh al-aqbat al-ma'ruf bi l-qawl al-Ibrizi li-l-'allama al-Maqrizi*. Edited by A. Diyab. Cairo: Dar al-Fadila.

———. n.d. *al-Khitat*. Vol. 4, 376. Cairo: Maktabat al-Adab.

Maraval, P. 1985. *Lieux saints et pèlerinages d'Orient: Histoire et géographie des origines à la conquête arabe*. Paris: Cerf.

Mar Mina Monastery. 2002. *The Holy Family in Egypt*. King Maryut: Saint Minas Monastery Press.

———. 2003. *The Great Saint Mena the Miraculous, the Most Famous Egyptian Martyr*. King Maryut: Saint Minas Monastery Press.

Marrou, H. 1939. "86–89. Lettres au supérieur du Monastère de la pénitence." In *Les papyrus Fouad I: Nos 1–89*, edited by A. Bataille et al., 175–202. Publications de la Société Fouad I de Papyrologie Textes et Documents 3. Cairo: IFAO.

Martin, M. 1971. *La laure de Dêr al Dîk à Antinoé*. Cairo: IFAO.

———. 1997. "Le Delta chrétien à la fin du XIIs." *OCP* 63:181–99.

Martin, M., C. Nispen, and F. Sidarous. 1990. "Les nouveaux courants dans la communauté copte orthodoxe." *Proche Orient Chrétien* 10:245–57.

Martindale, J.R., ed. 1980. *The Prosopography of the Later Roman Empire*. Vol. 2. Cambridge, UK: Cambridge University Press.

Maspero, G. 1915. *Guide du Visiteur au Musée du Caire*. Cairo: IFAO.

Maspero, J. 1913. "Rapport sur les fouilles entreprises à Baouît." *Comptes Rendus des Séances de l'Académie des Inscriptions et Belles-Lettres* 57:287–301.

Maspero, J., and E. Drioton. 1931. *Fouilles Exécutées à Baouît par Jean Maspero*. Cairo: IFAO.

Maspero, J., and G. Wiet. 1919. *Matériaux pour servir à la géographie de l'Égypte*. Cairo: Imprimerie de l'IFAO.

al-Masri, E.H. 1998. *The Story of the Coptic Church.* Book 2. Alexandria: Church of St. George, Sporting.
el-Masri, I. 1982. *The Story of the Copts: The True Story of Christianity in Egypt.* Book 2. Newberry Springs, CA: St. Anthony Monastery.
Mathews, T.F. 1971. *The Early Churches of Constantinople: Architecture and Liturgy.* University Park and London: Pennsylvania State University Press.
Mattaos, Bishop. 1985. *al-Difnar.* Beni Suef: Lagnat al-Tahrir wa-l-Nashr.
Matta'us al-Suryani. 2005. *al-Qiddis Anba Hadid al-Qiss wa tilmidhuhu al-Qiddis Yuhanna al-Rabban.* Wadi al-Natrun: Dayr al-Suryan.
McEnerney, J.I., trans. 1987. *St. Cyril of Alexandria: Letters 51–110.* Washington, DC: Catholic University of America.
———. 2010a. *Saint Cyril of Alexandria: Letters 1–50.* The Fathers of the Church 76. Washington: Catholic University of America Press.
———. 2010b. *Saint Cyril of Alexandria: Letters 51–110.* The Fathers of the Church 77. Washington: Catholic University of America Press.
McGuckin, J. 2004. *Saint Cyril of Alexandria and the Christological Controversy: Its History, Theology, and Texts.* Crestwood, NY: St. Vladimir's Seminary Press.
Megally, M. 1991. "Bashmuric Revolts." *CE* 2:349–51.
Meinardus, O.F.A. 1965. *Christian Egypt, Ancient and Modern.* Cairo: Cahiers d'histoire égyptienne.
———. 1970. *Christian Egypt: Faith and Life.* Cairo: American University in Cairo Press.
———. 1977. *Christian Egypt, Ancient and Modern.* 2nd rev. ed. Cairo: American University in Cairo Press.
———. 1979. "The Relics of Saint John the Baptist and the Prophet Elisha: An Examination of the Claims of Their Recent Invention in Egypt." In *Coptic Studies Presented to Mirrit B. Ghali,* edited by L. MacCoull, 26–63. Cairo: Society for Coptic Archaeology.
———. 1992a. *The Holy Family in Egypt.* 2nd rev. ed. Cairo: American University in Cairo Press.
———. 1992b. *Monks and Monasteries of the Egyptian Deserts.* Cairo: American University in Cairo Press.
———. 1999. *Two Thousand Years of Coptic Christianity.* Cairo: American University in Cairo Press.
———. 2002a. *Coptic Saints and Pilgrimages.* Cairo: American University in Cairo Press.
———. 2002b. *Monks and Monasteries of the Egyptian Deserts.* 4th ed. Cairo: American University in Cairo Press.
———. 2006. *Christians in Egypt: Orthodox, Catholic, and Protestant Communities, Past and Present.* Cairo: American University in Cairo Press.
Ménassa, L., and P. Laferrière. 1974. *La Saqia: Technique et vocabulaire de la roue à eau égyptienne.* Bibliothèque d'Étude. IFAO 67. Cairo: IFAO.
Menze, V. 2008. *Justinian and the Making of the Syriac Orthodox Church.* Oxford: Oxford University Press.
Merkle, S. 1932. *Carl Maria Kaufmann.* Cologne.

Messiha, H. 1975. "The Monastery (Temple) of Abu Sir and the Monastery of al-Zuggag." *Bulletin of the Institute of Coptic Studies* 1975:63–70.

Metzger, C. 1981. *Les ampoules à eulogie du Musée du Louvre.* Paris: Éditions de la Réunion des musées nationaux.

Meyer, B. 1992. "Les femmes et les bains publics dans l'Égypte grecque, romaine et byzantine." *Proceedings of the XIXth International Congress of Papyrology, Cairo 1989*, edited by A.H.S. el-Mosalamy, 51–60. Cairo: Ain Shams University.

Meyer, R.T. 1950. *The Life of Saint Antony.* Westminster, MD: Newman Press.

———. 1964. *Palladius: The Lausiac History.* Ancient Christian Writers 34. New York: Paulist Press.

Miedema, R. 1913. *De heilige Menas.* Rotterdam: W.J. van Hengel.

Mikhail, M.S.A. 2012. "The Coptic Tradition." In *The Orthodox Christian World*, edited by A. Casiday, 112. New York: Routledge.

———. 2014a. *From Byzantine to Islamic Egypt: Religion, Identity, and Politics after the Arab Conquest.* London and New York: I.B. Tauris.

———. 2014b. *From Christian Egypt to Islamic Egypt: Religion, Identity, and Politics after the Arab Conquest.* Cairo: American University in Cairo Press.

Mirecki, P.A., and J.D. BeDuhn, eds. 2001. *The Light and the Darkness: Studies in Manichaeism and Its World.* Leiden: Brill.

Moawad, S., ed. 2014a. *Die arabische Übersetzung der vier Evangelien (1253)*, by al-As'ad Abu al-Farag Hibatallah ibn al-'Assal. Cairo: Alexandria School.

Moawad, S. 2014b. "Coptic Historiography." In *Coptic Civilization: Two Thousand Years of Christianity in Egypt*, edited by G. Gabra, 11–18. Cairo: American University in Cairo Press.

Moftah, R., and M. Roy. 1991. "Music, Coptic." *CE* 6:1715a–1747b.

Mohamed, H.I. 2005. *Mariyut wa Aba Mina.* Cairo.

Mohrmann, C., G. Johannes, M. Bartelink, P. Citati, S. Lilla, and Evagrius. 1974. *Vita di Antonio.* Milan: A. Mondadori: Fondazione Lorenzo Valla.

Monneret de Villard, U. 1923. "La fondazione del Deyr el-Abiad." *Aegyptus* 4:156–62.

Montet, P. 1957. *Géographie de l'Égypte ancienne.* Vol. 1. Paris: C. Klincksieck.

Moschos, J., and N.H. Baynes. 1947. "The Pratum Spirituale." *OCP* 13:404–14.

Motzki, H. 1991a. "Ibrahim al-Jawhari." *CE* 4:1274.

———. 1991b. "Jirjis al-Jawhari." *CE* 4:1332.

MSAC. 1983. *Survey archéologique des Kellia (Basse-Égypte): Rapport de la campagne 1981.* Mission suisse d'archéologie copte de l'Université de Genève 1. Louvain: Peeters.

———. 1984. *Le site monastique des Kellia (Basse-Égypte): Recherches des années 1981–1983.* Mission suisse d'archéologie copte de l'Université de Genève EK 8184. Louvain: Peeters.

———. 1989. *Recherches archéologiques sur le site monastique copte des Kellia en Basse Égypte: Campagne de septembre et octobre 1988.* Mission suisse d'archéologie copte de l'Université de Genève. Louvain: Peeters.

Mubarak, 'Ali. 1887. *al-Khitat al-tawfiqiya al-gadida li-Misr wa-l-Qahira wa muduniha wa biladiha al-qadima wa-l-shahira.* 1st ed. Cairo: al-Matba'a al-Kubra al-Amiriya.

———. 1987. *al-Khitat al-tawfiqiya al-gadida li-Misr wa-l-Qahira wa muduniha wa biladiha al-qadima wa-l-shahira.* Vol. 6. 2nd ed. Cairo: al-Hay'a al-Masriya al-'Amma li-l-Kitab.

Müller, C.D.G. 1954a. *Die alte koptische Predigt: Versuch eines Überblicks.* Heidelberg: Darmstadt.

———. 1954b. "Einige Bemerkungen zur Ars Predicandi der alten koptischen Kirche." *Le Muséon* 67:231–70.

———. 1959. *Die Engellehre der koptischen Kirche: Untersuchungen zur Geschichte der christlichen Frömmigkeit in Ägypten.* Wiesbaden: Harrassowitz.

———. 1964. "Die koptische Kirche zwischen Chalkedon und den Arabereinmarsch." *Zeitschrift für Kirchengeschichte* 75:271–308.

———. 1970. "Aufbau und Entwicklung der koptischen Kirche nach Chalkedon, 451." *Kyrios* 10:202–10.

———. 1986. "Damián, Papst und Patriarch von Alexandrien." *Oriens Christianus* 70:118–42.

———. 1991a. "John III, the Merciful." *CE* 4:1337a–1338b.

———. 1991b. "John of Parallos, Saint." *CE* 5:1367–68.

Müller, C., et al., eds. 2013–14. *Body—Language—Communication: An International Handbook on Multimodality in Human Interaction.* Vols. 1–2. Berlin and Boston: De Gruyter Mouton.

Müller-Wiener, W. 1967. "Siedlungsformen in der Mareotis: archäologischer Anzeiger." *Jahrbuch des Deutschen archäologischen Instituts* 82, no. 2: 103–17.

Munier, H., ed. 1930. *La scala copte 44 de la Bibliothèque Nationale de Paris.* Bibliothèque d'Études Coptes 2. Cairo: SAC.

Munier, H. 1943a. *Recueil des listes épiscopales de l'Église copte.* Cairo: IFAO.

———. 1943b. *Recueil des listes épiscopales de l'Église copte.* Textes et Documents 2. Cairo: SAC.

Muscat, J. 2000. "The Tarxien Ship Graffiti Revisited." *Melita Historica* 13:49–57.

Muyser, J. 1944. "Contribution à l'étude des listes épiscopales de l'Église copte." *BSAC* 10:115–76.

Myers-Scotton, C. 2006. *Multiple Voices: An Introduction to Bilingualism.* Malden, MA: Blackwell.

Myśliwiec, K. 2000. "Rescue Excavations." In *Tell Atrib 1985–1995, I,* edited by K. Myśliwiec and Z. Sztetyłło, 9–49. Warsaw: Neriton.

Nakhla, K.S. 1943. *The History and Tables of the Patriarchs of the See of Alexandria.* Cairo: Committee of Coptic History.

———. 1951a. *Silsilat tarikh al-babawat batarikat al-kursi al-iskandari.* Vol. 1, *al-Baba Kyrilus al-Thalith.* Wadi al-Natrun: Dayr al-Suryan (reprint 2001).

———. 1951b. *Silsilat tarikh al-babawat batarikat al-kursi al-iskandari.* Vol. 1. 2nd ed., 2002. Wadi al-Natrun, Dayr al-Suryan.

———. 1952. *Silsilat tarikh al-babawat batarikat al-kursi al-iskandari.* Wadi al-Natrun: Dayr al-Suryan (reprint 2001).

———. 2011. *Silsilat tarikh al-batarika al-kursi al-iskandari.* Part 2. 3rd printing. Wadi al-Natrun: Dayr al-Suryan

Nicoll, A. 1821. *Bibliothecae Bodleianae codicum manuscriptorum orientalium catalogi.* Vol. 2, part 1, *Arabicos complectens.* Oxford: Clarendon Press.

Nigosian, S. 1991. "Armenians and the Copts." *CE* 1:234–35.

Nussbaum, O. 1961. "Zum Problem der runden und sigmaförmigen Altarplatten." *Jahrbuch für Antike und Christentum* 4:18–43.

———. 1965. *Der Standort des Liturgen am christlichen Altar vor dem Jahre 1000: Eine archäologische und liturgiegeschichtliche Untersuchung.* Bonn: Peter Hanstein Verlag.

O'Leary, D. 1926–30. *The Difnar (Antiphonarium) of the Coptic Church.* 3 vols. London: Luzac & Co.

———. 1937a. *The Saints of Egypt.* London: Society for Promoting Christian Knowledge.

———. 1937b. *The Saints of Egypt.* New York: Macmillan.

Oleson, J.P. 2000. "Water-lifting." In *Handbook of Ancient Water Technology*, edited by Ö. Wikander, 183–215. Leiden, Boston, and Cologne: Brill.

Orlandi, T. 1968. *Testi copti: 1. Encomio di Atanasio. 2. Vita di Atanasio.* Testi e documenti per lo studio dell'antichità 21. Milan: Istituto Editoriale Cisalpino.

———. 1968–70. *Storia della Chiesa di Alessandria.* 2 vols. Testi e documenti per lo studio dell'antichità 17 and 31. Milan: Istituto Editorale Cisalpino.

———. 1970a. *Elementi di lingua e letteratura copta: corso di lezioni universitarie.* Milan: La Goliardica.

———. 1970b. *Storia della Chiesa di Alessandria.* Testi e documenti 18. Milan: Cisalpino.

———. 1981. *Omelie copte: scelte e tradotte, con una introduzione sulla letteratura copta.* Turin: Società Editrice Internazionale.

———. 1991. "Cycles." *CE* 3:666–68.

———. 2013. "A Terminology for the Identification of Coptic Literary Documents." *JCS* 15:87–94.

———. 2014. "John of Parallos." In *Encyclopedia of Ancient Christianity*, edited by A. Di Berardino, 2:448a. Downers Grove, IL: IVP Academic.

Ostrogorsky, G. 1969. *History of the Byzantine State.* Translated by J. Hussey. New Brunswick, NJ: Rutgers University Press.

Papaconstantinou, A. 2001. *Le culte des saints en Égypte des Byzantins aux Abbassides: l'apport des inscriptions et des papyrus grecs et coptes.* Paris: CNRS Éditions.

———. 2006. "Historiography, Hagiography, and the Making of the Coptic 'Church of the Martyrs' in Early Islamic Egypt." *Dumbarton Oaks Papers* 60:65–86.

Partrick, T.H. 1996. *Traditional Egyptian Christianity: A History of the Coptic Orthodox Church.* Greensboro, NC: Fisher Press.

Patterson, P.A. 2012. *Visions of Christ: The Anthropomorphite Controversy of 399* CE. STAC 68. Tübingen: Mohr Siebeck.

Paulus di Tamma. 1988. *Paolo di Tamma: opere.* Rome: CIM.

Pearson, B., and T. Vivian. 1993. *Two Coptic Homilies Attributed to Saint Peter of Alexandria: On Riches, On the Epiphany.* Rome: CIM.

Peeters, P., trans. 1914. *Évangiles apocryphes.* Vol. 2. Paris: Picard.

Percival, H. 1892. *The Seven Ecumenical Councils*. Edinburgh: T&T Clark. http://www.ccel.org/ccel/schaff/npnf214.titlepage.html

Perry, B.E. 1964. *Secundus the Silent Philosopher*. Philological Monographs 22. Ithaca, NY: American Philological Association.

Perry, P. 2003. *Jesus in Egypt: Discovering the Secrets of Christ's Childhood Years*. New York: Ballantine Books.

Piccirillo, M. 1994. "Alcuni oggetti liturgici inediti del Museo della Flagellazione a Gerusaleme." In *Historiam pictura refert: Miscellanea in onore di Padre Alejandro Recio Veganzones O.F.M.*, 451–70. Studi di antichità cristiana 51. Rome and Vatican City: Pontificio Istituto di Archeologia Cristiana.

Piccirillo, M., and E. Alliata. 1998. *Mount Nebo: New Archaeological Excavations 1967–1997*. Jerusalem: Franciscan Printing Press.

Poggi, D. 2006. "Analyses." Report submitted to ARCE, July 24, 2006. Unpublished.

Price, R., and M. Gaddi. 2005. *The Acts of the Council of Chalcedon*. 3 vols. Translated Texts for Historians 45. Liverpool: Liverpool University Press.

Prinzivalli, E. 1987. *Didimo il Cieco e L'interpretazione dei Salmi*. L'Aquila and Rome: Japadre Editore.

Qanawati, G.Sh. 1992. *al-Masihiya wa-l-hadara al-'arabiya*. Cairo: Dar al-Thaqafa.

Quatremère, É. 1808. *Recherches critiques et historiques sur la langue et la littérature de l'Égypte*. Paris: Imprimerie Impériale.

Quibell, J.E. 1908. *Excavations at Saqqara (1906–1907)*. Cairo: IFAO.

———. 1909. *Excavations at Saqqara (1907–1908)*. Cairo: IFAO.

———. 1912. *Excavations at Saqqara (1908–1909, 1909–1910): The Monastery of Apa Jeremias*. Cairo: IFAO.

Ramsey, B. 1997. *John Cassian: The Conferences*. Ancient Christian Writers 57. New York: Paulist Press.

Ramzi, M. 1953–68. *al-Qamus al-jughrafi li-l-bilad al-misriya min 'ahd qudama' al-misriyin ila sanat 1945*. 6 vols. Cairo: Matba'at Dar al-Kutub al-Misriyia.

———. 1960. *al-Qamus al-jughrafi li-l-bilad al-misriya min 'ahd qudama' al-misriyin ila sanat 1945*. 2nd ed. Parts 1 and 2, vol. 2. Cairo: Matba'at Dar al-Kutub al-Misriya.

———. 1994. *The Geographical Dictionary*. Section 2, part 3. Cairo: General Egyptian Book Authority.

Rassart-Debergh, M. 1981a. "La décoration picturale du monastère de Saqqara: Essai de reconstitution." In *Acta ad Archaeologiam et Artium Historiam Pertinentia* 9, edited by H. Torp, J.R. Brandt, and L.H. Monssen, 9–124 and pls. I–XXVIII. Rome: Institutum Romanum Norvegiae, Giorgio Bretschneider.

———. 1981b. "Quelques remarques iconographiques sur la peinture chrétienne à Saqqara." In *Acta ad Archaeologiam et Artium Historiam Pertinentia* 9, edited by H. Torp, J.R. Brandt, and L.H. Monssen, 207–20. Rome: Institutum Romanum Norvegiae, Giorgio Bretschneider.

———. 1986. "Peintures des Kellia." In *Le site monastique copte des Kellia: Actes du colloque de Genève 13–15 août 1984*, edited by Y. Mottier and N. Bosson. Geneva: MSAC.

———. 1989. "Les peintures." In *Le site monastique copte des Kellia: Sources historiques et exploration archéologique, Actes du colloque de Genève, 13–15 août 1984*, edited by Y. Mottier and N. Bosson, 57–77. Geneva : Éditions du Tricorne.

———. 1991. "Kellia." *CE* 4:1396b–1410a.

———. 1992. "Quelques bateaux coptes et leur signification." In *BSAC* 31:55–75.

———. 2003. "Les décors." In *Kellia, l'ermitage copte QR 195*, edited by P. Ballet et al., 331–522. Cairo: IFAO.

Rassart-Debergh, M., and J. Debergh. 1981. "À propos de trois peintures de Saqqara." In *Acta ad Archaeologiam et Artium Historiam Pertinentia* 9, edited by H. Torp, J.T. Brandt, and L.H. Monssen, 187–205 and pls. I–II. Rome: Institutum Romanum Norvegiae, Giorgio Bretschneider.

Regnault, L. 1990. *La vie quotidienne des Pères du Désert en Égypte au IVe siècle*. Paris: Hachette.

Remondon, R. 1971. "Le monastère alexandrin de la Métanoia était-il bénéficiaire du fisc ou à son service?" In *Studi in Onore di Edoardo Volterra*, vol. 5, 769–81. Milan: Giuffrè.

René, M. 2014. "Contemporary Coptic Art." In *Coptic Civilization: Two Thousand Years of Christianity in Egypt*, edited by G. Gabra, 273–83. Cairo: American University in Cairo Press.

Révillout, Ch.E. 1873. *Première étude sur le mouvement des esprits dans les premiers siècles de notre ère: Vie et sentences de Secundus d'après divers manuscrits orientaux; Les analogies de ce livre avec les ouvrages gnostiques*. Paris. https://archive.org/details/premiretudesurl00revigoog

Riedel, W. 1902. "Der Katalog der christlichen Schriften in arabischer Sprache von Abu 'l-Barakat." In *Nachrichten von der Königl. Gesellschaft der Wissenschaften zu Göttingen*, edited by W. Riedel, 635–706. Philologisch-historische Klasse. Göttingen: Commissionsverlag der Dieterich'schen Universitätsbuchhandlung Lüder Horstmann.

Rituals Committee of the Coptic Orthodox Holy Synod. 2012. *The Synaxarium*. 2 vols. Cairo: al-Surian Monastery.

Rodziewicz, M. 1983. "Alexandria and District of Mareotis." In *Graeco-Arabica 2: First International Congress on Greek and Arabic Studies, Athens 1983*, edited by Association for Greek and Arabic Studies, 199–216. Athens: Rodamos Publications, Institouto Ellenoanatolikon kai Afrikanikon Spoudon.

———. 1988. "Remarks on the Domestic and Monastic Architecture in Alexandria and Surroundings." In *The Archaeology of the Nile Delta: Proceedings of the Seminar Held in Cairo, 19–22 October 1986*, edited by E.C.M. van den Brink, 267–76. Amsterdam: Netherlands Foundation for Archaeological Research in Egypt.

———. 1998a. "Classification of Wineries from Mareotis." In *Commerce et artisanat dans l'Alexandrie hellénistique et romaine: Actes du colloque d'Athènes 11–12 décembre 1988*, edited by J.-Y. Empereur, 27–36. Bulletin de Correspondance Hellénique, suppl. 33. Athens: École française d'Athènes.

———. 1998b. "From Alexandria to the West." In *Commerce et artisanat dans l'Alexandrie hellénistique et romaine: Actes du colloque d'Athènes 11–12 décembre*

1988, edited by J.-Y. Empereur, 93–103. Bulletin de Correspondance Hellénique, suppl. 33. Athens: École française d'Athènes.

———. 2003. "Philoxenité: Pilgrimage Harbor of Abu Mina." *BSAA* 47:27–47.

Roncaglia, M.P. 1991. "Didymus the Blind." *CE* 3:900a–900b.

Roussert, M.-O., and S. Marchand. 1999. "Tebtynis 1998: Travaux dans le secteur nord." *Annales Islamologiques* 33:185–262.

Rubenson, S. 1990. *The Letters of St. Antony: Monasticism and the Making of a Saint.* Studies in Antiquity and Christianity. Minneapolis: Fortress Press.

Rücker, A. 1920. "Über Altartafeln im koptischen und den übrigen Riten des Orients." In *Ehrengabe deutscher Wissenschaft dargeboten von katholischen Gelehrten*, edited by F. Fessler, 209–21. Freiburg im Breisgau: Herder.

Russell, N. 1981. *The Lives of the Desert Fathers: The* Historia Monachorum in Aegypto. Cistercian Studies 34. London: Mowbray.

———. 2007. *Theophilus of Alexandria.* The Early Church Fathers. London and New York: Routledge.

Ruszczyc, B. 1975. "Tell Atrib–Kôm Sidi Youssef 1969." *Études et Travaux* 3:335–40.

———. 1986. "Wykopaliska polsko-koptyjskie na komie Sidi Youssuf w Tell Atrib." *Rocznik Muzeum Narodowego w Warszawie* 30:331–53.

———. 1990. "Die Ausgrabungen in Tell Atrib (Kom Sidi Youssuf)." In *Coptic Studies: Acts of the Third International Congress of Coptic Studies, Warsaw, 20–25 August, 1984*, edited by W. Godlewski, 379–81. Warsaw: Éditions scientifiques de Pologne.

———. 1997. *Kościół pod wezwaniem Świętej Dziewicy w Tell Atrib.* Warsaw: Polska Akademia Nauk.

Rutschowskaya, M.-H. 1990. *Coptic Fabrics.* Paris: Adam Biro.

———. 2010. "Nouvelles peintures découvertes dans le monastère de Baouît." In *Études Coptes XI: Treizième journée d'études (Marseille, 7–9 juin 2007)*, edited by A. Boud'hors and C. Louis, 45–51. Paris: De Boccard.

al-Sadamanti, B. 1871–72. *al-Tashih fi 'alam al-Sayyid al-Masih.* Edited by Higoumenos Filutha'us [Ibrahim]. Cairo: al-Matba'a al-Qibtiya al-Ahliya.

———. 1884. *al-Burhan al-sadid fi-l-tathlith wa-l-tawhid.* Cairo: n.p.

———. 1890. *Matla' al-naja' fi-l-munaja'.* Cairo: al-Matba'a al-Wataniya.

———. 1895. *Fi i'tiqad al-kanisa al-qibtiya al-urthuduksiya.* Cairo: Matba'at al-Tawfiq.

———. 1925–26. "Risala fi tahdhib al-nafs." *Sahyun* 32:65–72, 81–96, 113–19, 129–37.

———. 1926a. *al-Qawl al-sahih fi 'alam al-Sayyid al-Masih.* Edited by Y. al-Maqari, S. 'Abd al-Sayyid, and A. al-Baramusi. Cairo: Matba'at Ramsis.

———. 1926b. "Maqala fi i'tiqad al-kanisa al-qibtiya al-urthuduksiya." *al-Karma* 12:226–32, 282–86.

———. 1972. *Introduction sur l'herméneutique.* Edited by P. van den Akker. Recherches, new series, B. Orient Chrétien 1. Beirut: Dar al-Machreq.

———. 1976. *Tilbat al-tadarru'at, matla' al-naja' fi-l-munaja'.* Cairo: Maktabat al-Karuz.

———. 2012a. "Khabar al-shab Isha'ya' wa ta'limuhu li-l-qiss Butrus al-Sadamanti." *Marqus*, February, 32–36; March, 33–37.

———. 2012b. "Khabar Babnuda al-Matrudi li-l-qiss Butrus al-Sadamanti." *Marqus*, April, 29–33; May, 33–37.

———. 2012c. "Khabar Isidhurus al-Iskandari li-l-qiss Butrus al-Sadamanti." *Marqus*, June, 34–37; September, 27–30; October, 26–30; November, 29–31; December, 29–31.

Sadek, A. 1987. *Popular Religion in Egypt during the New Kingdom*. Hildesheimer Ägyptologische Beiträge 27. Hildesheim: Gerstenberg.

———. 2005. "Un aspect de la religion populaire au Nouvel Empire égyptien: la quête du visage divin." In *Supplément aux ASAE*, Cahier 34, vol. 2, 279–86. Cairo.

Sadek, A., and B. Sadek. 2011. *Un fleuve d'eau vive: Trilogie sur l'Entrée du Christ en Égypte*. Vol. 1, *Les Sources*. Le Monde Copte 34. Limoges: Le Monde Copte.

Salah, I. 2014. *Fi sabil nazariya 'arabiya masihiya fi-l-tafsir, Butrus al-Sadamanti namudhajan*. Cairo: Dar al-Fikr al-Injili.

Salib, G. 2002. *The Church of the Great Saint Abu Sefein in Old Cairo: Art, History and Spirituality.* Cairo: Church of Abu Sayfayn.

Salib al-Qiss Dimitri. 1967. "al-Qiddis Anba Hadid al-Qiss." *al-Kiraza* 3–7:30–33.

Samaan, K.W. 1983. (= Kirillus, Coptic Catholic Bishop of Asyut). "Le Commentaire exégétique du récit de l'agonie par Butrus al-Sadamanti." PhD diss., Pontificia Universitas Gregoriana, Facultas S. Theologiae, Rome.

Samir, S.K. 1979. "Maqala tanfi al-shakk wa-l-kufr 'an al-nasara al-muwahhidin li Butrus al-Sadamanti." *Sadiq al-Kahin* 19:44–58.

———, ed. and trans. 1985. *Brefs chapitres sur la Trinité et l'Incarnation*, by al-Safi ibn al-'Assal. PO 43.3, no. 192. Turnhout: Brepols.

Samir, S.K. 1991. "Yusab." *CE* 6:2359.

———. 1994. "La version arabe des Évangiles d'al-As'ad ibn al-'Assal." *Parole de l'Orient* 19:441–551.

Samuel, Bishop. 1992. *Abu al-Makarim: History of the Churches and Monasteries in Lower Egypt in the Thirteenth Century*. Cairo: Institute of Coptic Studies.

———. 2000. *The History of Abu al-Makarim*. Part 2. Cairo: al-Naam Printing House.

Samu'il al-Suryani and N.K. Dawud, eds. [1987]. *Tarih al-aba' al-batarika li Anba Yusab usquf Fuwwa* [Pseudo-Yusab]. n.p.

Sarkissian, K. 1965. *The Council of Chalcedon and the Armenian Church*. New York: Armenian Church Prelacy.

———. 1970. *The Armenian Church in Contemporary Times*. New York: Prelacy of the Armenian Apostolic Church.

Saweros, I. Forthcoming. "Another Athanasius: Four Sahidic Homilies Attributed to Athanasius of Alexandria." PhD diss., Leiden University.

Sawirus ibn al-Muqaffa'. 1948. *History of the Patriarchs of the Egyptian Church Known as the History of the Holy Church*. Texts and documents, vol. 2, part 2, *Khael III–Shenouti II (880–1066 AD)*. Translated and edited by A.S. Atiya and Y. 'Abd al-Masih. Cairo: [SAC].

———. 1959. *History of the Patriarchs of the Egyptian Church Known as the History of the Holy Church*. Texts and documents, vol. 2, part 3, *Christodoulus–Michael*

(1046–1102 AD). Translated and edited by Y. 'Abd al-Masih and O.H.E. Burmester. Cairo: [SAC].

———. 1968. *History of the Patriarchs of the Egyptian Church Known as the History of the Holy Church*. Texts and documents, vol. 3, part 1, *Macarius II–John V (1102–1167 AD)*. Translated and edited by A. Khater and O.H.E. Burmester. Cairo: [SAC].

———. 1970. *Tarikh batarikat al-kanisa al-misriya: al-ma'ruf bi siyar al-bi'a al-muqaddasa*. Vol. 3, part 3. Edited and translated by A. Khater and O.H.E. Khs-Burmester. Cairo: SAC.

———. 1992. *The History of the Patriarchs*. Vol. 3. Cairo: al-Naam li-l-Tiba'a wa-l-Tawrid.

Sbath, Paul. 1929. *Vingt traités philosophiques et apologétiques*. Cairo: H. Friedrich et Co.

Schaff, P. 1859. *History of the Christian Church*. Vol. 4, *From Gregory I to Gregory VII, A.D. 590–1073*. New York: Scribner.

Schlumberger, G. 1919. "Les Fouilles de Jean Maspero à Baouît en 1913." *Comptes Rendus des Séances de l'Académie des Inscriptions et Belles-Lettres* 63:243–48.

Schmidt, J. 1986. *Dictionnaire de la mythologie grecque et romaine*. Paris: Larousse.

Schollmeier, J. 1962. "Drei Heiligenlegenden des Kopten Butrus as-Sadamanti." *Kyrios* 2:102–21.

Schroeder, C.T. 2007. *Monastic Bodies: Discipline and Salvation in Shenoute of Atripe*. Philadelphia: University of Pennsylvania Press.

Schulz-Flügel, E. 1990. *Tyranus Rufinus Historia monachorum sive de Vita sanctorum Patrum*. Berlin: W. de Gruyter.

Schwartz, E. 1928. "Cyril und der Mönch Viktor." *Sitzungsberichte der Wiener Akademie der Wissenschaften (Philosophisch-historische Klasse)* 208:1–51.

———, ed. 1933. *Acta Conciliorum Oecumenicorum*. Vol. 2, *Concilium Universale Chalcedonense*, vol. 1, pt. 2. Berlin and Leipzig: Walter de Gruyter.

Schwendner, G. 2014. "Working Memory and Scribal Process in PsT of Didymus the Blind." http://www.sbl-site.org/meetings/abstract.aspx?id=31357

Searle, J.R. 1969. *Speech Acts*. Cambridge, UK: Cambridge University Press.

Seeliger, H.R., and K. Krumeich. 2007. *Archäologie der antiken Bischofssitze*. Vol. 1, *Spätantike Bischofssitze Ägyptens*. SKCO 15. Wiesbaden: Dr. Ludwig Reichert Verlag.

Sellew, P. 1989. "Achilles or Christ? Porphyry and Didymus in Debate over Allegorical Interpretation." *Harvard Theological Review* 82, no. 1: 79–100.

Selwitz, C. 1988. *Cellulose Nitrate in Conservation*. Research in Conservation 2. Los Angeles: The Getty Conservation Institute.

Severin, G., and H.-G. Severin. 1987. *Marmor vom heiligen Menas*. Liebighaus Monographie 10. Frankfurt am Main: Liebighaus.

Seybold, C.F. 1904a. *Severus ben el-Moqaffa'*. Historia Patriarcharum Alexandrinorum 1. CSCO 52, Script 8. Beirut: Typographia Catholica.

———. 1904b. *Severus ben el-Moqaffa': Historia patriarcharum Alexandrinorum I*. CSCO 52. Louvain: Peeters.

———. 1912. *Alexandrinische Patriarchengeschichte von S. Marcus bis Michael I 61–767 nach der ältesten 1266 geschriebenen Hamburger Handschrift*. Veröffentlichungen aus der Hamburger Stadtbibliothek 3. Hamburg: Lucas Gräfe.

Shafiq, Mamduh. 2003. *al-Shahid al-'azim Mar Mina al-'Aja'ibi: Tarikh dayr Mar Mina bi Fumm al-Khalig*. 1st ed. Cairo: Matba'at 'Arabiya li-l-Tiba'a wa-l-Nashr.

Shashoua, Y., S.M. Bradley, and V.D. Daniels. 1992. "Degradation of Cellulose Nitrate Adhesive." *Studies in Conservation* 37:113–19.

Sheridan, M. 2002. "The Spiritual and Intellectual World of Early Egyptian Monasticism." *Coptica* 1:1–51.

———. 2006. "The Concept of the 'Useful' as an Exegetical Tool in Patristic Exegesis." *Studia Patristica*, vol. 34, edited by F. Young, M. Edwards, and P. Parvis. Papers presented at the Fourteenth International Conference on Patristic Studies held in Oxford, 2003, 253–57. Louvain: Peeters.

———. 2007. "Rhetorical Structure in Coptic Sermons." In *The World of Early Egyptian Christianity: Language, Literature, and Social Context: Essays in Honor of David W. Johnson*, edited by J.E. Goehring and J.A. Timbie, 25–48. Washington, DC: Catholic University of America Press.

———. 2015. *Language for God in Patristic Tradition: Wrestling with Biblical Anthropomorphism*. Downers Grove, IL: InterVarsity Press.

Shoucri, M. 1991a. "Cyril VI." *CE* 3:679–81.

———. 1991b. "Dayr Abu Mina." *CE* 3:706–707.

———. 1991c. "John XIX." *CE* 4:1351.

———. 1991d. "Mark VIII." *CE* 5:1538.

Sidarus, A. 1975. *Ibn ar-Rahibs Leben und Werk: Ein koptisch-arabischer Enzyklopädist des 7./13. Jahrhunderts*. Islamkundliche Untersuchungen 36. Freiburg im Breisgau: Klaus Schwarz Verlag.

———. 1976. "L'exégèse arabe chrétienne au XIIIe siècle: Butrus as-Sadamanti, édité par P. van den Akker." *Recherches de Science Religieuse* 64:463–67.

———. 1978. "Un exégète copto-arabe du VIIe–XVIIIe siècle: Butrus al-Sadamanti et son *Traité sur l'Herméneutique*." *Bibliotheca Orientalis* 35:21–25.

———. 1990. "Les lexiques onomasiologiques gréco-copte-arabes du moyen-âge et leurs origines anciennes." In *Lingua restituta orientalis: Festschrift Prof. Dr. Julius Assfalg*, edited by R. Schulz and M. Görg, 348–59. Ägypten und Altes Testament 20. Wiesbaden: O. Harrassowitz.

———. 1997. "Un recueil original de philologie gréco-copto-arabe: La *scala* copte 43 de la Bibliothèque Nationale de France." In *Scribes et manuscrits du Moyen Orient: Actes des Journées de codicologie et de paléographie des manuscrits du Moyen-Orient (Paris, juin 1994)*, edited by F. Déroche and F. Richard, 293–326. Pro-Libris. Paris: Bibliothèque nationale de France.

———. 2000a. "L'influence arabe sur la linguistique copte." In *History of the Language Sciences/Geschichte der Sprachwissenschaften/Histoire des Sciences du Langage*, edited by S. Auroux et al., 321a–325b. Berlin and New York: Walter de Gruyter.

———. 2000b. "La tradition sahidique de philologie gréco-copto-arabe (Manuscrits des XIIIe–XVe siècles)." In *Études Coptes VII: Neuvième Journée d'Études coptes (Montpellier, juin 1999)*, edited by N. Bosson, 265–304. Cahiers de la Bibliothèque Copte 12. Paris: De Boccard.

———. 2001. "Medieval Coptic Grammars in Arabic: The Coptic *Muqaddimat*." *JCS* 3:63–79.

———. 2002. "The Copto-Arabic Renaissance in the Middle Ages: Characteristics and Socio-Political Context." *Coptica* 1:141–60.

———. 2003. "Le modèle arabe en grammaire copte: Une approche des *muqaddimat* copto-arabes médiévales." In *Le voyage et la langue: Hommage à André Roman et Anouar Louca*, edited by J. Dichy and H. Hamzé, 253–67. Damascus: Institut Français du Proche-Orient–Institut Français d'Études Arabes.

———. 2004. "L'œuvre philologique copte d'Abu Shakir Ibn al-Rahib (XIIIe siècle)." In *Studies on the Christian Arabic Heritage (in Honour of Father Prof. Dr. Samir Khalil Samir at the Occasion of His Sixty-Fifth Birthday)*, edited by R. Ebied and H. Teule, 1–23. Eastern Christian Studies 5. Louvain and Paris: Peeters.

———. 2006. "La pré-renaissance copte arabe du Moyen âge (2ème moitié du XIIe, début du XIIIe siècle)." In *Eastern Crossroads: Essays on Medieval Christian Legacy*, edited by J.P. Monferrer-Sala, 191–216. Gorgias Christian Oriental Studies 1. Piscataway, NJ: Gorgias Press.

———. 2010. "La renaissance copte arabe du Moyen âge." In *The Syriac Renaissance*, edited by H.G.B. Teule et al., 311–40. Eastern Christian Studies 9. Louvain and Paris: Peeters.

———. 2012. "La philologie copto-arabe médiévale et le *Vat. copt.* 71." In *Coptic Treasures from the Vatican Library: A Selection of Coptic, Copto-Arabic and Ethiopian MSS (Papers Collected on the Occasion of the Tenth International Congress of Coptic Studies—Rome, Sept. 2012)*, edited by P. Buzzi and D.V. Proverbio, 85–107. Studi e Testi 472. Vatican City: Biblioteca Apostolica Vaticana.

———. 2013a. "Alexandre le Grand chez les Coptes (recherches récentes et perspectives nouvelles)." In *Orientalia Christiana: Festschrift für Hubert Kaufhold zum 70. Geburtstag*, edited by P. Bruns and H.O. Luthe, 477–95. Eichstätte Beiträge zum Christlichen Orient 3. Wiesbaden: Harrassowitz Verlag.

———. 2013b. "Coptic Dignitaries' Families *(Buyutat)* in the Ayyubid Period and the Golden Age of Coptic Arabic Literature." *JCS* 15:189–208.

———. 2013c. "Place et rôle de l'Antiquité gréco-romaine dans la littérature copte d'expression arabe." In *Græco-latina et Orientalia: Studia in honorem Angeli Urbani heptagenarii*, edited by S.K. Samir and J.P. Monferrer-Sala, 327–58. Series Syro-Arabica 2. Córdoba: Oriens Academic.

———. 2016. "Nouvelles données concernant la scala gréco-copto-arabe *Liber graduum*." In *Manuscripta Graeca et Orientalia: Mélanges ascétiques et patristiques en l'honneur de Paul Géhin*, edited by A. Binggeli et al., 563–81. OLA. Louvain: Peeters.

Simaika, M. 1937. *Guide Sommaire du Musée Copte et des Principales Églises du Caire*. Cairo: Publications of the Coptic Museum.

Simaika, M., and Y. 'Abd al-Masih. 1939. *Catalogue of the Coptic and Arabic Manuscripts in the Coptic Museum, the Patriarchate, the Principal Churches of Cairo and Alexandria and the Monasteries of Egypt in 3 Volumes.* Vol. 1 [The Coptic Museum]. Cairo: Government Press.

———. 1942. *Catalogue of the Coptic and Arabic Manuscripts in the Coptic Museum, the Patriarchate, the Principal Churches of Cairo and Alexandria and the Monasteries of Egypt in 3 Volumes.* Vol. 2 (in 2 fasc.) [The Coptic Patriarchate]. Cairo: Government Press.

Singleton, D., E. Miller, and P. Rose. 2006. "The Taharqo Wall Painting Rescue at Qasr Ibrim, Egypt." In *The Conservation of Decorated Surfaces on Earthen Architecture: Proceedings of an International Conference Organized by the Getty Conservation Institute and the National Parks Service, Mesa Verde, Colorado, September 22–25, 2004*, edited by L. Rainer and A.B. Rivera, 15–23. Los Angeles: Getty Conservation Institute.

al-Siniksar. 1978. Vol. 1. Cairo: Maktabat al-Mahabba.

Stefaniw, B. 2010. *Mind, Text, and Commentary: Noetic Exegesis in Origen of Alexandria, Didymus the Blind, and Evagrius Ponticus*. Frankfurt: Peter Lang.

———. Forthcoming. "The School of Didymus the Blind in the Light of the Tura Find." In *Rethinking Monastic Education*, edited by L. Larsen and S. Rubenson. Cambridge, UK: Cambridge University Press.

Stegeman, B. 1969–70. "Contrasting Philosophies of Monasticism in the Modern Church." *BSAC* 20:159–66.

Stephen, J.D. 1998. "Pilgrimage and the Cult of St. Thecla in Late Antique Egypt." In *Pilgrimage and Holy Space in Late Antique Egypt*, edited by D. Frankfurter, 303–39. Leiden and Boston: Brill.

Steppa, J.-E. 2002. *John Rufus and the World Vision of Anti-Chalcedonian Culture*. New York: Gorgias Press.

Stewart, R. 1991a. "Al-Bashmur." *CE* 2:349.

———. 1991b. "Bilbeis." *CE* 2:391.

———. 1991c. "Burullus, al-." *CE* 2:427.

———. 1991d. "Daqadus." *CE* 3:692.

———. 1991e. "Khandaq, al-." *CE* 5:1413.

———. 1991f. "Mareotis." *CE* 5:1526–27.

———. 1991g. "Samannud." *CE* 7:2090.

Störk, L. 1984. "Sakijeh." In *Lexikon der Ägyptologie*, edited by W. Helck and E. Otto, vol. 5, 358–59. Wiesbaden: Harrassowitz.

Strabo. 1997. *Strabon: Le voyage en Égypte; Un regard romain*. Translated by J. Yoyotte, P. Charvet, and S. Gompertz, XVII, 1, 7. Paris: Nil éditions.

Suciu, A. 2012. "Further Leaves from a White Monastery Codex Containing Texts Attributed to Athanasius of Alexandria." *Orientalia* 81:87–90, pls. XXII–XXVII.

Sulpicius Severus. 1969. *Dialogorum libri II, I 13*, 183–222. Patrologia Latina 20. Palermo.

al-Suriany, S. 1972. *The Diocese of Helwan and the Monastery of St. Barsum the Naked*. Helwan: Coptic Diocese of Helwan.

———. 2002. *Tarikh babawat al-kursi al-iskandari (1908–1971 A.D.) ma'a mujaz li mu'asirihim min asaqifat al-aqalim*. 2nd ed. Cairo: Matba'at Dayr al-Suryan.

Swanson, M.N. 2008. "Butrus al-Sadamanti." In *Historical Dictionary of the Coptic Church*, edited by G. Gabra, 52, 281. Cairo: American University in Cairo Press.

———. 2010. *The Coptic Papacy in Islamic Egypt (641–1517)*. The Popes of Egypt 2. Cairo: American University in Cairo Press.

———. 2012a. "Ibn Katib Qaysar." In *Christian–Muslim Relations: A Bibliographical History*, vol. 4 (1200–1350), edited by D. Thomas and A. Mallett, 453–56. History of Christian–Muslim Relations 17. Leiden and Boston: Brill.

———. 2012b. "Patriarch Cyril III ibn Laqlaq." In *Christian–Muslim Relations: A Bibliographical History*, vol. 4 (1200–1350), edited by D. Thomas and A. Mallett, 320–24. History of Christian–Muslim Relations 17. Leiden and Boston: Brill.

al-Syriani, Y. 1999. *The Holy Family*. Cairo.

Szymańska, H., and K. Babraj. 2005a. "The Ancient Port of Marea, Egypt: Four Seasons of Excavations by the Polish Archaeological Mission." *Minerva* (April):26–28.

———. 2005b. "Fouilles archéologiques de Marea en Égypte: Saisons 2002–2003." *Archeologia* 55:119–30.

———. 2005c. "Marea: Fifth Season of Excavations, 2004." *Polish Archaeology in the Mediterranean* 16:43–54.

———. 2005d. "Marea: Fourth Season of Excavations, 2003." *Polish Archaeology in the Mediterranean* 15:53–63.

———. 2006. "Polish Excavations in the Basilica at Marea (Egypt)." *BSAC* 45:107–17.

———, eds. 2008. *Byzantine Marea: Excavations in 2000–2003 and 2006, Marea*. Vol. 1. Biblioteka Muzeum Archeologicznego w Krakowie 4. Krakow: Muzeum Archeologiczne w Krakowie.

Szymusiak, J.M. 1987. *Athanase d'Alexandrie: Deux apologies à l'empereur Constance pour sa fuite*. Sources chrétiennes 56 bis. 2nd ed. Paris: Éditions du Cerf.

Taft, R.F. 2000. *A History of the Liturgy of St. John Chrysostom*. Vol. 5, *The Precommunion Rites*. OCA 261. Rome: Pontificum Institutum Studiorum Orientalium.

Tatwir al-mathaf al-qibti, AH 1404/AD 1984/AM 1700. 1987. Cairo: Matba'at Hay'at al-Athar al-Misriya.

Taylor, W. 2006. *Antioch and Canterbury: The Syrian Orthodox Church and the Church of England, 1874–1928*. Piscataway, NJ: Gorgias Press.

Tewfik, I. 1913. *Nawabigh al-aqbat wa mashahirihum fi-l-qarn al-tasi' 'ashr*. Vol. 2. Cairo: al-Tawfiq.

Thabet, A. 2015. "Misr wa ma'awiyat al-'ibada al-armaniya." *AREK* 56:15–16.

Thelamon, Françoise. 1981. *Païens et chrétiens au IVe siècle: l'apport de l'"Histoire ecclésiastique" de Rufin d'Aquilée*. Paris: Études augustiniennes.

Thirard, C. 2012. *Survivance des sites monastiques paléochrétiens dans le Proche-Orient*. Bibliothèque d'études coptes 20. Cairo: IFAO.

Thucydides. 1928. *History of the Peloponnesian War*. Translated by C.F. Smith. Loeb Classical Library 108. Cambridge, MA: Harvard University Press.

Till, W. 1935. *Koptische Heiligen- und Martyrerlegenden*. OCA 102. Rome: Pontificum Institutum Orientalium Studiorum.

———. 1958. "Johannes der Täufer in der koptischen Literatur." *MDAIK* 16:322–32.

Tillemont, S.L. de. 1732. *Mémoires pour servir à l'histoire ecclésiastique des six premiers siècles*. Venice: François Pitteri.

Timm, S. 1983. *Ägypten: Das Christentum in Mittelalter und Neuzeit*. Wiesbaden: L. Reichert.

———. 1984–92. *Das christlich-koptische Ägypten in arabischer Zeit*. 6 vols. Beihefte zum TAVO, series B (Geisteswissenschaften), 41, nos. 1–6. Wiesbaden: Ludwig Reichert Verlag. Available online at MENADOC.

———. 1984a. *Das christlich-koptische Ägypten in arabischer Zeit.* Vol. 1. Beihefte zum TAVO 41, no. 1. Wiesbaden: Ludwig Reichert Verlag.
———. 1984b. *Das christlich-koptische Ägypten in arabischer Zeit.* Vol. 2. Beihefte zum TAVO 41, no. 2. Wiesbaden: Ludwig Reichert Verlag.
———. 1985. *Das christlich-koptische Ägypten in arabischer Zeit.* Vol. 3. Beihefte zum TAVO 41, no. 3. Wiesbaden: Ludwig Reichert Verlag.
———. 1988. *Das christlich-koptische Ägypten in arabischer Zeit.* Vol. 4. Beihefte zum TAVO 41, no. 4. Wiesbaden: Ludwig Reichert Verlag.
———. 1991. *Das christlich-koptische Ägypten in arabischer Zeit.* Vol. 5. Beihefte zum TAVO 41, no. 5. Wiesbaden: Ludwig Reichert Verlag.
———. 1992. *Das christlich-koptische Ägypten in arabischer Zeit.* Vol. 6. Beihefte zum TAVO 41, no. 6. Wiesbaden: Ludwig Reichert Verlag.
Tkaczow, B. 2008. *Architectural Styles of Ancient Alexandria: Elements of Architectural Decoration from Polish Excavations at Kom el-Dikka (1960–1993).* Alexandria 8. Warsaw: Neriton.
Troupeau, G. 1972–74. *Catalogue des manuscrits arabes.* Part 1, *Manuscrits chrétiens*, 2 vols. Paris: Bibliothèque Nationale.
Tsuji, A. 2016. "Preliminary Report on Four Saints from the Mamluk Period: Hadid, Yuhanna al-Rabban, Barsauma al-'Uryan, and 'Alam." In *Coptic Society, Literature and Religion from Late Antiquity to Modern Times: Proceedings of the Tenth International Congress of Coptic Studies, Rome, September 17th–22nd, 2012,* edited by P. Buzi et al., 1153–60. Louvain: Peeters.
Turner, V., and E. Turner. 1978. *Image and Pilgrimage in Christian Culture: Anthropological Perspectives.* New York: Columbia University Press.
Ulbert, T. 1969. *Studien zur dekorativen Reliefplastik des östlichen Mittelmeerraumes (Schrankenplatten des 4.–10. Jahrhunderts).* Miscellanea Byzantina Monacensia 10. Munich: Institut für Byzantinische und Neugriechische Philologie.
Van Cauwenbergh, P. 1914. *Étude sur les moines d'Égypte depuis le Concile de Chalcédoine (451) jusqu'à l'invasion arabe (640).* Paris: P. Geuthner; reprint Milan: Cisalpino-Goliardica, 1973.
Van den Broek, R. 1996. "Der Bericht des koptischen Kyrillos von Jerusalem über das Hebräerevangelium." In *Studies in Gnosticism and Alexandrian Christianity*, edited by R. van den Broek, 142–56. Leiden: Brill.
Van der Vliet, J. 2006. "Bringing Home the Homeless: Landscape and History in Christian Egyptian Hagiography." In *The Encroaching Desert: Egyptian Hagiography and the Medieval West*, edited by J. Dijkstra and M. van Dijk, 39–55. Leiden: Brill.
———. 2011. "'What Is Man?' The Nubian Tradition of Coptic Funerary Inscriptions." In *Nubian Voices: Studies in Christian Nubian Culture*, edited by A. Łajtar and J. van der Vliet, 171–224. Warsaw: University of Warsaw.
———. 2013. "Ancient Egyptian Christianity." In *The Cambridge History of Religions in the Ancient World*, vol. 2, edited by M.R. Salzman and W. Adler, 211–34. Cambridge, UK: Cambridge University Press.
———. 2017. "The Wisdom of the Wall: Innovation in Monastic Epigraphy." In *Writing and Communication in Early Egyptian Monasticism*, edited by M. Choat and M. Giorda, 151–64. Texts and Studies in Eastern Christianity 9. Leiden: Brill.

Van Doorn-Harder, N. 1993. "Les vierges sages: le monachisme féminin contemporain dans l'Église Copte Orthodoxe." *Le monde Copte* 21–22:115–31.

———. 1995. *Contemporary Coptic Nuns*. Columbia: University of South Carolina.

———. 1997. "Kyrillos VI (1902–1971): Planner, Patriarch and Saint." In *Between Desert and City: The Coptic Orthodox Church Today*, edited by N. Van Doorn-Harder and K. Vogt, 231–44. Oslo: Novus-Forlag.

Van Loon, G.M. 2014. "Decoration of Coptic Churches." In *Coptic Civilization: Two Thousand Years of Christianity in Egypt*, edited by G. Gabra, 195–216. Cairo: American University in Cairo Press.

Van Moorsel, P. 1995. *Les peintures du monastère de saint Antoine près de la Mer Rouge*. Vols. 1–2. Cairo: IFAO.

———. 2002. *Les peintures du monastère de Saint-Paul près de la Mer Rouge*. Cairo: IFAO.

Van Moorsel, P., and M. Huijbers. 1981. "Repertory of the Preserved Wallpaintings from the Monastery of Apa Jeremiah at Saqqara." In *Acta ad Archaeologiam et Artium Historiam Pertinentia* 9, edited by H. Torp, J.R. Brandt, and L.H. Monssen, 125–86 and pls. A–G and I–XXX. Rome: Institutum Romanum Norvegiae, Giorgio Bretschneider.

Van Moorsel, P., M. Immerzeel, and L. Langen. 1991. *Catalogue général du Musée copte: The Icons*. Cairo: Supreme Council of Antiquities Press.

Vansleb, J.M. 1677a. *Histoire de l'Église d'Alexandrie fondée par S. Mark que nous appelons celle des Jacobites Copte d'Égypte, Écrit au Caire même en 1672 & 1673*. Paris: Clousier et Promé.

———. 1677b. *Nouvelle relation en forme de journal d'un voyage fait en Égypte en 1672 et 1673*. Paris: E. Michallet.

Veilleux, A. 1968. *La Liturgie dans le cénobitisme pachômien au quatrième siècle*. Studia Anselmiana 57. Rome: Herder.

———. 1980–82. *Pachomian Koinonia*. 3 vols. Cistercian Studies Series 45–47. Kalamazoo, MI: Cistercian Publications.

———. 1982. *Pachomian Koinonia*. Vol. 3, *Instructions, Letters, and Other Writings of Saint Pachomius and His Disciples*. Kalamazoo, MI: Cistercian Publications.

Venit, M.S. 2002. *Monumental Tombs of Ancient Alexandria: The Theater of the Dead*. New York: Cambridge University Press.

Viaud, G. 1975. *Les pèlerinages coptes en Égypte*. Bibliothèque des Études Coptes 15. Cairo: IFAO.

———. 1979. *Les pèlerinages coptes en Égypte, d'après les notes du Qommos Jacob Muyser*. Bibliothèque d'Études coptes 15. Cairo: IFAO.

———. 1991. "Pilgrimages." *CE* 6:1970–71.

Villecourt, L. 1924. "Les observations liturgiques et la discipline du jeûne dans l'Église copte." *Le Muséon* 37:218–43.

———. 1925. "Les observations liturgiques et la discipline du jeûne dans l'Église copte." *Le Muséon* 38:261–305.

Vincent, R.K. 2010. "Wall Paintings in the Coptic Museum in Cairo: Emergency Intervention." In *Preserving Egypt's Cultural Heritage: The Conservation Work of the American Research Center in Egypt 1995–2005*, edited by R. Danforth, 118–20. Cairo: American University in Cairo Press.

Virgil. 1999. *Eclogues. Georgics.* Translated by H.R. Fairclough. Loeb Classical Library 66. Cambridge, MA: Harvard University Press.

Vitruvius. 1956. *O architekturze ksiąg dziesięć.* Translated by K. Kumaniecki. Warsaw: PWN.

Vivian, T., ed. 2008. *Witness to Holiness: Abba Daniel of Scetis.* Cistercian Studies Series 219. Kalamazoo, MI: Cistercian.

Vogüé, A. de. 1996. *Histoire littéraire du mouvement monastique dans l'Antiquité.* Part 1, 3. Paris: Éditions du Cerf.

Vycichl, W. 1983. *Dictionnaire étymologique de la langue copte.* Louvain: Peeters.

Wace, H. 1877. *A Dictionary of Christian Biography and Literature to the End of the Sixth Century A.D. with an Account of the Principal Sects and Heresies.* London: Murray.

Wachsmann, S. 1998. *Seagoing Ships and Seamanship in the Bronze Age Levant.* College Station: Texas A&M University Press.

Wadi', A. 1997a. *Dirasa 'an al-Mu'taman Ibn al-'Assal wa-kitabihi* Majmu' Usul al-Din *wa-tahqiqihi.* SOCM 5. Cairo and Jerusalem: Franciscan Centre of Christian Oriental Studies.

———. 1997b. "Muqaddima fi-l-adab al-'arabi li-l-aqbat." *SOCC* 29–30:441–92.

———. 1998. "Introduzione alla letteratura arabo-cristiana dei Copti." *SOCC* 29–30, 491–441 (§39, pp. 471–470). SOCC. Cairo: Franciscan Centre of Oriental Christian Studies.

———. 2005. "Al-As'ad Ibn al-'Assal, *Muqaddima fi Qawa'id al-lugha al-qibtiyya.*" *BSAC* 44:113–32.

———. 2006. *Fihris makhtutat K=kulliyyat al-'ulum al-insaniya wa-l-lahutiya [bi-] l-Qahira al-Ma'adi.* Cairo: Kulliyyat al-'ulum al-insaniya wa-l-lahutiya [bi-] l-Qahira al-Ma'adi.

———. 2009. "Fihris makhtutat al-Ma'had al-Fransiskani bi-l-'Umraniyya, al-Jiza." *SOCC* 42:27–170.

———. 2012a. "Butrus al-Sadamanti." In *Christian–Muslim Relations: A Bibliographical History*, edited by D. Thomas and A. Mallet, vol. 4, 417–20. Leiden: Brill.

———. 2012b. "Butrus Sawirus al-Jamil." In *Christian–Muslim Relations: A Bibliographical History*, edited by D. Thomas and A. Mallet, vol. 4, 339–42. Leiden: Brill.

Walter, Ch. 1995. "The Byzantine Sanctuary: A Word List." In *Liturgy, Architecture and Art of the Byzantine World: Papers of the XVIII International Byzantine Congress (Moscow, 8–15 August 1991) and Other Essays Dedicated to the Memory of Fr. John Meyendorff*, edited by C.C. Akentiev, 95–106. Byzantinorossica 1. St. Petersburg: Publications of the St. Petersburg Society for Byzantine and Slavic Studies.

Walters, C.C. 1989. "Christian Paintings from Tebtunis." *JEA* 75:191–208, pls. XVI–XXIX.1.

Ward, B., trans. 1975a. *The Desert Christian: Sayings of the Desert Fathers, the Alphabetical Collection.* New York: Macmillan.

———. 1975b. *The Sayings of the Desert Fathers: The Alphabetical Collection.* London: Mowbrays.

Watson, J. 1996. *Abba Kyrillos: Patriarch and Solitary*. Lebanon, PA: Society of Coptic Studies (= *Coptic Church Review* 17, nos. 1–2: 1–48).

———. 2000. *Among the Copts.* Brighton and Portland: Sussex Academic Press.

Watts, E.J. 2006. *City and School in Late Antique Athens and Alexandria.* Berkeley: University of California Press.

———. 2010. *Riot in Alexandria: Tradition and Group Dynamics in Late Antique Pagan and Christian Communities.* The Transformation of the Classical Heritage 46. Berkeley: University of California Press.

Weatherhead, F.J. 2001. "Recording and Conservation of Painted Plaster from the Early Excavations at Amarna." In *Colour and Painting in Ancient Egypt*, edited by W.V. Davies, 53–59. London: British Museum.

———. 2007. *Amarna Palace Paintings.* London: Egypt Exploration Society.

Weidmann, D. 1986a. "Construction des plans des monastères: stéréotypes, normalisation ou respect des programmes individuels." In *Le site monastique copte des Kellia: Sources historiques et exploration archéologique, Actes du colloque de Genève, 13–15 août 1984*, edited by Ph. Bridel, 175–81. Geneva: Mission suisse d'archéologie copte de l'Université de Genève.

———. 1986b. "Dispersion et concentration des monastères: Réflexions sur le cas des Qouçoûr el-Izeila." *Le site monastique copte des Kellia: Sources historiques et exploration archéologique, Actes du colloque de Genève, 13–15 août 1984*, edited by Ph. Bridel, 257–60. Geneva: Mission suisse d'archéologie copte de l'Université de Genève.

———, ed. 2013. *Kellia: Kom Qouçour 'Isâ 1. Fouilles de 1965 à 1978.* Recherches suisses d'archéologie copte 4. Louvain: Peeters.

Weitzmann, K., ed. 1979. *Age of Spirituality: Late Antique and Early Christian Art, Third to Seventh Century. Catalogue of the Exhibition at the Metropolitan Museum of Art, November 19, 1977, through February 12, 1978.* New York: Princeton University Press.

Werthmuller, K.J. 2010. *Coptic Identity and Ayyubid Politics in Egypt, 1218–1250.* Cairo: American University in Cairo Press.

Wessel, S. 2004. *Cyril of Alexandria and the Nestorian Controversy: The Making of a Saint and a Heretic.* Oxford Early Christian Studies. Oxford: Oxford University Press.

Whitfield, P., N. Tomoum, and S. Marai, eds. 2010. *Coptic Art Revealed.* Cairo: Supreme Council of Antiquities.

Winstedt, E. 1906. "A Coptic Fragment Attributed to James the Brother of God." *JTS* 8:241–43.

Winter, M. 1992. *Egyptian Society under Ottoman Rule, 1517–1798.* London: Routledge.

Wipszycka, E. 1972. *Les ressources et les activités économiques des églises en Égypte.* Brussels: Fondation Égyptologique de la reine Élisabeth.

———. 1996. *Études sur le christianisme dans l'Égypte de l'antiquité tardive.* Studia Ephemeridis Augustinianum 52. Rome: Institutum Patristicum Augustinianum.

———. 2002. "Remarques sur l'identification de Philoxenité à la lumière de fouilles récentes." Paper delivered at the third conference on Mediaeval Alexandria at the Centre culturel français in Alexandria, 8–10 October. To be published in *Alexandrie médiévale* 3, edited by Ch. Décobert.

———. 2009. *Moines et communautés monastiques en Égypte (IVe–VIIIe siècles)*. Warsaw: Raphael Taubenschlag Foundation.

———. 2012. "Marea and Philoxenite: Where to Locate Them?" *Études et Travaux* 25:417–32.

Wortley, J. 2012. *The Book of the Elders: Sayings of the Desert Fathers: The Systematic Collection*. Cistercian Studies Series 240. Collegeville, MN: Liturgical Press.

———. 2014. *Give Me a Word: The Alphabetical Sayings of the Desert Fathers*. Popular Patristics Series 52. Yonkers, NY: St. Vladimir's Seminary Press.

Wray, A. 2008. *Formulaic Language: Pushing the Boundaries*. Oxford: Oxford University Press.

Wüstenfeld, F., ed. 1845. *Macrizi's Geschichte der Copten: Aus den Handschriften zu Gotha und Wien mit Übersetzung und Anmerkungen*. Göttingen: Dieterichsche Buchhandlung.

———. 1847. *Macrizi's Geschichte der Copten*. Vol. 3. Göttingen: Dieterichsche Buchhandlung.

———. 1879. *Synaxarium das ist Heiligenkalender der Koptischen Christen*. Gotha: Friedrich Andreas Perthes.

Xydis, S.G. 1947. "The Chancel Barrier, Solea, and Ambo of Hagia Sophia." *Art Bulletin* 29:1–24.

Yegül, F.K. 1992. *Baths and Bathing in Classical Antiquity*. New York: Architectural History Foundation; Cambridge, MA: MIT Press.

Youssef, Y.N. 1986–89. "La genèse de la légende sur le roi Dioclétien." *BSAC* 28:107–10.

———. 2000. "La translation des reliques des saints Jean et Siméon: Une contribution à l'étude de l'histoire de l'Église Copte." In *Études Coptes VII: Neuvième journée d'études, Montpellier 3–4 Juin 1999*, edited by N. Bosson, 339–50. Cahiers de la Bibliothèque Copte 12. Paris and Louvain: Peeters.

———. 2007. "The Archangel Michael and the Patriarchs in Exile in the Coptic Tradition." In *Actes du Huitième congrès international d'études coptes, Paris, 28 juin–3 juillet 2004*, edited by N. Bosson and A. Boud'hors, 645–56. Louvain: OLA 163.

———. 2012. "A Contribution to the Episcopal Lists of the Coptic Church." *Parole de l'Orient* 37:1–28.

Yusab, Bishop of Fuwwa. 1994. *The History of the Patriarchs*. Edited by S. al-Suriany. Cairo: al-Naam Printing House.

———. 2003. *Tarikh al-batarika*. Edited by M.M. Iskandar. Cairo: Maktabat al-Mahabba.

Zaborowski, J.R. 2005. *The Coptic Martyrdom of John of Phanijoit: Assimilation and Conversion to Islam in Thirteenth-century Egypt*. Leiden: Brill.

Zakrzewska, E.D. 2011. "Masterplots and Martyrs: Narrative Techniques in Bohairic Hagiography." In *Narratives of Egypt and the Ancient Near East: Literary and Linguistic Approaches*, edited by F. Hagen et al., 499–523. Louvain: Peeters.

———. 2015. "*L* as a Secret Language: Social Functions of Early Coptic." In *Christianity and Monasticism in Middle Egypt: Al-Minya and Asyut*, edited by G. Gabra and H.N. Takla, 185–98. Cairo: American University in Cairo Press.

———. 2017. "A 'Bilingual Language Variety' or 'the Language of the Pharaohs'? Coptic from the Perspective of Contact Linguistics." In *Greek Influence on Egyptian-Coptic: Contact-Induced Change in an Ancient African Language*, edited by E. Grossman, P. Dils, T.S. Richter, and W. Schenkel, 115–61. Lingua Aegyptia—Studia Monographica. Hamburg: Widmaier Verlag.

Zanetti, U. 1986. *Les manuscrits de Dair Abû Maqâr: Inventaire*. Cahiers d'Orientalisme 11. Geneva: Patrick Cramer Éditeur.

Zoega, G. 1810. *Catalogus codicum copticorum manu scriptorum qui in Museo Borgiano velitris adservantur*. Rome: Sacra Congregatio de Propaganda Fide.

Zotenberg, H. 1877. *Catalogue des manuscripts éthiopiens (Gheez et Amharique) de la Bibliothèque Nationale, Manuscrits orientaux*. Paris: Imprimerie nationale.